Media/Society

Media/Society

INDUSTRIES, IMAGES, AND AUDIENCES

David Croteau

Virginia Commonwealth University

William Hoynes

Vassar College

Pine Forge Press

Thousand Oaks ■ London ■ New Delhi

For information, address:

 Pine Forge Press
A Sage Publications Company
2455 Teller Road
Thousand Oaks, California 91320
(805) 499-4224
e-mail: sales@pfp.sagepub.com

Sage Publications Ltd.
6 Bonhill Street
London EC2A 4PU
United Kingdom

Sage Publications India Pvt. Ltd.
M-32 Market
Greater Kailash I
New Delhi 110 048 India

Production: Mary Douglas, Rogue Valley Publications
Copy Editor: Mary Roybal
Interior Designer: Lisa Mirski Devenish
Typesetter: Susan Rogin
Cover Designer: Terri Wright
Production Manager: Anne Draus, Scratchgravel Publishing Services
Print Buyer: Anna Chin

Printed in the United States of America
98 99 00 01 10 9 8 7 6 5 4 3 2

Library of Congress Cataloging-in-Publication Data
Croteau, David.
    Media/society : industries, images, and audiences / David Croteau, William Hoynes.
        p. cm.
    Includes bibliographical references and index.
    ISBN 0-8039-9065-0 (alk. paper)
    1. Mass media—Social aspects—United States.   2. Mass media—Political aspects—United States.   I. Hoynes, William.   II. Title.
HN90.M3C76   1997
302.23—dc21   96-45372
                                                                  CIP

 This book is printed on acid-free paper that meets Environmental Protection Agency standards for recycled paper.

For Bill Gamson,

with thanks, for helping us appreciate
the significance of mass media
and the value of teaching

About the Authors

David Croteau is Assistant Professor in the Department of Sociology and Anthropology at Virginia Commonwealth University in Richmond. He teaches courses on the sociology of media and on the news media. He is the author of *Politics and the Class Divide: Working People and the Middle-Class Left* (Temple University Press, 1995) and co-author of *By Invitation Only: How the Media Limit Political Debate* (Common Courage Press, 1994).

William Hoynes is Assistant Professor in the Department of Sociology at Vassar College in Poughkeepsie, New York, where he teaches courses on media, culture, and social theory. He is the author of *Public Television for Sale: Media, the Market, and the Public Sphere*(Westview Press, 1994) and co-author of *By Invitation Only: How the Media Limit Political Debate* (Common Courage Press, 1994).

About the Publisher

Pine Forge Press is a new educational publisher, dedicated to publishing innovative books and software throughout the social sciences. On this and any other of our publications, we welcome your comments and suggestions.

Please call or write us at:

Pine Forge Press
A Sage Publications Company
2455 Teller Road
Thousand Oaks, CA 91320
(805) 499-4224
e-mail: sales@pfp.sagepub.com

Visit our new World Wide Web site, your direct link to a multitude of on-line resources:
http://www.sagepub.com/pineforge

CONTENTS

LIST OF EXHIBITS

We live in a society that is increasingly saturated by mass media. For most of us, print, film, radio, music, and television are central parts of our daily lives. At the same time, the growth in "new" technologies has altered our understanding of what we mean by *mass media*. Computer networks, digital technologies, and interactive cable television are among the developments changing the media landscape. It is no surprise, then, that understanding the relationship between media and society has become an important topic in sociology, mass communication, political science, American studies, and other disciplines.

We have found that teaching about mass media works best as a collaborative process. Most students bring a great deal of media experience to the classroom. They have been readers, viewers, and listeners all their lives. In some cases, they have even become producers of mass media products. Their knowledge often results in lively and insightful classroom discussions. What students generally lack, though, is a broader framework for understanding the relationship between media and society. That is *our* contribution to the classroom.

In teaching about media, we try to build upon our students' experiential knowledge by providing resources to help them gain new insights about the media. This involves developing skills for critically evaluating both the conventional wisdom and our own often taken-for-granted assumptions about the social role of media.

In teaching about mass media at various colleges and universities— Boston College, Clark University, Keene State College, Tufts University, Vassar College, Virginia Commonwealth University—we have been frustrated by the lack of a "core" book around which a course and related readings could be organized. In sociology, there is a wide range of impressive scholarly works that examine specific media issues or individual components of the mass media. In mass communication, there are useful books that review media theory or explore the workings of the media industry. What we have not found is a text that is both *sociological* and *comprehensive* in its approach to mass media. This book is intended to fill that gap by covering the range of media in contemporary society and providing conceptual tools for making sense of the relationships among the media industry, media messages, and media audiences.

Media/Society: Industries, Images, and Audiences has at least four distinct features. First, *our approach is sociological.* By this we mean that our emphasis is on the "big picture," examining relationships between the various components of the media process. In the first chapter, we present a model of media and society (see Exhibit 1.5 on page 25) that notes the key relationships among the media industry, media products, audiences, technology, and the broader social world.

Second, because our approach emphasizes the sociological "big picture," *we integrate a wide variety of topics* into our discussion. Our analysis explores both different dimensions of the media process (production, content, and audiences) and different types of media (film, music, news, television, books, computer cyberspace, and so on). The issues we examine are diverse. They range from how government regulates the media to how audiences actively construct meaning; from how media personnel do their jobs to how changing media technology is having global repercussions; from how the economics of the media industry shape media products to how media products might influence audiences; from the portrayals of race, class, and gender in the media to the news media's impact on the world of politics. This diversity allows readers to see connections between mass media issues that are often treated separately. In addition, it allows instructors to use this text as a comprehensive survey of the field while tailoring supplementary readings to highlight issues of particular interest to them.

Third, our sociological focus on social relationships *highlights the tension between constraint and action* in the media process. For example, while we must understand the influence of the media industry in our society, we must also recognize how economic and political constraints affect the media. While we should be alert to the potential influence of media products on audiences, we must also recognize how audiences actively construct their own interpretations of media messages. While we ought to pay attention to the influences of technology on the media process, we must also see how social, economic, and political forces have shaped the development and application of technology. Examining these tensions helps us gain a more balanced and nuanced understanding of the role of media in society.

Finally, this book aims to be *current and accessible.* The particular details of current media debates change rapidly, but the types of debates that are occurring date back to the very origins of mass-mediated communication. Therefore, our analyses are historically grounded but draw upon current media debates, such as regulation of the Internet, the concentration of media ownership, portrayals of lesbians and gays in the media, and the growth of globally circulating media. By drawing upon recent examples, we concretize our broader theoretical points about media and society. We hope our approach will help make the text accessible and engaging for students and instructors alike.

We would like to take this opportunity to acknowledge the people who helped make this book possible. We are grateful to Matthew Dillard, David Hurley, Marilyn Kennepohl, and Kristin Monroe for their research assistance. Thanks to Ed Hedemann and Serge Levy for their photographs and the Vassar College Committee on Research for a grant from the J. R. Heimerdinger Fund in support of this project. Thanks to Steve Rutter and the folks at Pine Forge Press for their assistance and encouragement, and to Rogue Valley Publications and Scratchgravel Publishing Services for their work in producing this book. We are grateful to Pine Forge's reviewers, who provided very helpful comments on earlier drafts of this book: Marshall Battani, University of California, Davis; Bradley Buchner, Kutztown University; Tom Gerschick, Illinois State University; Kent Kedl, University of Minnesota; Arvind Rajagopal, Purdue University; Troy Zimmer, California State University, Fullerton.

We would also like to thank all the students who have taken our mass media courses. Their questions and concerns have provided wonderful fuel for thought. Nicholas Hoynes arrived during the final revision of the manuscript; he and his brother, Benjamin Hoynes, have given their father great incentive to complete this book. Finally, thanks as always to Deirdre Burns and Cecelia Kirkman—for everything.

PART ONE

Media/Society

CHAPTER 1

Media and the
Social World

The red display on the digital radio-alarm clock switches to 6:30 A.M., and Leonda awakens to the sounds of her favorite radio station. She lies in bed listening to a few songs, some ads, and a traffic update before she drags herself through her morning routine. She showers and dresses, putting on a T-shirt featuring a picture of her favorite rock band.

After going downstairs for breakfast, Leonda picks up the remote and clicks on the TV. She "channel surfs" until she comes across a network morning show that has the star of a big new Hollywood movie as a guest. While eating her bowl of cereal and listening to the show, she scans the morning newspaper and reads a review of the movie being discussed on TV. Meanwhile, her six-year-old brother is on the floor playing with some sort of power-mutant-adventure warriors based on a Saturday morning cartoon series.

After a short time, Leonda goes outside and waits for her friends to pick her up for school. While waiting, she notices a work crew pasting up a new ad on the billboard down the block. The ad is only half up, but it looks like some kind of liquor advertisement: a young and beautiful woman in a strapless black evening gown with a drink in her hand.

A compact car with half a dozen bumper stickers for local radio stations pulls up, and Leonda says hello to her friends as she climbs into the back seat. The car's tape player is pounding out a recent rap hit. Before they get to school, Leonda and her friends decide that tonight they will check out the new movie Leonda has just read about in the paper.

In Leonda's first-period class, the teacher turns on the television set mounted high on the wall. The students watch 15 minutes of a newscast—complete with commercials—developed for use in the classroom. After the broadcast, the teacher hands out copies of an article from a national weekly newsmagazine. The story is about the effects of media violence, a topic the students are discussing in this social-studies course.

Later in study hall, Leonda catches up with a friend and returns a CD she has borrowed—a soundtrack from a recent movie. She spends the rest of the period flipping through a "women's" magazine featuring articles—and many advertisements—on fashion, makeup, health, and personal relationships. She spends the last period of the day in computer lab,

*where she is learning about business practices through a program that
simulates a small business. She has also been using an Internet "bulletin
board" to post ideas and to read comments from dozens of other students
across the country who are also studying business.*

*At home after school, Leonda turns on the TV to a talk show and
then watches a tabloid news program claiming to give the inside story
about a high-profile celebrity murder case. Commercials for toothpaste,
fruit juice, and other products pepper the programs. Leonda also sees a
couple of campaign ads for the state's two gubernatorial candidates; each
accuses the other of lying and distorting the facts.*

*After dinner, some of Leonda's friends pick her up and drive to the
local mall's multiplex theater, where they catch the early show. After the
film, the group wanders around the mall. One of Leonda's friends is
checking out a pair of sneakers she is thinking of buying. The shoes are
on sale at a great price, and the store has prominently featured a big card-
board cutout of the well-known basketball star who endorses the product
in TV commercials.*

*When Leonda's friends drop her off at home, she walks into the living
room and joins her parents, who are watching television. The program,
though, is pretty bad, so she calls it a day and heads up to her room.
There she picks up a romance novel she has been reading and gets
through a couple of chapters before she falls asleep.*

The Importance of Media

The hypothetical story about Leonda highlights some of the many ways
that media are enmeshed in our lives. The particulars are different for different individuals, but in our daily lives media surround us—often from
the moment we wake up to the time we go to sleep.

Consider this: The U.S. Census Bureau (1995) reported that in 1994,
99 percent of American households had a radio and each household had
an average of 5.6 radios. In that year, 98 percent of households had a
television, with an average of 2.2 sets per household. Also, 79 percent of
U.S. households had at least one videocassette recorder (VCR), and 62
percent received some form of cable television. The equipment that provides access to electronic media is everywhere (see Exhibit 1.1). Most
people organize their living rooms around the television set; stereos are
key elements of many dorm rooms; most cars have a radio, a tape player,
or a CD player. Even the office in which this chapter is being written—on
a computer—has a radio and a tape player, as well as other forms of
media: stacks of books, magazines, and newspapers.

EXHIBIT 1.1 *Percentage of U.S. Households with Select Media, 1994*

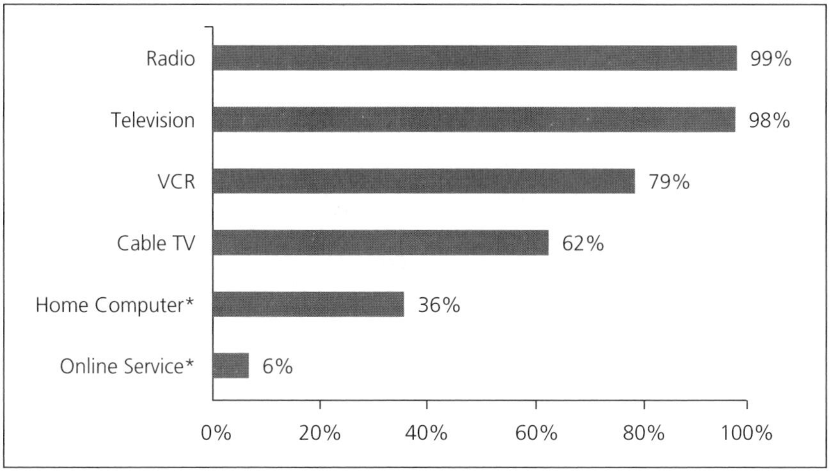

Sources: Statistical Abstract of the United States, 1995.

*Times Mirror Center for the People & the Press (1995). "Technology in the American Household: Americans Going Online . . . Explosive Growth, Uncertain Destinations." Data are from May 1995.

Americans spend an enormous amount of time watching, listening to, or reading these various forms of media. For example, television sets in U.S. households are turned on for an average of seven hours each day. Even by conservative estimates, individual Americans spend about two and a half hours a day—almost half of their available waking leisure time—watching television (Kubey and Csikszentmihalyi, 1990). Over the course of a year, two and a half hours a day adds up to more than 38 solid days of TV viewing! Imagine someone sitting in front of a television set 24 hours a day for well over a month! Every year, that's how much TV the typical American watches. Of course, this accounts only for television viewing. If you add the time we spend listening to the radio, playing CDs, reading, and using other media, it is easy to see that near-constant exposure to media is a fundamental part of contemporary life (see Exhibit 1.2). Indeed, some argue that the media have become the dominant social institution in contemporary society, supplanting the influence of older institutions such as the educational system and religion.

One way to recognize the importance of the media in our lives is to imagine life *without* the media. Imagine that you wake up tomorrow in a sort of "Twilight Zone" parallel society where everything is the same except that media do not exist: no television, no movies, no radio, no recorded music, no computers, no books or magazines or newspapers.

EXHIBIT 1.2 *How Americans Spend Their Leisure Time*

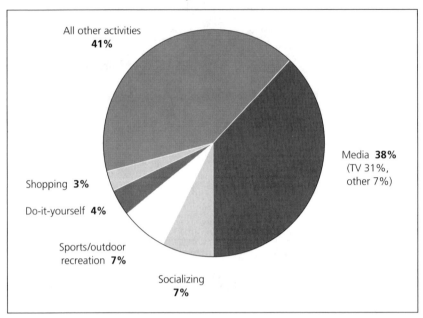

All other activities
41%

Media **38%**
(TV 31%,
other 7%)

Shopping **3%**

Do-it-yourself **4%**

Sports/outdoor
recreation **7%**

Socializing
7%

Source: Adapted from data in Jim Spring (1993). "Seven Days of Play." *American Demographics,* 15:50–53.

If the media were eliminated, *nothing* else would be the same. Our entertainment would be different. We would not follow sports teams in the newspaper, watch TV, or go to a movie for fun. We would not listen to recorded music at parties or for relaxation. Our understanding of politics and the world around us would be different because we would not have newspapers, television, magazines, and books to explain what is happening in our communities and beyond. Even our perceptions of ourselves would probably be different, since we would not have television characters and advertising images to compare ourselves against. For example, we might not concern ourselves so much with the latest fashions, music, or cars if ads did not imply that we *should* be concerned with such things.

With no television, no recorded music, no movies, and no radio, we would have a great deal of time on our hands. We would probably spend much of it interacting with other people. We might entertain ourselves by playing music or playing games. We might attend meetings and lectures or hold discussions on politics and current events to learn what was going on. We might take up hobbies or learn new skills to pass the time. Our social life—how we interact with other people—would also change in the absence of media.

Of course, changes would reach well beyond our private lives. The behavior of politicians, business executives, and leaders in other fields would change without media. Government would operate differently. Without advertising, business would be fundamentally different. Education, religion, and every other institution would also be different without media, as would social movements and citizens' organizations.

Given the pervasiveness of the media and their significance in our lives and in society, it's surprising to realize that the mass media are relatively new phenomena. Most forms of mass media are still in their infancy. Before we go any further in our discussion, we should take a brief look at the history and meaning of "mass media."

The Rise of Mass Media

The word *media* is the plural of *medium*. It is derived from the Latin word *medius,* which means "middle." The communication media are the different technological processes that facilitate communication between (and are in the "middle" of) the sender of a message and the receiver of that message. In this book, we will sometimes use the term "reader" rather than receiver or audience, because we want to highlight the active role of audiences in interpreting the messages they receive. In this sense, people "read" the sound and pictures of media messages just as they read the words of a written media message. Reading implies actively interpreting media messages. The same media product might mean very different things to two different people. For example, an MTV video of a hot new heavy metal band may elicit very different responses from a 15-year-old fan of the band and a parent concerned about stereotypically sexist images that might be present in such videos. The media product—the video—is the same, but different "readers" interpret it in very different ways. In studying media, then, it's important to consider readers, because they do not simply swallow the messages presented in the media.

Sociologists call the process of actively creating meaning in this way the "social construction of reality." This means that, while reality exists, we must negotiate the meaning of that reality. A student who sports a series of prominent tattoos is an objective reality. However, different people will interpret such body art in different ways. Is it a sign of conformity to a fad? A rebellious political statement? A playful snubbing of mainstream norms? A disgusting mutilation of the body? Or is it just an act of personal expression? The meaning of the tattoos must be constructed by those observing them. The same is true for the meaning of media messages. That is why the audience or "readers" are such an important part of the media process.

Our primary concern in this book is *mass* media, that is, media that reach a relatively large audience of usually anonymous readers. Writing a letter, sending a telegram, or placing a telephone call involves the use of different communication media, but scholars generally do not consider these to be mass media because messages in such media have a single, intended, known recipient. You know the individual who will receive your letter or answer your phone call. Mass media producers, though, have no way of knowing exactly who—or how many people—will read their book, watch their television program, buy their CD, or "hit" their Internet home page. The difference between mass media and other forms of communication is sometimes not simple or clear-cut. The distinctions have become even more blurred with the introduction of new technologies. Our primary concern in this book is the generally recognized mass media of print, film, radio, television, and sound recordings. We will also discuss communication media based on established or emerging computer technologies.

The Print Medium

When American revolutionaries founded the United States, there was only one form of mass media: print. (See Cassata and Asante, 1979; DeFleur and Ball-Rokeach, 1989; and McQuail, 1987, for summaries of the rise of mass media.) The technology for printing dated back to the beginning of the fifteenth century, when inventors in Korea first created the cast metal type that made printing possible. In 1450, Johannes Gutenberg made printing more practicable by converting a winepress into the first printing press with movable type. While the technology evolved, media content changed little. Reflecting the power of the Church in Europe at the time, the Bible, which scribes had previously hand-copied, was the book most often produced by early printers. Thus, as was true for later changes, social forces other than technology determined the direction of media development (see Exhibit 1.3).

For several centuries, print media—in the form of books, newspapers, and pamphlets—served as the only means for reaching a wide audience from a distance. However, the need for physical distribution limited print media products (unlike later electronic media). News, for example, traveled only as fast and as far as a horse, train, or ship could carry it. It routinely took four to eight weeks for information to travel from Europe to the United States. Even distances that we now perceive to be quite short—from New York to Washington, for example—were separated by

EXHIBIT 1.3   *Timeline of Media Development*

Year	Media-Related Event
100	Papermaking develops in China and spreads through Asia and the Arab world by the year 600
700	Arabs carry Chinese techniques for papermaking to the West
1000	Movable type made of clay is used in China
1400	Movable metal type is developed in Asia
1450	Gutenberg perfects movable metal type and handpress in Germany; the *Bible* is printed, 1456
1500	
1550	
1600	First "newspapers" appear in Germany, France, and Belgium
1650	
1700	1702 London's *Daily Courant* is first daily newspaper
1750	
1800	1833 Mass-circulation media begin with the first "penny press" newspaper, the *New York Sun*
	1837 Telegraph is first demonstrated
	1839 A practical method of photography is developed by Daguerre
	1844 Samuel Morse sets up telegraph link between Washington and Baltimore
1850	1876 First telephone message sent by Alexander Graham Bell
	1877 Edison develops first phonograph
	1879 Edison patents the electric light
	1884 Eastman perfects the roll film
	1895 Motion pictures are invented, and the first films are shown to the public
	1895 Radio messages are transmitted by Marconi
1900	1903 *Great Train Robbery* becomes model for storytelling with film
	1920 First regularly scheduled radio broadcasting, by KDKA in Pittsburgh
	1927 *The Jazz Singer* is first feature-length film with synchronized speech
	1933 TV is demonstrated by RCA
	1937 First digital computer is created from telephone parts
	1941 First commercial TV is broadcast
	1946 First mainframe computer is invented at the University of Pennsylvania
	1947 First transistor is developed by Bell Labs as alternative to vacuum tubes
	1948 Long-playing (LP) records, which rotate at 33-1/3 rpm, are introduced
	1949 Network TV begins in the United States
1950	1956 Videotape recording (VTR) is invented
	1957 *Sputnik,* world's first communication satellite, is launched by the Soviet Union
	1961 San Diego cable operator is first to import television signals from another city (Los Angeles) for distribution to subscribers

(continued)

EXHIBIT 1.3 *(continued)*

Year	Media-Related Event
1969	First nodes of the computer Internet are created in Pentagon plan to establish a decentralized communications system that can withstand nuclear attack.
1970	Early (and expensive) videocassette recorders (VCR) are introduced
1971	Invention of the microprocessor
1975	First microcomputer is marketed Fiber optics transmission begins HBO begins transmitting programming to cable TV systems by satellite
1977	Qube, the first interactive cable system, begins in Columbus, Ohio 200,000 VCR's sold; more affordable machines enter the market and sales boom
1990	World Wide Web (WWW) started as simple user interface for wide variety of data types
2000	

Sources: David Crowley and Paul Heyer (1991). *Communication in History.* New York: Longman. Everett M. Rogers (1986). *Communication Technology.* New York: The Free Press. Kenneth Jost (1994). "The Future of Television." *CQ Researcher,* 4 (48):1129–1152.

a vast communication gulf. The only way to communicate across such distances was for messages to travel physically between the two locations. While improved transportation technology increased the speed of communication throughout the nineteenth century, in the years immediately preceding the development of the telegraph it still took several days for news to travel from one city to the next (see Exhibit 1.4). Both routine and extraordinary information, from holiday greetings to news of the outbreak of war, traveled at a slow speed difficult to imagine today.

Not until the 1840s did the technological innovation of the telegraph allow for near instantaneous communication over long distances that were physically wired together. For the first time, there was a separation between transportation and long-distance communication. Since it did not reach a large audience, the telegraph was not a mass medium, but it did speed up the dissemination of information through newspapers. Reporters could send news stories instantaneously over a long distance to newspapers that would then print and distribute the story locally. The invention of the telephone in 1876 opened the way for more widely accessible personal long-distance communication as well as facilitating the work of reporters.

EXHIBIT 1.4 *Time (in days) Required for News to Travel from New York to Select Cities, 1794–1841*

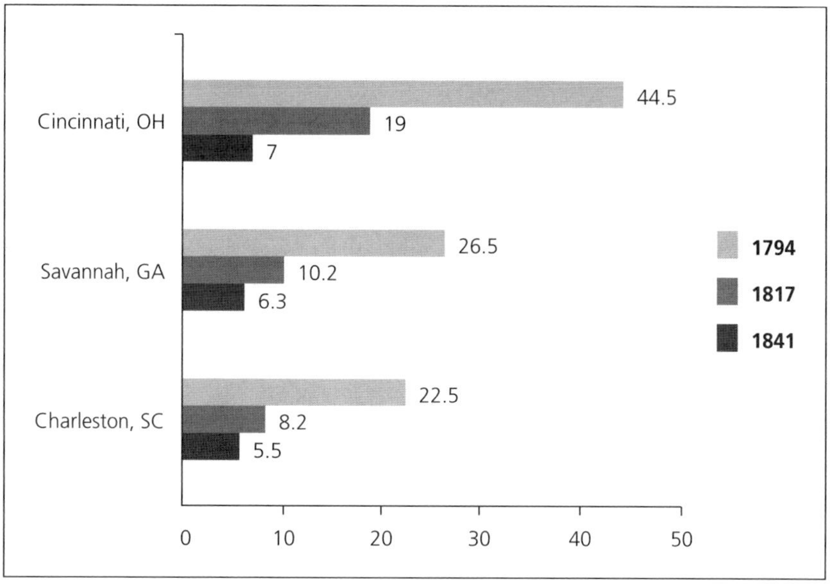

Source: Allan R. Pred (1973). *Urban Growth and the Circulation of Information.* Cambridge, MA: Harvard University Press.

Sound Recording and the Film Medium

In 1877, Thomas Edison developed the phonograph, which marked the beginning of the first new mass medium since print. In 1887, phonograph records were introduced and, later, other forms of sound recording proliferated. Magnetic tape originated in the 1920s and became most popular in its easy-to-use cassette form, introduced in the 1960s. In 1948, the long-playing (LP) 33-1/3 rpm record was launched by Columbia Records and became the recording industry standard for over 30 years. In the early 1980s, the compact disk (CD) emerged as the dominant format of popular sound recording. In 1895, Auguste and Louis Lumière invented the cinematograph, which subsequently led to "moving pictures." While the need to assemble a viewing audience in a particular location limited the reach of this new medium, movies proved to be enormously popular. By 1912, 5 million Americans *a day* were attending the cinema. Fifteen years later, the introduction of the first "talking picture" made moviegoing even more accessible and popular.

Broadcast Media

In the first decade of the twentieth century, innovations leading to the rise of radio presented new opportunities for communication. Radio was the first *broadcast* medium, and it introduced a new element to the media equation. No longer did media producers have to physically distribute their products (for example, to newsstands, bookstores, or movie theaters). Nor did the public have to travel physically to these locations to have access to mass media. Now, communicators could use the airwaves to transmit a media product directly to anyone who owned a radio receiver. Communicators could now cast media messages broadly.

Broadcasting made another advance with the introduction of television. When the Pioneer Corporation introduced the first television sets to the United States in the 1940s, their advertising boasted "We bring the revolution home" (Tichi, 1991, p. 12). They were not exaggerating. In the span of less than 10 years, between 1946 and 1955, television sets made their way into 65 percent of American households (Spigel, 1992). At the dawn of the twenty-first century, television so permeates our lives that it's easy to forget how recent its growth has been. Think of it this way: People who are over 55 years old in the year 2000—roughly 30 percent of the U.S. population—were born before the commercial introduction of television. It wasn't that long ago—as anyone over 55 will be happy to confirm! On the other hand, most Americans who are under the age of 45 in the year 2000 have a difficult time imagining life without the near-constant presence of television. That's how quickly the influence of television has spread.

The development of broadcasting fundamentally altered patterns of media consumption by creating the possibility of a largely privatized and individualized media experience. Consuming media or other forms of entertainment were often social activities, such as attending movies or going to concerts. These public activities have been replaced, or at least supplemented, by television, video rentals, and recorded music, which people usually experience in the privacy of their own homes.

"New" Media

In more recent years, technological innovation has again changed the face of mass media. Cable television, satellites, fiber-optic technologies, and especially computers have helped create an explosion in media products and formats. Ironically, much of this change has resulted in a move away from the mass broadcast audience toward smaller, more specialized niche populations—a process called "narrowcasting." With computer technology, users combine the specialization of media products with interactivity to make choices, provide responses, and customize media products. This interactive technology promises to bring new changes to tomorrow's media. Developers are planning to fuse telephone, television, fax, stereo, digital video, and computer into a single media center. As with the introduction of television a half century ago, the emergence of new technologies holds out the possibility of significant social change. But it is important to reiterate that changes in technology do not determine the evolution of media. Instead, as we will see, technology is only one of a number of interacting factors that shape the development and uses of media.

The rise of the Internet is a case in point. Changes in computer technology were a necessary but not sufficient condition for the existence of the Internet. It took government financing and regulation to help organize and launch the Internet system, primarily out of universities. The Internet was originally conceived as a decentralized communications network capable of functioning after a nuclear attack on central locations such as Washington, D.C. Much of the funding to develop the Internet, therefore, came from public tax dollars through the Pentagon budget. This is a clear example of an external social institution directly influencing the development of technology. As this technology is used more and more for private commercial applications, there is growing debate about the character and direction of the "information superhighway." It may be that, rather than transporting information, the Internet of the future will serve more as a "virtual mall," with corporations trying new ways to sell us all sorts of products. Perhaps here, too, interaction at home with electronic media will replace the social experience of going shopping. The point is that, throughout the history of media, technology by itself has never led unambiguously in a specific direction; rather, broader social forces have channeled the development and application of technological capabilities.

Media and Society

Because media are such an integral part of our lives, they generate a great deal of popular interest and debate. Does television have too much sex and violence? Are the news media biased? Have TV talk shows gone too far with their sensationalized topics? Should the content of the Internet be regulated? In order to address such questions, we need a better understanding of the mass media and their role in contemporary social life.

A sociological perspective, which underlies this book, can help us understand the media. For both students of mass media and citizens in the twenty-first century, sociology provides a set of tools to help make sense of the dizzying array of media-related issues. A sociological perspective asks us to consider the role of media in our individual lives (the micro level) in the context of social forces such as the economy, politics, and technological development (the macro level). Most of all, sociology suggests that if we want to understand the media and their impact on our society, we must consider the relationships (both micro and macro) between media and the social world.

Mass Media in Socialization

One way in which individuals are connected to the larger social world is through socialization. Socialization is the process whereby we learn and internalize the values, beliefs, and norms of our culture and, in so doing, develop a sense of self. We might, for example, learn as children that the United States is a democracy whose citizens have fought valiantly in the name of freedom and have excelled in science, business, entertainment, and the arts. Such information, coupled with socializing rituals such as Fourth of July parades, Labor Day, pledging allegiance to the flag in school, and playing the national anthem at sporting events, encourages us to take pride in being an "American," thus helping to form one aspect of our identity.

Through the socialization process, we also learn to perform our social roles as friend, student, worker, citizen, and so forth. The process of socialization continues throughout life, but it is especially influential for children and adolescents. If socialization proceeds smoothly, we hardly notice it. The dominant values, beliefs, and norms of our society become "our" values and norms. The internalization of the lessons of socialization means that our culture becomes taken-for-granted. We learn to hold "appropriate" values and beliefs. We learn to behave in socially acceptable ways.

We realize the learned, taken-for-granted nature of our beliefs and values only when someone calls them into question or contradicts them. A diverse society such as the United States incorporates many different cultures, and, consequently, different groups of people are sometimes socialized into adopting distinctly different norms, beliefs, and values. These cultures can sometimes clash. It can be startling to learn, for example, that the civics-book version of U.S. history that socialized us to be proud Americans often glosses over the less noble incidents in our complex history.

We also can become aware of the learned nature of our beliefs when we travel abroad and experience a different culture or hear about other people's travels. The idea of experiencing "culture shock" suggests that we are not equipped—we were not socialized—in the ways and norms of a particular culture. A simple example of this occurred as we prepared this chapter. One of our graduate assistants was a Swedish woman who had recently moved to the southern United States. She was surprised to find that in casual conversation Americans would inquire about her religious affiliation. In Sweden, she noted, organized religion is not nearly as influential as it is in the United States. More important, she had been taught that religion is a highly personal and private affair that is not casually discussed. Conversely, she was surprised to find Americans so reticent and ill-prepared to discuss political issues, since politics was a staple of Swedish social conversation. This student had to relearn the subtle norms of casual social conversation in order to meet the expectations of her acquaintances in a new culture.

Part of the explicit responsibility of some social institutions, such as the family and schools, is to promote socialization. We expect families to pass on core values, a sense of responsibility, an appropriate work ethic, and so forth. Educators often gear schools toward teaching children the necessity of submitting to authority, of being punctual and orderly, and of following instructions—skills and orientations that help produce a reliable, compliant worker for future employers.

Other socializing agents, such as adolescent peers, usually have a less intentional, though just as powerful, socializing influence. Often, however, these unofficial socializing agents can promote messages that contradict the ones being espoused by the "powers that be." When parents chastise their teenage kids for hanging around with "the wrong crowd," they are implicitly aware that the potential socializing influence of peers can work to counter parental influence. Parents and teachers might be promoting hard work and study as important values, while peers may be suggesting that partying is a more interesting way to spend one's time.

In contemporary society, the mass media serve as a powerful socializing agent. By the time an average American student graduates from high school, she or he will have spent more time in front of the television than in the classroom (Graber, 1980, p. 2). Viewers learn and internalize some of the values, beliefs, and norms presented in media products. Take the example of crime. Although the FBI reported a decline in violent crime in many areas between 1989 and 1994, the number of crime stories on network news tripled. At the same time, there has been a considerable increase in the degree to which American citizens fear violent crime. Do media reports of crime heighten the fears of citizens?

Some researchers argue that we "learn" about crime even while we are watching entertainment television. For example, watching a lot of police crime shows seems to cultivate two beliefs. First, heavy viewers are more likely than light viewers to see their community as a dangerous, violent place where they are likely to become crime victims. Second, heavy viewers of crime shows tend to develop empathy for the police—even when television police are clearly violating someone's civil rights. The result of such media exposure seems to be an increased likelihood that viewers will adopt a tough law-and-order attitude supportive of authority figures such as the police (Carlson, 1985, 1995).

Of course, the more controversial discussions of media as a socializing agent usually involve media products that seem to challenge convention and authority; music videos, rap lyrics, and pornography immediately come to mind. We will explore those issues later. Media influence on socialization is not direct and unambiguous, and we will also explore some of the debates in this area of research. For now it's enough to note that the media play a role, however qualified, in socializing us into our culture.

Mass Media in Social Relations

From a sociological perspective, the media play a crucial role in almost all aspects of daily life. However, their influence is not limited to *what* we know. The sociological significance of media extends beyond the content of media messages. Media also affect *how* we learn about our world and interact with one another. That is, mass media are bound up with the *process* of social relations.

This impact is most obvious when we look at the ways in which the mass media literally mediate our relationships with various social institutions. For example, we base most of our knowledge of government on news accounts rather than experience. Not only are we dependent on the media, then, for *what* we know, but the media's connection to politics also affects *how* we relate to the world of politics. Before mass media, political debates usually took place in a public forum where a crowd was physically present. Today, instead of attending a political event, we are more likely to read or watch the news of a political debate—followed by instant analysis and commentary—in the isolation of our home. Rather than take part in community action, we might satisfy a desire to participate in political life by calling a radio talk show. In turn, politicians rely heavily on the media to communicate their message. Gone are the days when candidates and their campaign workers pounded the pavement and knocked on doors to talk with voters. When such practices take place today, they are likely to be staged by politicians for the benefit of the media. We see similar dynamics at work with televised sports, televangelist preachers, and other "mediated" aspects of social life.

In more subtle ways, media are often part of our most routine relations with our families and close friends. Couples talk over the radio at breakfast as they read the morning newspaper. Families often watch television together, huddled around the "electronic hearth." Friends sit attentively and listen to music together, and groups of young people go to the movies or rent a video. Time-strapped parents sometimes use the TV as a surrogate baby-sitter, allowing their children to watch hours of television at one sitting. In all these cases, media products are connected to the ways we interact with other people on a daily basis. Media products provide a diversion, a source of conflict, or a unifying force.

The impact of media—both in content and in process—on all areas of society is undeniable. Talking about social life without including a discussion of the role of mass media risks missing an important element of contemporary society.

A Sociology of Media

Sociologists are not the only ones who study the mass media. Political scientists are sometimes interested in the media's role in politics. Literary scholars might examine the media as cultural texts. Some psychologists are interested in the effect of media exposure on individual behavior. Most important, mass communication scholars explore a wide range of media issues that often emphasize the structure and practice of media institutions.

The lines between the different approaches to the media are rarely clear. Instead, the differences tend to be ones of relative emphasis. It is common to see references to sociological theories and concepts in the mass communication literature. In fact, some mass communications scholars were trained as sociologists before turning their attention exclusively to the media. In turn, sociologists draw upon the work of mass communications scholars. But although they can overlap, there is a difference between the disciplines of mass communication and sociology. The field of mass communications is defined by a particular substantive area of interest, while sociology is a perspective that is applied to a wide range of substantive areas, including the media. Not all sociologists study the media, and not all mass communications researchers use a sociological perspective.

One of the best-known articulations of the sociological perspective came from C. Wright Mills, an American sociologist. Mills (1959) once argued that a sociological perspective—what he called the "sociological imagination"—enables us to see the connections between "private troubles" and "public issues." Such a perspective suggests that we can understand the condition of the individual only by situating that person in the larger context of society.

For example, students make very personal and individualized decisions about why they want to attend college. However, if you step back a moment, you can see that the individual, private choice of attending college makes sense only in the larger public context of society. We can understand this "individual" choice in the broader context of an economy in which a college education is now required for more and more occupations, or we can understand some students' choice in light of a larger culture that highly values formal education, as evidenced by their parents' (key socializing agents) pressure on them to attend school. Thus, social structure inextricably links the private lives of college students to the public world of economics (jobs), politics (public universities, government loans), and culture (the value of learning).

In contemporary society, it is media that most often act as the bridge between people's private lives and their relation to the public world. That is, people often learn about their place in larger society through mass media. The lessons media products might be teaching and the experience of participating in a mass-mediated society, therefore, are of crucial interest to anyone who wants to understand how society functions.

Throughout this text, we will note examples of media research that implicitly or explicitly employ a sociological perspective. A sociological perspective also informs our organization of this text. This book is not a historical overview of the evolution of media, nor is it a mass communications account of how the media industry functions. Such works are important, but what we highlight in this text is a sociological approach that emphasizes social relations, especially in the form of the tension between structure and agency, which we explain below.

The Importance of Social Relations

Sociologists believe that the individual is, to varying degrees, a product of social relations. The language we use, the education we receive, and the norms and values we are taught are all part of a socialization process through which we develop and embrace a sense of self. We become who we are largely through our social relations with others. At its most basic level, this means that our sense of identity and individuality emerges from our social interaction with others.

For example, we develop an identity by routinely imagining how others see us. Imagine a self-conscious interaction such as an important job interview. We dress up for the part of "serious" applicant and play the role we think the employer wants to see. We might feel very nervous because we are trying to sense how the employer views us. We ask ourselves questions: "Am I dressed appropriately?" "Did I answer that question well?" "Did the employer like me?" and so on. We put ourselves in the shoes of the employer and imagine how we must appear to him or her. We then imagine the employer's judgment of us, and we experience a feeling—such as pride or embarrassment—as a result of this imagined judgment. One sociologist (Cooley, 1902/1964) called this the "looking glass self." In social interactions, we try to see ourselves as if we were looking in a mirror. Our behavior is often affected by what we think others expect from us. Usually, our social interactions are not as tension-filled as a job interview, but the process still applies to a wide range of our daily interactions.

Furthermore, our daily activities usually take place within the context of larger groups and institutions. (The job interview mentioned above might take place in the context of a corporation, which, in turn, exists in the context of a larger economy, and so on.) Family, friendship circles, school, team, work, community—these are the collective contexts in which we develop our roles and identities as daughters or sons, friends, students, athletes, employees, citizens, and so forth. Each role brings with it a set of expectations about our actions; being a "good" student, employee, or friend usually involves conforming to those expectations. Sociology teaches us, therefore, that if you want to understand people's actions, you must consider the larger social context in which they occur.

Understanding the importance of social relations lies at the heart of thinking sociologically. Sociologists often try to look at the "big picture" to see the interplay between parts of social systems. In considering the mass media, we will emphasize three types of social relations:

- Relationships *between institutions,* for example, the interactions between the media industry and the government.

- Relationships *within an institution,* which involve the interaction of individuals occupying their institutional roles and positions—for example, the relationship between a screenwriter and the head of a motion picture studio.

- Relationships *between institutions and individuals,* who are always part of larger social groups—for example, the use of media products by audiences or readers.

Seeing the operation of social relations on different levels is also important to recognizing some of the different roles the media play in our society. One reason why the media are often controversial is that different groups expect the media to play different—and often incompatible— roles. For audiences, the media can serve as entertainment and diversion and as sources of information about the world beyond direct experience. For media workers, the media industry offers a job, with resulting income, prestige, and satisfaction, as well as a place for the development of a professional identity. For media owners, the media are a source of profit and, perhaps, a source of political power. For society at large, the media can be a way to transmit information and values (socialization), and can serve as a check on the abuse of political and economic power. Many of the debates about the media relate to the relative prominence of each of these divergent roles.

Structural Constraint and Human Agency

Sociologists often link discussions of social relations to the concepts of structure and agency. In this context, structure suggests constraint on human action, and agency indicates independent action. Each social relationship noted above is characterized by a tension between structure and agency. Because the tension between social structure and human agency is at the heart of this book, these ideas deserve our closer attention.

Structure

Structure is not something physical. In the broadest sense, social structure describes any recurring pattern of social behavior. For example, we can talk about "family structure" as a pattern of behaviors associated with the culturally defined idea of "family." The "traditional family" is actually a quite recent, historically specific phenomenon (Coontz, 1992). However, during the post–World War II years in Western countries, the "traditional family" usually meant married, heterosexual couples with children. In such relationships, the expected role of the wife was to work at home raising children. The expected role of the husband was to work for a paycheck to cover the household bills.

When sociologists speak of the change in family structure, they are referring to the changes in expected family behavior. Traditional expectations that a "family" include two parents, that the parents be married, that they be heterosexual, that a woman work only in the home, and so forth have changed dramatically. Single-parent families, blended families, two-income families, unmarried couples, and gay or lesbian couples, to name a few, have supplemented the "traditional" family. The family structure—the pattern of behavior associated with families—has changed.

It's easy to see from today's perspective that the traditional family structure was an attractive one for some people. It enabled them to fit neatly into clearly defined roles that brought them significant rewards. Husbands and children were nurtured and cared for. Wives were spared the pressure of holding down a job outside the home, while often enjoying autonomy in the home. However, it is also easy to see that such a structure limited the options of many people. It constrained their behavior by encouraging or coercing them to conform to the accepted standards of family-related behavior. For example, husbands were denied the experience of participating significantly in raising children, while wives were denied the opportunity to use their skills outside the home in paid employment.

A more immediate example of social structure is the complex pattern of institutions that make up the educational system in the United States, within which students, teachers, and administrators fulfill their expected roles. This structure can be enabling to students who successfully navigate through the system and eventually receive diplomas. Schooling often helps these students achieve a better life. However, as all students know, the educational structure can also be very constraining. Required courses, assignments, deadlines, and grades are all part of a structure that limits the actions of students and teachers. It is this constraint feature that is most important when considering structure.

Agency

When sociologists discuss structure, they often pair it with agency. Agency is intentional and undetermined human action. In the education example, the structure of education constrains students; but students also have a great deal of leeway in what they study, how much time and energy they spend on schoolwork, and so forth. Indeed, some students reject the educational structure entirely and drop out. Students in fact have the capacity for independent action in schools—they have agency. However, the regulations and norms of the educational system—the "structural constraint" —limit that agency.

It is important to note that human agency reproduces social structure. The education system or the traditional family structure continued only as long as new generations of people accepted the roles they were asked to fill. Daily activities within the family and school help to reproduce social structures, and they can also be a source for changing them. As long as most women saw themselves primarily as mothers and housewives and men accepted the role of primary wage-earners, the traditional family structure was able to continue. However, when enough women began to demand the right to choose from a wider set of possible roles, including having a career outside the home, family structure began to change. Thus, while structure constrains agency, it is human agency that both maintains and alters social structures.

Structure and Agency in the Media

With respect to the media, the tension between structure and agency is present on at least three levels, which correspond to the three types of social relations discussed earlier. We can express these three levels of analysis as three pairs of questions about structural constraint and agency.

- *Relationships between institutions.* How do nonmedia social structures, such as government and the economy, affect the media industry?
  How does the media industry influence nonmedia social structures?
- *Relationships within an institution.* How does the structure of the
  media industry affect media personnel (and indirectly media products)? How much do media personnel influence the media products
  (and indirectly the media industry)?
- *Relationships between an institution and the public.* How do the mass
  media influence the readers (audiences) of media messages? How do
  readers interpret and use media messages?

These basic social relations underlie our discussion throughout this book.

Relationships Between the Media and Other Social Institutions

First, our broadest level of analysis is the tension between structure and
agency produced by different institutions. We cannot adequately understand
the media industry without considering the social, economic, and political
context in which it exists. Institutions outside the control of media personnel set certain legal and economic limits within which the media must
operate. In turn, media have agency in the sense of acting on their own
and perhaps influencing other social institutions. A totalitarian regime, for
example, is likely to exert extreme constraint upon the press in that society. There would be little room for agency by the mainstream media,
although underground media may emerge to challenge the status quo.
Labeling a society democratic, on the other hand, includes the suggestion
that, at least in theory, the media are free of severe constraint by the government and thus have significant agency. Indeed, media in democratic societies can themselves exert a constraining influence over other institutions.

In the real world, there is always a mixture of structural constraint
and independent agency. Media researchers, therefore, examine both how
social structures external to the media impact the industry and how the
media affect other social structures. This level of analysis includes questions such as the following: Does advertising revenue influence the content of popular magazines? Should music lyrics be "rated" as movies are?
How have media affected the organization of political campaigns? Does it
matter who owns major publishing houses or newspapers?

Relationships Within the Media Industry

Second, to understand the decisions made by journalists, writers, producers, filmmakers, media executives, and other media personnel, we must
understand the context in which they labor. This means that we must be

familiar with both the internal workings of mass media organizations and the processes of professional socialization. The sociological emphasis here is on social positions, roles, and practices, not on particular individuals. Relevant issues of concern include the structures of media institutions, who wields power within them, what professional norms and expectations are associated with different positions, and so forth.

Within the media industry, the tension between structure and agency is related primarily to how much autonomy media personnel have in doing their work. The amount of autonomy will vary depending on the position an individual occupies. The questions raised include the following: To what extent do standard journalistic practices shape the process of news reporting or the content of the news? How much do economic considerations enter into the decision-making process of Hollywood movie-making? How "free" are musicians to create their music? In the language of sociology, structural considerations may significantly affect the individual agency of media personnel. At the same time, the collective agency of those who work in the media has the potential to alter the structures that constrain individual media professionals.

Relationships Between the Media and the Public

A third kind of social relationship occurs when the media deliver messages to readers. Here the issues of interest involve how readers interact with media products and media technology. Readers are not passive sponges that soak up the many messages they come across in the media. This would imply a one-way relationship, with the media determining the thoughts and behavior of listeners and viewers. Instead, readers of media products must actively interpret media messages.

When we interpret the words of someone speaking with us face to face, we have an excellent resource at hand: the speaker. We interactively construct the conversation. We can elicit more information from the speaker by asking a question ("What do you mean?") or by using appropriate facial expressions to convey our reactions. We can comment on statements and thereby affect the course of the conversation. Such interaction between speakers helps promote mutual understanding about the messages being communicated.

Mass media messages, however, do not allow for the intimate interaction of sender and receiver that characterizes personal communication. We cannot ask a stand-up comedian on television to explain a joke. We either get it or we don't. If a television reporter mentions the National Labor Relations Board and we do not know what she is referring to, we cannot ask for a clarification. Audiences, therefore, must rely on other resources to make sense of media messages.

Relevant resources available to audiences might include knowledge and information gained from personal experience, other people, formal education, or other media products. These resources are neither randomly nor equally distributed. The interpretive skills that people bring with them to their viewing, listening, and reading are shaped by aspects of social structure such as class and education. Thus, in constructing their own individual interpretations of the media, people constantly draw upon collective resources and experiences that are shaped by social factors. Although media messages are impersonal and subject to multiple inter-pretations by audiences, the construction of meaning does not take place in individualized isolation.

Active audience interpretation is important, but we must also realize that the thousands of hours people spend with the media do have some influence on them. Readers are not completely immune to the impact of media content and media technology. The structure and agency frame-work suggests that we have to explore the dynamic tension between the power of social structure and the (always partial) autonomy of human activity. How powerful are media images in shaping how we think and feel? Do they affect how people are likely to behave? For example, does violent television programming encourage children to be more aggressive? What are the differences in the ways different people respond to these images? How does media technology affect our social relationships? Ultimately, these are complex questions that do not lend themselves to easy answers involving all-encompassing media power or complete indi-vidual freedom. The relationship between structure and agency helps illu-minate the various levels at which mass media images, whose meanings are neither fixed nor arbitrary, influence but do not determine our under-standing of the world.

A Model of Media and the Social World

How can we begin to make sense of the complex relationships we have identified? Exhibit 1.5 provides a graphic representation of these rela-tions. The model illustrates the fundamentals of a sociological perspective on the media. As noted above, we cannot understand the media without looking at them as one aspect of a larger social world. Our model repre-sents this by showing that all components of the media, as well as the audience, exist within the broader framework of the social world (the shaded area).

Four components, each represented by a separate box in the diagram, make up the core of our model. We must understand that all four ele-ments are simultaneously a part of the social world and surrounded by

EXHIBIT 1.5 *Simplified Model of Media and the Social World*

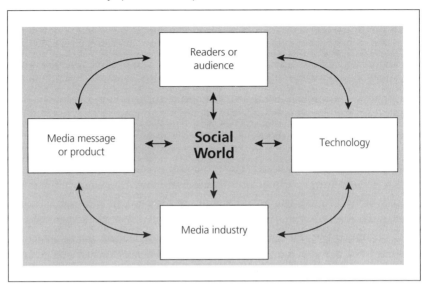

the social world. We must also remember that the graphic organization of these four elements is arbitrary. There is no "top" or "bottom" to the process; rather, it is a circular, multidimensional process. Arrowheads represent the potential relationships between these components. (Not all relationships will be relevant in all situations.) We will first describe the elements represented by the four large boxes (proceeding clockwise from the bottom) and then turn our attention to the unique status of the "social world" (represented by the shading), which is both in the center of the model and simultaneously surrounding it.

The box at the bottom of the model represents the "media industry," by which we mean the entire organizational structure that makes up the media, including all media personnel. The media industry is affected by changes in "technology" (e.g., the invention of television) but is also instrumental in influencing the direction and application of technology (e.g., the use of computers for film animation).

The "media industry" is the producer of the "media message or product." For example, a book is written by an author, designed, typeset, printed, distributed by a publisher, and sold in a bookstore. However, the conventions of particular genres of media products also influence the creators of the product. The murder mystery genre, for example, requires the existence of a crime.

"Readers or audiences" may be influenced by the media messages they see (e.g., learning about an impending snowstorm from the weather report), but they must actively interpret and construct meaning from those messages and products (e.g., deciding whether or not to believe the forecast and whether to act differently as a result).

The direction and development of "technology" is affected by how the "readers or audiences" choose to use it—or not to use it. In the early and mid-1990s there was relatively little enthusiasm for early experiments in interactive television, but there was a great deal of public interest in the capabilities of the Internet, especially e-mail. In turn, technology has a potential impact on the public. For example, television viewing usually requires close attention because the medium communicates via both sound and images. This contrasts with radio. The technology of radio makes it a very mobile medium that does not demand our full attention. Unlike television, which we must watch in order to fully follow the programs, radio allows us to do other things while still attending to it, such as drive a car, jog, cook dinner, or work. Books demand more attention than television or movies. We can carry on a conversation while watching TV or sitting in a movie theater, although we risk missing a scene or being scolded by another viewer. It is far more difficult to read a book and carry on a conversation at the same time. Each medium, therefore, tends to produce a different experience for the readers. This is one effect of technology.

The middle, and broader context, of the model is the "social world." We theorize this to be all the social elements not included in the four main boxes. Some of these elements are crucial for an understanding of the workings of the media and thus can be thought of as being at the center of the model. For example, in this book we will examine the role of government and broader economic forces; these are nonmedia social factors that influence all the elements of our model.

Notice that the top and bottom elements of our model include human agents—real people—while the left and right boxes are human creations. People are the medium through which media messages and technology affect each other. Similarly, the relationship between the media industry and most members of the audience is mediated by media products, technology, and other factors in the social world.

Note, too, that any single component of the model simultaneously relates to other components. For example, the reader of a media message simultaneously experiences the impact of technology (the medium) and other social forces (including things such as race, class, and gender). Thus, readers do not interpret media messages in isolation. Similarly, media products are simultaneously influenced by the media industry that creates them, the readers who interpret them (or choose to ignore them), and other aspects of the social world, such as government regulation.

Our simplified model is meant to identify some of the key components in a sociology of media and to clarify some of the relationships between these components. Like all models, it cannot fully account for the infinite complexities of the "real" social world. However, using the model to analyze the media can help us clarify the workings and social significance of mass media.

Applying the Model: The Civil Rights Movement

To illustrate briefly how the model can alert us to important real-life issues, let us consider the modern U.S. civil rights struggles of the 1950s and 1960s (Branch, 1988; McAdam, 1982; Morris, 1984). We can think of this social movement as a part of the nonmedia "social world" insofar as it exists independent of our four components of the media model. For the moment, then, imagine the civil rights movement as being the element of the social world that occupies the center position in our model.

Using this premise, and moving clockwise around our model, we see that the media industry created media messages about the civil rights movement, while the genre norms of "news" coverage influenced the media personnel reporting the news. Reporters wrote stories about the movement, but because these stories constituted "news," they were supposed to be a balanced presentation of facts.

The media messages about the civil rights movement affected the viewing and reading audiences, who, in turn, were interpreting the meaning of those messages. Readers are influenced by the words and images about race-related issues that appear in a wide variety of media products, including news reports, television sit-coms, Hollywood movies, music, best-selling books, and popular magazines. In our case, some supporters in the North, for example, were moved by media accounts to make financial contributions to movement organizations in the South, while others sympathized with the forces of segregation. The media messages were having an impact, but the readers could interpret the meaning and significance of the messages.

Audiences made use of technology, especially the newly emerging television technology in the 1950s and 1960s, to access media messages. Meanwhile, technology may have indirectly influenced readers, in this case with the immediacy and impact of television pictures of police violence against demonstrators. Technology was also affecting the media industry; lighter hand-held cameras allowed reporters more mobility. The industry, in turn, influenced the use of the new technology by applying it to the coverage of demonstrations.

Now let us move to the center of the model. The civil rights movement has clearly had an impact on the media industry (and other social institutions), which, like all major industries, has changed its hiring and promotion practices to comply both with cultural changes and with laws against discrimination. The limited racial diversity that exists today in the media industry would not have come about without the influence of this social movement and the resulting changes in legislation and social norms. This is one example of how the "social world" influences the "media industry."

However, the media industry also had an impact on the civil rights movement. Because social movements are aware of the potential effect the media may have on society at large, they have often crafted strategies that try to take advantage of potential media coverage (Ryan, 1991). In modern society, social movement strategies, such as marches and demonstrations, are important as much for the media coverage they generate as for the actual events themselves (see Exhibit 1.6). Many social movements, therefore, have become media-conscious in their efforts. Thus, the impact of the media industry—in the form of its personnel and its organizational routines—on such movements is evident even before the media produce any coverage of the group.

"Media messages" affected the civil rights movement as it tried to develop favorable media coverage and, in some cases, altered strategies that generated negative coverage. The movement probably did not affect media messages directly but instead did so indirectly by influencing the media industry. Thus, changes in the social world can filter through the media industry and affect media products. An industry that employs more people of color in positions of power, for example, is more likely to be sensitive to race issues in its media products.

The civil rights movement has had a direct impact on citizens who are also "readers" of media products. The presence of this movement has meant more social equality and direct material and psychological benefits for many people. At the same time, citizens have acted as social agents creating the social movement in the first place, illustrating the interaction between these two components of the model.

The "technology" of the 1950s that the civil rights movement relied upon to communicate its messages may seem ancient by today's standards, but it was an integral part of the ongoing organizing effort. Movement organizers influenced the application of the existing technology by using it for their own ends. For example, if a leaflet announcing a meeting needed to be distributed, stencils might be cut for hand-cranked mimeograph machines. Computer desktop publishing, laser printers, high-speed copiers, and fax machines would have seemed like science fiction at the time. Perhaps more important is the indirect manner in which technology —through the media industry—affected the movement. In the 1950s, a

EXHIBIT 1.6 *Social Movements and the Media*

In part because they do not have regular access to the media, many social movements must adopt dramatic tactics that will attract attention and increase their chances of gaining media exposure. A common strategy is the public demonstration or picket. Here, under the watchful eye of police, demonstrators carry signs with their anticensorship message. Media photographers and videographers (on the right) capture the image for possible transmission to the public.

The demonstrators pictured here were protesting a chain bookstore's 1989 decision to not carry Salman Rushdie's book *The Satanic Verses*. Rushdie's life was threatened by Islamic fundamentalists who considered the book to be blasphemous. *(Photo by Ed Hedemann)*

new generation of cameras allowed news teams to readily cover social movement events, sometimes producing dramatic images of the clashes between civil rights marchers and police. (In the 1990s, the availability of home video cameras made it possible for the media to broadcast graphic images of brutality inflicted by the Los Angeles police upon black motorist Rodney King. The incongruity between these stark images and the initial acquittal of the police officers involved played an important role in the 1992 Los Angeles riot. Also, the introduction of additional channels through cable technology facilitated the rise of programming oriented specifically toward racial minorities—like that on BET, Black Entertainment Television.)

This brief sketch of the civil rights movement illustrates the utility of a sociological approach to understanding how media interact with the social world. This interaction is always multidimensional, and each element of our model will receive closer attention in later chapters.

Conclusion

It is difficult to overestimate the importance of media in today's society. From the privacy of our living rooms to the public forums of presidential debates, the media serve as the informational network connecting the many elements of our society. There is no doubt that the media are significant and worth studying. A sociological approach to the media allows us to identify the key questions and reminds us to keep the "big picture" in mind when we discuss media issues.

The remainder of this book is organized into sections on media production, content, and audiences, with a concluding chapter on the future of the media in a global culture. The model of media and the social world presented in Exhibit 1.5 is the underlying framework for the rest of the book. At the most general level, this sociological framework helps us identify questions we should ask when we study the media. In this case, those questions concern the multidirectional relations between components of our model: the social world, the media industry, media products, audiences, and technology. Examining the relationships between these key elements is the first step toward developing a nuanced understanding of the role of mass media in our society.

Production
The Media Industry and the Social World

We begin our examination of the mass media by looking at the source of media products: the media industry. In particular, Part Two explores the social forces that influence the media industry, first highlighting relationships *between* institutions. In Chapter 2, we look at the economic forces that shape the industry and the consequences for media content. Chapter 3 turns to the political constraints on the media industry, exploring various debates about government regulation of mass media.

We also examine how the organization of the media industry helps shape media products. Here the concern is with relationships *within* the media industry. Chapter 4 analyzes the professional routines and organizational norms at work in various sectors of the media.

The emphasis in Part Two is on the broad structural constraints on media production; how these economic, political, and organizational forces shape decision making and influence media content; and how actors within the media industry interpret and respond to these constraints. This "production perspective" has been the principal lens through which much contemporary sociology has looked at mass media. As we will see, it has a great deal to offer in highlighting several key issues.

However, since a production-oriented perspective has little to do with things such as *how* people use or interpret media products, it is important to remember that it is only part of our larger model of media and the social world. Issues of media content, the role of active audiences, and media influence will be addressed in Parts Three and Four. Production, though, is an important piece of this larger media puzzle. ■

CHAPTER 2

The Economics of the
Media Industry

This chapter focuses on the economics of mass media. Most of the media in the United States are for-profit businesses. Like all businesses, they are influenced by issues such as profitability, cost containment, and evolving ownership patterns. To understand the mass media, then, we must have some sense of the economic dimension of the media industry. Chapter 2 explores this topic by focusing on media ownership, the for-profit orientation of most media, and the impact of advertising.

The types of questions we ask, and the general orientation of this chapter, build upon the framework outlined in Chapter 1. We emphasize a sociological perspective that argues that social structures shape—and are in turn shaped by—human behavior. An emphasis on this tension between agency and structural constraint suggests that human activities and attitudes must be understood in relation to broader social forces. In this case, we cannot understand the media industry without understanding the forces that affect the industry. The individuals and groups that create the newspapers we read, the television we watch, the music we listen to, or the movies we attend are not fully autonomous actors. They do not work in isolation from the social world. Instead, they work within the constraints of an existing organization, a broader media industry, and a larger social context.

A sociological perspective suggests that we cannot look at media products in a vacuum, either. Instead, we should see media products as the result of a social process of production that occurs within an institutional framework. Some researchers call this kind of institutional approach a "production perspective" (Peterson, 1976; Crane, 1992) because it emphasizes the media production process rather than either specific media products or the consumption of those products. The production perspective highlights the fact that mass media products are not free-floating texts; they do not just appear out of thin air. They are the result of a complex production process that, in turn, is shaped by a variety of social structural forces that operate on various levels, some affecting the industry as a whole, some affecting particular actors or groups of actors within the industry. Producers create media products under conditions that are always changing as economic, technological, political, and social changes occur in the broader society. Therefore, if we are to better understand media products, we must take into account the historically specific context in which people create them.

Within the explicitly sociological literature, researchers have applied the production perspective most widely to the news media. Therefore, much of this chapter explores the ways the production perspective explains news. We also use the production perspective to examine several nonnews media examples, including the music industry and new media technologies.

Changing Patterns of Ownership

Who owns the media? This is a central question about the economic organization of the mass media. The assumption behind the question is that owners of the media influence the content and form of media products by their decisions to hire and fire certain personnel, to fund certain projects, and to give a media platform to certain speakers. In its least subtle version, such a question might imply a kind of conspiracy theory, in which a small group of powerful owners uses the media to control the thoughts of the rest of us. With its Orwellian connotations of mind-control, this extreme version of the question is far too simplistic and therefore not particularly illuminating. Still, a substantial body of research has explored this topic in a more helpful way.

Concentration of Ownership

One of the clearest trends in media ownership is its increasing *concentration* in fewer and fewer hands. In *The Media Monopoly*, Ben Bagdikian (1992) argues that ownership of media has become so concentrated that in 1992 only 20 national and multinational corporations dominated the mass communication industry. His examples are striking. While there are more than 3,000 book publishers in the United States, only 5 companies account for more than half the annual revenue in the book industry. Only 2 corporations receive the majority of annual revenues in the magazine industry, and 11 companies control the majority of daily newspaper circulation in the United States. In all three cases, the numbers represent significant increases in concentration since 1983, when Bagdikian produced the first edition of his book. As Exhibit 2.1 shows, the comparable figure for newspapers had been 20 companies (instead of 11), for magazines 20 (instead of 2), and for book publishing 11 (instead of 5). Concentration in both the television and the film industries remained largely unchanged between 1983 and 1992, but both industries were

EXHIBIT 2.1 *Changing Media Ownership Concentration, 1983–1992*

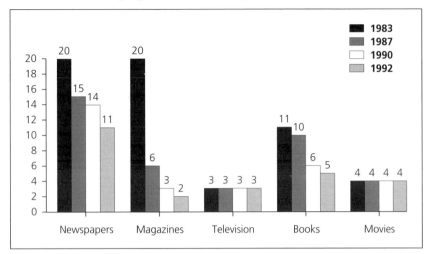

Source: Ben Bagdikian. *The Media Monopoly.* Boston: Beacon Press, 1983, 1987, 1990, 1992.

This graph shows the number of corporations that, collectively, controlled 50 percent or more of the market in each industry sector. (The number of companies controlling 50 percent or more of the total media market fell from 46 in 1983 to 29 in 1987, 23 in 1990, and 20 in 1992.)

already highly concentrated in 1983, with four motion picture studios and three television networks dominating these industries. (As we will see, new developments have weakened the dominance of the three television networks, who lost one-third of their audience between the late 1970s and 1990. Still, in the 1990s, ABC, CBS, and NBC continue to hold more than a 50 percent share of the prime-time audience.)

These figures may surprise many readers, who are exposed to so many individual media outlets every day. Ownership seems to change so often that it can be hard to keep up with which company owns which media outlet. In the world of newspapers, for example, chains such as Gannett, Knight-Ridder, and Newhouse own newspapers all over the country. Each paper has a different name, and it is not always immediately apparent to readers that a paper is part of a national chain. In book publishing, the major companies have so many different imprints that even a conscientious reader is unlikely to know the common owners of the different imprints. For example, Random House publishes Knopf, Times Books, Ballantine Books, Pantheon, Vintage, and others; Macmillan publishes the Free Press, Atheneum, Collier Books, Twayne, and Scribner's, among others.

EXHIBIT 2.2 *Anatomy of Media Conglomerates**

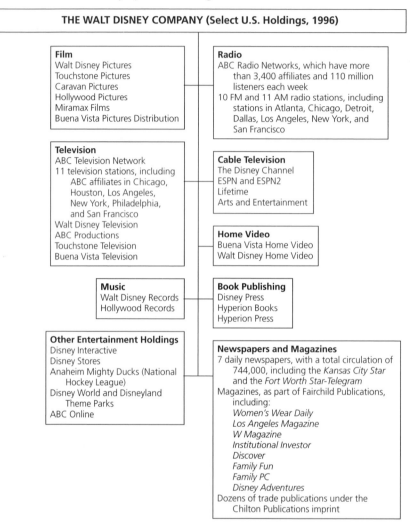

THE WALT DISNEY COMPANY (Select U.S. Holdings, 1996)

Film
Walt Disney Pictures
Touchstone Pictures
Caravan Pictures
Hollywood Pictures
Miramax Films
Buena Vista Pictures Distribution

Radio
ABC Radio Networks, which have more
    than 3,400 affiliates and 110 million
    listeners each week
10 FM and 11 AM radio stations, including
    stations in Atlanta, Chicago, Detroit,
    Dallas, Los Angeles, New York, and
    San Francisco

Television
ABC Television Network
11 television stations, including
    ABC affiliates in Chicago,
    Houston, Los Angeles,
    New York, Philadelphia,
    and San Francisco
Walt Disney Television
ABC Productions
Touchstone Television
Buena Vista Television

Cable Television
The Disney Channel
ESPN and ESPN2
Lifetime
Arts and Entertainment

Home Video
Buena Vista Home Video
Walt Disney Home Video

Music
Walt Disney Records
Hollywood Records

Book Publishing
Disney Press
Hyperion Books
Hyperion Press

Other Entertainment Holdings
Disney Interactive
Disney Stores
Anaheim Mighty Ducks (National
    Hockey League)
Disney World and Disneyland
    Theme Parks
ABC Online

Newspapers and Magazines
7 daily newspapers, with a total circulation of
    744,000, including the *Kansas City Star*
    and the *Fort Worth Star-Telegram*
Magazines, as part of Fairchild Publications,
    including:
    Women's Wear Daily
    Los Angeles Magazine
    W Magazine
    Institutional Investor
    Discover
    Family Fun
    Family PC
    Disney Adventures
Dozens of trade publications under the
    Chilton Publications imprint

*These charts do not reflect the formal corporate structure of the companies.

There has been much debate about the potential effect of ownership concentration on media products. We discuss these debates in some detail later in this chapter. First, though, we take note of two other trends related to media ownership: conglomeration and integration.

Conglomeration and Integration

Concentration of media ownership means that fewer corporations own the media. At the same time that concentration of ownership has been

EXHIBIT 2.2 *(continued)*

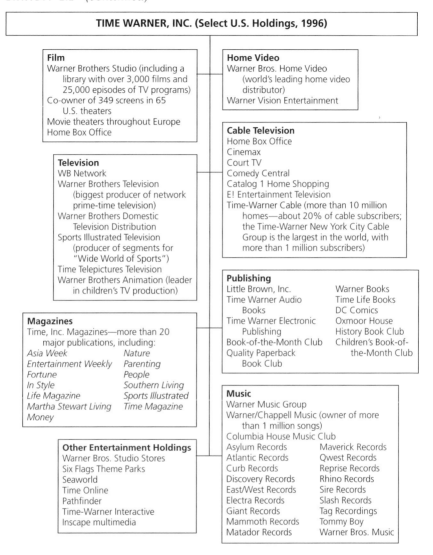

TIME WARNER, INC. (Select U.S. Holdings, 1996)

Film
Warner Brothers Studio (including a
    library with over 3,000 films and
    25,000 episodes of TV programs)
Co-owner of 349 screens in 65
    U.S. theaters
Movie theaters throughout Europe
Home Box Office

Television
WB Network
Warner Brothers Television
    (biggest producer of network
    prime-time television)
Warner Brothers Domestic
    Television Distribution
Sports Illustrated Television
    (producer of segments for
    "Wide World of Sports")
Time Telepictures Television
Warner Brothers Animation (leader
    in children's TV production)

Magazines
Time, Inc. Magazines—more than 20
    major publications, including:
Asia Week   Nature
Entertainment Weekly   Parenting
Fortune   People
In Style   Southern Living
Life Magazine   Sports Illustrated
Martha Stewart Living   Time Magazine
Money

Other Entertainment Holdings
Warner Bros. Studio Stores
Six Flags Theme Parks
Seaworld
Time Online
Pathfinder
Time-Warner Interactive
Inscape multimedia

Home Video
Warner Bros. Home Video
    (world's leading home video
    distributor)
Warner Vision Entertainment

Cable Television
Home Box Office
Cinemax
Court TV
Comedy Central
Catalog 1 Home Shopping
E! Entertainment Television
Time-Warner Cable (more than 10 million
    homes—about 20% of cable subscribers;
    the Time-Warner New York City Cable
    Group is the largest in the world, with
    more than 1 million subscribers)

Publishing
Little Brown, Inc.   Warner Books
Time Warner Audio   Time Life Books
    Books   DC Comics
Time Warner Electronic   Oxmoor House
    Publishing   History Book Club
Book-of-the-Month Club   Children's Book-of-
Quality Paperback   the-Month Club
    Book Club

Music
Warner Music Group
Warner/Chappell Music (owner of more
    than 1 million songs)
Columbia House Music Club
Asylum Records   Maverick Records
Atlantic Records   Qwest Records
Curb Records   Reprise Records
Discovery Records   Rhino Records
East/West Records   Sire Records
Electra Records   Slash Records
Giant Records   Tag Recordings
Mammoth Records   Tommy Boy
Matador Records   Warner Bros. Music

occurring, *conglomeration* has been taking place. That is, media companies have become part of much larger corporations, which own a collection of other companies that may operate in highly diverse business areas
(see Exhibit 2.2).

As mass media have become big businesses, major corporations with
many nonmedia holdings have increasingly turned their attention to
media operations. In the United States, media properties are among the
most attractive properties to both potential investors and buyers. As

shown by the merger that created Time Warner in 1989, the 1993 high-stakes bidding between QVC and Viacom for the purchase of Paramount, the 1996 merger of Disney and Capital Cities/ABC, and the growth of major chain newspapers, the process of conglomeration continues at a rapid pace. As manufacturing jobs move to other parts of the globe, media—in both news and entertainment forms—have become a key segment of the American economy. The media industry is producing high visibility, high profits, and a major item for export to other countries.

Concentration has affected the relationship between various media organizations within a single conglomerate. Economic analysts have long used the terms "horizontal integration" and "vertical integration" to describe two types of ownership concentration in any industry. In the media industry, vertical integration refers to the process by which one owner acquires all aspects of production and distribution of a single type of media product. For example, a movie company might integrate vertically by acquiring talent agencies, production studios, theater chains, videocassette manufacturing plants, and a chain of video rental stores. The company could then better control the entire process of creating, producing, marketing, and distributing movies. Similarly, a book publisher might integrate vertically by acquiring paper mills, printing facilities, bookbinderies, a trucking firm, and a chain of bookstores (see Exhibit 2.3).

Horizontal integration refers to the process by which one company buys different kinds of media, concentrating ownership *across* differing types of media rather than "up and down" through one industry. In horizontal integration, media conglomerates assemble large portfolios of magazines, television stations, book publishers, record labels, and so on to mutually support one another's operations. For example, Time Warner released the blockbuster film *Batman* with the help of a prominent review in *Time* magazine and heavy promotion on Time Warner–owned Home Box Office (Miller, 1990). The opportunity for cross-promotion is one of the driving forces behind the growth of horizontally integrated media companies.

Consequences of Conglomeration and Integration

While the trends in media ownership may be of interest in themselves, our prime concern is with the relationship between ownership and the media product. What are the consequences of integration, conglomeration, and concentration of ownership?

EXHIBIT 2.3 *Vertical and Horizontal Integration in the Media Industry**

Example of vertical integration:

MUSIC	BOOKS	FILM
Musicians	**Authors**	Actors
Talent agencies	**Literary agencies**	Talent agencies
Record labels	**Publishers**	Film studios
Sound recording manufacturers	**Printers and paper mills**	Film and videocassette manufacturers
Record clubs	**Trucking firms**	Movie theaters
Record stores	**Bookstores**	Video rental stores

Example of horizontal integration:

MUSIC	BOOKS	FILM
Musicians	Authors	Actors
Talent agencies	Literary agencies	Talent agencies
Record labels	**Publishers**	**Film studios**
Sound recording manufacturers	Printers and paper mills	Film and videocassette manufacturers
Record clubs	Trucking firms	Movie theaters
Record stores	Bookstores	Video rental stores

*Shaded, bold-faced companies are owned by the same corporation.

Integration and Self-Promotion

The economic factors propelling both vertical and horizontal integration are clear: Owners perceive such arrangements as both efficient and profitable. The cultural consequences are more ambiguous. However, an institutional approach suggests that such ownership patterns are likely to affect the type of media product created. In particular, integrated media conglomerates—seeking the benefits of what industry insiders refer to as "synergy"—are likely to favor products that can best be exploited by other components of the conglomerate. For example, horizontal integration may well encourage the publication of books that can be made into movies and discourage the publication of those that cannot. It may encourage the promotion of new music releases on television programs and the popularization in magazines of celebrity personalities who star in company-owned television programs or movies. More generally, promotion and marketing are likely to dominate the decision-making process within a horizontally integrated media industry.

Vertical integration becomes especially significant when the company that makes the product also controls its distribution. For example, a corporation that owns a mail-order "book-of-the-month" club is likely to prominently feature its own publications, limiting competitors' access to a lucrative book-buying market.

The possibilities for fully utilizing horizontal and vertical integration are startling. Bagdikian (1992) presents a hypothetical all-encompassing case, which he characterizes as the fondest scenario of the new owners:

> A magazine owned by the company selects or commissions an article that is suitable for later transformation into a television series on a network owned by the company; then it becomes a screenplay for a movie studio owned by the company, with the movie sound track sung by a vocalist made popular by feature articles in the company-owned magazines and by constant playing of the sound track by company-owned radio stations, after which the songs become popular on a record label owned by the company and so on, with reruns on company-owned cable systems and rentals of its videocassettes all over the world.

The growth of global media giants like Disney, Viacom, and Time Warner has made such a scenario increasingly plausible. One consequence of integration, then, is an increase in media cross-promotion and, perhaps, a decrease in media products that are not suitable for cross-promotion.

The Impact of Conglomeration

What has the growth of large multimedia firms in the 1980s and 1990s meant for the news, television, radio, films, music, and books we receive? In other words, to what extent does conglomeration affect the media product? The loudest warnings about the impact of conglomeration have come from within the news industry, in part because some news media had traditionally been sheltered from the full pressure of profitmaking. For example, respectable television news divisions were understood to represent a necessary public service commitment that lent prestige to the major networks. They were not expected to turn a substantial profit.

However, that has changed with the takeover of news operations by major corporate conglomerates. Ken Auletta's *Three Blind Mice* (1991) paints a vivid picture of the clash between the new corporate owners of the three major television networks and their news divisions in the mid-1980s. For those who worked at, for example, NBC News, the purchase of the network by General Electric led to conflicts about the meaning and role of television news. In most of these conflicts, the new corporate owners ultimately prevailed. As Auletta (1991, p. 564) tells it, the new owners of NBC "emphasized a 'boundaryless' company, one without walls between News, Entertainment, Sales, and other divisions. . . . At NBC's annual management retreat in 1990, many of the 160 executives questioned why Sales or Entertainment couldn't have more input into news specials, or why News tended to keep its distance from the rest of the company, as if it were somehow special." General Electric chair Jack Welsh even specified that "Today" show weather reporter Willard Scott should mention GE light bulbs on the program. According to former NBC news president Lawrence Grossman, "It was one of the perks of owning a network. . . . You get your light bulbs mentioned on the air. . . . People want to please the owners" (Husseini, 1994, p. 13).

Conglomeration has affected print journalism as well. Some critics argue that corporate takeovers of print media have put the emphasis on attracting and entertaining consumers, rather than on informing citizens (Squires, 1993). In this context, newspapers become increasingly colorful, focus attention on the lives of celebrities, and print sensationalistic stories about dramatic and bizarre happenings. An additional sign of the change is the training required for top-level editorial positions at newspapers. As marketing has become the focus of many local papers, MBAs with background in the business world have begun to replace people with journalistic experience in executive positions (Underwood, 1993). Conglomeration, therefore, has led to increased bottom-line pressure, even in areas of the media that used to be partially insulated from such pressure.

The Effects of Concentration

As with integration and conglomeration, a key concern with the concentration of media ownership has been its impact on the media product—especially the potential homogenization of media products. A broader concern, however, to which we first turn, is the growing concentration of power and the limitation of media access.

Media Control and Political Power

Can concentrated media ownership be translated into undue political influence? Most people recognize the importance of such a question in examining the government's control of media in totalitarian nations. It is clear in such situations that state ownership and exclusive access are likely to affect media products. In the United States, most discussion about the First Amendment and free speech also focuses on the possibility of government censorship. This discussion is generally blind, however, to the impact of corporate ownership.

In addressing this concern, Bagdikian (1992) has argued that the United States has a "private ministry of information," metaphorically referring to the type of government-led propaganda system that exists in totalitarian societies. In the case of the contemporary United States, however, private interests, not the government, largely control this information system. Bagdikian suggests that when a small number of firms with similar interests dominate the media industry, it begins to function in a way similar to a state information system. It is hard to question the underlying argument that those who own large media conglomerates have at least the *potential* to wield a great deal of political power.

How might ownership of media translate into political power? It is possible that those amassing political power could use the media as a direct resource. In Italy, the 1994 national election produced a new prime minister, Silvio Berlusconi, who is a media magnate and the dominant force in Italian broadcasting. For Berlusconi, ownership of media was clearly of great political value; he owned strategic assets that were unavailable to other political actors. However, the reign of his conservative coalition was short-lived, an indication of the limitations of media ownership as a source of power. He resigned in late 1994 after only eight months in office. One of the many issues that plagued him was the apparent conflict of interest between his role as prime minister and that of media magnate.

The situation in the United States is even more complex, largely because of the vast size of the U.S. media industry. One line of argument suggests that owners of media companies have direct control over media products and thus are able to exert political influence by promoting ideas that enhance their interests. For example, conservative media magnate Rupert Murdoch financed the start-up of the high-profile conservative U.S. magazine *The Weekly Standard*. However, some media outlets, especially news outlets, rely on a perception of objectivity or evenhandedness to maintain their legitimacy. It is not likely, therefore, that major news media outlets will consistently and blatantly promote a single political agenda. Viewers are more likely to find such an approach among smaller cable stations and satellite networks such as the conservative National Empowerment Television, established in 1993.

However, there are more subtle processes at work in mainstream media that do have serious political consequences. The process of using media to promote a political agenda is more complex than simply feeding people ideas and images that they passively accept. Owners can use media sites to disseminate a specific position on a controversial issue or to help legitimize particular institutions or behaviors. Just as important, owners can systematically exclude certain ideas from their media products. While control of information or images can never be total, owners can tilt the scales in particular directions quite dramatically.

Ownership by major corporations of vast portfolios of mass media gives us reason to believe that a whole range of ideas and images—those that question fundamental social arrangements, under which the media owners are doing quite well—will rarely be visible. This does not mean that all images and information are uniform. It means that some ideas will be widely available, while others will be largely excluded. For example, images critical of gridlock in the federal government are frequent; images critical of capitalism as an economic system are virtually nonexistent. There is no way of proving the connection, but the media's focus on the shortcomings of the government, rather than of the private sector, seems consistent with the interests of the corporate media owners.

This process is most obvious in products that directly address contemporary social and political events, but it also happens in entertainment products. Consider, for example, the depiction of gays and lesbians on prime-time television. Most obvious is the scarcity of gay and lesbian characters. Also, those that do appear face constraints that heterosexual characters do not; for example, they do not kiss, even as popular television continues to become more explicit in depictions of heterosexual sex. There is no conspiracy here. More likely, a small number of profit-making firms that rely upon mass audiences and major advertisers are simply avoiding potential controversies that might threaten their bottom line. We return to these issues in Chapters 5 and 6 when we explore the content of mass media.

The political impact of concentrated corporate ownership, however, is both broader and subtler than the exclusion of certain ideas in favor of others. Herbert Schiller (1989) argues that "the corporate voice" has been generalized so successfully that most of us do not even think of it as a specifically corporate voice. That is, the corporate view has become "our" view, the "American" view, even though the interests of the corporate entities that own mass media are far from universal. One example of this is the entire media-generated discourse—in newspapers, television, radio, and magazines—about the American economy, in which corporate success provides the framework for virtually all evaluations of national economic well-being. Quarterly profits, mergers and acquisitions, productivity, and fluctuations in the financial markets are so widely discussed that their relationship to the "corporate voice" is difficult to discern. The relationship between corporate financial health and citizen well-being, however, is rarely discussed explicitly.

One possible political consequence of the concentration of media ownership is that, in some ways, it becomes more difficult for alternative media voices to emerge. Because mass media outlets in all sectors of the media industry are large mass-production and mass-distribution firms, ownership is restricted to those who can acquire substantial financial resources. In the age of multimillion-dollar media enterprises, freedom of the press may be left to those few who can afford to own what has become a very expensive "press." Ownership of the means of information becomes part of larger patterns of inequality in contemporary societies. In this sense, mass media institutions are no different from other social institutions; they are linked to the patterned inequality that exists throughout our society.

Media Ownership and Content Diversity

Does a change in the pattern of media ownership change the nature or range of media products? As this question suggests, macro-level patterns and specific media products need to be understood in relation to each other. Such a link is imperative for media sociology and moves us into the realm of social relations. The key is to explain the specific nature of the relations between broad institutional forces and the everyday world of mass media.

As media ownership has become more concentrated, researchers have been particularly interested in the ways such ownership patterns influence the diversity of the media in terms of both form and content. One widely adopted argument has been that media owned by a few will lead to products that lack diversity; that is, as ownership becomes increasingly concentrated, the content of media will become increasingly uniform. This relationship is a *hypothesis,* a proposition to be studied. However, research shows that the relationship between ownership concentration and diversity is not as straightforward as we might think. We will look at how researchers have studied this relationship in the news and the popular music industries.

The Homogenization Hypothesis

Bagdikian (1992) has provided the best-known examination of the concentration of media ownership. While Bagdikian is not a sociologist, his work is full of sociological questions about the relationship between ownership and diversity. His most important contribution is the way he draws connections across the various media, showing how, for example, companies that are giants in the music industry have a similar position in film. The combination of ownership concentration and growing horizontal integration leads Bagdikian to conclude that the absence of competition in the media industry will lead inevitably to homogeneous media products that serve the interests of the increasingly small number of owners.

While Bagdikian's homogenization hypothesis seems plausible, research on the relationship between competition and diversity reveals a more complex situation. We turn now to some of these studies.

The Local Newspaper Monopoly

Entman (1989) looked at local newspaper competition and asked whether or not monopoly ownership matters. While this study investigates only one component of the broader media monopoly that Bagdikian describes, it does provide an interesting test of his argument.

By the late 1980s, only 27 American cities had two or more competitive newspapers. (This number has continued to decline.) A variety of critics, particularly journalists, mourned the death of the "two-paper town," which has been replaced by local newspaper monopolies. In 1995, for example, the city of Houston became a one-paper town. The chain-owned *Houston Chronicle* purchased its rival, the *Houston Post,* and then closed it down, making the *Chronicle* the only daily in town.

Consistent with Bagdikian's homogenization hypothesis, it had become widely accepted that the decline in local newspaper competition was, in itself, a threat to the ideal of a free press. Entman, though, argues that we need to subject this commonsense assumption to closer scrutiny before accepting it as fact. Rather than assuming that monopoly inevitably leads to an absence of diversity, Entman set out to closely study the issue.

Entman argues that diversity in news content can be understood in both vertical and horizontal terms (not to be confused with vertical and horizontal integration). Vertical diversity refers to the range of actors mentioned and the degree of disagreement in a *single newspaper*. Horizontal diversity refers to the differences in content between *two newspapers*. Those concerned about the consequences of the media monopoly implicitly argue that monopoly papers will be less diverse than competitive papers in terms of both the actors mentioned and the degree of conflict. Information will be narrower—that is, less diverse—in one-paper towns.

Additionally, "joint-ownership" agreements have proliferated, whereby the same company owns two papers or two companies jointly operate two papers in the same town, a situation Entman labels "quasi-monopoly." Critics have argued that these jointly owned papers will differ less from each other than will two competitively owned papers. Local newspaper monopoly, then, should lead to less vertical diversity, and joint ownership ("quasi-monopoly") should lead to less horizontal diversity. In either case, the critique of monopoly suggests that genuine competition will lead to increased diversity in both vertical and horizontal terms.

Entman's analysis focuses on the content of 91 newspapers: 26 monopoly, 33 quasi-monopoly, and 32 competitive. He finds no consistent relationship between newspaper competition and news diversity. In fact, on measures of vertical diversity, papers in all three categories perform virtually the same, mentioning a narrow range of actors and exhibiting a small degree of disagreement. The comparison of quasi-monopoly and competitive papers shows very little difference between the two pairs of papers. Papers in competitive circumstances do not differ from each other any more or less than do jointly operated papers in the same market. In both cases, the difference between the pairs of papers was minimal.

Entman's findings on the nature of local newspaper monopolies have no bearing on Bagdikian's broader claims about the concentration of power inherent in the growth of national media giants. They do, however, suggest that we need to think carefully about the way news organizations operate and about why we expect competitive papers to be somehow "better" than noncompetitive papers. On this front, the romanticization of newspaper competition is the central issue.

Americans tend to be suspicious of monopolies and confident about the benefits of economic competition. Especially in the post–Cold War era, the superiority of the free market has taken on mythic proportions. According to this largely uncontested view, free markets and democratic political systems go hand in hand, with one being the precondition for the other. Commentators often see economic competition as a guarantor of a healthy press, which they perceive as central to democratic societies.

Entman's study suggests that there is little evidence for the argument that competition leads to either higher-quality or more diverse news. Instead, the incentives built into the structure of a for-profit news industry actually have little to do with producing high-quality, diverse news. Genuine economic competition—the commonsensical protector of the news—may in fact exacerbate the problem by encouraging news organizations to minimize costs and produce a least-common-denominator product that appeals to mass-market advertisers and as broad an audience as possible. Competitive papers often try to attract the same mass audience and court the same advertisers. As a result, they may face even stiffer pressures, which contradict quality and diversity, than their noncompetitive counterparts.

It is difficult to argue with Entman's conclusion that economic competition is no panacea, especially since it is free-market economic forces that produced the local newspaper monopoly in the first place. In the news industry, ownership structure does not explain in any direct way the content of the news. However, by asking about this potential relationship, researchers have helped us see some of the underlying dynamics at work in the news industry. Entman's study reveals that concentration of ownership does not create homogenization. *That is because all the newspapers in his study had very limited diversity!* In order to understand the content of the news, we must move beyond questions of ownership and explore the impact of the for-profit orientation and the role of advertisers. We will address these topics later in the chapter. Now we consider another study of how ownership patterns influence diversity and media, this time in the popular music industry.

Concentration and Diversity in the Music Industry

The newspaper industry is not the only branch of mass media that became increasingly concentrated in the 1980s and 1990s. In the popular music industry, between 1969 and 1990, the four largest firms dramatically increased their share of the top 100 albums from 54.5 percent to 82 percent (Lopes, 1992). The question is, what are the implications of this ownership concentration for the diversity of the music we hear?

In their analysis of the postwar music industry, Peterson and Berger (1975) argue that high market concentration leads to homogeneity, while a competitive market leads to diversity. This is, in essence, the same relationship we explored within the newspaper industry. In this case, however, Peterson and Berger provide a historical analysis that demonstrates the relationship between market concentration and several measures of music diversity.

The fundamental premise of their argument is that the late 1950s and 1960s produced a great deal of innovation and diversity in the popular music industry, representing a dramatic shift from the more homogeneous and standardized music available in the 1940s and early 1950s. The cause, they argue, was the opening of the popular music market to increased competition. Radio's shift from a national orientation to a focus on local markets helped spur this opening. Independent record companies entered the newly opened market and produced new and innovative styles of music, breaking the homogeneity-producing control of the major record companies. Peterson and Berger base their conclusion about the relationship between competition and diversity on analyses of both ownership trends within the music industry and *Billboard* magazine's singles chart from 1949 to 1972.

Peterson and Berger suggest two key components of musical diversity. First, they analyze the sheer number of different songs that made the top-10 list each year, arguing that an increase in number reflects an increase in diversity. Second, they analyze the number of "new" and "established" artists who made the top 10, from the premise that new artists are a reflection of diversity and established artists are a reflection of standardization. They found that the measures associated with increased diversity (number of songs and number of new artists) increased at times when market concentration (domination of the popular music industry by a small number of firms) decreased. They conclude that a loosening of market concentration through increased competition permits greater innovation and diversity in popular music. However, their data suggest that in the 1970s market concentration was again increasing. Thus, they foresaw a return to the oligopoly (control by a small number of firms) of the 1940s and predicted a renewed homogeneity within the popular music industry.

Sociologist Paul Lopes (1992) revisited the same question more than 15 years after Peterson and Berger. Using a similar method of analysis—one that focused on the degree of concentration of the industry and the degree of diversity exhibited on the *Billboard* charts—Lopes found that the dynamics in the popular music industry have become more complex since the 1960s.

In line with Peterson and Berger's prediction, market concentration increased substantially between 1969 and 1990, with the top four record companies controlling the vast majority of hit music. However, the accompanying decrease in diversity that Peterson and Berger predicted did not follow. Instead, the number of new artists and established artists fluctuated throughout the 1970s and 1980s, reaching roughly the same number in 1990 as in 1969. Although significant market concentration occurred during this period, Lopes found little evidence that musical diversity had suffered.

The explanation, according to Lopes, is that the system of production within the music industry changed from what he characterizes as a "closed" system to an "open" system. The key change is in the ratio of record *labels* to record *firms*. As in other sectors of mass media, notably the book-publishing industry, the major music firms own multiple record labels and maintain links with smaller, independent labels. Among the companies producing the top 100 albums, the ratio of labels to firms changed dramatically, from less than two labels per firm in 1969 to approximately four labels per firm by 1990.

Peterson and Berger suggested that a "closed" system of record production dominated the industry during the 1940s and early 1950s. In this system, major companies used a limited number of familiar channels to produce and distribute the music that dominated the charts. Lopes, however, argues that the substantial increase in the number of labels per firm suggests new processes at work. In this "open" system, the major record companies control large-scale manufacturing, distribution, and publicity but draw upon semiautonomous independent producers to maintain the vitality of the popular music market. This open system is the key to the continued diversity within the industry despite high market concentration. The open system allows for innovation and diversity, which helps the major companies maintain both their profitability and their control of the industry.

These two studies of the popular music industry remind us that there is no single effect of concentrated ownership within mass media industries. Clearly, ownership and control within oligopolistic media industries matter. Controlling companies adopt strategies that determine, to a great degree, production and distribution systems within media industries. However, we need to explore the specific conditions under which concentration exists before we can make sense of the relationship between concentration and diversity. As changes occur in the composition and tastes of the audience, the methods of distribution, and the technologies of production, the organization of media industries will likely respond in ways that enhance the bottom-line profitability of the major firms. Even when a small number of companies control media industries, increased diversity may prove to be an effective strategy in a profit-making industry.

Mass Media for Profit

In a capitalist system, mass media organizations must focus on one under-lying goal: the creation of products that will earn financial profits. This for-profit orientation is central to any sociological explanation of mass media. It provides the context within which media personnel make deci-sions. However, the focus on profits does not work in a uniform way across media industries or in different time periods. The example above of the popular music industry shows how the same industry responded to similar profit pressures in different ways under different conditions.

Prime-Time Profits

One of the most sensitive treatments of how profit requirements influence media production is Todd Gitlin's (1985) analysis of network television. In *Inside Prime Time*, Gitlin explores the decision-making processes at the three major networks, suggesting that bottom-line profit pressures set the framework for programming decisions. The goal for network executives is steady profits. Executives achieve profits by broadcasting programs that will attract large audiences that will, in turn, lead to the sale of advertis-ing time at premium rates. The problem is that there is no sure-fire for-mula for successful programming. Even the most sophisticated methods for predicting success are much better at determining which shows will *not* succeed than at identifying which programs will become hits.

One reason why this is the case is that failure is the norm in network television. Writers offer the networks thousands of ideas each year, but networks develop only a few hundred into scripts. Perhaps 100 of these scripts become pilots, of which a few dozen make it onto the fall schedule. Of those that make the schedule, networks renew only a handful. At each stage, executives and producers weed out another layer of programs. Only a small number of programs are ultimately successful in commercial terms.

If failure is the norm in network television, how is the system prof-itable? In a situation similar to that in the music, film, and book indus-tries, the big hits—as few as 10 percent of the products, depending upon the particular industry—can provide profits large enough to make up for the vast number of programs that break even or lose money. Network television has an additional advantage: Even in the age of cable television, major advertisers still perceive the networks to be the most effective medium to promote products to a national market. Given the number of households that tune in to even a low-rated program—an audience of 5 million households does not add up to a successful prime-time program —advertisers have good reason to continue to support programs that have less-than-impressive ratings.

As part of the all-encompassing search for steady profits, network programmers follow a "logic of safety" that revolves around minimizing the risk of losing money on programs. Risky programs are those that seem unlikely to attract a mass audience or, even worse, a large advertiser. This formula might appear to be simple. If safety is the cardinal rule, executives will avoid at all costs programs that appear to be obvious ratings losers. However, as we have seen, ratings "hits" are rare. Gitlin explains, for example, that between 1957 and 1980 the testing division at CBS predicted that almost two-thirds of the programs *that made the network schedule* would be ratings losers, and the prediction of failure was correct more than 90 percent of the time.

One consequence of the profit-driven logic of safety is the general tendency to avoid controversy, even when it might bring high ratings. The logic of safety, however, has much broader consequences than the avoidance of controversial programs. Network executives are never sure what audiences will watch or why some programs succeed and others fail. Therefore, Gitlin suggests that the corollary to the logic of safety is the notion that "nothing succeeds like success." As a result, network television constantly imitates itself, creating copies and spin-offs that can reach bizarre proportions. Hit programs like "The Mary Tyler Moore Show" ("Rhoda," "Phyllis," "Lou Grant") and "All in the Family" ("The Jeffersons," "Maude," "Good Times," "Gloria," "Archie's Place") produced multiple spin-offs and new programs for the stars. More recently, "Hill Street Blues," the 1980s hit police drama with an ensemble cast, spun off the sit-com "Beverly Hills Bunz," a short-lived ratings loser about a police officer's move from New York to Los Angeles, and a large number of imitations. "Cheers" led to both the short-lived sit-com "The Tortelli's" and the hit program "Frasier." The success of the 20-somethings of "Friends" spawned a rash of imitators trying to cash in on the concept. Whether it be gritty police programs, medical dramas, courtroom law programs, or 20-something sit-coms, each network tries to exploit what appears to be the prevailing trend. Without any other accepted method for making programming decisions and with profit demands moving from an annual to a quarterly or weekly basis, programmers choose shows that resemble the latest hit on another network. However, these imitations are frequently not satisfying for audiences and are rarely commercial successes.

The same profit-oriented dynamic is the driving force behind the recent resurgence of tabloidlike newsmagazine programs. Such programs are inexpensive to produce, often relying on already existing news staffs and easily accessible video footage, and are sufficiently entertainment-oriented to attract a substantial prime-time audience. For network news divisions facing increased profit pressures following the ownership changes of the mid-1980s, these programs appear to be the perfect answer. They combine a low-cost product with the potential for a large audience. Similar economic forces have driven the development of programs such as "Cops" and "Emergency 911," so-called "reality TV." These programs require very modest production budgets and are titillating enough to attract significant numbers of viewers.

Profit and the News Media

How do such profit pressures influence the content of news media? News outlets, like any other company, have two ways to enhance their profits: They can either cut costs or increase revenues. In the highly competitive news industry of the 1990s, both of these approaches are evident. To cut costs, news outlets rely on several or all of the following strategies:

- Decrease the number of journalists.
- Cut back on long-term investigative reporting that produces a small number of stories.
- Use a larger percentage of wire services reports.
- At television stations, use video public relations segments (reports that have been prepared and provided free of charge by public relations firms) in newscasts.
- Rely on a small number of elites (who are easy and inexpensive to reach) as regular news sources.
- Focus the news on preplanned official events (which are easy and inexpensive to cover) instead of less routine happenings.
- Focus coverage on a limited number of institutions in a handful of big cities.

All these methods allow news organizations to lower the cost of gathering and producing the news. While they may be effective at cutting costs, however, they do have consequences. Such cost-cutting measures are likely to make news coverage oriented more toward elites and government, with little focus on events or perspectives outside the official world.

At the same time, news organizations try to increase revenues by maximizing their audience and advertiser base. The most straightforward approach for audience maximization is to create a light, entertainment-oriented news product that makes watching or reading the news fun. Since upsetting or offending any segment of the audience carries with it real costs, there will be a tendency to avoid controversy and to report the news in an upbeat, reassuring manner. Personality-oriented journalism that highlights intrigue, titillation, and scandal is another strategy for attracting large audiences.

Profit pressures have intensified in the 1990s as a result of increased competition in the overall media sector and the demand by corporate owners for a substantial return on their investments. The result is that newspaper editors, increasingly trained in the world of business instead of news reporting, focus more on marketing and packaging the news. Profit pressures have different consequences for different media outlets. Still, the combination of cost-cutting and audience-enhancing demands is one of the key reasons why different news outlets, all responding to a comparable set of profit pressures, produce news that looks so similar.

The Impact of Advertising

As we have seen, profit requirements provide incentives for the operators of mass media outlets to keep costs down and to create a product that will bring in sufficient revenue. We must weigh one additional factor: the specific source of revenue. In both of our previous examples, television and newspapers, the key source of revenue is advertising. This is the case with all mass-market print and commercial broadcast media. In the print world, receipts from sales account for roughly one-third of revenue, with advertising providing approximately two-thirds of operating costs. In broadcast media, advertising is the only substantial source of revenue. As a result, it should be no surprise that the magazines we read often seem more focused on the full-page glossy ads than on the articles that are buried between ad pages, or that television commercials frequently seem more clever and interesting than the programs they surround. Advertising is, after all, what pays the bills for print and broadcast media.

Because advertisers are doing the most important buying, the principal "products" being sold are *the audiences,* not the newspapers, magazines, or programs produced by media organizations. Advertisers are not interested in media products, except as a kind of bait to lure audiences and expose them to the ads. As the phrase goes, media are in the business of "delivering audiences to advertisers." Our attention is what is being bought and sold, and competition for that attention has intensified as technologies such as the remote control and the VCR make it easier to avoid ads. Advertisers' perception that public attention is hard to attract leads to a continual search for new ways to reach consumers.

One result of this ongoing search is the growth of advertising in realms of media that had previously been largely ad-free. Take movies, for example. Movie theaters have always run ads for their snack bar, along with previews of "coming attractions," a form of industry advertising. Now many theaters run advertisements for local or regional merchants and service providers before the "coming attractions."

Videocassettes, initially advertising-free, now contain ads and pre-views before the "feature presentation" (although VCR technology makes these easy to skip by fast-forwarding). And advertisements do not stop when the movie begins. Product placement within movies—whereby a character sips from a can of a well-known brand of soft drink or flies on a prominent airline—has become a big business as a new, subtler way to promote products (Miller, 1990). The use of products on screen or the mention of brand names by star actors can bring in big money, helping to offset the rising costs of film production. From the standpoint of advertisers, these plugs are a smart investment, in part because theatergoers cannot turn the page or flip the channel to avoid the "ad."

Advertisements also make their way, through various media, into unlikely places such as the high-school classroom and the doctor's office. Whittle Communications pioneered the art of producing media products, with ample room for advertisements, that reach "captive" audiences and ensure that other media are not available to compete for consumer attention. These captive audiences—students in classrooms and patients in waiting rooms—led to the development of a classroom television news program, "Channel One," and several advertiser-friendly magazines for distribution to participating doctors. In both cases, the media products were provided free of charge, and "Channel One" supplied participating schools with television and video equipment as part of the deal. What did Whittle Communications get in return? In the case of schools, Whittle received a commitment to show the news program—along with advertisements—to students on a regular basis as a required part of the school day. Doctors' offices agreed to carry Whittle publications exclusively. In both cases, producers created new media products with the specific aim of sending advertising messages to audiences in situations where they would be most likely to receive them. Educators and doctors, in essence, exchanged the attention of those they serve—students and patients—for media products. In cases where the content of the media product is explicitly incidental, serving only to provide a context for the presentation of advertising, the dynamics of advertising-supported media become clearer and the interrelationship of media, advertising, and audiences comes into sharper focus.

Advertising and the Press in the Nineteenth Century

Advertising is a central force in the workings of contemporary mass media, providing the bulk of the revenue for newspapers, magazines, television, and radio. Additionally, as we have seen, advertising needs can generate new media products and appear in forms of media that once existed without ads. But what influence does advertising have on the content of these media? One way to explore this question is to look at the historical development of advertising in relation to a particular kind of mass media in order to see how the introduction of ads shaped the media product. One well-documented example is the impact of advertising on the British and American press in the 1800s.

The British Press

James Curran's (1977) historical account of the British press provides an important institutional analysis of the relationship between news and advertising. Traditionally, historians have argued that British newspapers gradually won their freedom from government and party control as they shifted to a financial structure that relied upon advertising. In this view, newspapers achieved a kind of economic independence, permitting the press to take up its contemporary role as the "fourth estate." Curran, however, argues that the simple equation of advertising with press freedom neglects the substantial influence this new economic structure had on the radical, working-class press in England. His approach is a textbook example of how the production perspective provides new insight into the workings of mass media systems by asking questions that researchers would otherwise not explore and by examining relationships that researchers had previously neglected.

Certainly, the shift away from financial dependence on the government had great significance for the British press. But we cannot understand the movement away from a state-supported press to an advertiser-supported press as linear movement from a "captive" press to a "free" press. Such an explanation ignores the ways in which advertising revenue relates to a larger set of relationships among, in this case, capitalism, the state, and the press.

During the first half of the nineteenth century, according to Curran, a radical, working-class press thrived in England, breaking circulation records. At the same time, efforts by the government to control the press —through libel laws and press taxes—were largely ineffective. Rather than being constrained by government action, the British working-class press was undermined by the changing economics of the newspaper business whereby the less politically inclined middle-class papers turned to advertisers, instead of readers, as a central source of revenue. The resulting impact suggests the significant, albeit often unintended, power of advertising to shape the content of media systems.

Curran argues that the growth of advertising changed the playing field and led to the decline of the British radical press. Advertising made circulation figures (the number of readers) less important than the patronage of advertisers. In the early years of advertising, radical papers did not receive the support of advertisers, even though they had large numbers of readers. More mainstream papers, meanwhile, were able to make profits with a substantially smaller readership base. Advertisers' political interests were dramatically different from the ideas espoused by the radical press. In essence, the working-class press presented a political critique of industrial capitalism, while potential advertisers were generally beneficiaries of that same system. Given a choice of which newspaper to support, advertisers elected not to support their political opponents. This is, to be sure, only a partial explanation. The political interests of advertisers were not uniform, and we should not discount the economic attractiveness of a large-circulation newspaper.

Still, advertisers had economic reasons for avoiding the radical press. Radical newspapers appealed largely to a working-class audience, and even though the papers were widely read, advertisers did not perceive the readers to be a valuable market. To advertisers, reaching smaller numbers of upper- or middle-class readers seemed to be a better sales strategy than reaching large numbers of working-class readers who did not have the necessary resources to buy many of the advertised goods and services.

In addition, advertising changed the meaning of economic viability within the newspaper industry. With new resources coming in, the advertiser-supported papers were able to produce papers with more pages, containing both news and ads. This pushed up the cost of producing a competitive newspaper. At the same time, with advertising revenue as a base, the cover price of papers dropped dramatically, making it difficult for papers without advertising to compete.

The consequences of the rise of advertising were grave for the radical press and tell us a good deal about the broader impact of advertising on the news. Without advertising support, even several high-circulation working-class papers ceased publishing because they could be underpriced by competitors, who also had the resources to produce and distribute a more attractive product. One important consequence of advertising, then, was the end of a national radical press in Britain. Owners transformed those papers that did survive in one of two ways. Some publications became small-circulation papers, much like our "alternative" press today. These papers did not even try to compete with the national press. Other papers moved away from their working-class audience by focusing on items of interest to upper- and middle-class audiences. By losing their radical political commitments, these newspapers were better able to attract advertisers. Either way, from the standpoint of the working class and its radical supporters, the shift to an advertising-based press did not represent progress toward press freedom. Instead, the introduction of advertising and the subsequent decline of the radical press resulted in newspapers that provided a more limited view of events than they had before.

The U.S. Press

The move toward advertising-supported newspapers also had a significant impact on the content of the U.S. press. Until the late 1800s, U.S. newspapers had been largely funded and controlled by political parties, politicians, and partisan organizations. Then the news shifted from a partisan, politically based press to a commercially based press. A principal consequence of this shift was a change in the definition of a newspaper's very purpose. As advertising became the key to success, news moved from the realm of politics and persuasion to the realm of business (Baldasty, 1992). This was no small change. Newspapers were no longer partisan, and they no longer perceived their readers as voters or citizens. On the contrary, newspapers made an effort to avoid partisanship as much as possible and instead looked upon their readers as consumers. There is, in fact, good reason to believe that the historical roots of what we now refer to as "objectivity" in journalism lie in this process of commercialization, whereby the news industry developed a new nonpartisan framework for reporting news.

The move toward a commercial press in the United States shaped news content in two significant ways (Baldasty, 1992). News purveyors began to avoid controversy, preferring instead a blander product that would be likely to attract (and not offend) large numbers of readers as well as advertisers interested in reaching those readers. This shift went beyond a nonpartisan style or voice. As advertisers' desires became intertwined with news values, political news itself—even that without any intentional partisanship—became problematic because of its inherent focus on difficult, sometimes unpleasant issues. As a result, newspapers shifted their focus away from substantive political news.

If news shied away from political issues, what did newspapers write about? Much like contemporary newspapers, the commercial press in the late nineteenth century contained a variety of features—including sports, fashion, recipes, and entertainment—that existed largely to support the accompanying ads. Then, as today, such items may have been of substantial interest to readers. The point to be made here is that they became part of the daily newspaper at a time when the medium, because of its emerging financial base, sought new forms of news that would be both advertiser-friendly and entertaining for potential readers.

Commercialization led to one additional consequence of lasting significance. Newspapers became advocates for their newfound economic patrons. According to Baldasty (1992, p. 141), "early nineteenth-century newspaper editors were unabashed *advocates for political parties.* Late-nineteenth-century newspaper editors were advocates as well, *advocates for business,* for their advertisers." There may be good reason for celebrating the movement of news away from political partisanship. Certainly, our contemporary sensibilities suggest that news should be independent of political control. However, independence from direct political influence was achieved only by introducing a new business influence. The financial role of advertising shaped daily practices within the news industry and transformed the meaning of news for both producers and consumers.

Advertising and the Contemporary News Media

Advertising continues to exert a powerful influence on the news media. Some critics have suggested that advertisers have the ability to dictate the content of the news (Collins, 1992). Advertisers are still the dominant source of revenue for news media; journalists, editors, and producers are well aware of who pays the bills. At the same time, most journalists do not set out to intentionally produce news that is advertiser-friendly. The dynamics are not so simple as either routine intervention by advertisers to protect their interests (although this does happen) or daily compliance with advertiser agendas by reporters. Rather than directly determining news content, advertising is a force that provides both incentives and constraints that influence the news in a generally predictable way. Let's look at how this works.

At the most general level, news usually depicts advertisers' products and their broad interests in a favorable light. This does not necessarily mean that journalists live in fear of criticizing their advertisers, nor does it mean that powerful editors routinely keep reporters in line in order to protect their advertisers. The influence is more subtle and operates on several levels. Reporters and editors may not perceive themselves as defending their advertisers' interests, but there is no doubt that they are fully aware of the economic role of their major advertisers. As a result, the dominant influence in this regard is probably more akin to self-censorship, perhaps unconscious, on the part of journalists. Self-censorship refers to the ways reporters doubt themselves, tone down their work, omit small items, or drop entire stories to avoid pressure, eliminate any perception of bias, or advance their careers. Even though many critics express outrage at such a scenario, this kind of response by journalists should not be surprising. Professionals are not isolated from the social world around them, nor can they be entirely unmindful of their economic patrons. Lawyers serve their clients' interests; academics are often aware of tenure decisions and funding priorities when they are choosing their research projects; doctors respond to the financial situations of hospitals and insurance companies. Journalists are no different.

Of course, the ways journalists respond to advertiser interests is complex. Rarely is one particular advertiser important enough that journalists need to avoid any hint of criticism, and media outlets can often replace unhappy sponsors with new ones. There are other ways to protect advertisers; for example, network news producers will often pull ads from an oil company on the evening that a large oil spill is in the news. More generally, though, news organizations and broadcasters need to pay attention to the interests of the entire class of advertisers, not individual sponsors. The example of the radical press in Britain illustrates this point quite clearly. In practical terms, news personnel will tend to avoid content that is too critical of the system of consumer capitalism, since this system is at the core of the interests of advertisers as a collective.

Some types of news reporting are more vulnerable to influence than others. In local newspapers, real estate and automotive coverage is notorious for its reverence of local advertisers. There are clear economic reasons for this. Local real estate agencies and local automobile dealers generally fill the bulk of these sections with their ads, often perceiving that they virtually own the pages. With other advertisers unlikely to pick up the slack, reporters writing in these two areas have little freedom to deviate from traditional, light, industry-pleasing coverage.

This dynamic works in a more affirmative way in a variety of news settings. Editors and producers create new sections in newspapers and new features on radio and television to attract new advertisers. Coverage of music, computers, food, health, and fashion, for example, is prominent in our news because it attracts advertising revenue from companies that sell products in these industries. "Life-style" coverage is an advertiser's dream, because much of it focuses on a variety of forms of consumption. Entertainment-oriented coverage meets advertisers' agenda in an additional way. News should, at the very least, maintain a tone that contributes to—and certainly does not undermine—a "buying mood" (Baker, 1994). If news content is consistently negative or upsetting, audiences are not likely to be in an appropriate frame of mind to respond to the ads that accompany it. When news is in some way negative, as it often is, there is generally an attempt to brighten the picture and reassure the audience. One example is the convention of television news to end a broadcast with an upbeat story.

Finally, since news outlets need to court advertisers for financial support, there is an incentive to produce news that will appeal to an audience the advertisers want to reach: the well-off. As competition for sponsors increases, news outlets face increased pressure to deliver an upscale audience. One result of this pressure is that there is rarely news about the poor, except when they commit crimes, violate basic social norms, or become objects of charity. In essence, editors and producers generally restrict news about the poor to stories about how the poor affect the middle and upper classes. Much of the style and fashion coverage is geared toward people with high incomes. Of course, not all news is successful at reaching an upscale audience. Still, news outlets that we can most easily identify as upscale—the *New York Times,* PBS' "NewsHour" (formerly the "MacNeil/Lehrer NewsHour"), "Nightline," the *Wall Street Journal, the Washington Post*—are also perceived by industry observers to be the "best" news in the business.

In the end, advertising does not directly determine news, but news cannot be entirely independent of advertising. Individual editors, journalists, and producers will not all respond the same way, and individual advertisers will not all perceive the news or their interests in the same way. However, both historical and contemporary analysis indicates that the language we use to talk about news—discussions of "objectivity," the meaning of "quality" or "prestige" journalism, the very categories that are defined as news—is derived, in part, from the central role of advertising in the news industry.

Advertising, MTV, and "New" Media

News is not the only area in which we can see the impact of advertising on mass media products. Music videos must be analyzed in light of their essentially promotional role (Goodwin, 1992). Music videos are themselves forms of advertising for the music industry. The connection between the music-video-as-advertising and the founding of MTV is so close that we cannot meaningfully separate them. MTV developed as a result of the opportunities created by the growth of cable television and the music industry's need to develop new ways to promote its music to a young audience. Cable television opened doors for new programming, and the music industry provided that programming to MTV at no charge. MTV was economically viable because it had virtually no programming costs; all the initial content—the videos—was advertising for the music industry. From the standpoint of the music industry, this arrangement was efficient because its only costs were those associated with the production of the video; placement on MTV was free. At least in its early years, then, the very existence of MTV was a result of the music industry's promotional needs and the status of the music video as a new form of advertising.

Andrew Goodwin (1992) goes one step further, arguing that the "promotional demands" of music videos help determine what the videos actually look like. In particular, Goodwin focuses on the control of the video by the record company and its chosen director, rather than the musicians. The video versions of songs, in most cases, are the result of marketing decisions made by record companies, not the artistic expression of the musicians. Music videos are also used to develop and promote "star identities," which is the key to long-term economic success in the music business (Goodwin, 1992).

New media technologies, often characterized as revolutionary developments, will not be immune to the institutional influence of advertising. Their adoption will depend, in large part, on the financial support of advertisers. The wide-scale introduction of "interactive" television and newsmagazines on CD-ROM, both heralded as examples of the grand potential of the "communications revolution," have been hindered by a lack of enthusiasm on the part of advertisers. At the same time, "home shopping" on cable television continues to proliferate. Already, those in the advertising industry are ahead of the game, exploring how the new media can provide new methods for delivering commercial messages to potential consumers. The result of their exploration will likely play a key role in determining which new media become staples of our lives in the coming decades.

What kinds of on-line computer services will advertisers find most suitable to their aims? Applications that are consumption-oriented and target high-income or corporate users will certainly be the first wave. An institutional analysis of the role of advertising in the media industry suggests that the future of the "information superhighway" will be intimately connected to the future of advertising.

As consumer markets change, however, the specific nature of the relationship between advertising and mass media is likely to evolve as well. The most immediate social issue that will influence this relationship is the increasing fragmentation of the mass audience. The concept of "mass media" has been based on a communication structure in which a small number of "senders" direct messages to a large number of "receivers," hence, a mass audience. Given the "mass" dimension of the media, advertising has encouraged the production of homogeneous, least-common-denominator media products.

New technological capabilities and the identification of new consumer markets may be changing the mass orientation of media. Already, observers use the term "narrowcasting" to refer to cable television programs that target specific audience segments instead of aiming for a mass audience. To a company that markets cookware and kitchen appliances, a cooking show with a smaller audience may be more valuable than a highly rated sit-com. With a cooking show, the advertiser is guaranteed to reach an audience that already has an interest in cooking-related products. This is not the case with a sit-com.

Advertisers, perhaps more than others in the industry, are aware of the potential benefits of narrowly targeted media products. As long as advertisers want to spend money to reach specific groups of people, as opposed to a mass audience, "special interest" media will likely be financially viable. Advertising has long been a homogenizing force in the media world. In the future, it may play a key role in diversifying the content of some media. This will occur, however, only if formerly underserved audiences are identified as growing consumer markets and new media products are directed at them. Those who are considered unimportant by advertisers, especially poor people, are likely to continue to be left out of advertiser-driven media.

Conclusion

This chapter has examined the ways in which economic versions of the production perspective help us understand the media industry. We have explored the kinds of questions asked by researchers from this tradition, some of the key arguments they make, and the underlying social processes at work. Such an approach is essential, but a focus on the economics of the production of media is a limited lens from which to view the relationship between mass media and society.

One line of argument suggests that the approach outlined in this chapter has a tendency to present an "overdetermined" view of the mass media, that is, it overemphasizes the ways in which economic forces determine the nature of media products. *Determine* is the key word here, for this critique suggests that the economics of the production process cannot fully define the specific nature of mass media. According to this argument, the production process involves too many additional intervening variables. Media production is directed by human beings who make judgments and interpretations at every stage. As a result, there is more variability within media than some production-oriented critics imply, and the institutional constraints on production are not all-encompassing. We accept the basic contours of this criticism but see no need to discard the insights gained from the production perspective. We cannot ignore, nor should we overstate, the impact of economic forces on media production.

The economic dimension of the media industry is certainly a critical component for sociological analysis. However, as the next two chapters will show, more than economics is involved in understanding the contours of the media industry and the processes of media production. We must also consider political and organizational factors.

CHAPTER 3

Political Influence
on Media

In George Orwell's novel *1984,* the "Ministry of Truth" controlled mass media. It used its power to promote a fictional account of the world intended to limit the range of acceptable thought among citizens. Through the omnipresent "telescreen," which covered almost an entire wall in every home, the Ministry of Truth fed a constant stream of propaganda. Citizens could not turn off the screen; they could only dim it. "Big Brother" was able to shape public discourse and social thought because it controlled media outlets, media-related technology, and media content.

A half-century after Orwell wrote, Big Brother does not threaten us in the way Orwell envisioned. However, even if it is not the extreme stuff of science fiction, the relationship between government and the mass media gives rise to many basic questions and concerns. In this chapter, we examine how political forces influence the nature of mass media. Later, in Chapter 7, we will look at the media's influence on politics.

The state in all nations serves as an organizing structure that can, to varying degrees, constrain or promote the free activity (or agency) of the media. This is the tension between structure and agency as it applies to media and the political world. Although our focus in this chapter is on the role of government, we also address the more informal political pressure that various actors directly or indirectly bring to bear on the media. These actors include media advocacy groups, public interest organizations, religious groups, and media critics.

Clearly, in order to better understand media, we need to understand the political environment in which they operate. This becomes obvious when we consider the drastic differences between media in a democratic society and those in totalitarian nations. State control of the mass media is a routine element of totalitarian systems. Here the structural constraint of the state largely dominates the potential agency of the media industry. In extreme cases, state-owned news agencies, broadcast media, and film studios act as propaganda arms of the state, promoting a single set of government-sanctioned images and messages. Audiences in such nations must become adept at "reading between the lines" in decoding such propaganda efforts. The emergence of illegal underground media is also common in such situations, affirming the active agency of citizens in even the bleakest of circumstances.

Democratic societies, on the other hand, pride themselves on protecting freedom of the press and freedom of expression. Such societies are usually characterized by a more diverse mix of public and privately-owned media outlets offering a variety of arts, news, information, and entertainment. The media in such societies are still subject to government regulation, but they are usually given much greater latitude to operate independently.

You might expect the key argument about media regulation in a country like the United States to be whether or not the government should intervene in the media industry. However, this is not the case. Despite the frequent rhetoric about deregulation, virtually everyone involved with the media—including liberal and conservative politicians, industry executives, and public interest advocates—wants government regulation. What these groups disagree about is *what kind* of government regulation should exist. Different actors are constantly trying to influence the scope and direction of the government's media regulation, a classic example of how outside social forces influence the media industry.

In turn, the media industry has a well-organized and powerful political arm that finances political candidates and lobbies elected officials. And, of course, the media industry controls the biggest soapbox in society. One Federal Communications Commission (FCC) official pointed out that one reason broadcasters are such a powerful Washington lobbying group is because they control the air time given to members of Congress on local stations (Hickey, 1995). Politicians courting favorable media coverage for reelection are likely to be highly conscious of legislation that can affect the media industry.

Government laws and regulations affect all facets of media production. Best known are the legal regulations affecting the *content* of media. However, other forms of regulation have at least as great an impact. Most important among these are regulations concerning the *ownership* of media outlets and media-related technology. Ownership is important because some critics argue that a version of Big Brother may yet appear—not in the form of a government official, but rather as a corporate media executive.

The Relationship Between Government and Media

Some of the complexities involved in the relationship between government and media are illustrated in the 1991 Hollywood film *Pump Up the*

Volume. In the movie, Mark Hunter (played by actor Christian Slater) is a teenager whose family has recently moved from the East Coast to Arizona. Shy and alienated in his new suburban environment, Mark rebels by using radio equipment to secretly broadcast a program from the basement of his parents' house. With an electronically disguised voice and the on-air pseudonym of "Hard Harry," Mark creates an obscenity-laced show featuring a mix of music, philosophical musings, and angry diatribes against an unjust, hypocritical society. The program becomes a cult hit among the local teens, while angry school and city officials try to identify the anonymous broadcaster. After the program incites chaos at the local high school and a listener commits suicide, officials from the FCC are brought in to shut down Mark's operation.

At first glance, Mark might appear to be exercising his constitutionally guaranteed freedom of speech. But that's not the case. The Constitution does not protect someone like Mark. In the eyes of the U.S. government, he is running an illegal "pirate" radio station and thus attracts the attention of the Federal Communications Commission, the agency responsible for enforcing communications regulations.

Mark's right to free speech did not apply because he was using a broadcast medium (radio). As a consequence, he was subject to different regulations than are the print media. If Mark had used a computer and copy machine to produce a magazine, he would have been on more solid legal ground (though his status as a minor would have raised some difficulties). The Constitution *does* protect the freedom of the press. But government and the courts have treated broadcast media differently because they must use the public airwaves to reach an audience. There is a limited spectrum of available electromagnetic frequencies, and the government regulates who can use certain frequencies. (A radio station's call number—for example, 98.6 or 101—refers to the frequency at which the station broadcasts.) The government does this by issuing licenses, which Mark did not have, to stations that seek to broadcast at a certain frequency. When it comes to government regulation, therefore, not all media are alike. In this chapter, we highlight print and broadcast media, but we also consider the emerging area of computer cyberspace.

What appeared to be government intrusion from the perspective of Mark and his listeners makes good business sense from the media industry's perspective. Mark's signal was not strong, but it might have been interfering with the signal of another station that was legally licensed to use the same, or a nearby, frequency. The absence of government regulation of the airwaves might lead to chaos as multiple stations tried to drown each other out at the same frequencies. The result would be akin to a street and highway system with no lanes, signs, stoplights, or speed limits. In fact, it was precisely this sort of chaos in the early days of radio that led—at the request of the radio industry—to regulation and the practice of requiring broadcast licenses. (License requirements began in 1912, even before commercial broadcasting began, because other maritime communications traffic was interfering with the Navy's radio communications.)

Regulation constraining the behavior of one actor benefits others. Some government regulations, like broadcast licenses, are intended to protect the financial interests of media businesses. Indeed, the media industry could not exist in its current form without active government regulation and control. That is why the media industry actively supports *some* regulations, namely, those that benefit the industry.

Other regulations, as we will see below, are created to protect the interests of the public against the influence of the powerful media industry. The media industry usually cites the merits of *deregulation* when it is faced with such constraints, while at the same time it is directly benefiting from other forms of government regulation. In considering regulation, therefore, it is important to ask "Who benefits from such regulation?" as well as "Who is constrained?" This approach can explain a great deal about regulation debates.

The current collection of media rules and regulations has evolved along with changes in technology and the political climate. On the technological side, for example, new computer-based technologies have opened up a whole new set of debates about the role of regulation. Changes in the political climate have also had a profound impact on regulation debates. At various times, different actors have had the upper hand in shaping the nature of the government's relationship with the media. For example, the mid-1990s saw a dramatic swing of the political pendulum in favor of the media industry as the government relaxed or eliminated regulation of the industry in key areas.

Technological change and evolving legislative initiatives make media regulation a fast-changing field. Indeed, the particulars of existing media regulation at the time of this writing are likely to be different by the time you read this. Our concern, therefore, is less with the details of media legislation than with the general trends and orientations that characterize the relationship between government and media of all types. From a sociological perspective, this relationship illustrates both the constraining and enabling nature of political structures. It also reveals the socially constructed nature of ideas such as "freedom of the press" and "public interest."

The "First Freedom"

Most Americans are familiar with the First Amendment to the U.S. Constitution, which guarantees, among other things, "freedom of the press." The amendment in its entirety reads: "Congress shall make no law respecting an establishment of religion, or prohibiting the free exercise thereof; or abridging the freedom of speech, or of the press, or the right of the people peaceably to assemble, and to petition the government for a redress of grievances."

What does "freedom of the press" really mean? Since the amendment begins with "Congress shall make no law . . ." it seems to imply that the government should take a "hands off" approach toward the media. This has led some observers to argue that regulation of the media by the government is an illegitimate pursuit that contradicts the goal of the First Amendment. But the reality is more complex than this.

We do not have to go any farther than the U.S. Constitution to see another dimension of the government's relationship with the media. Section 8 of Article I lists the "Powers of Congress," among which is the power "to promote the progress of science and useful arts, by securing for limited times to authors and inventors the exclusive right to their respective writings and discoveries." Here the Constitution explicitly gives Congress the right to intervene in the communications marketplace to protect the interests of authors and inventors with copyrights.

The copyright clause of the Constitution, along with the enforcement mechanisms of the U.S. government, protects the sale and distribution of this book. If you flip to the beginning of this book, you will find a copyright page that includes the publication date of the book, the name and address of the publisher, and a statement of copyright. This copyright statement reads: "All rights reserved. No part of this book may be reproduced or utilized in any form or by any means, electronic or mechanical, including photocopying, recording, or by any information storage and retrieval system, without permission in writing from the publisher." This statement, enforced by government laws and regulations, makes it illegal for someone to simply copy and sell this book without permission from the publisher. The language of copyright statements has evolved over time to address new technologies such as photocopying, sound recording, and electronic scanning devices. All such forms of reproduction for sale are illegal. Such regulations exist to protect both the publisher, who collects income from the sale of books, and the authors, who receive a royalty payment from the publisher for each copy of the book that is sold. Because they have invested the time and money necessary to create the book you are holding, the law says that they should control the right to sell, distribute, and profit from such sales. If the copyright laws didn't exist, there would be no way for publishers to earn a return on their investment.

Over the years, the government and the courts have extended copyright laws to include a wide variety of visual, sound, and computer software products under the rubric of "intellectual property rights." For example, it is illegal to copy and sell music CDs, movies, and computer software. Likewise, it is illegal to electronically scan a copyrighted photograph and use it in a commercial publication, and so forth. We had to acquire permission to use all the photographs you see in this book. (We were unable to include some photos we wanted because the copyright holders would not grant us permission to use them.) The media industry may not want government regulation in some matters, but in this case it certainly *does* want government intervention. The government's protection of copyright is crucial to the continued functioning of the media industry. Without government enforcement of copyright laws, the for-profit media industry would be unable to survive.

Thus, the relationship between government and media is more complex than a simple "freedom of the press" slogan might suggest. We must take into account other issues, which vary depending upon the type of medium being discussed. As a result, the rules regulating media have historically differed among the three basic types of communication media: print media, broadcast media, and common carriers.

The third category refers to communication systems whose operators must provide equal access in their service of the public, usually because they have some type of protected monopoly. The mail system is a common carrier. The government, in another example of how regulation helps the media, uses the mail service to subsidize the print media through the establishment of lower mail rates for newspapers, magazines, and books. Legally, the telephone, the telegraph, and some computer networks are also common carriers. As we noted in Chapter 1, though, these media generally are not mass media systems in the usual sense and thus are not of central concern here.

We must also understand the constitutional notion of "freedom of the press" in historical context. When the founders of the nation originally wrote the First Amendment, it referred to the only form of existing mass media at the time: the print media. The framers of the Constitution knew all too well how European governments had persecuted authors, printers, and publishers. Throughout Europe, governments limited the right of printers through tactics such as requiring licenses, heavily taxing newsprint, and aggressively prosecuting libel (Eisenstein, 1968).

The U.S. legal and legislative system took a different route. It protected the freedom of the press in several key ways. First, it treated the licensing of the press as a case of illegal "prior restraint." Second, it developed a tradition of opposing special taxes on the press. Third, it greatly restricted criminal libel suits. This was the "hands off" dimension of public policy embodied in the First Amendment.

The creators of the First Amendment's provision on "freedom of the press" designed it for the print media. The later emergence of broadcast media presented new challenges, resulting in a different set of rules. The more recent emergence of cable systems, satellite transmissions, and computer-based communication systems once again presents new challenges, the implications of which we are only beginning to understand.

Before we move on in our discussion, it is worth taking a moment to briefly describe the government agency most directly responsible for media regulation—the Federal Communications Commission (FCC). (If you have access to the World Wide Web, you can get more information on the FCC at www.fcc.gov, where we found some of the following information.) The government established the FCC in 1934 to consolidate the regulatory responsibilities of the Federal Radio Commission and other existing agencies. The FCC's responsibilities now include the regulation of U.S. interstate and international communications by radio, television, wire, satellite, and cable. The FCC is also responsible for the issuance of licenses, the setting of some charges, and the enforcement of communication rules. Five commissioners, appointed by the President and confirmed by the Senate for five-year terms, head the FCC. The FCC is organized into seven regulatory bureaus:

1. The Common Carrier Bureau regulates telephone and telegraph.
2. The Mass Media Bureau regulates television and radio broadcasts.
3. The Wireless Bureau regulates private radio, cellular telephone, and pagers.
4. The Cable Bureau regulates cable TV and other cable services.
5. The International Bureau regulates international and satellite communications.
6. The Compliance and Information Bureau investigates violations and answers questions.
7. The Office of Engineering and Technology evaluates technologies and equipment.

Our concern will be with the FCC's functions as they affect various mass media.

The "Public Interest"
and the Regulation Debate

There is a fundamental debate about the wisdom of government regulation as carried out by the FCC. Supporters of some deregulation generally assert that the "free-market" system is adequate for accommodating the needs of both media producers and media consumers. They argue that consumers have the ultimate power to choose to tune into or buy media products and that there is no need for government interference in the form of media regulation. The marketplace serves as a quasi-democratic forum in which consumers, not government agencies, get to decide the fate of media.

But, as we noted earlier, almost all calls for deregulating media are, in fact, calls for *selective* deregulation, leaving in place many of the laws and policies that benefit the media industry. These remaining laws then become all the more important.

In its pure form, the deregulation approach is largely a negative prescription for policy. That is, deregulation advocates suggest what they are *against* (regulation), not what they *favor*. While they clearly support the "free-market" *process*, there is little or no discussion about the *outcome* of this process. In this vision, what would the media look like? The answer is not clear, except that media products would reflect changing market tastes. But what if explicit sex and graphic violence are what market tastes demand? Should the government involve itself in the regulation of content? This is a central dilemma raised by the deregulation position.

In contrast to the deregulation approach, support for media regulation is usually based on a desired *outcome*. The most common standard for assessing this outcome is the "public interest." The idea that media should serve the public interest goes back to the earliest days of radio broadcasting when, because broadcast media were using publicly owned airwaves, the government tied serving the public interest to the granting of licenses. But what is the "public interest"? This is a central dilemma raised by the pro-regulation position.

FCC policymakers generally express agreement with the importance of serving the "public interest," and they share some common ground in understanding the term (Krugman and Reid, 1980). For example, policymakers commonly believe that the FCC serves the public interest by attempting to balance the interests of various groups, suggesting that there is no single public interest. They also stress that the government cannot write media regulation in stone for all eternity, since technological and economic changes are constantly occurring. Finally, they believe that regulation that promotes diversity in programming and services is in the public interest. However, beyond these broad parameters, much disagreement remains about what is or is not meant by the "public interest." Defining the meaning of this malleable term is one way in which different actors have influenced the construction of public policy.

Regulation in International Perspective

All governments, because they understand the political and social importance of the media, develop some policies aimed at regulating and controlling them. Obviously, the method by which governments try to achieve such control varies. Some nations have taken direct authoritarian control of media through state ownership and the banning of opposition media. But most nations engage in media regulation that is nonauthoritarian in nature, combining government influence with free-market forces.

The role of the U.S. government in regulating the media has always been minuscule compared to many other nations. In Europe, for example, broadcast regulation began early as an outgrowth of regulations affecting wireless telegraphy (Hills, 1991). In contrast to the chaos created by American free-market commercialism in the early days of radio, European nations adopted an approach that involved direct government operation of the media as a technique to avoid signal interference. The result was a system that (1) emphasized public service, (2) was national in character, (3) was politicized, and (4) was noncommercial (McQuail, de Mateo, and Tapper, 1992).

In many countries, this approach meant adopting a state monopoly system. The British Broadcasting Corporation (BBC), established in 1922, was the first such system. Within four years, Italy, Sweden, Ireland, Finland, and Denmark had copied the BBC model. Over time, more nations developed similar arrangements, and many variations developed as well. Most monopolies, for example, were nationwide. But in countries such as Belgium, where both Flemish and French were widely spoken, each linguistic group had a separate public broadcasting service. Also, although some countries maintained a state monopoly, other nations— for example, Britain since the 1950s—adopted an approach that coupled state-run with privately owned systems.

In most European countries, the government controlled the organization and financing of broadcast services, while programming was largely run independently. Here, too, there was no single model. Producers outside the state-run system often created the actual programming. However, unlike in the United States, public broadcasting in Europe was always a central force in broadcasting. The point of government control was to ensure that broadcasting could deliver quality programming that served the public interest. As in the United States, the interpretation of "public interest" was debated in Europe. However, people generally considered the purpose of public service broadcasting to be to provide citizens with a diverse range of high-quality entertainment, information, and education. This in turn was generally understood to mean the production of a broad range of programs rather than only programs that were highly profitable (Hills, 1991). Thus, unlike in the United States, success in the purely commercial marketplace has not been the dominant model for most media in Europe.

Government media, however benignly run, present difficulties. In some countries, controversy regarding the political content of programs has plagued public service broadcasting. France, for example, has engaged in rancorous debates about the impartiality of news coverage. In part because of such debates, in part because of changes in technology, and in part because of shifts in the political winds, European broadcasting has undergone dramatic changes since the 1980s. Governments have significantly reduced regulations concerning the structure and financing of broadcasting. The shift has been toward more open competition between public broadcasters and commercial stations. Regulators have introduced advertising into public stations and have added new commercial stations. The results have been increases in advertising, increases in imported programming (which is often cheaper to air than original domestically produced programming), and the consolidation of media companies into ever larger corporate conglomerates that buy up formerly independent producers (Hills, 1991).

Ironically, deregulation in structure and finance has been followed by increased regulation of media content, in part because free-market competition has led to more violent and sexually explicit images as a way to attract audiences. In response, some governments have introduced new limits on programming and have regulated the amount and frequency of advertising. For example, in some countries, governments require that news, public affairs, religious, and children's programming run for 30 minutes before a commercial break (Hirsch and Petersen, 1992). Also, France, Great Britain, and Sweden (along with Canada and Australia) have restrictions against broadcasting violent programs during children's hours, with broadcasters subject to stiff fines for violation (Clark, 1993).

The issues that have characterized European debates are not far removed from those debated in the United States. The following sections of this chapter discuss some common U.S. debates about media regulation and the public interest. We group the issues into those concerning the regulation of *ownership and control* and those concerning the regulation of *content*.

Regulating Ownership and Control

In this section, we review examples of the debates over regulating media ownership and technology in the United States (Brenner and Rivers, 1982; Noam, 1985; Pool, 1983; and Tunstall, 1986). We do not attempt to provide any sort of comprehensive review; rather, our primary goal is to show how debates about the relationship between politics and the media represent one kind of tension between agency and structure in the social world.

Regulating Ownership of Media Outlets

When early government officials crafted the First Amendment, media ownership was largely a local, decentralized affair. As a result, the First Amendment closely links "freedom of speech or of the press" because in colonial times the two were very similar. Individual printers or shops employing just a couple of people created the media products of the day. The written word, therefore, was largely an extension of the spoken word.

In this context, the issue of ownership was of little concern. The equipment needed to operate a press was relatively straightforward and affordable for purchase or lease to those with modest capital. In theory, there was no limit on the potential number of different presses. Over time, however, communication media have changed in significant ways.

First, media *technology* has changed. Broadcast media enabled producers to reach millions of people through a networked system that blanketed the country. This ability has transformed the nature of the media by dramatically expanding their reach and potential influence. Also, the technologically accessible range of the electromagnetic spectrum limited the number of free broadcast stations that could operate in any market, creating the scarcity that was crucial in justifying broadcast regulation.

Second, *ownership* patterns have changed. The amount of investment capital necessary to produce state-of-the-art media products is now enormous. As the wry saying goes, freedom of the press exists only for those who can afford to own one. With changes in technology and in the scale of production, most competitive media ownership is affordable only for those with substantial capital. As a result, media have moved away from their independent localism, and more and more media outlets are part of national and international corporate entities. Larger media conglomerates, for example, now own many "local" newspapers. Magazine and book publishers are now largely national, or international, enterprises. The days of "free speech" protecting the small publisher of pamphlets are largely over. Instead, the control of media has become centralized in the corporate offices of media giants like Time Warner and Viacom.

These changes have led to the regulation of media ownership. For example, the FCC has regulated the number of television and radio stations a single company can own, although the limit has changed over time. By the early 1990s, the government prohibited companies from owning more than 12 television stations or from owning stations that reached more than 25 percent of the nation's audience. Regulations also limited companies to owning a total of 20 AM and 20 FM radio stations, with no more than 2 AM and 2 FM stations in any one city. The aim was to limit the potential monopolistic power of a media conglomerate and encourage diverse media ownership. However, changes introduced in the 1996 Telecommunications Act eased restrictions on both television and radio station ownership and raised the ceiling on television audience limits to 35 percent of the viewing public.

Following the same logic, since 1975 the FCC usually has not allowed cross-ownership of print and broadcast outlets in a single city. The owner of a local newspaper, for example, cannot also own a local television station. Here the aim is to prevent monopolistic control of media in a local market. However, a company is not prevented from owning a newspaper in one city and a television station in another city; it simply cannot control a single market.

One clear way in which government can intervene in the media industry, then, is by regulating ownership of media outlets. By preventing monopoly ownership of media, the government attempts to act in the public interest, since control of media information by a few companies may well be detrimental to the free flow of ideas. Through such regulations, the government prevents media giants from acquiring control of the media market.

Media companies usually oppose such restrictions and work to have such limits relaxed, as they did successfully in 1996. Some observers see an unprecedented threat emerging from the consolidation of media ownership into fewer and fewer hands. Reuven Frank, former president of NBC News, suggested that "it is daily becoming more obvious that the biggest threat to a free press and the circulation of ideas is the steady absorption of newspapers, television networks and other vehicles of information into enormous corporations that know how to turn knowledge into profit—but are not equally committed to inquiry or debate or to the First Amendment" (quoted in Shales, 1995).

Regulating Ownership of Programming: The Case of "Fin-Syn" Rules

The most far-reaching intervention of government into the media market is in its protection of the ownership of media products. As we noted before, copyright laws protect the interests of artists, writers, and the media industry by banning the unauthorized use or reproduction of many media-related products. In this case, government structure clearly has empowered, rather than constrained, the media industry.

While the government is concerned with protecting the rights of the owners of media property, however, it has also been concerned with avoiding monopolistic ownership of that property. One example of this concern was the FCC's regulation of ownership and control of television programming through so-called "fin-syn" (financial interest and syndication) rules (Crawford, 1993; Flint, 1993; Freeman, 1994a, 1994b; Jessell, 1993). Most people do not realize that, until recently, the television networks generally did not own the programs they broadcast. They merely bought the rights to broadcast programs produced by others. The fin-syn rules, established in 1970, limited the ability of the three major TV networks (ABC, CBS, NBC) to acquire financial interests or syndication rights in television programming. (In syndication, a producer sells the rights to rebroadcast a program.) In its words, the FCC "imposed these constraints to limit network control over television programming and thereby encourage the development of a diversity of programs through diverse sources of program services" (FCC, April 5, 1995). The fear was that the three networks—who shared an oligopoly in television broadcasting in 1970—could also dominate programming industrywide if they were able to own and control the creation and syndication of programming. Regulators theorized that, by forcing the networks to buy programming from independent producers, they could encourage the emergence of a more competitive marketplace of program producers.

For over two decades, the fin-syn rules were the law of the land. During that period, though, the landscape of American television broadcasting changed dramatically. Many new independent television stations, cable stations, and even new television networks emerged. The audience share controlled by the three networks declined, and fear of a network monopoly subsided. Finally, in 1993, a U.S. District Court ruled that networks were not subject to many of the FCC's fin-syn regulations because competing cable stations and the emergence of new networks and independent stations precluded them from monopolizing production and syndication. In this case, changes in technology were a factor in changing how government regulates media.

The changed FCC rules meant that, among other things, networks could now acquire financial interests in and syndication rights to *all* network programming. The stakes in such a change were high. For example, in the early and mid-1990s, "Home Improvement" was a popular half-hour situation comedy that aired on the ABC network. However, it was coproduced by Wind Dancer Entertainment and Touchstone Television.

In 1994, the producers sold the program into syndication for $3 million per episode, and "Home Improvement" found a second life on independent television stations. With over 130 episodes in existence at the time, the sale netted the producers nearly $400 million—money that would have gone to the networks if they had owned the program (Freeman, 1994a).

The changes generated by the new regulations were swift. Before the new regulations, network production was limited to a maximum of 20 percent of a network's prime-time programming. One year after the changes in regulation, the "Big Three" networks either produced in-house or had financial interests in about half of all prime-time programming. Independent producers were quick to feel the pinch. Some of them argued that when networks negotiated production deals, they took advantage of the lack of regulations to extract better terms for themselves at the expense of small, independent producers.

The fin-syn debates, in all their inside details, illustrate some of the basic tensions that exist in the media industry. The unbridled growth of major media conglomerates threatens small media producers. In turn, major conglomerates argue that we live in a diverse media world where monopolistic control is no longer possible. The question for policymakers is whether the government needs to use any regulatory constraint to control the actions of the growing media corporations.

These debates are yet another illustration of the tension between structure and agency. In this case, the same regulatory structure that protects the media industry's copyright claims constrained its ability to produce and resell its products. However, the agency of the media industry is seen in its ability to promote changes that favored the major networks. Meanwhile, the relaxing of the old regulations may end up harming the viability of smaller media producers. Once again, regulations constrain some and benefit others.

Regulating Ownership and Control of Technology

Some observers believe that we are currently in the most revolutionary period of media development since the introduction of printing (Jost, 1994a; Hickey, 1995). The underlying reason for such dramatic claims can be found in two numbers: 0 and 1. These two numbers represent the basis of binary code—the basic bits of information that make up a digital signal. Such digital information is most familiar to us in computer applications. However, the technology of digitization has now spread to all forms of information. Compact disks, for example, provide digitized music recordings. Their sound is remarkably clean because the digital information is "read" by a laser and sounds the same each time we play a CD.

Some of the impact of digital information is medium-specific, as in the case of music CDs. However, the most significant consequence of digitization is that producers can easily transform digital information from one medium to another. Digital television or video, digital CDs, digital telephone, and digital computers can, in effect, all "talk" with one another. With digitization, the basic format of the information each transmits is the same.

The impact of digitization is enhanced further when coupled with fiber optics. Rather than transmitting information over a copper wire, as is usually done, fiber optics allows information to travel by way of laser-beam light over a tiny, pure-glass fiber no thicker than a human hair. This format greatly increases the capacity for transmitting vast amounts of information at high speed. Boosters of new technologies paint a vision of information access that is just beginning to emerge today. Computer networking through the Internet, to take just one example, will link individuals to commercial sites, community organizations, government agencies, and other individuals. From a home computer, individuals will be able to complete banking transactions, shop, pay bills, take an on-line educational course, check electronic want ads, engage in political discussion, register their child for the local Little League, e-mail a government official, and access local bus schedules. However, the precise nature of these informational sites and the question of who will control the information available on them is still being debated.

The commercial nature of current on-line services raises some disturbing possibilities. For example, in 1990 the commercial on-line service Prodigy (which was a joint venture between Sears and IBM) decided to raise its rates for customers sending frequent e-mail messages. Some angry customers began posting e-mail messages of protest as well as contacting Prodigy's on-line advertisers to threaten a boycott. Prodigy read and censored the protesters' messages and removed the dissenters from the service. In an opinion piece for the *New York Times*, a company spokesperson wrote that Prodigy would continue to restrict on-line speech as it saw fit—including speech that criticized the company (Shapiro, 1995). The public would likely have met such action with widespread outrage if it had been carried out by the government. In this case, censorship by a private corporation elicited little public notice.

Digitization and fiber optics are leading to a convergence of mass media formats. The lines between cable television, broadcast television, telephone, computer, and so on will become less and less identifiable. The result will be the emergence of more integrated "multimedia" services. We will examine the implications of such technology in more detail in Chapter 9, but it is important to note here that such changes raise critical issues for the regulation of technology.

Formerly, the government protected against monopolies by regulating the ownership and control of some technologies. Telephone companies, for example, could not enter the cable TV business, and vice versa. In the 1990s, however, all this changed because of the merging of different media forms. In 1996, Congress revised federal laws limiting ownership of cable television. The government allowed the seven regional local telephone companies—the so-called "baby Bells"—to enter the cable television business. In turn, deregulation opened local phone service to competition from cable providers who wanted to carry phone service over their cables. Some hailed this change as a step toward more competitive, integrated media. Others worried that phone companies would have a substantial advantage in funding new cable ventures, given their steady stream of income from phone services. Many critics were concerned about the specter of a "single-wire" monopoly, that is, a single company providing a wire that could bring cable television, telephone, and computer services to a home.

The telephone and cable television "merger" is just one of many similar changes in media technology. Some changes have international implications. With the advent of satellite-based television and the Internet, media products now easily cross national boundaries. In an attempt to control the social implications of such information, the Chinese government has pressured Western media companies to limit the content of some news broadcast via satellite in China. In 1996, the Chinese government announced that all Internet users would have to register with the government and that all Internet service providers would be subject to close supervision by various government agencies. These actions suggest that changes in technology will spark new initiatives by media corporations and governments around the globe. The dust from these technological changes has not yet settled.

Regulating Media Content

While the regulation of the ownership and control of media outlets, programming, and technology raises basic questions about the relationship between government and media, a different set of issues is raised with respect to the regulation of media content. However, the basic dynamic of structure and agency remains.

Regulating the Media Left and Right:
Diversity vs. Property Rights

In the everyday political world, calls for media regulation come from both liberals and conservatives. However, the intended target of the regulation differs based on political orientation. The sides do not always line up neatly, but conservatives and liberals generally tend to approach the topic of regulation differently.

Liberals and the left usually see the government's role in media regulation as one of protecting the public against the domination of the private sector. (Conservatives see this as government meddling in the free market.) As we have seen, this view manifests itself in liberal support for regulating media ownership of outlets, programming, and technology, with the aim of protecting the public interest against monopolistic corporate practices. Inherent in this approach is the belief that the marketplace is not adequately self-regulating and that commercial interests can acquire undue power and influence.

Liberals and the left also tend to support regulation, such as the Fairness Doctrine, that encourages diversity in media content. We discuss the Fairness Doctrine below. Finally, liberals also support publicly owned media such as the Public Broadcasting Service (PBS) and National Public Radio (NPR) because such outlets can sometimes provide a less commercialized alternative to mainstream media. A central theme for liberals and the left is the need for diversity in all facets of the media.

Conservatives and the right tend to respond to such arguments with staunch support for property rights and the free-market system. When it comes to regulating ownership and control of media, conservatives tend to advocate a *laissez faire* approach by government. They caution against the dangers of bureaucratic government intervention and, more recently, the tyranny of "politically correct" calls for diversity. They are often enthusiasts for the ability of the profit motive to lead to positive media developments for all. Conservatives generally see the marketplace as the great equalizer, a place where ideas and products stand or fall based on the extent of their popularity. They often portray ideas like the Fairness Doctrine or public television as illegitimate attempts by those outside the American mainstream to gain access to the media.

Although conservatives abhor the idea of limiting, restricting, or regulating private property rights, they are often quite comfortable with restricting the content of media products, especially in the name of morality. The problem with a pure free-market system for the media is that it leads to things such as graphic violence and pornography. Media images of sex and violence are popular and profitable. However, nearly all observers agree that some restrictions on the content of media are necessary, especially to protect children and minors. In fact, it is conservatives who have often led the call to regulate material they deem unfit for minors. So while conservatives oppose government regulation, such as the Fairness Doctrine, that requires additional content for the sake of diversity, they are generally comfortable with regulations that restrict or prohibit the dissemination of material they deem unsuitable. The result has been both voluntary and mandatory regulation of media content. We turn now to some of the more common forms of content regulation.

Regulating for Diversity: The Fairness Doctrine

While media have tremendous potential to inform citizens about events and issues in their world, they also have unparalleled potential for abuse by political partisans and commercial interests. One way in which the government attempted to protect against potentially abusive media domination was the establishment of the Fairness Doctrine (Cronauer, 1994; Frank, 1993; Jost, 1994b; Simmons, 1978; Wiley, 1994). The goal of the doctrine was to promote serious coverage of public issues and to ensure diversity by preventing any single viewpoint from dominating coverage. The Fairness Doctrine provides an interesting example of the rise and fall of a government attempt to regulate media content in the public interest.

In 1949, the FCC adopted a policy that reaffirmed the congressional precedent that "radio be maintained as a medium of free speech for the general public as a whole rather than as an outlet for the purely personal or private interests of the licensee." To achieve this goal, the FCC required, first, that licensees "devote a reasonable percentage of their broadcasting time to the discussion of public issues of interest in the community served by their stations" and, second, "that such programs be designed so that the public has a reasonable opportunity to hear different opposing positions on the public issues of interest and importance in the community" (13 FCC 1246 [1949] in Kahn, 1978, p. 230). While the specific dimensions of the Fairness Doctrine evolved over time, the two basic provisions—requiring broadcasters both to cover public issues and to provide opportunity for the presentation of contrasting points of view—remained intact.

The goal in the application of the doctrine was to ensure diversity of views within the program schedule of a station. The Fairness Doctrine, for example, did not interfere with conservative radio talk shows but rather required the station to provide other programming that included differing points of view. Thus, the Fairness Doctrine never suppressed views, but it sometimes required additional speech for balance. The goal was not to stifle criticism but instead to ensure the airing of vigorous debate and dissent. FCC involvement in any Fairness Doctrine case came only *after* someone filed a complaint.

Over time, competing actors tried to use, and in some cases abuse, the Fairness Doctrine. The Kennedy, Johnson, and Nixon administrations, for example, harassed unsympathetic journalists by filing complaints under the Fairness Doctrine (Simmons, 1978). In many cases, the doctrine allowed the airing of opposing views that the public would not otherwise have heard. That was the intent of the regulation.

The broadcast industry challenged the legality of the Fairness Doctrine, but in 1969 the Supreme Court unanimously upheld the policy. The Court based its decision, however, on the scarcity of broadcast frequencies, agreeing with the FCC that because the airwaves were a scarce public resource broadcasters should use them to serve the public interest. As part of the Reagan-era push for government deregulation, the FCC voted in 1987 to repeal the Fairness Doctrine. Failed attempts to revive the Fairness Doctrine have occurred periodically ever since.

The key argument used against the Fairness Doctrine is that the premise of broadcast-frequency scarcity upon which it was built is no longer an issue. Critics note that when the government introduced the Fairness Doctrine in 1949, there were 51 television stations and 2,600 radio stations in the United States. By the mid-1990s, there were over 1,500 television stations and over 11,500 radio stations. However, the scarcity discussed in the 1969 Supreme Court decision referred to the availability of frequencies, not to the number of media outlets. While the number of media outlets has exploded over the years, the demand has kept pace. There is still more demand for prime frequency use than space allows. Some new technologies, such as personal communications equipment, require more space on the limited waveband. So, despite the technological changes, a kind of scarcity still exists in broadcast media.

Cable technologies raise different issues. In 1995, almost two-thirds of American households received some form of cable service, although only about one-third of U.S. households received "premium" cable channels. Cable technology enables subscribers to receive literally hundreds of different channels. However, unlike broadcast media, cable is "hard-wired" directly into homes and is available only to those who can afford it. Less affluent households are disproportionately without cable service. Cable, therefore, is generally exempted from the debates regarding public service, because it does not use the public airwaves.

The debate over the Fairness Doctrine highlights an important issue that is easy for us to forget: The airwaves are a public resource, *not* private property. By applying for a license, broadcasters, much like automobile drivers, agree to adhere to the rules of the road. Supporters of the

Fairness Doctrine believe that one of those rules should be the requirement that stations air differing points of view. Opponents argue that government regulation inherently inhibits the free expression of ideas. At this writing, opponents of the Fairness Doctrine have prevailed.

Relying upon the scarcity argument to support the Fairness Doctrine ignores a more fundamental issue. Allowing the marketplace to exclusively determine the content of media can mean that only popular—and thus profitable—ideas are regularly heard and seen in commercial media. The commercial marketplace operates on the basis of providing what is most popular to the greatest number. This approach may work reasonably well with consumer products, but when the "commodity" at hand is ideas, democracy is not likely to be well served by paying attention only to the popular and fashionable.

Since the abandonment of the Fairness Doctrine, the FCC no longer requires stations to seriously address issues of public interest. If stations do address public issues, they can now create entire program schedules that communicate a single viewpoint without ever seriously considering alternative opinions. Some argue that further fragmentation in our media culture will occur as partisans tune into stations that reflect only their point of view and ignore the possible merits of differing opinions. One possible result is the further entrenchment of political division. We must also remember that commercial interests drive almost all mass media. It is likely, therefore, that corporate owners of media outlets, unfettered by balance constraints, will feel no need to air the views of consumer advocates and business critics.

Regulating for Morality

In May 1995, then presidential candidate Bob Dole made a speech in Los Angeles—the capital of the U.S. entertainment industry—on the "evil" in popular culture. According to Dole, "One of the greatest threats to American family values is the way our popular culture ridicules them. Our music, movies, television and advertising regularly push the limits of decency, bombarding our children with destructive messages of casual violence and even more casual sex." Dole scolded "the corporate executives who hide behind the lofty language of free speech in order to profit from the debasing of America." He argued that "[w]e must hold Hollywood and the entire entertainment industry accountable for putting profit ahead of common decency."

But Dole affirmed his support for the free-market system. "Our freedom to reap the rewards of our capitalist system has raised the standard of living around the world. The profit motive is the engine of that system, and is honorable. But those who cultivate moral confusion for profit should understand this: we will name their names and shame them as they deserve to be shamed. . . . For we who are outraged also have the freedom to speak. If we refuse to condemn evil it is not tolerance but surrender. And we will never surrender."

One particular target of Dole's criticism was media giant Time Warner. He asserted that some of the company's products, especially "gangsta rap" music, "debase our nation and threaten our children for the sake of corporate profits." Such criticism spurred Time Warner to sell its 50 percent interest in Interscope Records, the producers of the rap music in question. However, there is an important footnote to Dole's apparent hostility toward Time Warner. His "shaming" of Time Warner came despite the fact, which Dole later revealed, that the company had contributed $23,000 to his campaigns. More important, less than two weeks after his harsh speech Dole led the battle for passage of sweeping deregulation of the telecommunications industry—a bill of enormous benefit to Time Warner.

The incident reflects some of the peculiarities in the debate over controlling media. On the one hand, in the conservative tradition, Dole invoked citizen pressure—not government action—in shaming the media industry into changing its practices. On the other hand, he helped pass legislation that will likely lead to a larger, more centralized media industry that will be increasingly immune from citizen pressure. Dole's actions are in line with a long tradition of conservative thought. While supporting a hands-off approach to regulating media ownership, conservatives are often at the forefront of calls to control media content.

Ratings and Warnings

One way content is regulated is by industry self-regulation, rather than formal government involvement. The best-known examples of this are the rating and warning systems devised for different media (Cronauer, 1994; Frank, 1993; Jost, 1994b; Simmons, 1978; Wiley, 1994). The National Association of Broadcasters, an industry lobbying group, has established a set of regulations regarding the form and content of programming. The best known of these self-regulation systems is that used for the motion picture industry. Before the 1960s, the movie industry, in the form of the Motion Picture Association of America (MPAA), used an internal system of self-regulation that essentially prevented the making or release of any film the MPAA considered indecent. All that changed in the 1960s when directors and studio executives began challenging the authority of the MPAA president more forcefully. More films emerged that challenged public standards by including nudity and explicit language.

This new generation of Hollywood films explicitly dealing with mature themes led to public concern and increasing calls for control. Congress seemed poised to require a rating system. To ward off government regulation, the MPAA in 1968 collaborated with theater owners and film distributors to develop a rating system that film makers would adopt voluntarily. An anonymous panel of citizens representing a national cross section of parents would implement the new rating system by a process of majority vote.

For years the rating system used G to indicate material appropriate for general audiences, PG to suggest parental guidance because some material might not be suitable for young children, PG-13 to caution that some material might be inappropriate for preteenagers, R to restrict access to adults or to those under 17 accompanied by a parent or guardian, and X to indicate a film intended only for adults.

The rating system presented some problems. First, theaters were notoriously lax in enforcing the supposedly restricted access of R-rated films, a rating given to about half of all movies. This problem continues today. A recent Gallup Poll found that more than one-third of all minors age 12–17 had attended an R-rated film without being accompanied by a parent or guardian (Sandler, 1994).

More significantly, the public came to associate the X rating not with adult-oriented themes but with hard-core pornography. Part of the problem was that the MPAA applied the X rating only to about 4 percent of all films and in most of these cases used the rating for films that consisted almost entirely of graphic sex scenes. There was no way for the public to distinguish between these X-rated movies and the few mainstream films that also received an X rating because of mature subject matter. (For example, the MPAA gave *Midnight Cowboy* an X rating because of its adult-oriented subject matter, but the film won the 1969 Academy Award for best picture.)

Pornographers exacerbated the problem of the public associating X-rated films with hard-core pornography by informally adopting the rating of X—or better yet, XXX—as a selling point in their advertising. This self-labeling had no connection with the MPAA's rating system, although much of the public did not know this. However, since the MPAA had failed to acquire trademark protection for their rating system, the problem persisted. The X rating could mean the kiss of death for a mainstream film because many newspapers would not carry advertising for X-rated films and many theater owners refused to show such films.

In 1990, the MPAA moved to replace the X rating with a new NC-17 rating, indicating that theater owners would not admit children under the age of 17. It also made sure to acquire a trademark for this new system. The development pleased artists and producers, who hoped it would lead to the possibility of more viable adult-oriented films. Some religious and conservative groups, though, denounced the move as an attempt to acquire mainstream legitimacy for sexually explicit material.

The story of movie ratings is one example in which the perceived threat of government regulation was enough to spark industry self-regulation. A similar dynamic developed in the debate over the labeling of music lyrics (Clark, 1991a; Harrington, 1995). Responding to the increasingly graphic sexual language in popular music lyrics, a group of Washington, D.C., parents formed the Parents' Music Resource Center (PMRC) in 1985. These weren't just any parents, however. Their founding ranks included the spouses of 6 U.S. Representatives and 10 U.S. Senators (most notably, Tipper Gore, wife of then-Senator Al Gore of Tennessee), as well as one cabinet member. After organizing a well-publicized congressional hearing—dubbed by the media the "Porn Rock" hearings—the PMRC persuaded the recording industry to adopt a system of voluntary parental-warning labels. At first, each record company designed its own labels, but in 1990 the companies adopted a standardized label that read "Parental Advisory: Explicit Lyrics." In that year, 93 heavy-metal, rap, blues, pop, and comedy albums carried the label (see Exhibit 3.1).

By 1995, the founders of the PMRC had moved on, but a new generation of members had taken up the fight. The PMRC's new president, Barbara Wyatt, argued that the labeling system had been largely ineffective, noting that song lyrics had only gotten "worse." While still opposing government regulation, the organization now argued that stores should not sell music recordings that carried the warning label to minors. Other prominent conservatives, notably former Education Secretary William Bennett (whose wife, Elayne, became a PMRC board member in 1987) and Senator Bob Dole, argued that music companies should not produce such material in the first place.

Outlawing and Controlling Distribution

The suggestion that stores should not sell recordings with explicit lyrics to minors is an example of a more active approach to regulating the media industry for its moral content. It is an approach most often associated with obscene material. Obscene material is different from both *pornography,* or sexually arousing material, and *indecent material,* or material morally unfit for general distribution or broadcast. Pornography and indecent material are legal, although the government may regulate their broadcast or distribution. The government outlaws only obscene material. (The major exception is that the government also outlaws sexually explicit materials involving children, regardless of whether it judges such material to be obscene.)

EXHIBIT 3.1 *Warning Labels*

In response to well-publicized criticisms of some popular music lyrics, the music industry uses a voluntary system of advisory labels. As this photo shows, the nature of the advisory is rather vague, noting that the warning is about "explicit lyrics," and the advisory label itself is very small. Some critics have suggested that by carrying a warning to parents, the music may in fact be more attractive to children, who are the primary consumers. Do warning labels protect the public, or do they merely attract more curious listeners? *(Photo by Serge Levy)*

The United States has a long history of regulating sexually explicit material. As early as 1711, the "government of Massachusetts prohibited publication of 'wicked, profane, impure, filthy and obscene material'" (Clark, 1991b, p. 977). The debates that have ensued ever since often focus on the definition of *obscenity*. The courts have used these definitions to limit the production and distribution of printed materials, films, and, most recently, computer-based material. A 1973 Supreme Court decision set the standard for determining what is and is not obscene. For material to be considered obscene—and thus beyond First Amendment protection—it had to fail a three-prong obscenity test that asked (1) "whether the average person, applying contemporary community standards, would find that the work, taken as a whole, appeals to prurient interest; (2) whether the work depicts or describes, in a patently offensive way, sexual conduct specifically defined by applicable state law; and (3) whether the work, taken as a whole, lacks serious literary, artistic, political or scientific value" (in Clark, 1991b, p. 981). The court intended to limit the label of obscenity to only "hard-core" pornography. However, four justices dissented from even that limited application, with Justice William O. Douglas writing "The First Amendment was not fashioned as a vehicle for dispensing tranquilizers to the people. Its prime function was to keep debate open to 'offensive' as well as to 'staid' people. . . . The materials before us may be garbage. But so is much of what is said in political campaigns, in the daily press, on TV or over the radio" (in Clark, 1991b, p. 981).

Various laws also regulate materials that are sexually explicit but not obscene. For example, merchants cannot legally sell pornographic magazines and videos to minors. Laws also restrict what broadcasters can air on radio and television. The FCC has set times—for example, 10:00 P.M. to 6:00 A.M. during much of the 1970s and 1980s—during which broadcasters may air indecent programming. The idea in this situation was to protect children from being exposed to material that may be too mature for them. Periodic attempts have been made to remove all indecent programming from the airwaves, but the courts have generally supported the position that the First Amendment protects indecent material. In the 1990s, radio "shock jock" Howard Stern propelled his career by pushing the boundaries of radio decency standards. The station where his program originates was hit with an FCC fine for these violations.

The computer Internet has raised new questions about the need to limit sexually graphic material. Minors with access to a computer can easily obtain sexually explicit written or visual materials from on-line sites. They can also take part in on-line discussion groups that involve sexually explicit material. Should the government ban such on-line material because it is available to minors? Producers of sexually explicit material argue that the Internet should be treated like the print media and thus remain unregulated. Internet producers are not distributing or broadcasting the material, and there is no use of public airwaves; minors must take the initiative in order to access sexually explicit on-line sites. However, advocates of treating the Internet more like a broadcast medium subject to government regulation of content won a victory when the 1996 Telecommunications Act outlawed the transmission of sexually explicit and other indecent material. Accessing an Internet site, they argued, is no different from tuning in to a particular television channel. However, opponents of regulation won their own victory in June 1996 when a Philadelphia federal district court issued a preliminary injunction against the "indecency" provisions of the Communications Decency Act (CDA). One month later, a New York court called the CDA "unconstitutional." The issue continues to be debated in the courts.

Another issue that has arisen with the growth of the Internet is the traditional "community standard" clause of the obscenity definition. Since material on the Internet may originate in one place but be accessible worldwide, which community is supposed to set the standard? The notion of a self-contained community implicit in the Supreme Court's 1973 decision is not applicable to the growth in global communications and media. For example, at the end of 1995, a German judge ruled that over 200 sexually explicit discussion groups and picture data bases on the Internet violated German pornography laws. Fearing prosecution but unable to easily limit access to only German users, CompuServe, Inc., an on-line service provider, blocked access to the 200 Internet sites for all its subscribers around the world. Many subscribers in the U.S. and elsewhere saw this as a case of cyber-censorship and organized protests to force CompuServe to reverse its decision.

The Issue of Violence

Violence in the media is another area of content regulation that has received a great deal of attention (Ballard, 1995; Clark, 1993; Lazar, 1994; Schlegel, 1993). Violence on television is usually at the center of this debate because it is so accessible to children. For example, the American Psychological Association estimates that an average American child will see 8,000 murders on television before finishing elementary school (in Clark, 1993, p. 267).

An enormous amount of research—over 3000 studies by one count (Clark, 1993, p. 269)—has been done on the effects of media violence. Some researchers contend that for some children violent programming can lead to more violent behavior (aggressor effect), to increased fearfulness about violence (victim effect), or to increased callousness about violence directed at others (bystander effect). While such findings still inspire debate, there is growing consensus that prolonged exposure to violent programming affects some people. One study reanalyzed over 200 existing major studies on television violence (Paik and Comstock, 1994, p. 516). It concluded that although the various studies showed different degrees of influence, there is "a positive and significant correlation between television violence and aggressive behavior."

Producers of violent media products often argue that they are merely reflecting the violence that already exists in society. However, polls repeatedly show that most Americans believe violence in the mass media contributes to violence in society. As a result, there has been fairly widespread popular support for the regulation of violent programming, especially on television.

There are four basic approaches to responding to television violence.

First, some argue that the marketplace should determine programming and, therefore, no government interference is needed. Second, a few critics argue for a total ban on television violence, calling it a threat to public health. Third, and perhaps most common, is support for limiting violent programming to certain times of the day when young children are less likely to be watching, say, 10 P.M. to 6 A.M. Finally, a recently initiated technological solution is the introduction of violence-chips, or "v-chips." In 1996, Congress passed a law requiring manufacturers to install a computer chip in television sets to identify programs that had been electronically labeled as containing violence or material otherwise inappropriate for children. Homes where parents had activated the v-chip in their television would be unable to receive such programs. Networks agreed to provide a rating system for their programs.

Support for regulation of violent programming is not new. Concerns about violence on television date back almost to its introduction. The level of concern grew dramatically in the 1960s, though, as more programming regularly included violence. Movies, too, came under attack for depicting increasingly explicit violence.

In 1972, the Surgeon General released a major five-volume report on the impact of television violence, concluding that, for children predisposed to aggression, there was a causal effect from television violence. However, the 1970s saw increases in the level of explicit violence on television, and the FCC took no significant action to stem the media violence.

Meanwhile, citizen and professional organizations were demanding action. In 1976, the American Medical Association passed a resolution proclaiming TV violence to be a threat to "the health and welfare of young Americans" (in Clark, 1993, p. 278). The National Parent-Teacher Association (PTA) passed a resolution demanding that networks reduce the amount of violence on television, especially between 2 P.M. and 10 P.M. A 1982 report from the National Institute of Mental Health found that TV violence affects all children, not just those predisposed to aggressive behavior.

The 1980s, however, were an era of deregulation, and Congress did not enact restrictions on children's television. Instead, the government deregulated children's television and relaxed or eliminated many existing rules, such as those controlling the amount of advertising on children's television. One result was the development by toy manufacturers of children's cartoons that served as program-length commercials for their toys. The first of these was the "He-Man" cartoon, which promoted action figures and accessories of the same name. Over time, program-length commercials were selling children everything from "GI Joe" to "Teenage Mutant Ninja Turtles." Many of these programs were violent and war-related, and between 1983 and 1986, just after deregulation, war toy sales increased by 600 percent (Lazar, 1994).

Violence is universal and easily understood in any culture. Producers conscious of the increasingly important international market, therefore, are likely to continue to produce violence-filled programming. The creation of such shows will no doubt generate more concern among people worried about the effects of media violence. Here, too, we see the relationship between elements of the media and the social world.

Regulating for Accuracy: Advertising

Another area of content regulation worth noting is regulation that affects advertising (Clark, 1991a). A number of different agencies regulate the advertising industry because of its broad and varied commercial dimensions, which encompass all forms of mass communication. For example, the Federal Trade Commission (FTC) handles most cases of deceptive or fraudulent advertising practices. The Securities and Exchange Commission is responsible for the advertising of stocks and bonds, while the Transportation Department oversees airline advertising. The Treasury Department's Bureau of Alcohol, Tobacco and Firearms regulates most tobacco and alcohol advertising, and the FCC is responsible for overseeing children's television ads.

This collection of regulatory agencies addresses two basic concerns. First, the agencies protect the public against fraudulent or deceptive advertising. Segments of the advertising industry have a reputation for hucksterism that involves, at best, the distortion of fact. The most egregious violators are usually small companies that advertise—for everything from miracle cures to bust enhancers—in the classified ads in the back of magazines. The promises made in such deceptive ads sometimes echo turn-of-the-century patent medicine claims. But misleading ads can come from major corporations as well.

The second major area in which government regulations affect advertising involves ads featuring potentially dangerous products, especially when the ads are targeted at children and minors. Thus, the government regulates advertising for products such as alcohol and tobacco. Cigarettes, for example, cannot be advertised on television. In 1995, a new government initiative to further limit tobacco advertising even banned the use of tobacco company ads at sporting events that were televised. This meant a ban on everything from cigarette billboards at baseball games to tobacco company logos on professional race cars.

The government has also acted at times to limit the total amount of advertising aimed at children. For example, the 1990 Children's Television Act limited advertising during children's programs to 12 minutes per hour on weekdays and 10.5 minutes per hour on the weekend. The advertising industry opposes these limits, arguing that the free market should determine the appropriate amount of advertising for children.

Deregulation in the 1980s eliminated FCC limits on the overall amount of time radio and television stations can devote to advertising, and within eight years the amount of money spent on advertising almost doubled from $66 billion (in 1982) to $130 billion (in 1990). Since 1965 the number of commercials on network television has more than tripled, and in the early 1990s it was increasing by 20 percent a year (Clark, 1991a, p. 661). At the same time, the rise of "infomercials"—30-minute commercials that look very much like programs, often including a "live" studio audience—blurred the line between advertising and programming.

While most people know that the government controls and regulates advertising in the media, they are less likely to be familiar with laws that help business and the advertising industry. Most important is the fact that most advertising is a tax-deductible business expense, saving businesses millions of dollars annually and helping to support the advertising industry. Other ways government laws help advertisers include government financing of election campaigns, much of which is spent on commercial advertising; Department of Agriculture subsidies for advertising particular commodities; and postage rate subsidies for magazines and newspapers that are filled with advertisements. Finally, the government is a direct purchaser of advertising, spending hundreds of millions of dollars annually on military recruiting and other ads (Schudson, 1984).

In this area, too, fundamental issues of constraint and agency emerge as government seeks to protect the public from misleading sales pitches and advertisers, in turn, seek to protect the benefits they receive from government.

Regulating in the "National Interest": Media and the Military

During the Civil War, Union generals regularly read Southern newspapers to gain information about troop strength and movement. Ever since then, a tension has existed between the media's right to provide information to the public and the government's need to protect sensitive information during times of war. The nature of this tension has varied at different points in history. During World War II, for example, the media voluntarily complied with military restrictions on information and in many ways helped promote the Allied war effort.

A dramatic change in this cordial relationship occurred during the Vietnam War, when television, in particular, began reporting information the military did not wish to make public. The military felt that media were sometimes irresponsible in reporting information. Some reports were even said to have endangered the safety of troops.

From the media's perspective, the military's publicity apparatus had lost credibility with the press and a significant portion of the U.S. public. Well-publicized incidents of the Pentagon lying to the press and the public contributed to a highly skeptical tone in the media. As the war in Vietnam dragged on, the press corps so distrusted the information being provided by the Pentagon that they dubbed the afternoon military press briefings the "Five O'clock Follies." The Vietnam War was also the first to be given extensive television coverage. While the government repeatedly claimed that victory was near, network television images of dying American soldiers and dissenting American demonstrators revealed a different reality.

The experience in Vietnam led the military to take the offensive on two separate fronts. First, it developed a massive public relations machine to project a more positive image of the military. Ironically, part of this effort involved the hiring of press personnel (at officer status) to provide expertise on how to handle the media. The military became very adept at promoting information it wanted publicized in the media. From the military's perspective, its effort was an attempt to educate journalists and sensitize them to issues of military concern.

Second, the military began developing a strategy for controlling the dissemination of information through the media to the public. The central element of this strategy was the press pool (see Cheney, 1992, and critical views in Bennett and Paletz, 1994; Denton, 1993; Jeffords and Rabinovitz, 1994; Mowlana, Gerbner, and Schiller, 1992; Taylor, 1992). Tested in the invasions of Panama and Grenada and fully implemented during the Persian Gulf War, the press pool system was the Pentagon's attempt to control the information that journalists would report during a conflict by limiting the access of media personnel. The military argued that limiting access was necessary in order to protect journalists in the field and to curb the ever-growing number of media personnel seeking access to areas of conflict. In order to fight effectively, they argued, they needed to restrict the movement of journalists.

By choosing which media personnel would be included in the press pool, controlling their means of transportation in the field, and permitting access only to predetermined locations, the military was able to effectively control information about military operations. Military press personnel even monitored interviews with soldiers and screened media dispatches before publication. Journalists bristled at the new restrictions, but the major media complied. Some Americans were startled during the Gulf War to find a notice on the front page of their newspapers stating that

U.S. military censors had approved all information about the war. Many critics thought the military had gone too far in restricting the press, but the majority of the public supported the restrictions.

In the last half-century, the basic tension between an active press and a constraining military has centered on the definition of "sensitive information," which the military wishes to control. The military considered information sensitive if it might endanger U.S. troops or affect troop morale. The press had no problem with the first criterion and willingly complied with restrictions on information that might endanger U.S. troops. However, many journalists objected to the censoring of information that might indirectly and adversely affect troop morale. The military would likely consider "sensitive" anything that might undermine public support for the war effort, because reduced public support might undermine troop morale. For example, during the Gulf War the military did not allow the media to film the flag-draped coffins of U.S. soldiers being unloaded from planes that had returned to the United States. These images clearly did not threaten the safety of U.S. troops, but they did threaten public support for the war. Such blatant censorship was a startling development in the government's effort to ensure public support and raised profound questions about the role of government restriction on a free press, even in times of conflict. As a result of the restrictions, much information about the war that might have been controversial—such as the high civilian death toll or the fact that the U.S. military used huge bulldozers to bury Iraqi troops alive in their trenches—did not reach the public until well after the end of the war.

Press pools remain the official policy of the Pentagon, and it will likely use them in the next major deployment of American military force overseas. The issues of constraint and agency raised by this policy will also likely return during the next conflict.

Informal Political, Social, and Economic Pressure

This chapter has focused primarily on formal government regulation and informal government pressure on the media. However, it is important to remember the political role played by other actors in debates concerning the media. These varied actors often play a pivotal role in either directly influencing the media or prompting the government to act in relation to the media.

The most obvious players in the debates over the media are media critics and media-related think tanks, who produce much of the information that forms the basis of popular media criticism. Some of these critics are academics whose area of specialty is the mass media. Others are affiliated with privately funded think tanks that produce analyses and policy recommendations relating to the media. Such critics span the political spectrum, and knowing a little about their funding sources can give us insight into their perspectives on the issues at hand.

More important than media critics are the citizen-activists who write, educate, lobby, and agitate about the media. Some organizations not exclusively devoted to media issues have played an influential role in pressuring media organizations and the government. Religious groups, for example, often lead the fight for less violence and sex on broadcast television, creating significant social pressure on the media. In addition to political organizations that address media issues as part of a much broader agenda, dozens of local, regional, and national organizations are devoted exclusively to a range of media-related issues, from violence in Hollywood films to political diversity in the news to children's television to public access to the Internet. These groups, too, span a wide spectrum of political orientation.

Citizens' groups have legal status when it comes to renewing broadcast licenses. In the early years of broadcasting, the government allowed only those with an economic stake in the outcome to significantly participate in FCC proceedings regarding radio and television licenses. This changed in the mid-1960s when the Office of Communication of the United Church of Christ won a court case allowing it to challenge the granting of a television license to a station in Jackson, Mississippi. The Church of Christ contended that the station discriminated against black viewers. The U.S. Court of Appeals for the District of Columbia Circuit ruled that responsible community organizations, including civic associations, professional groups, unions, churches, and educational institutions, have a right to contest license renewals. While ensuing challenges rarely succeeded, activists discovered that some broadcasters were willing to negotiate with community groups to avoid challenges to their license renewals (Longley et al., 1983).

Challenges to license renewals comprise only a tiny part of the action repertoire of citizen groups. The Fairness Doctrine, when it was in effect, served as a useful tool for groups advocating more substance and diversity in the coverage of public issues. Some groups have testified before Congress on matters related to media. Others have employed a more grassroots approach, encouraging consumers to communicate their concerns to local media outlets. Some groups have even conducted their own studies and analyses of media coverage as part of their critique. While various forms of activism have ebbed and flowed, citizen group pressures from both liberals and conservatives have been a constant in the media debate.

Media organizations, and especially advertisers, are sometimes very sensitive to action organized by citizen groups. Nowhere is this truer than in the case of boycotts. There have been numerous attempts to put political pressure on media by organizing boycotts of advertisers who sponsor certain controversial programs or of stores that carry controversial books and magazines.

Conclusion

As this cursory survey of regulatory history makes clear, forces outside the media have had significant impact on the development and direction of the media industry. When we consider the role of media in the social world, we must take into account the influence of these forces. The purpose, form, and content of the media are all socially determined, and, as a consequence, vary over time and across cultures. The particular form our media system takes at any time is the result of a series of social processes. As we have seen, the world of government and politics can significantly influence the media industry.

Media organizations operate within a context that is shaped by economic and political forces beyond their control, but the production of media is not simply dictated by these structural constraints. Media professionals develop strategies for navigating through these economic and political forces, and media outlets have their own sets of norms and rules. In Chapter 4, we examine these media organizations and professionals.

Media Organizations and Professionals

Chapters 2 and 3 highlighted the ways in which economic and political forces constrain the media industry. However, we must keep in mind that action does not follow inevitably and directly from structural constraint. At most, broad structural constraints will influence behavior by making some choices more attractive, some more dangerous, and some almost unthinkable. Despite working within certain constraints, those who help create media products make a series of choices about what to make and how to produce and distribute the final result. People—Hollywood directors, network television executives, book editors, news reporters, and so on—are not simply cogs in a media machine. They do not churn out products precisely in accord with what our understanding of social structure tells us they should.

Our task, then, is to make sense of the dynamic tension between the forces of structure, which shape but do not determine behavior, and the actions of human beings, who make choices but are not fully autonomous. To adapt an often cited comment by Marx: Media professionals make their own products, but they do not make them just as they please; they do not make them under circumstances chosen by themselves, but under circumstances directly found, given, and transmitted from the past.

This chapter focuses on the structure–agency dynamic *within media organizations*. We explore how professionals create media products, the ways in which media work is organized, the norms and practices of several media professions, the social and personal networks that media professionals cultivate, and the ways the organizational structure of media outlets shapes the methods of media work.

The Limits of Economic and Political Constraints

As we have seen in earlier chapters, economic and political forces can be powerful constraints. As we examine below, media personnel actively respond to these constraints, often limiting their impact.

Working Within Economic Constraints

Let's briefly return to our discussion in Chapter 2 of the commercial logic of prime-time television. Recall that profit demands shape programming decisions in network television. Profits result from high ratings and desirable demographics, which lead to strong advertising sales. Network executives, facing severe pressure to schedule programs that will attract large audiences, select programs that are "safe," trying not to offend any significant constituency. It is the commercial logic of network television, then, that leads to the fact that programs on different networks look so much alike.

In Chapter 2, we emphasized the constraining power of the commercial organization of network television. However, Gitlin's (1985) study provides a nuanced analysis of the tension between these economic constraints and the agency of network programmers, producers, and writers. The people who actually create and select television programs work in an environment in which the decisions they make carry real costs. If you write too many scripts that are considered to be commercially unviable, your future as a television writer may be in jeopardy. Likewise, if you choose unorthodox programs for your network's prime-time lineup and they are ratings flops, you will be looking for a new job in short order. The economics of prime-time television, then, may shape the decision-making environment, but decisions are still made at various stages by various players. And since audience tastes appear to be both dynamic and unpredictable, these decisions cannot use any one simple formula to determine which programs will be profitable and which will not. As a result, people who work in the world of television must interpret both the current "mood" of the audience and the "appeal" of particular programs in order to create and select shows that will meet profit requirements.

Here the structure–agency dynamic is quite clear: Economic forces identify the goals and shape the terrain of the decision-making process, but human actors must assess both program and audience in their effort to deliver the "correct" product. The fact that the vast majority of programs do not succeed tells us that this is not easy terrain to master. Despite the difficulty of the field, however, players within the television world still try to navigate it safely; along the way, they adopt certain rules or conventions to smooth out and routinize the decision-making process. Imitation, for example, has been routinized in the television world. One basic rule of thumb is to create programs that look like those that are currently popular. Throughout this chapter, we will give attention to the conventions that media professionals adopt, because they provide an insightful window on production processes within media industries.

Responding to Political Constraints

Political forces, particularly government regulations, also play a significant role in shaping the environment within which media organizations operate. Even here, where federal laws require or prohibit specific actions, the constraints of government regulation do not determine what media organizations will do. Instead, the media sometimes ignore, reinterpret, challenge, or preempt regulations.

In the first place, passing laws is one thing, but enforcing regulations is another. The Federal Communications Commission historically has been reluctant to be a firm enforcer, in large part because of the complexities of its relationship to the U.S. Congress and to the media industries it is supposed to regulate. As a result, communications regulations can often simply be ignored, with few consequences.

Second, government regulations are almost always subject to interpretation, giving media organizations the power to read regulations in ways that match their broader agendas. For example, the 1990 Children's Television Act required stations to include educational television in their Saturday morning lineups but left a good deal of room for interpretation of the meaning of "educational" programming. As a result, broadcasters were willing to define almost anything as educational, including cartoons such as "The Flintstones" and "The Jetsons." While regulations were on the books, broadcasters found an innovative way to respond, demonstrating that regulation is, at best, only a partial constraint.

Sometimes government efforts are more successful at shaping the actions of media organizations. The Pentagon was quite adept at controlling the content of news reports during the Persian Gulf War, in large part because the government regulated access to information. There was little need for more direct censorship, because the government had a near monopoly on the strategic resource—information—that news organizations required. Even in this case, though, control of information was not total, nor was it met with complete acquiescence. A handful of enterprising journalists ignored military restrictions in an effort to gather independent information, and a group of alternative publications took legal action against the Pentagon for restricting access so tightly.

This action suggests a third route that media organizations can take in order to avoid the constraints of government regulation. If they have the resources, they can challenge regulations to try to alter them or rescind them altogether. Media organizations can adopt a legal strategy, challenging the constitutionality of specific regulations, or they can use a political strategy, lobbying potentially supportive politicians and threatening opponents in an effort to win new legislation more to the liking of the industry.

Finally, media industries can preempt external regulation by engaging in a public form of self-regulation. This is the strategy that the motion picture and popular music industries have adopted. They have used voluntary film ratings and warning labels on music products to stave off more direct government regulators. The television industry has also recently headed in this direction by agreeing to voluntarily rate the content of TV programs.

Ultimately, just as economic forces do not fully determine the actions of media professionals, media organizations are not passively compliant in the face of political constraints. In both cases, media personnel are active agents, making decisions and pursuing strategies within particular economic and political frameworks. Media personnel try both to control the environment as much as possible and to operate most effectively given specific constraints. Their actions sustain, and sometimes help change, the basic structural constraints, but they are not determined by them.

So far, we have focused our attention primarily on the broad environment within which media producers and consumers exist. We now move more directly into the world of those who produce media in order to examine how their work is organized.

The Organization of Media Work

In a widely cited book, sociologist Howard Becker (1982, p. 28) suggests that "producing art requires elaborate cooperation among specialized personnel." We can make the same statement about the production of media content. Whether we are talking about films, books, music, radio, magazines, newspapers, or television, the production and distribution of the message becomes the work of many people. Even the apparently most individualistic media presentation—a solo album by a singer-songwriter —still requires many other actors, including the music producer, the representatives of the music label, the designer of the album cover, the publicists who promote the music, and so on.

Becker goes on to ask an important question about the many people who do media work: "How do they arrive at the terms on which they cooperate?" Some researchers have argued that the behavior of media personnel is shaped by the "needs" of an organization (Epstein, 1973). In other words, maintaining the existence of the organization points different individuals within that organization in the same direction. The difficulty in such an analysis is that it relies on the sticky concept of "organizational need." How are we to assess what organizations need in order to sustain themselves? Is it really appropriate to assert that organizations have "needs" in the first place? In its strongest application, this approach is usually too constraining to account for the independent action of media personnel.

Another way we might account for the collaboration of media workers is to suggest that they must negotiate the terms of their cooperation before each new endeavor. This approach emphasizes the capacity for independent action, but it ignores the constraints under which media personnel labor.

In line with what sociologists who study occupations have found, Becker pursues a more practical approach that recognizes the tension between structure and agency. He tells us that "people who cooperate to produce a work of art usually do not decide things afresh. Instead, they rely on earlier agreements now become customary, agreements that have become part of the conventional ways of doing things" (1982, p. 29).

A convention is a practice or technique that is widely used in a field. It is much easier to identify something as conventional than it is to explain the source and meaning of the convention. All of us could likely identify some of the conventions that govern news reporting, pop music, or advertising. For example, nearly all U.S. evening news broadcasts take place on a studio set that includes a counter or desk behind which anchors sit. This format is an obvious convention of broadcast news. More important, the form of news is similar from one day to the next, even though the specific events change. Conventions are found in all spheres of media: The sound of top-40 music rarely surprises us; most pop songs follow the verse/refrain/verse structure; most magazine covers have the publication's name in large letters at the top and feature a large, dominating graphic; fashion advertisements seem to draw on the same stock of images, even if the clothes and models are different. Even media products that break from convention appear striking and innovative only because both producers and audiences are accustomed to conventional forms.

Conventions are not arbitrary, even though they may often seem to be. They are the result of the routinization of work by media professionals. To understand media content on the basis of its conventions, we need to consider where conventions originate, how they are followed in the work process, and how they lead to the production of media that we perceive as "conventional."

News Routines

What is news? This is not a question we ask ourselves with great frequency. The answer seems self-evident: News is information about recent important events. We read the newspaper over coffee in the morning or watch the evening news in order to find out what of significance has happened beyond our direct experience.

We usually do not explore the definition of news. How do we know what makes an event "important"? How do we know what information about an important event is relevant? We leave it to professional journalists to handle these questions. As a result, we rely upon journalists to make judgments about what is or is not important, or *newsworthy*, and to provide us with factual accounts about these newsworthy events. Ultimately, if we are to understand what news really is, we need to understand how journalists form their judgments and construct their accounts. In other words, we need to examine the day-to-day work of the professional journalist, because this is where news is defined and news stories are written.

Let's look at the process from the perspective of people within a news organization. Every day, a news staff must generate enough copy to fill up a newspaper, regardless of what did or did not happen that day. This means that editors and reporters must find news each and every day. At the same time, literally thousands of things "happen" each day: People eat meals, walk their dogs, buy and sell goods, commit crimes, announce new policies, argue court cases, participate in sporting contests, lie on the beach, fight wars, campaign for elected office, and so on. The list is virtually endless. News outlets, however, cannot report on all the things that happen; only some "happenings" are defined as important enough to be news. For reporters, the difficulty is determining which events are newsworthy and gathering enough information to cover these newsworthy events.

On the face of it, news reporting may seem to be an impossible job. How can journalists know which events to report and which to ignore? They cannot go to dozens of different events before deciding which one to cover; they would never meet their deadlines. How do reporters find out about relevant happenings in the first place? We rely on journalists to tell us about the important things that have happened, but how do they find out about these events?

Two classic sociological studies (Tuchman, 1978; Fishman, 1980) argue that we can find answers to these questions in the routine practices of journalism. Since news organizations cannot "start afresh" each day, the processes of news gathering and news reporting must be rationalized. In other words, news organizations must be able to anticipate where news will happen—before it happens—and structure their reporters' assignments accordingly. Within news organizations, reporters follow routines that tell them where to look for news and how to gather it efficiently. When the same basic routines are adopted as professional norms, as they are in contemporary American journalism, different news outlets will make similar judgments about newsworthiness. This state of affairs makes it difficult to see that any judgments are being made at all.

What are these journalistic routines? Tuchman (1978) adopts the metaphor of the "news net" to explain the standard practice for gathering news. News organizations cast a "net"—made up of wire services, full-time reporters, and stringers—to "catch" newsworthy happenings. The net, however, does not catch everything; like all nets, it is full of holes and catches only the "big fish." This is not an error on the part of news organizations. The netlike nature of news gathering serves as an initial filter, sorting out those happenings that do not meet the standard criteria for news.

The organization of news gathering shows which criteria determine how the news net is constructed. Newspapers will have staff or bureaus in places they define as important. For example, news outlets typically have bureaus in Washington and London, but not Houston and Lisbon. As a result, happenings in and around these predefined important places are more likely to become news, while happenings outside of these areas are more likely to be ignored.

News organizations also establish "beats" at prominent organizations where news can be expected to occur. In practice, this means that a series of official locations—police stations, courthouses, city hall, the state house, Capitol Hill, the White House—become sites where reporters are stationed. Each day, the reporter on the city hall beat will be responsible for providing one or more stories about the happenings there. It is likely that the city government will have a media-relations staff who will be more than happy to provide the beat reporter with daily doses of news in the form of press releases, public announcements, press conferences, and so forth. Finally, areas such as sports, business, and the arts are topical beats that are expected to produce news each day, so reporters establish relationships with key players in these areas in order to guarantee a regular supply of news.

Beats are central to how reporters "detect" events (Fishman, 1980). They are structured to bring reporters in contact with "news" and "newsmakers" by focusing the reporters' attention on a specific set of institutions or locations. But even within this structure, each beat covers so much potential territory that reporters have to develop strategies for detecting the newsworthy events. Fishman (1980, p. 33) uses the example of a local paper's "justice" beat, which included, among other things, "three law enforcement agencies: city police, county sheriffs, and an FBI office; four penal institutions . . . ; two juvenile facilities; two entire court systems; an extensive drug subculture. . . ." With such a vast terrain to cover, Fishman notes, reporters develop complex work routines that he calls "rounds."

The round structures the workday and defines what events the reporter will be exposed to in the first place. In essence, the round is a process by which beat reporters develop a schedule for visiting locations and talking to sources that are likely to produce news. Such work routines are built around the bureaucratic organization of the institutions that make up the beat. For example, a justice reporter will build a work routine around the schedules of the courthouse, police department, and district attorney's office in order to be on hand for meetings, press conferences, and prescheduled events and to gain access to official records. The reporter may also check in on a regular basis—perhaps hourly—with a range of sites to see if anything is "happening." For example, a beat reporter might call each prison, juvenile facility, law enforcement agency, and courthouse to make sure that important events do not go undetected.

We can see that, before anything even happens on a given day, news organizations have already made decisions about where they intend to look for news. The flip side, of course, is also true: The routine practices associated with news gathering virtually ensure that certain happenings will be excluded from the news. Because reporters on a deadline must produce a news story for their employers, we should not be surprised that news work is routinized in this way. How else could reporters gather news in an efficient, consistent manner while meeting the needs of their news organization? The problem, however, is that we rarely talk about the news in these terms. We usually prefer to treat newsworthiness as an inherent characteristic of events, rather than something that is constructed each day by professional journalists and news organizations.

A sociology of news work gives us insight into the making of news by demonstrating the significance of the ways in which journalists respond to the demands of news organizations. The standard practices for gathering news, and the corresponding definition of where news is likely to happen, help explain why so much of our daily news focuses on the activities of official institutions. Television news, with its focus on the visual quality of events, requires different work routines than the print media, although it is likely to rely on similar definitions of what is newsworthy. In either case, the news we get needs to be understood as the end result of these professional routines, which generally focus on the activities of legitimate, bureaucratic institutions.

Objectivity

We have seen that the specific definitions of "news" and "newsworthiness" are, in large measure, the result of the ways reporters organize their work. However, there is more to be learned by exploring the profession of journalism. Consider the concept of "objectivity." Most contemporary evaluations of the performance of the American news media begin or end with claims about their adherence (or lack thereof) to the standard of objectivity. Politicians routinely criticize the press for its supposed lack of objectivity, charging journalists with taking sides, being too opinionated, or having a routine bias.

In 1993, for example, Bill Clinton accused the "knee-jerk liberal press" of not giving him enough credit (Wenner and Greider, 1993). Throughout 1995, the Speaker of the U.S. House of Representatives, Newt Gingrich, claimed that some of the national press lacked objectivity and urged advertisers to withdraw support from these "biased" news outlets. In 1992 and 1995, debates about the continuation of federal funding for public television and radio focused on whether PBS (Public Broadcasting Service) and NPR (National Public Radio) were sufficiently objective. Both critics and defenders of public broadcasting used the language of objectivity as a principal framework for assessing its merits. Interest groups often make similar complaints. Those unhappy with news reports regularly charge journalists with violating their most fundamental professional standard: objective reporting.

Popular discussions of news media, as well, often focus on the question of objectivity. When we talk about the news with friends or family, an implicit (and sometimes explicit) basis for evaluation is whether or not we think the reporting is sufficiently objective. The following statements may sound familiar: "I read the *New York Times* because its reporters are the most objective." "That reporter really seems to have an axe to grind; I can't believe that anyone could call his reports objective." "I expect to read opinions on the editorial page, but I thought the front page was supposed to be objective." The central position of objectivity in American journalism is something we take for granted. We all seem to "know" that the news is supposed to be objective; the problem is that the news often does not live up to this widely shared expectation.

Rather than ask Is the news objective? however, sociological analysis of news media asks: Where did the value of "objectivity" come from? Why are we so concerned with it? How does the ideal of objectivity affect the daily practice of journalism? Michael Schudson's (1978) important study, *Discovering the News*, treats the ideal of objectivity as something to be explained, rather than something to be taken for granted. It is a perfect example of how studying professional norms and practices can help us better understand the media.

The Origins of Objectivity

What do we mean by "objectivity"? Schudson (1978, p. 6) provides a useful definition: "The belief in objectivity is a faith in 'facts,' a distrust of 'values,' and a commitment to their segregation." Objectivity is more than simply getting the facts straight; it is a doctrine that perceives the separation of "fact" and "value" as a messy business that requires the use of a method, or set of practices, to ensure their separation. This method is objective journalism. But where does this view of the world and this journalistic approach come from? According to Schudson, the concept of objective journalism is a relatively recent development. Even though we often talk about objectivity as if it has always existed, only in the years after World War I did it become the dominant value in American journalism.

Prior to World War I, reporters did not subscribe to a belief in what we now term objectivity. The Associated Press—the first wire service—tried to present news in a way that would be acceptable to many different papers, and the *New York Times* utilized an "information" model of reporting to attract an elite audience. But journalists did not think about the separation of facts and values, nor did they believe that facts themselves were at all problematic. Rather, to journalists before World War I, the facts spoke for themselves. The goal of fact-based journalism was simply to uncover these facts, and doing so did not require a method of objective reporting. The task was straightforward: Find and report the truth. In this era, journalists were confident of their ability to identify the relevant facts and to report them accurately.

This faith in facts held by American journalists was thrown into doubt in the 1920s. Many American reporters had participated in wartime propaganda efforts during World War I. The success of such efforts made them uncomfortable with any simple understanding of "facts." Having seen how easily facts could be manipulated, journalists became more cynical. They began to mistrust facts, realizing that facts could be made to serve illusion as well as the truth.

At the same time, the field of public relations emerged, and professional publicists became early "spin doctors." They fed information to reporters, carefully controlling access to their powerful clients, and they staged events such as the press conference or "photo opportunity" expressly for the media. With PR professionals spinning the facts, dispensing information strategically, and shaping a good deal of news content through the use of official handouts or press releases, journalists' emerging cynicism became even more pronounced.

The recognition that information could be manipulated and the rise of a profession—public relations—expressly dedicated to the shaping of public attitudes left journalists with a crisis of confidence about their own ability to report the "facts" in a "neutral" way. In Schudson's account, objectivity emerged as a "scientific" solution to this crisis of confidence. By training would-be reporters in the "scientific" method of objectivity, journalists transformed their fact-based craft into a profession with a particular method. Objectivity, therefore, can be seen as a set of practices or conventions that the professional journalist is trained to follow.

What practices make up this method? W. Lance Bennett (1988), synthesizing the research on the professional norms of journalism, identifies six "key practices": (1) maintaining political neutrality, (2) observing prevailing standards of decency and good taste, (3) using documentary reporting practices, which rely on physical evidence, (4) using standardized formats to package the news, (5) training reporters as generalists instead of specialists, and (6) using editorial review to enforce these methods. The practical implication of belief in the ideal of objectivity is adherence to these basic practices.

Objectivity as Routine Practices

The day-to-day routine practices of journalism, more than some abstract conception of objectivity, are key to understanding the news media. For example, we have all probably noticed that news reports from different outlets look very much alike. Flip the channels during the evening news, and you will find the networks covering many of the same stories, often in a very similar way. Pick up a couple of daily newspapers, and you will probably notice many of the same stories prominently featured.

News accounts have a tendency to look similar because reporters all follow the same basic routines. They talk to the same people, use the same formats, observe the same basic do's and don'ts, and watch one another closely to make sure that they are not out of step with the rest of the profession. If we understand objectivity to be a set of routine journalistic *practices,* we can see why all news coverage is pretty much the same. Journalists adhere to the same methods, so they produce similar news. In fact, if news differed substantially from outlet to outlet, questions would be raised about the method of objective reporting, likely signaling a new crisis for the profession.

Most reporters do not consider the similarity in news coverage to be the result of following the standard *practices* of objectivity. Instead, they see similarity in coverage as a confirmation that they have lived up to the *ideal* of objectivity. However, following a common set of practices does not ensure the achievement of the ideal of objectivity, that is, the separation of values from facts. Indeed, it can be argued that adherence to the practices associated with objectivity directly benefits particular political interests.

The Political Consequence of Objectivity

Implicit in our discussion of news routines has been the argument that the content of the news is fundamentally shaped by these practices. We have already seen that the news-gathering structure includes certain happenings as news and excludes others. In particular, things that happen in and around established institutions, especially official agencies, are defined as news. Happenings outside of these boundaries are likely never to be detected by journalists. Even if they are detected, they are not likely to be defined as newsworthy by the established definitions of importance. This is one of the principal reasons why so much news is about the world of officialdom, even when such stories are often routine and predictable. Journalists and news organizations rely upon, and build their work around, the routineness and predictability of these established institutions.

Newsworthiness, then, is socially constructed. It is not a property inherent in events but is instead something that is attached to happenings by journalists. Once we realize this, the traditional ways we talk about news begin to seem inappropriate. In particular, the metaphor of news as a "mirror"—a simple reflection of events—no longer works. Even a mirror cannot reflect the whole world. It must be facing a particular direction, including some subjects in its reflection and excluding others. The space and time constraints of the news media generally preclude a complete discussion of even the narrowest topic. The result is often the exclusion of some positions and the forgoing of historical context. Thus, the image propagated by the media is far from complete. At best, it "reflects" only a small part of society.

Additionally, the objects being reflected in the media are not passive. Instead, people holding different interests, wielding different amounts of power, and enjoying different relationships to those producing the news actively attempt to influence the content of the news. Thus, the resulting images often reflect the relative power of actors in our society rather than some "objective" reality.

News is the product of a social process through which media personnel make decisions about what is newsworthy and what is not, about who is important and who is not, about what views are to be included and what views can be dismissed. None of these decisions can be entirely objective. The *ideal* of objectivity—separating values from facts—is ultimately unobtainable, although some would argue it is a valuable goal. The *practices* associated with objectivity give those in power enormous visibility in the media, while those outside the centers of power are largely ignored. Thus, "objective" journalism, by highlighting the views and activities of officials, can be seen on balance to favor those in power.

As we have seen, news media production is the result of a series of conventions and routines that enable professionals collectively to do their jobs and meet the demands of the organizations for which they work. These conventions incorporate fundamental professional norms (e.g., objectivity) and basic organizational goals (e.g., gathering news). Routine media practices shape, to a great degree, the final media products.

Journalists are not the only media professionals who use routine practices. Analyzing work practices and professional norms can help us understand other media as well. Let's turn to two additional examples: photographers and book editors.

Occupational Roles and Professional Socialization

One type of media image we consume regularly is the photograph. We see photographs in newspapers and magazines, on billboards and in books, even on computer screens. But where do these photo images come from? To most people, photographs are not much of a mystery. At one time or another, you have probably taken pictures at a family gathering or during a vacation. The camera you used may have been quite simple, requiring few choices, and largely automated, reducing the chance of serious errors. Your pictures were probably developed by a local photo shop instead of in a darkroom. Amateur photographers use snapshots to tell stories, remember distant friends or places, or display their artistic talent. What separates those of us who take photos from someone who is a photographer?

The easiest answer to this question is talent. Professional photographers have a vision for their pictures that the rest of us lack. There is undoubtedly something to this distinction, but we would be hard pressed to put it to practical use. Who should define this talent or vision? How do we decide who is worthy of the status of "photographer" and who is just a weekend picture taker? It is more useful to think about photographers as people who take on the *role* of photographer and behave according to the norms of that role. Of course, there are different types of photography and, therefore, different versions of this role.

The concept of "role" has a long history in sociological theory and research. It has helped clarify the relationship between society and individuals, between the forces of structure and agency. We also use the term in everyday conversation: We know that actors play specific roles, we might refer to a member of a basketball team as a role-player, and, upon learning of a recent dispute at the local bar, we might ask our friends what role they played in the squabble. Sociologically, roles can be thought of as the bundles of expectations that are associated with different social positions. For example, students know the basic requirements of their role: attend class, complete assignments, show a certain measure of respect for teachers, and so on.

We rarely think about the specific content of roles, because we have largely internalized them. A person who has learned a role tends to "just do it" and not think about it as a role. In fact, roles become part of our sense of self. You would say, "I am a student," not "I play the role of a student."

However, sometimes the socially constructed nature of roles becomes apparent, for example, when role expectations are obviously breached. Take the classroom as an example. If a student were to fall into a deep sleep in class, begin snoring loudly, and perhaps even slide onto the carpeted floor to get a bit more comfortable, others in the class would feel a bit uneasy. They would be uncomfortable, in large part, because the snoring student had rather blatantly violated a key component of the student role. Students are expected not only to attend class but to show some interest—even if feigned—in what goes on there. The level of interest expected to be shown may be quite modest, but curling up for a good nap clearly violates even the minimal role expectation. These kinds of situations clarify role norms; seeing what we *shouldn't* be doing reaffirms what we *should* be doing.

Another time when we become aware of roles is when we have to learn a new one. Think about starting a new job that involves a kind of work you have never done. During the first few days, the bundle of expectations associated with this new role—whether it be waitress, teacher, or stockbroker—is likely to be a bit unclear, even confusing. Eventually, though, you must "learn the ropes" in order to be successful in your new job. You do this by following instructions, watching others do the work, and getting feedback on your own efforts.

The process by which we learn the basic ground rules of a role is called *socialization*. Every media occupation that we will encounter in this book—journalist, photographer, writer, filmmaker, musician, and so on—requires a kind of socialization into that role. We tend to think of this kind of work as *creative*, done by people who have a special talent. However, we need to keep in mind that even these creative media jobs are performed by people who must fulfill the expectations of their role and must fit into the expectations of the organizations with which they work.

On one hand, the concept of role highlights the significance of external social controls. Specific roles, we might say, serve as a social control mechanism by clarifying what is expected of us. Since other members of a social group also know the norms of the role, the expectations are enforced by our interaction with others. We generally do not consider role expectations oppressive, because the social control is not simply imposed on us. We internalize, to varying degrees, the components of the role, often so thoroughly that we hardly acknowledge any social control.

The role concept, then, explains how individual behavior is both patterned by and influenced by broader social forces.

This is, however, only half of the story. Roles are not rigid; they do not dictate specific behaviors. On the contrary, individuals often have a good deal of room for negotiation within the framework of the roles they occupy. Parents, for example, can relate to their children in a variety of ways without violating the norms of the parent role. However, there are limits. Certain actions will be widely perceived as violating basic norms, and some actions may even lead to the removal of children from the home, an effective termination of the parent role.

Roles also are not static. The parent example illustrates the dynamic nature of roles. What is expected of parents today is different from what was expected 50 years ago. Nor are roles permanent. Changing social conditions both create and eliminate the need for particular roles. In the following sections we explore how roles and socialization apply to media professionals.

Photography

It is tempting to view different styles of photography as simply the result of different creative visions. However, we want to look at the relationship between photography and the role expectations that different photographers face. We begin by noting that photographers in different work settings take on different roles. In other words, the photojournalist and the advertising photographer may use similar basic equipment, but each has a different role—with different sets of tasks, expectations, and norms.

Rosenblum's (1978) study *Photographers at Work* shows that role expectations and organizational demands are central to explaining the different *styles* of photography in newspapers and advertising as well as the different *conceptions of creativity* held by photographers in the two settings. Rosenblum (1978, p. 4) suggests—as we did at the outset of this chapter—that it is not enough to note the existence of conventions. We also need "to discover the underlying general social processes that create the conventions which shape and condition human behavior."

News photos and advertising photos draw upon distinct stylistic conventions that make the images quite different from each other. News photos look different from ad photos in ways that are readily apparent even to the untrained eye. Think about this for a moment. If you were to look at a group of photo images, some that were news and others that were ads, would you be able to determine which pictures fit in each category? There is a high likelihood that you would be quite expert at this task (see Exhibit 4.1). We have all seen so many news and ad photos that, even if

EXHIBIT 4.1 *Photographic Conventions*

a

Can you tell whether these photographs are from the news or from an advertisement? The contrast between photographs (a) and (b) illustrates the different level of control that the news and ad photographers have over their pictures. Photograph (a), a news photo, documents an independently existing event; it is not staged for the photojournalist (although the demonstrators likely sought news coverage of the event). Notice the incomplete sign on the left, the partially visible person on the right, and the sense of emotion that the photo evokes. *(Photo by Serge Levy, courtesy of Poughkeepsie Journal)*

Photograph (b) is an advertisement for an early home computer system, and it looks significantly different from photograph (a). From the smiling children to the helping father to the plastic plant in the background, nothing is left to chance in this picture. It has been created, down to the last detail, by the ad photographer to evoke the image of the computer as a family activity.

What about photograph (c)? This photo appeared in a newspaper, but it is a portrait of a newsmaker that has been staged specifically for this photograph. Does it make use of the conventions of the news photo in photograph (a), or the ad photo in photograph (b)? What does this suggest about the status of the newsmaker portrait as a form of photojournalism? *(Photo by Serge Levy, courtesy of Poughkeepsie Journal)*

EXHIBIT 4.1 *(continued)*

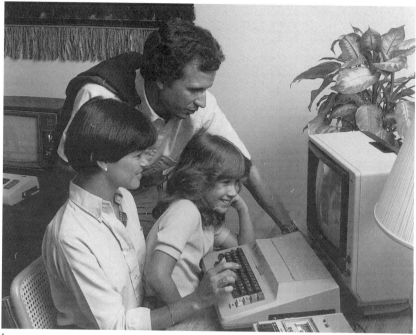

b

c

we cannot remember specifics, we have a sense of the look or style of the two different types of photos. Photo images selling jeans or perfume in *Vanity Fair,* for example, are easily distinguishable from a front-page photo illustrating the lead story in the *New York Times.* If the photo styles and their associated conventions are different, the sources of this difference can be found in the socialization of photographers, their work roles, and the organizational goals the pictures need to meet.

Socialization of Photographers

We begin our discussion with socialization. We have already seen that socialization refers to the process by which people learn the expectations of a particular role. It is likely that young news and ad photographers begin with a similar set of skills. Each knows the basic technical requirements of taking pictures. Socialization allows the beginner to move beyond the technical aspects of the work and learn how to conceptually "see" images in ways that are distinct to the professional photojournalist or the ad photographer. This distinct vision must be learned in order for each photographer to produce suitable pictures. One underlying assumption here is that ways of seeing images are socially constructed. Photojournalists and ad photographers must learn to see images in ways that are in line with their professional and organizational roles.

Entry-level photographers have to learn and internalize the basic norms of the organizations they work for and, at the same time, learn the culture of their profession. A beginning photojournalist learns the kind of news that the paper features and, more important, becomes acquainted with the "picture selection process" at that paper. If you have ever seen photojournalists on assignment, you have probably noticed that they are likely to take a large number of pictures of various aspects of the scene. When you pick up the paper in the morning, however, only one of these shots will have made it into print. The photo editor is responsible for selecting which pictures to run in the paper. Part of the process of socialization, then, is learning the norms of the selection process in order to be able to produce the kind of pictures that the photo editor will select. After all, one of the principal goals of photojournalists is getting their pictures into the paper.

It is one thing to know what your editors expect; it is another to be able to produce it. The beginner must learn the *role* of the press photographer. In order to produce suitable news photos, press photographers usually believe that they should not behave in such a way that their presence changes the unfolding of events. This is one of the fundamental professional norms of photojournalism: Pictures should document happenings, not transform them. While pictures inevitably provide selective snapshots of complex phenomena, the commitment to unobtrusiveness is central to the ideology of photojournalism. News photographers, then, have to learn techniques to stay out of the way yet still get good pictures.

Taking pictures that are suitable for the paper while remaining unobtrusive is no easy task. Because the events that photographers cover are almost all either prescheduled (e.g., press conferences, parades, sporting events) or fit into standard story formats (e.g., fires, accidents, crimes), photographers learn that they will be successful if they can anticipate what they will see in order to plan the kinds of shots they will take. This anticipation allows photographers to locate themselves in strategic spots, use the appropriate lenses, focus on the setting or people that are central to the event, and produce the kinds of pictures that will be acceptable to their editors. Thus, the socialization of the photojournalist involves learning how to anticipate action and plan shots in advance.

Advertising photographers must learn a set of organizational and professional norms that are different from those of photojournalism. One difference is that advertising photographers learn to leave nothing to chance; every aspect of each photo is the responsibility of the photographer. We are exposed to so many ad images each day that we can easily forget that everything about an ad photo has been staged. This staging is most obvious in respect to lighting and setting, but it extends to every last detail: the hairstyles, clothing, and jewelry of the models; items that sit in the background of the picture; the specific nature of any key props for the shot. Should the woman in the lingerie ad wear a wedding ring? If so, how will she hold her hand to both look natural and display the ring? The ad photographer must learn how to exert precise control and develop the technical skills required to accomplish it.

Advertising photographers learn that ad photography is a collective process; managing relationships with art directors and representatives of the advertiser is a key part of the job. The ad photographer learns that success requires not only vision or skill in creating compelling images, but also the ability to negotiate with—even please—those who have creative control over the advertisements. In practice, this means that photographers learn that there is little room for individualists who perceive themselves as pure artists. The profession requires that ad photographers see their role as just one part of a collective process driven by the logic of commerce.

Photographers' Work Roles and Organizational Goals

The division of labor within newsrooms shapes the kinds of pictures that photojournalists take. Newspaper photography involves various people in coordinated activities: the person who decides on the assignment, the photographer, the photo editor who selects the pictures, the printer, the editor of the paper who decides which stories to run. Newspapers are highly developed bureaucracies that rely upon clearly defined rules and classification systems. This kind of organization leads photographers to take "standard" pictures, the kinds of photos that we would be likely to recognize as news photos. The key is the system of classification, in which events are grouped into types: the disaster, the war, the political campaign, the court case. In producing news coverage, news organizations impose a standard script—including images—on these basic types of stories. Photographers are expected to produce images that fit the standard scripts. When images that do not fit the script are routinely weeded out by the photo editors, photographers soon learn not to take these kinds of pictures in the first place.

Role expectations also provide the framework for definitions of creativity. Editors expect photographers to have good news judgment, to be willing to use initiative to get good pictures, and to produce pictures that can tell various aspects of the story. Moreover, photographers are expected to regularly provide the kind of standard pictures that can accompany standardized stories, which both editors and readers come to expect. This expectation does not leave much room for the independent creativity of the photojournalist. The subject matter is assigned, and the organizational norms suggest the kinds of pictures that are appropriate. As a result, photojournalists generally see themselves not as creative artists but as reporters who take pictures.

Ad photographers, in contrast, take on the role of "merchants" since they must sell their services to an ad agency and an advertiser, follow the lead of the art director, and produce pictures that are generally prescripted. Thus, much ad photography is reduced to technical work. The photographer must have the knowledge and skills to effectively carry out the wishes of those making the creative decisions. Much of the day-to-day work of the ad photographer involves creating scripted images and adding small variations—in angle or lighting, for example—so that art directors have several different versions of the picture from which to choose.

For the vast majority of ad photographers, creativity is not in the conception of the images but in the ability to capture the desired image. They often achieve this by devising solutions to technical problems in the photographic process. Creativity in ad photography, then, is being innovative enough to figure out how to get the image the art director wants when standard techniques do not work. The creativity of ad photography is not in the vision but in a kind of technical mastery (Rosenblum, 1978).

Photographers, then, are not all the same. They work in different kinds of organizations that place different demands on them. They are socialized into different professional roles and take different kinds of pictures.

Organizational and professional norms provide the context for understanding the pictures photographers take, the daily routines in the workplace, and the ways photographers evaluate their own work. One of the central lessons to be learned from our focus on photographers is that authority relations within the workplace can tell us a good deal about the kind of work that media professionals do. Photographers, in both news and advertising, have specific superiors whom they must satisfy by producing appropriate pictures. Most of the time, they carry out the creative wishes of others rather than conceptualizing on their own. What about media professionals who are higher in the organizational hierarchy? What norms or social forces affect how they organize their work? A look at the work of book editors will help us answer these questions.

Editorial Decision Making

Book publishing is a dynamic, multifaceted industry. Books are published on a wide range of subjects, packaged in various formats, sold in many different settings, and bought by many types of readers. Additionally, there are several different kinds of publishing companies, from large commercial houses that sign prominent authors to six-figure advance-payment contracts to small presses that publish scholarly monographs.

In all publishing firms, the key decision is which manuscripts to publish. Regardless of whether the house is aiming for the best-seller list, with sales in the millions, or for adoption by college professors as a classroom text, where "success" might mean only a few thousand copies sold, all publishers have to sift through many submissions and proposals and select the few that will become books. These selection processes take place in other media industries as well. Record labels sign a small number of musicians, Hollywood studios produce a limited number of films, and the television networks add only a handful of new programs to their prime-time schedules each year. In each of these industries, decision makers need to make a large number of choices for projects about which they have only partial knowledge. These decisions, of course, have substantial consequences—they dictate the books, music, films, and television programs that will be available.

Different industries, and the various sectors within each industry, have different rules that govern the decision-making process. The search for steady profits by commercial media companies makes evaluations of the potential for economic success a central feature of the decision-making process. Those in decision-making roles need to develop strategies for evaluating the potential profitability of a particular movie or book.

Two common approaches are to copy current hits and to sign up producers of recent hits. The underlying assumption in both cases is that hits and their makers beget more hits. We saw in Chapter 2 how the commercial dynamic of network television helps create the conditions for rampant imitation on the small screen. We can see this dynamic in other media industries. The commercial success of the group Nirvana prompted the big music labels to look for other "grunge" bands that might ride the same wave. Authors of popular mass-market books, such as Stephen King, Patricia Cornwell, and John Grisham, are paid huge sums of money for the rights to their future works. Virtually every hit movie seems to produce a sequel.

However, there is no sure-fire formula for popularity or economic success. Many products that were *supposed* to be popular failed to meet expectations. Witness the remarkable failure of Arnold Schwarzenegger's 1993 film, *The Last Action Hero,* a movie that was designed to be a blockbuster hit. A variation on a fairly standard and successful format, starring a proven box-office draw, ended up being a multimillion dollar dud. Thus, imitation does not guarantee economic success, but as a kind of informal operating assumption, it is one way for media organizations to try to maximize the likelihood of success.

Different segments of the media industry feature different definitions of and approaches to economic success. This makes it difficult to generalize across the various industries. It is useful, therefore, to explore the dynamics of one media sector to see how a particular form of cultural decision making is organized by a set of *practices* and *premises.* Our example will be the book editor.

The Work of the Book Editor

In most publishing houses, the people who solicit, evaluate, and sign manuscripts are called acquisitions editors. It is their job to get high-quality books for the press, to weed out titles that do not fit, and to work with authors to produce books that will meet organizational goals. Acquisitions editors have varying degrees of autonomy and different editorial mandates at different presses, but they are ordinarily the principal filter through which the decision to publish is made.

One study of publishing (Coser et al., 1982) found that a key factor in whether or not a manuscript is published is the channel that brings a potential author to a publisher's attention. Abstract measures of the "quality" or "significance" of a book manuscript are far less important—at least in determining whether a book is published—than the way the manuscript comes in the door. There are different "lines" of authors (perhaps a better image is piles of manuscripts) awaiting the eyes of editors. These different piles are organized according to how they were received. The longest, and by far most unsuccessful, line is made up of authors who send their unsolicited manuscript to a publishing house, hoping that it will be impressive enough to be accepted for publication. Unfortunately for aspiring authors, there is very little likelihood that this route will pay off. One large publisher estimated that only 3 or 4 out of 10,000 unsolicited manuscripts are published each year (Coser et al., 1982).

Other avenues are more likely to lead to publication. Unsolicited manuscripts that are addressed to the appropriate editor by name are more likely to be considered seriously than those not directed at an individual. More important, personal contacts are what really facilitate the publication of a book. Manuscripts that come through informal networks —other authors, friends, or professional meetings—go into a much smaller pile that is taken more seriously. And authors who have agents are placed in yet another pile.

These piles are not likely to exist in any concrete form (although the volume of unsolicited manuscripts is so high that it is hard to believe they sit anywhere except in piles on an editorial assistant's desk); the pile metaphor suggests that publishing houses organize work, even if unconsciously, along these lines. Organizationally, this system operates like a kind of obstacle course with different entry points. Depending on where each manuscript starts the course, it will face different hurdles, opportunities, time frames, perhaps even personnel until it completes the course or is rejected. The specific nature of the obstacle course depends on the particularities of the organization of the publishing house.

Scholarly Publishing

Walter Powell (1985) studied the operating procedures that govern the process of manuscript selection in two scholarly publishing houses. Scholarly publishing is a particularly useful example because it is a segment of the book industry that is not so clearly oriented to profitability. As a general rule, books need to be able to sell enough copies to pay for the costs of production and meet the house's criteria for scholarly quality. However, editors do not have to focus their attention on signing up bestsellers. As a result, acquisitions editors at scholarly publishing houses have a more ambiguous goal than their counterparts at the large commercial houses, where sales potential is the dominant goal.

Editors follow a set of routines, governed by standard operating assumptions, that help them make decisions about what to publish. The volume of manuscripts is so high that it is impossible to attend to each project. As a consequence, routines allow editors to make decisions and still manage their schedules.

Potential manuscripts are not organized, evaluated, or responded to on a first-come, first-served basis. Manuscripts from unknown authors who have never had contact with the publishing house do not receive much editorial attention and are, therefore, unlikely to be published. Manuscripts from an author with previous connections to the house or those solicited by an editor receive much more thorough, and quicker, attention. Additionally, editors make use of prominent academics who serve as "series editors" to help attract new authors or evaluate manuscripts. In this way, editors can farm out evaluations to a stable, trusted group of scholars who may be more expert in the particular field. Most scholarly houses also use outside reviewers—people the editor selects to anonymously assess the quality of the manuscript. Editors use all these practices to manage their work load in ways that are consistent with their editorial goals and their obligations to their authors, colleagues, and friends. All of this suggests a good deal of autonomy for editors; they can draw upon series editors when they choose to, send manuscripts to an outside reviewer who is likely to be supportive (or not), and give closer attention to projects that involve scholars they already know.

Powell's research uncovered some of the informal controls, or organizational premises, that shape editorial work. He is particularly candid about the development of his own understanding of publishing. At first, he accepted editors' explanations that they had wide discretion in acquiring books. However, Powell later noticed several things that made him skeptical: Editors had a clear sense of which authors deserved priority service and which could be put off for long periods; editors never proposed atypical books, demonstrating their sense of boundaries; and there was a high turnover rate among editors yet stability in the kinds of decisions that were made. Additionally, Powell found that his observation at the houses had made him an expert in predicting which manuscripts would be signed and which would be rejected. In essence, he had learned the informal rules so well that the decision-making process was no longer a mystery.

Our description of scholarly publishing is similar to our earlier discussion of photography. Through a process of socialization, acquisitions editors learn the values and preferences of their publishing houses. This socialization process is one of the mechanisms by which organizations assert a kind of unobtrusive control. The key to the socialization of editors is learning about the "types" of books the press publishes. As part of their socialization, editors learn about the history and traditions of the house; they may already be familiar with the prominent books and authors that the house has published. In short, successful editors must understand the house's "list"—its currently available books, including new releases and the backlist of older titles. New books must "fit" with the list; that is, they must complement other titles. Editors understand this constraint and adopt it as a norm in their own editorial decisions. In this way, choices about new books are shaped, in important ways, by the types of books that a house has previously published. Additionally, most outside reviewers are authors who have published with the house, thus reinforcing a similar set of norms for each new year's crop of books. Finally, the process of signing a book—the paperwork and formal evaluations leading to approval of a contract—follows a standard operating procedure each time, adding another step at which editors must pay attention to organizational goals. Most editors anticipate this procedure and do their homework in advance to ensure that their projects meet organizational requirements.

Powell attributes his finding that editors rarely had their selections rejected by their superiors to their internalization of the basic norms of the publishing house. Editors do not have their projects rejected, because they have already weeded out those that did not fit. The manuscripts that they send on for approval by superiors fit with the house list. This is what makes them good editors, and it is what allows them to have a good deal of autonomy in their work.

A focus on the practices that editors use to organize their work and on the organizational premises that guide these decisions shows the dynamic relationship between human agency and structural constraint in media production. While organizational premises—structure—may make change more difficult, small changes in routine practices may help alter these premises, leading to the publication of new types of books. The backlist is the concrete embodiment of the relationship between agency and structure. It represents the accumulation of decisions made by prior editors, a tradition that shapes current decisions. But those current decisions will alter the backlist and, in turn, affect the framework for future decisions. In this example, we see both the stability and the potential dynamism of the socialization process.

Emerging Norms on the Internet

The three occupations we have explored—journalism, photography, and editorial work—are relatively stable professions. The workplaces we have examined are also long-standing organizations. As a result, our view of professional practices and organizational norms has demonstrated the ways in which the activities, choices, and perspectives of media professionals are connected to established professional and organizational forces. But what about new forms of media?

In the case of the growing information superhighway, clear rules of conduct are only just emerging. There is no established professional culture to which new recruits must be socialized, and the highly decentralized nature of computer networks makes it more difficult to see the role of organizational values. In fact, the notion of "virtual" space out there on the Internet might tempt us to think that social activity in cyberspace is totally autonomous, that is, free from the kinds of conventions that seem so central to the production of more traditional forms of media.

This is, to be sure, one of the great appeals of cyberspace. Participants in virtual culture can take on new roles. They can change sex or age or occupation and interact electronically with an altered identity. Additionally, computer networks challenge the distinction between a "producer" and "receiver" of media messages, combining characteristics of "mass" communication with one-to-one communication. This has led some critics to argue that computer networks are a kind of liberated zone, free from stifling labels, big bureaucracies, and arcane tradition—a place that is all agency and no structure.

It is difficult to disagree with the claim that cyberspace permits new forms of interaction and challenges our assumptions about the nature of mass-mediated communication. However, anyone who has spent any time surfing on the Internet is likely to have a sense of an emerging set of norms that govern behavior in cyberspace, as well as a set of potential consequences for violators.

In short, our relationships and our behavior in virtual spaces are patterned. Those who have constructed and are expanding the networks that connect us to one another—through discussion groups, databases, e-mail, and World Wide Web sites—certainly are technological innovators. At the same time, they both draw upon and create conventions that help structure our interaction within these networks. This process is, in important respects, an organizational matter. The network is not some random collection of access points. For example, network sites are classified by subject, which sets boundaries on the direction of the hypertext files that we move through. In addition, we need some kind of navigational software to connect us to the vast array of data and services. This requirement imposes very concrete patterns on our behavior. Users of Netscape, for example, will become familiar with and follow a similar set of procedures each time they log on.

We also construct a language that helps users understand the new technology. This may seem purely instrumental; after all, we need some way to talk about and describe cyberspace. However, language also helps impose a kind of logic onto cyberspace by in essence formalizing conventional ways of perceiving, even behaving on, the network. Terms widely used in cyberspace—such as "home page," "newsgroup," "flaming," "spamming," and "lurking"—characterize some of the ways our virtual behavior is both predictable and patterned. Some cyberspace terms, such as "newbie" and "moderator," even explicitly describe particular cyber-roles, with accompanying expectations.

Since the early 1990s, a cottage industry of Internet user's guides has proliferated. Go to the computer section of any large bookstore or your local software outlet, and you'll find shelves full of materials to help you understand the fundamentals of cyberspace. Much of what these materials provide is knowledge about the organization of the network—how and where to get access, basic terminology, strategies for negotiating through the mass of information. This knowledge gives you a framework that shapes the ways we use (or don't use) the network.

We can think of cyberspace as a site where anyone with access can be the producer of media messages. It is useful, then, to consider the norms and practices that these "producers" follow. McLaughlin and her colleagues (1995) pursue this question by exploring the "standards of conduct" in electronic newsgroups. In effect, they examine the expectations associated with the role of on-line newsgroup participant. In particular, they argue that there are specific types of "reproachable" network behavior, that is, actions that violate the basic norms of the Internet. As regular cyberspace visitors will know, the body of norms on the net is commonly referred to as "netiquette," and these standards are taken quite seriously.

What are the behaviors that elicit reproaches from other network users? One involves the incorrect use of the technological apparatus and is generally associated with novices who have not mastered the net. An example is a user who accidentally posts a message to an entire newsgroup that was intended only for a single recipient. A second norm-violating behavior is wasting "bandwidth" by using an excessive amount of the network, posting long messages, or sending out the same messages to many different newsgroups. A third is the violation of a basic network convention, such as failing to include your electronic signature with your message or neglecting to include a previous message about which you are commenting. Users who behave in these reproachable ways are likely to be admonished on-line by fellow users who are committed to the orderly functioning of the group. Such admonishment may be, at least initially, gentle and intended to be educational in nature. But admonishment can become rather venomous, referred to as "flaming." Many violators likely will learn from their mistakes, seek out help with the technology, be more careful about bandwidth, and learn network conventions. Those who persist in their reproachable behavior may be threatened with loss of access to the group, and repeat offenders will ultimately be expelled from the newsgroup.

Newsgroup norms are powerful shapers of virtual behavior. Perhaps that is why the vast majority of newsgroup subscribers are perpetual "lurkers," reading the messages but not posting their own. One widely held newsgroup norm, in fact, is to follow a group for some time before posting a message. This allows newcomers to become socialized into the ways of the group, to learn about the group's history and traditions, and to see the kinds of issues that are generally on the group's agenda. Additional practices help socialize new members of newsgroups. Upon subscribing, members receive an electronic "how to" manual for participation in the group, which includes both technical advice on the workings of the system and instructions on appropriate conduct. Archives of previous group discussions are often available, and new group members are encouraged to read through them. In addition, a file of "frequently asked questions" (FAQs) is sent to new members so that they do not clutter up the network with the same questions. All of these support materials serve the same general role as the publisher's backlists.

Why do such standards of conduct develop in the first place? One answer is that they provide a foundation for the maintenance of the identity of the newsgroup. This identity is passed along to new members through socialization into the norms of the electronic "community" and is enforced when new members are admonished for not adhering to the ground rules. Where do these standards come from? There are both practical and technological sources of the basic norms of the net. For example, regular users are aware of the cost of surfing the Internet and thus have incentive to limit the size of their messages and not waste bandwidth. Shorter messages that are not "cross-posted" to several different groups save everyone time and money. Other conventions, such as using an appropriate subject line on a posting, enable users to follow "threads" for days or weeks at a time. Each posting on the same discussion should use a subject line that identifies it as part of that thread. Users can sort through their messages by following the subject line on each posting. Those who use subject lines inappropriately or leave the line blank make participation in the virtual community both more confusing and more time-consuming. Also, without a set of technical conventions on the net, the millions of messages criss-crossing the world might become unworkable.

Technological conventions may seem trivial, and notes of reproachment for violations may seem nasty, but the requirement of maintaining some kind of order in cyberspace is their driving force. Perhaps most important, McLaughlin and her colleagues argue that there are underlying social roots to the cyber-conventions. These conventions reinforce and protect the collective identities of the electronic communities and can be used to ward off newcomers who pose a threat to these identities or to the stability of the group. Like other producers of media, users of the

Internet are part of a social world in which tradition, organizational history, group identity, and the routinization of daily activities help shape the norms and practices that pattern even our virtual behavior.

Hits, Stars, and Decision Making

We have seen that media products are created by professionals who follow a relatively stable set of practices, routinizing the production of creative work. But not all media professionals are in the same boat. One of the principal resources in the media industry is "fame," or "stardom," and media stars operate under a different set of rules. Why are stars so important to the media industries, and how does this reputational resource—fame—shape decision making in the media world?

Let's look at the question of stardom from the perspective of the public. For moviegoers, bookbuyers, popular music fans, and television junkies, the stars are the ones who are the dominant figures. A large celebrity-producing apparatus promotes the stars, making them seem almost omnipresent. We know about their personal lives, often refer to them by their first name, and follow their careers, and their stardom is a significant inducement in our selection of films to attend, compact disks to buy, and so on. Media stars are so prevalent that it is difficult to imagine what our media would look like without them.

The principal reason why stars are so visible and seem to dominate our mass media is because the production of "hits"—which draw upon existing stars and create new ones—is the major economic goal of most mass media organizations. Publishers want best-sellers; record labels are looking for top-40 songs and platinum albums; movie studios seek blockbuster films. Since most movies, songs, and books lose money, hits compensate for the losses and produce profits. They also create more publicity for the stars, making them even more attractive properties to the media industries. In short, the "hit system" is the underlying operating principle of most major media companies. If hits are the goal, the simplest path to success is seen to be the acquisition or manufacture of a star who can attract audiences for hit products and have a lengthy career as a hit producer.

This star principle is so widely adopted as a basic norm of the media world that we see its manifestation in apparently unlikely places. Broadcast journalism, with its heavy promotion of network anchors such as Peter Jennings, Tom Brokaw, and Dan Rather, vies for the news audience by selling the appeal of the big names. These anchors and a handful of other network reporters are full-fledged celebrities who make appearances on talk shows, are the subjects of high-stakes bidding wars, and have programs created for the purpose of giving them even more exposure. The college textbook industry also adopts the star system, seeking well-known professors as authors of high-volume introductory texts, even when unknown coauthors do most of the writing. Given a market that is dominated by a small number of standard-bearing texts—the equivalent of the hit song or blockbuster film—it is no surprise that textbook publishers seek the prestige and visibility that come with academic "stars."

Because acquiring already existing stars is both expensive and difficult, most media organizations will try to create their own. This is, of course, a difficult task, and even the best publicists have been known to miscalculate in their assessments of who has star quality. We might think that all new media products have an equal chance to be hits and that their main players have an equal chance at stardom. They are all thrown out to the audiences, who are the only true judges—it is audience interest that makes hits and stars. This view suggests that the true stars rise to the top because audiences love them, but it is a misleading view.

All media products do not have the same chance for hit status, nor do all media personalities have the same chance at stardom. Hits and stars are rare, and the resources to produce them are limited. So before audiences ever get to see them, media organizations make advance decisions about which products and people have the best chance of success. It is virtually impossible to be a star if the firm that produces and distributes your work has already decided that you do not have what it takes. On the other hand, you have a chance, though no guarantee, of stardom if you are deemed a possessor of star quality.

Films that are seen as potential hits, for example, are slotted for heavy promotion. This might include full-page newspaper ads, frequent television commercials, talk show appearances by the stars-to-be, wide distribution of the film's theme song, and release of the film to theaters all over the country. Movies not seen as potential hits will receive much less promotion and will be released to a much smaller number of theaters. The next time you go to the video store, take note of the large number of films on the shelves that you have never heard of; many come and go from the theaters so fast, with so little advertising, that only true film enthusiasts know they exist. Some never even make it to the theater but instead are released directly to video. As a result, only those films that the movie studios identify as potential hits will ever get the visibility to have a chance to become blockbusters.

The same dynamic is at work in the music industry. Acts are split into "potential earning divisions," with some being classified as big-time and others as possessing only minor or specialized appeal (Frith, 1981). The first hurdle for musicians, then, is to get through the initial classification process, which occurs before the first album is even released. Those who are identified as potential big-timers will have much more opportunity, and many more resources, than those who are categorized as minor players.

We can see a similar process in the book industry. Publishers decide how to package a book, how many copies to print, what to price the book at, how to promote it, and where to distribute it based on advance judgments of sales capability. These judgments are often made before the final draft is completed. Likewise, the key decision for television programs, once they are selected for the prime-time lineup, is where they will be scheduled. Which program will they follow or precede? What will the competition be on the other networks? Obviously, some time slots are more favorable than others; programs that seem unlikely to attract top-level ratings are generally scheduled in a way that practically guarantees they will be cancelled in short order.

Media organizations are attempting to produce hits—products that will be popular with audiences and, therefore, big money makers. It stands to reason that stars, who are also perceived to be popular and money makers, will be a key part of their strategy. The logic goes something like this: Hits make money, stars make money, and hits have stars; therefore, hits *need* stars. In a media world in which uncertainty is a constant, decision makers seek rules to make their decisions less arbitrary. The deep commitment to stars, and to the importance of reputation more generally, is one of the principal ways that the fluidity and ambiguity of the media industry are brought under control.

Movie-making, for example, is a very uncertain business. Without any method for ensuring commercial success and with so many players involved in the production and distribution of a film, the presence of a star helps reduce the perception of risk. Stars make people more comfortable with the risks they are taking, even if they are not demonstrably less risky. The presence of the star, in essence, rationalizes the entire process by providing an agreed-upon currency for assessing potential projects. The star system is a useful coping mechanism in such an uncertain industry (Prindle, 1993).

The dynamic in television is similar. Programmers rely on producers of prior hits as a strategy for legitimizing their decisions (Bielby and Bielby, 1994). In much the same manner as the film industry, network programmers operate in a situation in which hits are hard to come by and even harder to predict. Programmers have to satisfy various constituencies—advertisers, local station managers, and network executives—and they have to demonstrate that their programming decisions are not arbitrary. In this case, reputation—the result of the prior production of a hit—is the key currency. The various players within the television industry agree that past hit production is a legitimate criterion for selecting programs. They even try to sell viewers on this notion when promotional commercials emphasize that a new series is brought to you "by the producers of" a previous hit.

However, the "stars = hits = success" formula may not be as accurate a description of media products as industry common sense would suggest. For example, the films of major Hollywood stars such as Meryl Streep, Robert De Niro, Richard Gere, and Burt Reynolds lost money in the domestic box office in the 1980s (Prindle, 1993). Each may have made a hit or two, but they also made several duds that financially outweighed their money-making pictures. Of course, there are other sources of revenue for major motion pictures, in particular, videocassettes and the foreign market, and many films that do not break even at the domestic box office find substantial revenue elsewhere. For another example, a recent study found that television program pilots that are linked to established producers—those who have produced previous hits—are much more likely to be selected for the network fall schedule but end up being no more commercially successful than programs from new producers (Bielby and Bielby, 1994).

These examples suggest that the "stars produce hits" formula has holes in it. But the organization of production in the film and television industries and the ambiguities of these creative businesses help explain why the hit–star relationship continues to shape decision making—even in the face of conflicting evidence.

Conclusion

This chapter has rounded out our discussion of media production by showing how professional norms, institutional premises, and organizational structures shape the day-to-day work of media producers. We have seen that human agents—reporters, photographers, book editors, and Internet users—are active participants in the construction and reconstruction of production routines. These routines serve as conventions that help organize the collective work of media production.

Routines and conventions are shaped by economic, political, and organizational forces in each sector of the media industry. However, media production routines are not the simple and direct result of such forces. Routines and conventions are (and have been) actively developed by professionals who work under varying degrees of structural constraint. They serve as a framework within which media professionals adopt norms and practices for media production. Conventions can change, although this change is likely to be slow. Ultimately, conventions themselves become a form of structural constraint, producing guidelines for action and decision making by future media professionals.

A production perspective helps us understand the media messages that are part of our lives. In Part Three, we turn to the content of mass media, focusing on questions of inequality and ideology.

Content

Media Representations of the Social World

Part Two emphasized processes of production within the media industry. However, most of us never actually see these processes taking place. What we are exposed to—what we watch, read, and listen to—are media products, the movies, books, CDs, television shows, newspapers, and magazines that are the result of the production process. These media products are the most common way most of us experience the mass media.

In Part Three, we turn our attention to the content of these media products, exploring the ways in which mass media represent the social world. Chapter 5 examines how media portray central social cleavages in contemporary society, focusing on issues of race, class, gender, and sexual orientation. The chapter looks at how various groups are depicted in mass media, how such depictions have changed over time, and how these representations relate to social reality. Chapter 6 shifts the focus to the question of ideology, exploring the values, beliefs, and norms that mass media products routinely display. The chapter looks at the underlying perspectives in the images that confront us every day, as well as the potential contradictions and ambiguities that are built into mass media texts. ■

CHAPTER 5

Social Inequality and Media Representation

The examination of media content traditionally has been the most common type of media analysis, perhaps because of the easy accessibility of media products. The production process takes place in the relative remoteness of movie lots, recording studios, and editors' offices. In contrast, media products surround us and are within easy reach of the researcher.

Whatever the reason, there is an enormous volume of research and commentary on the nature of media content. Rather than try to review this vast literature, we have organized this chapter on media content around the single theme of representation. We explore the question "How do media representations of the social world compare to the external 'real' world?" As we discuss below, this is not the only possible line of investigation related to media content. However, given our sociological interest in the relationship between the media and the social world, it is a central one.

Further, our discussion focuses on the issue of social inequality. We argue that the creators of media content have often reproduced the race, class, and gender inequalities that exist in society. This is not to say that the media have acted as a mirror, passively reflecting the inequalities of society. Rather, white, middle- and upper-class men have historically controlled the media industry, and media content has largely reflected their perspectives on the world. Therefore, the inequalities in the social world have affected the organization of the media industry that produces media products.

In turn, those who have developed alternative media have routinely challenged this mainstream perspective by telling their own stories through words and pictures. More recently, progressive social change movements have succeeded in altering some facets of social inequality in society at large. This human agency has created changes in the social world, which, in turn, have affected the organization of the media industry. Contemporary media content reflects these changes to varying degrees.

Comparing Media Content and the "Real" World

Does media content reflect the realities of the social world? Based on the accumulated volume of media research, the answer is an emphatic "no." Content analyses of media products have repeatedly shown them to be quite different from key measurable characteristics of the social world. This gap between the "real world" and media representations of the social world is the subject of this chapter.

"How do media representations of the social world compare to the external 'real' world?" is an important question, since we conventionally organize media according to how closely they represent reality. We talk, for example, about fiction versus nonfiction, news or public affairs versus entertainment, documentaries versus feature films, and so on. The impact of media, as we will see in Part Four, can actually become more significant if media products diverge dramatically from the real world. We tend to become more concerned, for example, when media content lacks diversity or overemphasizes violence, sex, or other limited aspects of the real world.

The question "How do media representations of the social world compare to the external 'real' world?" also raises several issues. First, the literature in media and cultural studies reminds us that representations are not reality, even if media readers or audiences may sometimes be tempted to judge them as such. Representations—even those that attempt to reproduce reality such as the documentary film—are the result of processes of selection that invariably mean that certain aspects of reality are highlighted and others neglected. Even though we often use the "real-ness" of the images as a basis for evaluating whether we like or dislike particular representations, all representations "re-present" the social world in ways that are both incomplete and narrow.

Second, the media usually do not *try* to reflect the "real" world. Most of us would like news programs, history books, and documentary films to represent happenings in the social world as fairly and accurately as possible. (After examining the production process, we now know how difficult it is to achieve this, if only because of limited time and resources.) But by its very nature, a science fiction film, for example, is likely to diverge significantly from contemporary social life. Without that gap between reality and media image, the genre would cease to exist.

We cannot push this point too far, however, because even "fantasy" products such as science fiction films hold the potential for teaching us something about our society. Often, this is the attraction of the genre. When Captain Kirk and Lieutenant Uhuru of "Star Trek" kissed on prime-time television in the 1960s, it was the first interracial kiss on a

U.S. television series. This media content, though clearly embedded in a fantasy science fiction about the future, just as surely was making a statement about race relations in contemporary America. Social commentary continued in later "Star Trek" spin-offs when producers cast an African-American as the commander of "Deep Space Nine" and a woman as captain of "Voyager." Both of these programs were clearly science *fiction,* yet both were commenting on social conditions at the time of their creation.

The point is that there is potential social significance in all media products—even those that are clearly make-believe fantasies. Creators of media products are often aware of this fact and use entertainment media to comment upon the real social world. In turn, readers and audiences develop at least some sense of the social world through their exposure to both entertainment media and news media. It behooves us, therefore, to attend to what these media messages might be. That includes looking at media forms—including science fiction, soap operas, music videos, and romance novels—that clearly do not claim to accurately reflect society.

A third issue raised by the question "How do media representations of the social world compare to the 'real' world?" concerns the troublesome term "real." In an age in which sociologists teach about the social construction of reality and postmodernists challenge the very existence of a knowable reality, the concept of a "real world" may seem like a quaint artifact from the past. We generally agree with the social constructionist perspective, which suggests that no representation of reality can ever be totally "true" or "real" since it must inevitably frame an issue and choose to include and exclude certain components of a multifaceted reality. However, some social facts seem solid enough to be used as a measure of reality. To give a simple example, we have a pretty good idea of the age distribution in the United States. In 1991, for example, the Census Bureau reported that about 21 percent of the U.S. population was under the age of 15. Imagine that, for some unknown reason, television situation comedies became inundated with children, who made up, say, two-thirds of all characters. We could then reliably state that, compared to the real world, such programs featured three times as many children. Such a claim is possible only because we have a reasonably accurate way of measuring age distribution in the population as a whole.

The legitimacy of the question becomes much more dubious, however, with other examples. Is media content more liberal than society at large, as some contend? That depends on how you go about defining "liberal" and how you attempt to measure it in both the media and the "real" world. Such a concept is much more ambiguous than age, and therefore we have to be careful about claims of "bias" leveled at the media. In the end, we can make some useful comparisons between the content of media and society, but our limited ability to measure the social world necessarily limits such claims.

Finally, the question "How do media representations of the social world compare to the 'real' world?" seems to imply that the media *should* reflect society. This premise is not agreed upon. For many people, media are an escape from the realities of daily life. Therefore, how "real" media products are is irrelevant to many people. However, it is not necessary to believe that the media should accurately reflect society in order to compare media representations with the social world. Gaps between media content and social reality raise interesting questions that warrant our attention.

The Significance of Content

While this chapter focuses on the content of media, it is important to realize that many researchers study media content to make inferences about other social processes. In other words, they study media content to assess the significance of that content. There are at least five ways in which researchers can assess the significance of media content. They involve linking content to producers, to audience interests, to society in general, or to audience effects or examining content independent of context.

To illustrate, let's return to our hypothetical example about children and situation comedies. If researchers found that child characters appeared on situation comedies three times as often as children do in the real world, then several lines of interpretation would be possible. Each of these different approaches tries to explain the source and significance of media content.

Content as Reflection of Producers. First, it would be possible to infer that this child-centered content reflected the intent of the program writers and producers. This line of interpretation—linking content to producers— encourages us to investigate the social characteristics of situation-comedy writers and producers. We might find that such creative personnel are disproportionately "thirty-somethings," with children of their own, who draw upon their own family lives for story inspiration. As a result, a disproportionate percentage of programs feature children. Or perhaps corporate advertisers have expressed strong interest in sponsoring child-related programs, influencing producers to create more such programs. Determining this connection would require research that moved beyond media content and studied media personnel and the production process more generally (exactly the kind of research we examined in Part Two). Content analysis would alert us to this issue but by itself could not provide an adequate explanation for the heavy population of children on such programs.

Content as Reflection of Audience Preference. Second, we might infer that perhaps the high number of child characters reflects the audience for situation comedies. This does not necessarily suggest that children constitute a large percentage of the audience. It may simply mean, for example, that many viewers are parents who enjoy watching the antics of young children on situation comedies. Here the implication is that media personnel are merely responding to the interests of their likely audience, not to their own interests or to the influence of the production process. This approach suggests that content is a reflection of audience preference. The idea that media producers are only "giving the people what they want" also implies that people want what they get. To test such claims, researchers must explore more than media content. They must move into the area of audience research.

Content as Reflection of Society in General. Third, some researchers investigate media content as a gauge of social norms, values, and the interests of society in general—not just the audience. Some analysts might suggest that child-dominated situation comedies reflected a high level of social concern for children. They might reflect the fact that we live in a child-centered society where people value children highly. The difficulty in firmly making such sweeping assessments should be clear. To support such claims, research would need to extend well beyond the boundaries of media content.

Content as an Influence on Audiences. Fourth, researchers sometimes examine media content for potential effects on audiences. Perhaps the preponderance of children on television will encourage couples to have children or to have more children. Here, too, the researcher would have to link content analysis with research on audience interpretations—a topic examined in Part Four. The influence of media is so diffuse, however, that a direct link is usually very difficult to establish. The emphasis in this case—in contrast to the first three—is not on content as a *reflection* of the production process, audiences, or society. Instead, it is on content as a social *influence* on audiences.

Content as Self-Enclosed Text. Finally, a substantial body of work addresses media content on its own terms. That is, it usually makes no attempt to link content to producers, audiences, or society but instead examines media as a self-enclosed text whose meaning is to be "decoded." For example, an analysis of the film *Rambo* might show

> how this film follows the conventions of the Hollywood genre of the "war film," which dramatizes conflict between the United States and its "enemies," and provides a happy ending that portrays the

victory of good over evil. It would study the strictly cinematic and formal elements of the film, dissecting the ways that camera angles present Rambo as a god or how slow-motion images of him gliding through the jungle "code" him as a force of nature. One would also notice that images of Rambo being tortured adopt familiar crucifixion iconography, valorizing him as a Christlike martyr, and images of his headband and clothing code him as an individualist, thus appropriating 1960s countercultural iconography for the political right. (Kellner, 1995, pp. 10–11)

This tradition has many variations associated more with the structuralism and semiology found in literary studies and linguistics than with the content analysis found in the social sciences. However, researchers sometimes combine this approach with studies of production and audience reception under the rubric of cultural studies. It is often difficult or impossible to assess the validity of the claims of such analyses, because no standard methods exist in this field. Still, such work can be useful for those whose concerns lie with issues such as the relationship between elements of a text or the language, grammar, and vocabulary of image production.

Having sketched out the different ways in which researchers assess the significance of media content, we now turn to the content itself. As you will note, it is impossible to examine content without touching upon the role of producers, audiences, or larger social norms. However, we will focus primarily on media content per se. We will also limit our discussion to a few basic characteristics—race, class, gender, and sexual orientation —that are illustrative of a sociological approach to content analysis and that relate to our theme of inequality.

Race and Media Content: Inclusion, Roles, and Control

Nearly all sociologists and anthropologists now recognize that "race" is a socially constructed concept whose meaning has evolved over time. There is no biologically valid difference in the genetic makeup of different "races." In fact, different blood types might be more biologically significant than different racial classifications. However, racial distinctions have powerful social meaning with profound real-world consequences. Social scientists chart the development and implications of these socially constructed distinctions, especially as they influence discriminatory structures and practices.

Since race is a cultural or ideological construct, it is not surprising that there has been much interest in content analysis that examines how media messages treat the issue of race. In the United States, the issue of race has been most evident—and most studied—in Black–White race relations. This situation is rapidly changing, however, as the population of other racial minorities increases and as scholars examine the history and legacy of other people of color.

Historically, the U.S. media have taken "Whites" to be the norm against which all other racial groups are measured. The taken-for-granted nature of "whiteness" means that it need not be explicitly identified. For example, we generally do not talk about "white culture," or "the white community," or "the white vote," and so forth. We do, however, often hear reference to "black culture" or "the Latino community," and so on. The *absence* of a racial signifier in this country usually signifies whiteness. The pervasiveness of white perspectives in media is perhaps its most powerful characteristic.

To understand how racial difference is portrayed in the mass media, we must recall the earlier roots of racial stereotyping in American culture. Throughout much of U.S. mass media history, Blacks, Native Americans, Asians, Latinos, and other racial minorities have been, at best, of little consideration to the media industry. Because such minorities comprised a relatively small part of the population, mainstream media did not see them as an important segment of the audience. When it came to media content, racial minorities were either ignored or stereotyped in such roles as the Black Mammy, the Indian Maiden, the Latin Lover, or the sinister Asian Warlord. Such stereotypical images were the product of white media producers and bore little resemblance to the realities of the different racial groups (Wilson and Gutierrez, 1995).

When we consider how racial differences have been portrayed in the media, three crucial issues emerge. First is the simple issue of *inclusion.* Do media producers include the images, views, and cultures of different racial groups in media content? The second issue of concern is the nature of media *roles.* When producers do include members of racial minorities in media content, how do they portray them? Here the history of racial stereotypes takes center stage. Finally, the *control* of production is crucial. Do people from different racial groups have control over the creation and production of media images that feature different racial groups? This last issue is more about the production process and the nature of the media industry than about media content in itself. However, the history of media suggests that content very often reflects the views of those in control.

Racial Diversity in Media Content

A sample of some research findings on racial images in the modern media will help provide historical context and alert us to the changes that have occurred over time. The inclusion of different racial groups in the media has changed dramatically. In early Hollywood films of the 1920s and 1930s, for example, Blacks were largely absent or were relegated to two roles: entertainer or servant (Cripps, 1993). Not until after World War II did more African-Americans begin appearing on the screen. Even then, there were a limited number of available roles, and progress since then has been halting. The trend, though, seems to be toward more racial diversity in films.

On television through the 1940s and 1950s, the presence of Blacks was limited largely to their traditional, stereotypical roles as entertainers and comedians. There were virtually no serious dramatic roles for Blacks in this period. Instead, comedies and variety shows were the only regular forum for black talent (Dates, 1993). In the 1960s and 1970s, this began to change as television programs featured more Blacks and, to a lesser extent, other racial groups. By the 1969–70 season, half of all dramatic television programs had a black character. Surveys conducted from this period through the early 1980s show that whereas roughly 11 percent of the population was black at that time, 6–9 percent of all television characters were black (Seggar et al., 1981). By the 1991–92 season, Blacks made up 12 percent of the population and 11 percent of prime-time characters and 9 percent of daytime characters (cited in Greenberg and Brand, 1994). Few other racial groups, though, were regularly portrayed. On television too, then, we see a gradual trend toward more representation of Blacks, but underrepresentation is still the norm.

Minorities have also historically been underrepresented in other areas. In 1984, only 4 percent of lead performers on MTV music videos were black (Brown and Campbell, 1986). On news and public affairs programming, racial minorities continued to lack visibility. A study of guests on the two preeminent public affairs television programs, "Nightline" and the "MacNeil-Lehrer NewsHour," found that nearly 9 out of 10 guests were white (Croteau and Hoynes, 1994). Studies of advertising have repeatedly found underrepresentation of minorities. A study of *Cosmopolitan, Glamour,* and *Vogue* in the late 1980s found that only 2.4 percent of ads featured black women (Jackson and Ervin, 1991). One review of research findings on broadcast advertising concludes that, compared to earlier years, "there are more Black faces, but they get less time, are less visible, may be buried in a sea of faces, and rarely interact with Whites" (Greenberg and Brand, 1994, p. 292).

Race and Media Roles

For much of U.S. history, most white-produced images of other racial groups have been unambiguously racist. As early as the late 1700s, the "comic Negro" stereotype of "Sambo" appeared in novels and plays. On the stage, Dates and Barlow (1993, p. 6) note, this racist character "was cast in a familiar mold: always singing nonsense songs and dancing around the stage. His dress was gaudy, his manners pretentious, his speech riddled with malapropisms, and he was played by white actors in blackface." Such images in popular culture are the precursor of racist stereotypes in the mass media.

Early Images of Race

Racist stereotypes were peppered throughout popular culture in the nineteenth century. In the novel *The Spy,* James Fenimore Cooper introduced the stereotypical image of the loyal, devoted, and content house slave who doubled as comic relief because of his superstitious beliefs and fear of ghosts. This image reappeared in many later books and films. Whites in blackface performed racist stage acts, portraying Blacks as clownish buffoons. In the 1830s, a white actor named Thomas Dartmouth Rice copied a song-and-dance routine he saw performed on a street corner by a young slave boy. Rice used burnt cork to blacken his face, dressed in tattered clothes, and popularized the "Jump Jim Crow" routine. Early minstrel shows consisted of Whites in blackface copying black music and dance traditions. Native Americans, too, were ridiculed in stage performances. One popular play was titled *The Original, Aboriginal, Erratic, Operatic, Semi-Civilized and Demi-Savage Extravaganza of Pocahontas* (Wilson and Gutierrez, 1995). Popular songs, sung on the stage and printed in sheet music, also featured many racist stereotypes. Even well-intentioned works like Harriet Beecher Stowe's antislavery novel, *Uncle Tom's Cabin,* perpetuated a "positive" image of Blacks as gentle, suffering victims with childlike innocence.

The end of slavery brought different but equally racist images. The "contented slave was taken over by the faithful servant: the female side of this stereotype became the domestic mammy caricature, while the male side matured into elderly Uncle Toms" (Dates and Barlow, 1993, p. 11). The folksy character of "Uncle Remus," speaking in black dialect, became the prototypical apologist for postbellum plantation life. Free black men began appearing as angry, brutal, and beastlike characters in novels. When D. W. Griffith's 1915 film, *Birth of a Nation,* featured similar characters, it was an indication that producers would fill the new film medium, as well, with racist images.

By 1920, the United States had fought in World War I "to make the world safe for democracy," according to President Wilson. However, early U.S. films were routinely presenting racist images of white supremacy. Blacks were viciously attacked in films such as *The Wooing and Wedding of a Coon* (1905) and *The Nigger* (1915). The Mexican government banned films, like 1914's *The Greaser's Revenge,* that portrayed Mexicans as bandits, rapists, and murderers. Movies portrayed Asians as a threat to American values, as in the film *The Yellow Menace.* Early films openly advocated white supremacy over American Indians, as in the 1916 film *The Aryan* (Wilson and Gutierrez, 1995).

As the film industry matured and grew in the pre–World War II years, it continued to use stereotypically racist images, albeit in less crude forms. Cliched portrayals of Native Americans filled the popular "western" film genre. Movie directors transferred the faithful black servant image to the silver screen, leading to the first Oscar for a black actor when Hattie McDaniel won the award for her portrayal of Scarlet O'Hara's servant in *Gone With the Wind.* Hollywood responded to complaints—and to declining distribution sales in Mexico and Latin America—by largely replacing the earlier "greaser" image with the exotic "Latin lover" stereotype. Asians were either violent villains, in the mold of Dr. Fu Manchu, or funny and clever, as in the enormously popular Charlie Chan film series.

Slow Change and "Modern" Racism

It is out of this long legacy of racist imagery that the modern media's portrayals of racial minorities emerge. Media images have changed over the years. Since World War II, and especially since the 1960s, the trend has been toward more inclusiveness and growing sensitivity in media of all types. The media, though, have followed the shifting winds of change. Sometimes, progress in changing stereotypical images has been a case of "one step forward, two steps back." The civil rights struggle for racial equality influenced Hollywood, and discrimination against Blacks became the theme of a number of prominent movies in the late 1950s and 1960s. The more militant black power struggles in the late 1960s and early 1970s were accompanied by the rise of "black exploitation" films with nearly all-black casts. The 1980s and 1990s witnessed the huge success of some black performers, such as Whoopi Goldberg and Denzel Washington. Directors cast these black stars in a wide variety of roles, from comic to dramatic.

Meanwhile, white guilt over the domination of Native American Indians surfaced in a series of movies. The 1970 film *Little Big Man* suggested that, since General Custer had engaged in years of atrocities against American Indians, he got what he deserved at the Little Big Horn massacre. Films in the 1990s began to create a different stereotype: the idealized Indian. *Dances with Wolves* (1990) and *Geronimo* (1993), for example, extended the theme of white guilt and Indian dignity. Film portrayals of other racial groups followed this general trend toward a new set of roles for people of color (Wilson and Gutierrez, 1995).

Blatantly racist images of minority groups are no longer widespread in the mainstream U.S. media. Certainly, it is still possible, without much effort, to identify stereotypical racial images in film, television, novels, and other media, but the clear trend has been away from such unabashed stereotyping. Some researchers, however, believe that in recent years the legacy of racism has manifested itself in more subtle but perhaps equally powerful ways.

In a study of local Chicago news coverage of Blacks and Whites, Robert Entman (1992) illustrates the complicated dynamics present in contemporary images of race. In his work, Entman distinguishes between two forms of racism. "Traditional racism" involves open bigotry usually based on beliefs about the biological inferiority of Blacks. "Modern racism" is a "compound of hostility, rejection and denial on the part of whites toward the activities and aspirations of black people" (p. 341). Modern racism, therefore, is much more subtle. It eschews old-fashioned racist images, and as a result, according to Entman, "stereotypes are now more subtle, and stereotyped thinking is reinforced at levels likely to remain below conscious awareness" (p. 345). Is this "modern racism" found in the news media? Entman argues that it is, but at first some of his claims can seem counterintuitive.

One of his findings was that the local news prominently covered the activities of politically active Blacks. We could easily see the *exclusion* of such activities as racially motivated, but here Entman says that the form of their *inclusion* suggests a racist image. Entman found that "black activists often appeared pleading the interests of the black community, while white leaders were much more frequently depicted as representing the entire community" (p. 355). Thus, Entman argues, it is possible for viewers to get the impression that Blacks are pursuing a politics of "special interests" rather than one of public interest. The cycle of racial stereotypes becomes difficult to break. Political marginalization as a result of years of racism may spur black leaders to agitate on behalf of the "black community." The news media duly cover this activism. Such coverage unintentionally conveys a message that Blacks are seeking special treatment, thus fostering white resentment and perpetuating the political marginalization of Blacks.

Wilson and Gutierrez (1995) note a similar problem in the media coverage of minority issues in general. They argue that in recent years "the coverage of minority issues often focused inordinate attention on the more bizarre or unusual elements of minority communities, such as youth gangs, illegal immigration, or interracial violence" (p. 26). While these are legitimate issues, the near-exclusive emphasis on such negative stories "resulted in a new stereotype of racial minorities as 'problem people,' groups either beset by problems or causing them for the larger society."

In his study, Entman (1992) criticizes the portrayal of politically active Blacks as being inadvertently racist. However, he also criticizes the regular use of Blacks who "did not talk in angry or demanding tones" (p. 357). He is referring to black newscasters, who are generally "unemotional, friendly but businesslike" (p. 357). Station managers often use a black newscaster as a co-anchor, with a white newscaster, for the local news. While this practice may be seen as a very positive step, Entman suggests that

> the innocuous black anchors may also reinforce whites' impatience with the poor or demanding blacks who appear so frequently as news subjects. The anchors' very presence suggests that if blacks just keep quiet and work hard, the system will indeed allow them to make progress and even earn more money than most whites. Showing attractive, articulate blacks in such a prestigious public role implies that blacks are not inherently inferior or socially undesirable—and that racism is no longer a serious impediment to black progress. (p. 358)

Entman's arguments are provocative, though speculative. His work was based on content analysis of news programs, not on a study of news audiences. There is no way to tell from his work how audiences interpret what they are seeing. However, his suggestions raise difficult questions about African-American media images in the future. For example, if the *exclusion* of Blacks from news anchor positions reflects underlying racism and the *inclusion* of Blacks in such positions inaccurately implies that racism no longer exists, then what should the media industry do? Entman's analysis suggests that we have to understand race and the media in a holistic fashion. Racially diverse news anchors really don't indicate much progress if, at the same time, the content of news remains racially skewed. Real change will come when all aspects of the media—including media content—more accurately reflect the racial diversity of society.

Entman suggests that we must pay closer attention to how the *process* of media production influences the *content* of the media. Entman believes that the production norms of news are linked with the perpetuation of stereotypical images. To create dramatic stories, for example, reporters will often choose "sound bites" from black leaders that are emotional and suggestive of conflict. Such dramatic quotes, though sometimes misleading, follow media conventions for "good television." The unintended result is that such norms and practices contribute to stereotypical images of African Americans.

Race and Class

Entman's study hints at—but does not explore—the intervening issue of class in the portrayal of African Americans. He is, in effect, contrasting black anchors who exude upper-middle-class manners and confidence with the poor and working-class Blacks featured in many news accounts. To understand contemporary media images of different racial groups, therefore, it is important to consider their class (and, as we will see, their gender). There is no longer any single image of African Americans in the mainstream media.

The intervention of class in the portrayal of Blacks on television has resulted in a bifurcated set of images (Gray, 1989). On one hand, middle-class Blacks have become mainstream in prime-time entertainment programs. Epitomized by "The Cosby Show" of the 1980s, these programs portray African-American families who have succeeded in attaining a piece of the traditional "American dream." On the other hand, news coverage and documentaries about Blacks tend to focus on poor African Americans in the so-called "underclass," mired in drugs, crime, and violence. One implicit message in these contrasting images may be that, since some Blacks have clearly succeeded, the failure of other Blacks is their own fault.

In their conclusion to a sweeping review of black images in television, radio, music, films, advertising, and public relations, Dates and Barlow (1993, p. 527) suggest that the tension between white-produced images of Blacks and black cultural resistance "has become increasingly entangled in more complex social conflicts and concerns. In effect, the primacy of the 'color line' is being challenged by generational, gender, and class differences." We have moved beyond the point where we can say that a single set of media images represents African Americans—or any other racial group.

Some media have begun to change their treatment of minorities for simple economic reasons. Growing racial diversity in the population as a whole means that people of color make up larger segments of the market than in the past. Advertisers, in some cases, have become more interested in reaching this growing market. The Census Bureau reports that, in 1993, 83.3 percent of Americans were classified as White, 12.5 percent as Black, and 3.4 percent as Asian or Pacific Islander. In addition, the Bureau further identified 9.8 percent as Hispanic (or Latino), a category that includes people of any race who trace their origins to Spain, Latin America, or the Caribbean. In the 13 years since the 1980 census, the percentage of Whites decreased by 6 percent, while the percentage of Blacks increased by 5.9 percent, Asians increased by 112.5 percent, and Latinos increased by 53.1 percent. The future clearly will hold an even more racially diverse population.

In what may be a sign of things to come, most Americans are not seeing or reading about this growing diversity in mass media. The growth of media outlets gives some indication that media audiences are growing even more segregated, gravitating toward programming specifically aimed at them. For example, in 1994, 25 television series on the four major networks (ABC, CBS, NBC, and FOX) featured African Americans in either leading or major roles. However, for the 1993 season, *none* of the 10 most popular television programs in black households were among the top 10 rated programs overall (Wilson and Gutierrez, 1995, p. 99). It has been suggested that, ironically, as racial minorities finally make their way into mainstream media, only members of their own race are watching. This segmentation of media audiences has stirred concern that the media are losing their role as a common socializing agent.

Controlling Media Images of Race

The absence or stereotyping of different racial groups in the media highlights a fact often taken for granted: Affluent, white men have historically controlled the mainstream mass media. But although Whites have often propagated racist images of Blacks, it is important to note that, historically, African Americans have responded by producing a culture of resistance. From the slave chronicles of Frederick Douglass to the poetry of Langston Hughes, from the blues of Bessie Smith to the rap of Public Enemy, from the diverse work of Paul Robeson to the films of Spike Lee —to name just a few of the better-known personalities—black activists and artists have created a counterculture that opposes the racist stereotypes being propagated in white-owned media and culture. *Freedom's Journal* was the first African-American newspaper in the United States. Its editors wrote in the first 1827 edition, "We wish to plead our own cause. Too long have others spoken for us. Too long has the publick been deceived by misrepresentations" (in Rhodes, 1993, p. 186). Such sentiments have continued to underlie the efforts both of those working in alternative media and of those charting new territory in the mainstream media.

People of color, as well as women and people promoting the interests of the working class and poor, have had to confront a basic dilemma:

They have had to choose between developing alternative media and struggling to change mainstream media from within. The first strategy—developing alternative media—has the advantages of being feasible with more limited financial resources and of promising control for the producers. However, it usually means sacrificing the chance of reaching a mass and broad audience in favor of a smaller, narrower one, in part because media operations working on a shoestring budget cannot hope to match the slick, seductive production quality of the mainstream media.

The second strategy—changing the mainstream media from within—offers an opposite set of advantages and challenges. Mainstream success can result in access to major financial resources that allow a product to reach millions of people. However, ownership and control of mainstream media are still predominantly in the hands of wealthy, white men. While some people of color and some women have worked their way into positions of authority and influence, they are still vastly underrepresented. For example, in 1995 minorities made up about 11 percent of U.S. newsroom personnel (up from 4 percent in 1978), but minorities were concentrated at lower levels of the newsroom hierarchy (*Editor & Publisher*, 1995; Foote, 1994). Gray (1995) notes that in 1989 only 7 percent of television shows with minority characters had minority producers.

Gender and Media Content

In some ways, the media's history of portraying women parallels its history of portraying people of color. Women were often marginalized in all types of media. Simple, blatantly stereotypical images dominated the earlier years of mass media. As media audiences and the media industry felt the influence of movements struggling for women's rights, these stereotypical images gave way to a wider diversity of images and roles for women. Here too, then, we see a history of injustice, inequality, and change.

Women: Presence and Control in the Media

Reviews of the extensive literature on gender and the media reveal a fundamental inequality in the frequency of appearance of women and men. Television, for example, features more portrayals of men than women, and men appear more often in lead roles (Fejes, 1992). Only 12 percent of MTV videos broadcast in 1984 featured a female lead (Brown and Campbell, 1986). However, family and heterosexual relationships are central to the plots of many films, music videos, and television programs, ensuring that women (unlike racial minorities) are regularly included in these media, though in secondary roles.

Control of the creation and production of media images is also in male hands. Consider the news media, for example. In the early 1990s, just over one-third of the journalistic work force was made up of women. However, the upper levels of major corporate media organizations are almost entirely male (Duckworth et al., 1990). In addition, women occupied only 25 percent of middle management and 6 percent of top newspaper management positions (Lafky, 1993). In 1994, women occupied the position of news director at only 20.6 percent of television stations (Stone, 1996). In 1995, women wrote only 19 percent of front-page stories in major newspapers and female correspondents presented only 20 percent of television news reports (Bridge, 1995). This kind of inequality exists in other media as well. Hollywood directing, for example, has historically been a male bastion entered only rarely by female directors.

The trends are similar or more pronounced in other nations. H. Leslie Steeves (1993) reviewed studies on gender and global media from around the globe. She concluded that women were "grossly underrepresented" in all forms of entertainment media—film, print, radio, and television. Existing work also suggests that "much magazine content for women—including the popular *fotonovelas* [romance stories in comic-book form] of Latin America—as well as broadcast content (e.g., soap operas), reinforce traditional ideologies of oppression and encourage escapism" (p. 41).

In news coverage, too, women are underrepresented. In all countries with available data, the media featured women in less than 20 percent of news stories. In most countries, the percentage was much lower. The little news coverage of women that did exist tended to highlight their role in the family and emphasized issues concerning physical appearance.

The dynamics relating to gender are similar to those found in the discussion of race. Women are generally not in positions of control and, perhaps as a result, are less likely than men to be prominently featured in media products. However, like racial images, the situation of women in media is undergoing what one observer calls "a long, slow journey" (Lafky, 1993, p. 87).

Because of the enormous export of U.S. media products abroad, American images of women have infiltrated the global community. Western images—with all their merits and faults—are now a central part of the global flow of media products. In the face of inadequate or unsatisfactory mainstream media images, many women's organizations focus on the development of alternative media. However, the number of periodicals for women in different countries starkly highlights the uneven development of such projects. In 1992 the United States had over 609 periodicals for women. Only nine other countries had more than 10 each: Canada (59), England (51), Germany (38), Argentina (21), Australia (21), the Netherlands (17), France (11), Italy (11), and Switzerland (11). The development of indigenous alternative media has certainly not yet taken place on a large scale.

Changing Media Roles for Women . . . and Men

The media images of women and men reflect and reproduce a whole set of stereotypical but changing gender roles. On television, we are more likely to find men in action and drama roles and less likely to find them in situation comedies and soap operas (Fejes, 1992). Men are also more likely than women to be portrayed as having high-status jobs—in traditionally "male occupations"—and are less likely to be shown in the home. Producers are likely to portray men as more dominant than women and as more prone to engage in violence. In situation comedies, men are more likely to disparage women than vice versa, but overall men are more often the object of humor or disparagement. Even simple camera techniques used on women and men seem to differ. Television camera shots are more likely to feature women's entire bodies while more often showing men in close-ups of only their faces.

Fejes (p. 12) concludes that "men, as portrayed on adult television, do not deviate much from the traditional patriarchal notion of men and masculinity." They are portrayed in the media as generally powerful and successful. They "occupy high-status positions, initiate action and act from the basis of rational mind as opposed to emotions, are found more in the world of things as opposed to family and relationships, and organize their lives around problem solving." Alerting us to the intersection of different identities, Fejes (p. 12) points out that "the masculinity portrayed on television is a white, middle-class heterosexual masculinity." While important distinctions exist, we can make similar observations about advertising, film, music, and other media.

Women's roles have often reflected similar stereotypes about femininity. Over the years, the dominant roles for women have been as mother/homemaker or sexual object. The media industry, though, responded to feminists organizing for social change. As with racial stereotypes, the industry has muted the blatant simplicity of stereotypical gender images in more recent years. There is certainly a wider palette of roles and media images of women in the 1990s than there was 25 years ago, despite what some have called a "backlash" (Faludi, 1991) in the 1980s against feminist gains. However, the inequality that women still face in society as a whole is clearly reflected in the unequal treatment women receive in the media. Some of this unequal treatment, such as that in sexist advertising and degrading pornography, is straightforward and easy to spot, as are some of the stereotypical roles writers still create for women on television situation comedies and dramas. However, like racist stereotypes, sexist stereotypes have often taken subtler forms.

Media coverage of women's sports, for example, has changed as more women have entered organized sports at all levels. Messner and his associates (1993) note that

> sport is still dominated by men at nearly all levels, and still serves to construct culturally dominant ideals of "exemplary masculinity.". . . But the dramatic increase in female athleticism in the past two decades directly challenges the assumed naturalness of the equation of men, muscles, and power. In short, the institution of sport has become a "contested terrain" of gender relations and ideologies. (p. 122)

Messner and his associates examined the role of the media in this "contested terrain." Previous research showed media coverage of women's sports to be minuscule compared to men's sports, accounting for less than 10 percent of all sports coverage in newspapers and on television. In sports magazines for children, visual images of male athletes outnumber those of female athletes by two to one. The only area offering hope for increased coverage of women's sports seems to be cable television.

However, the relative absence of media coverage of women's sports tells us nothing about the quality of the coverage that does exist. Studies conducted in the 1970s and early 1980s found that on the rare occasions when women athletes were covered on television, they "were likely to be overtly trivialized, infantilized, and sexualized" (p. 123). Such media images of women's sports is the area that Messner examines. The examples Messner and his associates studied were the television coverage of the 1989 men's and women's NCAA (National Collegiate Athletic Association) basketball tournaments and coverage of various matches in the 1989 U.S. Open tennis tournament. What they found is symptomatic of the subtle ways in which media both reflect and re-create gender inequality.

First, they note that their study "revealed very little of the overtly sexist commentary that has been observed in past research" (p. 125). They did find that camera angles, especially in tennis, tended to differ a bit between women and men and perhaps subtly framed women athletes as sexual objects. However, the main focus of their study—verbal commentary—did not do so. We can consider this finding qualified good news, since it contrasts with the overtly sexist coverage researchers found in earlier studies.

Second, though, they found that commentary did frame women's and men's sports differently. One finding was that gender was constantly "marked" in women's basketball coverage. For example, the coverage mentioned—77 times during three games—both verbally and graphically that it was the "NCAA *Women's* National Championship Game" or *"women's* basketball." (This does not even count gender-marked team names, like the "Lady Tigers," which were mentioned 102 times.) Not a single instance of gender marking occurred in coverage of men's basketball. Television coverage referred to men's competition in a universal way: "The Final Four," "The NCAA National Championship Game," and so on. It did not mention gender.

Tennis coverage showed roughly equitable treatment—for example, in references to the "men's doubles finals," "women's singles semifinals," and so on. However, gender differences did occur in discussing the athletes. The researchers note that "in the mixed-doubles match, the commentators stated several times that Rick Leach is 'one of the best doubles players in the world,' where Robyn White was referred to as one of 'the most animated girls on the circuit'" (p. 126). More gender marking occurred when CBS used pink graphics for the women's matches and blue graphics for the men's matches.

The naming of athletes also differed by gender. The announcers called women "girls," "young ladies," and "women." They never called men "boys," only "men," "young men," or "young fellas." Commentators covering tennis matches referred to female athletes by first name seven times as often as they did male athletes. In basketball, the ratio was about two to one. Messner and his associates remind readers that "research has demonstrated that dominants (either by social class, age, occupational position, race, or gender) are more commonly referred to by their last names (often prefaced by titles such as Mr. [or Professor!]). Dominants generally have license to refer to subordinates (younger people, employees, lower-class people, ethnic minorities, women, etc.) by their first names" (p. 128).

Finally, an array of differences appeared in the language used to describe athletes. Male coaches "yelled," while female coaches "screamed." Announcers described female tennis players as having "confidence," but they never applied this term to male players. Was it because announcers took for granted that men were confident? While an excellent shot by a female player was "lucky," excellent play from a male player showed that he was "imposing his will all over this court." Announcers described success differently as well. "Men appeared to succeed through a combination of talent, instinct, intelligence, size, strength, quickness, hard work, and risk taking. Women also appeared to succeed through talent, enterprise, hard work, and intelligence. But commonly cited along with these attributes were emotion, luck, togetherness, and family" (p. 130).

Language is never neutral. Media coverage, in this case of sports, reflects—and helps to construct and affirm—a particular framing of the social world. When media personnel use language in a way that represents stereotypical gender roles, it helps perpetuate such roles. Conversely, when they use language self-consciously to counter stereotypes, it can be influential in changing social realities.

Class and the Media

Interestingly, researchers have not given a great deal of attention to class in media content. There are many fewer studies about class in television, for example, than about either race or gender. Yet class permeates media content, and it is useful to examine both the class distribution of people in the media and the roles given to characters of different class status. It is also important to keep in mind the relationship between class and the media industry.

"Some People Are More Valuable Than Others"

Class underlies the media industry in a distinctive way. Class considerations connect advertisers, producers, content, and audiences. The for-profit, advertiser-driven nature of all commercial media means that advertisers are keenly interested in the economic status of media consumers. They want to reach people with enough disposable income to buy their products. You can guess which class a media product reaches by examining the ads that accompany it. Everybody has to buy toothpaste and breakfast cereal, but when a program or publication features ads for jewelry, expensive cars, and investment services you know it is aimed at an affluent audience. (Take a look at one of the national weekly newsmagazines, for example. Whom do you think advertisers are trying to reach?) Media outlets, in turn, want to attract affluent consumers and often gear their content to a more affluent reader or viewer.

The influence of class can sometimes take on strange dimensions. For example, one of the lesser-known strategies sometimes employed in the newspaper business is to *reduce* circulation to increase profits. While at first this may seem to be an impossible strategy, here is how publishers make it work. Newspapers receive about two-thirds of their revenue from advertisers, not readers; therefore, they must be sensitive to advertiser needs in order to stay in business. In turn, as noted above, advertisers want to reach only readers with enough disposable income to buy their products. In the information that major newspapers send to potential advertisers, they usually tout the affluence of the consumers who read their paper, because these are the readers advertisers want to reach. To sell advertising space at a premium, newspapers want to improve the demographic profile (in terms of average household income) of their readership. They can do this in two ways: Attract more affluent readers, and/or get rid of poorer readers.

The first approach is reflected in media content that is clearly aimed at more affluent households. This content includes major business sections with extensive stock market reports and "style" sections with articles that highlight fashion, culture, and other upscale consumer activities. The second strategy is more direct. Some papers have made it difficult for poor people to buy their product. Publishers sometimes limit the paper's distribution in poor neighborhoods and in some cases even *raise* the price of the paper in these areas while *reducing* it in wealthier areas! The *Los Angeles Times,* for example, raised its daily sales price in inner-city neighborhoods from 35¢ to 50¢. At the same time, it reduced the price to 25¢ in affluent surrounding counties (Cole, 1995).

Newspaper publishers are not the only ones who recognize that affluent people are more important for the media industry than poor or working-class people. In the 1970s, ABC issued a profile of its viewing audience, highlighting its desirable demographics. The network titled the profile "Some People Are More Valuable Than Others" (Wilson and Gutierrez, 1995, p. 23). It is important, therefore, to keep in mind the underlying profit-oriented nature of the media when we examine class in media content.

Class and Media Content

Overwhelmingly, the American society portrayed in the media is wealthier than it is in the real world. The real world is predominantly working class, with the vast majority of Americans working in service, clerical, or production jobs. Media, however, portray the social world as one heavily populated by the middle class—especially middle-class professionals. Images showing comfortable middle-class life fill magazines, films, and television programs. These images are most obvious in advertising. Simply put, advertisements aimed at selling products do not feature poor people and rarely feature working-class people. Instead, comfortable middle-class and affluent upper-class images reign in ads.

Entertainment Media

Entertainment is little different from advertising. Butsch (1992) examined 262 family-based situation comedies that aired from 1946–1990. Because programs based in a workplace—such as police shows—would dictate the occupation of the main characters, he intentionally excluded these.

EXHIBIT 5.1 *Social Class in Prime-Time Programs*

The class status of a television family is communicated to viewers in various ways, most obviously through the occupation of the major characters. Another signal of class is the set used to represent home life.

Most prime-time programs feature families that are middle- to upper-middle-class. The "Home Improvement" photo shows a distinctly middle-class set: beautiful glass doors open onto a backyard with an expensive-looking jungle gym, the dining room furniture appears to be high-quality, tasteful artwork decorates the wall, and books fill the shelves. (Here the father is teaching his sons proper table manners.) Notice how many prime-time programs feature such "tasteful" and upscale sets. *(Photo © 1996 CAPITAL CITIES/ABC, INC./Fred Sabine)*

The focus of domestic-based situation comedies is home life away from work. Thus, creators of such programs are free to give their characters a wide range of potential occupations. Butsch found that only 11 percent of such programs featured blue-collar, clerical, or service workers as heads of the household. Over 70 percent of home-based situation comedies featured middle-class families. In 1992, professionals made up roughly 15 percent of the U.S. work force. In Butsch's study, fully 44.5 percent of families—three times as many—were headed by professionals. And these weren't your run-of-the-mill professionals, either. The elite professions were vastly overrepresented. Doctors outnumbered nurses nine to one, professors outnumbered school teachers by more than three to one, and lawyers outnumbered less glamorous accountants by more than nine to

EXHIBIT 5.1 *(continued)*

In contrast to the usual middle-class fare, the set of "Roseanne" illustrates what is probably closer to reality for working-class Americans of more modest means. There is an eat-in kitchen instead of a dining room, and the trappings of the set are much less fancy: the furniture appears to be worn, the wall is decorated with an Elvis Presley plate and discount department store artwork instead of "tasteful" art, and there are no book-lined shelves on the set. *(Photo © 1996 CAPITAL CITIES/ABC, INC./Don Cadette)*
What other devices are used to signal the class status of television characters?

one. All these high-paying jobs for television characters meant lots of disposable income, and families in these situation comedies overwhelmingly lived in beautiful middle-class homes equipped with all the amenities (see Exhibit 5.1). More than one out of every five families even had a servant!

Try to think of domestic-based situation comedies in which the head of the household had a working-class job. A number of well-known programs may come to mind. Archie in "All in the Family" was a dock worker. Ralph in "The Honeymooners" was a bus driver. On the prime-time cartoon "The Flintstones," Fred was a "crane" operator in a rock quarry. The short-lived FOX program "ROC" featured an African-American garbage collector and his wife, who was a nurse. The main character in "Roseanne" held various jobs, including a factory worker, waitress, and shampooer in a beauty salon, while her husband struggled as a construction worker and mechanic. The father in "Family Matters" was a police officer. "Married With Children" featured a shoe salesman, and Homer in "The Simpsons" was a woefully underqualified technician in a nuclear power plant. (Interestingly, several of these working-class programs highlight their characters' aspirations for middle-class life through the launching of small businesses. For example, Archie Bunker became a bar owner in the later program, "Archie's Place." Both parents on "Roseanne" opened up businesses of their own: an unsuccessful motorcycle shop and a diner.) You can probably come up with a few more examples of family-based situation comedies with working-class main characters—but you can't come up with *many* more, because, as Butsch has shown, they simply don't exist. The exceptions here prove the rule.

Now think of domestic-based situation comedies in which the head of the household had a middle-class job. The list of lawyers, doctors, architects, advertising executives, journalists, and businesspeople should be quite long. Butsch argues that the predominance of middle-class characters in these television situation comedies conveys a subtle but significant message. The few working-class characters who do populate some programs are the deviant exception to the norm, and therefore it must be their own fault that they are less economically successful. (This observation is quite similar to the one Gray [1989] made when examining the portrayal of Blacks in the media. As you may remember, Gray argued that middle-class Blacks on entertainment programs were the "norm" against which real-life Blacks in the news were contrasted.)

The message that people in the working class are responsible for their fate is a quintessential middle-class idea that ignores the structural conditions that shape social class. It is also an idea reinforced by another tendency identified by Butsch. In contrast to most middle-class television families, the father in working-class families is usually ridiculed as an incompetent, though sometimes lovable, buffoon. Ralph Kramden, Fred Flintstone, Al Bundy, and Homer Simpson are perhaps the most obvious cases. All, to varying degrees, were simpletons who pursued foolish get-rich schemes and wound up in trouble because they simply weren't very smart. Each of these shows portrayed the female main character as more level-headed and in control. Often, these programs even portrayed the children of working-class men as smarter and more competent than their fathers. Here, too, the father on "Roseanne" and the lead character on "ROC," for example, were notable exceptions that illustrate the possibility of more sympathetic portrayals of competent working-class fathers.

Butsch acknowledges that this kind of program sometimes also ridiculed middle-class fathers, but not nearly as often as working-class fathers. Instead, the norm in comedies with middle-class families—from "Father Knows Best" and "Leave It to Beaver" to "Bewitched" and the "Brady Bunch" to the "Cosby Show" and "The Wonder Years"—is for middle-class fathers to be competent at their jobs and often to be wise and capable parents. The implication, argues Butsch, is that working-class families struggle because of incompetence and lack of intelligence, while middle-class families succeed because of competence and intelligence. Such images help reinforce the idea that class-based inequality is just and functional.

If media rarely show working-class folks, they are even less likely to show working people in labor unions. And as Puette (1992) has shown, the media's portrayal of unions has been anything but sympathetic. Like the stereotypical images of racial groups and women, the media stereotypes of unions have evolved over the years. After examining the image of labor unions in Hollywood movies, television dramas, TV news, and editorial cartoons, Puette argues that there are some basic "lenses" that color and distort media portrayals of organized labor and its leaders. Among these media images are the stereotypes that unions protect and encourage unproductive, lazy, and insubordinate workers; that unions undermine America's ability to compete internationally; that union leaders, because they do not come from the educated/cultured (privileged) classes, are more likely to be corrupted by power than are business or political leaders; and that unions are no longer necessary. Certainly, unions are far from perfect organizations, and they are fair game for media criticism. However, with very few exceptions, Puette's analysis points to a systematic and relentless disparagement of the most visible effort at collective empowerment by working Americans.

News Media

Class enters directly into news media content as well. News tends to highlight issues of concern to middle- and upper-class readers and viewers. Take the example of stock market reports. Four out of five American families do not own stock (Folbre, 1995) and are unlikely to be interested in such reports. (In fact, 85 percent of the nation's stock is owned by just 10 percent of the nation's families.) Most Americans do not even understand stock listings and reports. Yet stock market reports are a prominent feature of news programs and newspapers. Now think for a moment. When was the last time you saw a news story explaining how to apply for welfare benefits or reviewing the legal rights of workers to form a union or to learn about health and safety hazards in the workplace? Even suggesting such stories might seem odd, because it contradicts our taken-for-granted notion of what news is "supposed" to be.

On the whole, the news reflects a middle- and upper-class view of the world. In this world, newspaper business pages flourish, but labor reporters are almost an extinct breed. News may address "regular" people as consumers, but it almost never addresses them as workers. Even consumer-oriented stories are scarce because they have the potential to offend advertisers. In 1995, for example, the *San Jose Mercury News* published an innocuous feature story advising consumers on how to buy a new car. The prospect of well-informed customers apparently concerned a group of 47 local auto dealers. They retaliated by collaborating and canceling 52 pages of advertising in the paper's weekly "Drive" section—a loss of $1 million for the paper. While pressure from local car dealers is infamous in the newspaper industry, this time the paper went to the Federal Trade Commission, which ruled that the auto dealers had illegally conspired. The dealers reached an agreement with the FTC and agreed not to boycott the newspaper in the future (Chiuy, 1995). This episode is a dramatic illustration of how advertisers can influence media content—directly or indirectly. Advertisers do not want media content to interfere with the "buying mood" of the public.

The people who populate news and public affairs programs also represent a skewed sample of American life. "Hard news" usually features people in positions of power, especially politicians, professionals, and corporate executives. We might argue that, for many journalists, the very working definition of news is what those in power say and do. As we saw in Chapter 4, the organizational structure of journalism also favors coverage of the wealthy and powerful. The industry organizes its news beats around powerful political institutions such as the city hall, the state house, and federal offices. People with substantial resources and influence can also command attention from the media by supplying journalists with packaged information such as press releases, press conferences, and pseudo-events. The only regular features on working-class and poor people are likely to come from the reporter on the crime beat.

Unlike straight news broadcasts, public affairs programs offer a great deal of flexibility in the list of guests who are invited by producers to comment on and analyze current issues. Yet the class characteristics of the guests on such programs are also heavily skewed toward professionals. On the prestigious public affairs programs "Nightline" and the "MacNeil-Lehrer NewsHour," politicians and professionals dominate the guest lists (Croteau and Hoynes, 1994). Representatives of organizations speaking on behalf of working people are almost nonexistent on such programs. Public television in general is skewed toward professional sources, usually leaving the public out of the picture (Croteau, Hoynes, and Carraggee, 1996).

Sexual Orientation: Out of the Closet and into the Media?

Finally, let's consider one more group in society that suffers unequal treatment both in and outside the media: lesbians and gays. For decades lesbians and gays have been either ignored or ridiculed in nearly all media accounts. Like the movements for racial equality, women's rights, and organized labor, the gay and lesbian movement has both developed alternative media and worked for more positive portrayals of gays and lesbians in the mainstream media.

Reviewing the literature on lesbians, gays, and the media, Fejes and Petrich (1993, p. 397) argue that until the early 1930s, film portrayals of homosexuals were used either as "comic devices," as "a form of erotic titillation," or "to depict deviance, perversion and decadence." From the mid-1930s to the early 1960s, more conservative norms reigned in Hollywood, and producers severely restricted and censored images of gays and lesbians. The lesbian and gay images that emerged in the 1960s were usually quite negative in tone. Fejes and Petrich (p. 398) note that during this period "homosexuality was portrayed at best as unhappiness, sickness, or marginality and at worst perversion and an evil to be destroyed." They cite one review of all the films made between 1961 and 1976 that featured a major homosexual character. Thirty-two such films appeared in this period. Eighteen of these films featured a homosexual character who ends up being killed by another character, 13 featured a homosexual character who commits suicide, and the one remaining film featured a gay man who lives—but only after being castrated. The portrayal of gays and lesbians in films has improved since then—there was no place to go but up. However, realistic and positive portrayals are still a rarity, although independent films by lesbians and gays have served as an important source in providing a broader range of images.

Television has followed much the same route as Hollywood. From comic drag queens to threatening villains, television routinely disparaged homosexuals. Fejes and Petrich (p. 400) cite a 1967 CBS documentary in which the host, Mike Wallace, concluded, "The average homosexual, if there be such, is promiscuous. He's not interested in, nor capable of a lasting relationship like that of a heterosexual marriage." As the gay and lesbian movement gained strength in the 1970s and 1980s, it more actively sought fairer television portrayals of homosexuals. A 1974 episode of the medical drama "Marcus Welby" featured a homosexual child molester and suggested that homosexuality was a treatable disease. The program angered gay activists, who responded by organizing media watch efforts that challenged the negative media portrayals of gays and lesbians. Because of such efforts, gay and lesbian characters began to appear on prime-time programs, especially in episodes that revolved around homo-sexuality. Such programs, though, almost always framed these images as a "heterosexual view of homosexuality. Dramatic programming por-trayed homosexuality as a problem disrupting heterosexuals' lives and expectations" (Fejes and Petrich, p. 401).

In the 1980s and 1990s, gay and lesbian characters began appearing in more serious and realistic portrayals, especially in roles highlighting the issue of AIDS. This time, it was conservative and religious fundamen-talist groups who organized to challenge the media images. They objected to the positive portrayals of lesbians and gays and organized boycotts against advertisers on such programs. Limits still exist on television por-trayals of gays and lesbians. Television almost always presents homosex-ual characters in isolation, not as part of a gay community. They are almost never major, recurring characters. Also, displays of physical affec-tion between homosexual characters are still taboo on American televi-sion. One episode of "Thirtysomething" showed two gay men talking in bed. After the episode aired, conservative activists organized protests, sev-eral advertisers withdrew from the show, and the network dropped the episode from its summer rerun schedule.

News coverage of lesbians and gays has also changed over the years. Rarely mentioned before the 1960s, homosexuality entered the news as a result of gay and lesbian activism. The AIDS epidemic in the 1980s prod-ded the news media to address issues related to the gay community more directly. The move toward more positive coverage of lesbians and gays has taken place primarily in larger metropolitan areas with large, active, and visible gay and lesbian organizations. Smaller, more conservative communities have often lagged behind in their coverage of gay and les-bian issues.

As with the evolution of media coverage of women and racial minori-ties, the media's portrayal of lesbians and gays has slowly become less blatantly stereotypical. While coverage is still significantly limited, con-temporary media have at least displayed a sense of tolerance toward gays and lesbians. This is a start, but there is a long way to go before media provide truly equitable coverage. "Tolerance" of homosexuality is a far cry from a media position that no longer privileges heterosexuality.

Fejes and Petrich (p. 412) note that the changes in mass media images of gays and lesbians did not occur spontaneously. Such changes "were not brought about by more enlightened social attitudes. Rather, the activism of gays and lesbians in confronting and challenging negative stereotypes played a decisive role in the change." This important point applies to all the groups we have examined. Women's organizations and civil rights groups, as well as lesbian and gay organizations, were significant social factors, in the form of collective human agency, in influencing the media industry to change the nature of media content. Labor unions and other organizations representing working-class and poor people have not had the same impact on media coverage of their constituents.

Conclusion

Entertainment and news media do not reflect the diversity of the real world. However, by its lack of diversity, media content does reflect the inequality that exists in the social world—and in the media industry.

The dynamic relationship between media content and the social world is complicated. Is media content cause or effect? A sociological approach would suggest that it is both. The social world affects media producers and media products. For example, we have seen how the efforts of social-movement organizations have influenced changes in media content. In this case, human agency has altered the operations of a major institutional structure. In turn, media content certainly influences our understanding of the social world, because media content can communicate underlying messages about the nature of reality. It can provide models of norms, values, and behaviors. This brings up the issue of ideology, the topic of the next chapter.

CHAPTER 6

Media and Ideology

Most media scholars believe that media texts articulate coherent, if shifting, ways of seeing the world. These texts help to define our world and provide models for appropriate behavior and attitudes. How, for example, do media products depict the "appropriate" roles of men and women, parents and children, or bosses and workers? What defines "success," and how is it achieved? What qualifies as "criminal activity," and what are the sources of crime and social disorder? What are the underlying messages in media content, and whose interests do these messages serve? These are, fundamentally, questions about media and ideology.

Most ideological analyses of mass media products focus on the content of the messages—the stories they tell about the past and the present —rather than the "effects" of such stories. In this chapter, then, we focus primarily on media messages. Part Four of this book will turn to the relationship between media messages and their audiences.

What Is Ideology?

Ideology is a decidedly complicated term with different implications depending on the context in which it is used. In everyday language, it can be an insult to charge someone with being "ideological," since this label suggests rigidity in the face of overwhelming evidence contradicting one's beliefs. When Marxists speak of "ideology," they often mean belief systems that help justify the actions of those in power by distorting and misrepresenting reality. When we talk about ideology, then, we need to be careful to specify what we mean by the term.

When scholars examine media products to uncover their "ideology," they are interested in the underlying images of society they provide. In this context, an ideology is basically a system of meaning that helps define and explain the world and that makes value judgments about that world. Ideology is related to concepts such as "worldview," "belief system," and "values," but it is broader than those terms. It refers not only to the beliefs held about the world, but also to the basic ways in which the world is defined. Ideology, then, is not just about politics; it has a broader and more fundamental connotation.

When we examine the ideology of media, we are not so much interested in the specific activities depicted in a single newspaper, movie, or hit song as in the broader system of meaning of which these depictions are a part. For ideological analysis, the key is the fit between the images and words in a specific media text and ways of thinking about, even defining, social and cultural issues.

Media critics are interested in the images of women, or African Americans, or immigrants—and how these images may change over time—because they contribute to the ways we understand the roles of these groups in society. In this case, the question is not whether such media images are "realistic" depictions, because analysts of ideology generally perceive the definition of the "real" as, itself, an ideological construction. Which aspects of whose "reality" do we define as the most real? Those that are the most visible? The most common? The most powerful? Instead of assessing the images and making some judgment about levels of realness, ideological analysis asks what these messages tell us about ourselves and our society.

Politicians have long perceived mass media, both news and entertainment forms, as sites for the dissemination of ideology. That is one reason why media are so frequently the subjects of political debate. For example, during just a few short weeks in the spring and summer of 1995, virtually every form of contemporary mass media was singled out for a scolding by prominent politicians. In the wake of the April 1995 bombing of the Oklahoma City federal building, President Clinton identified extremists on talk radio as purveyors of hatred, implying that these radio hosts were disseminating a worldview that condoned violence. Senate Majority Leader Robert Dole focused his attention on the entertainment industry, condemning what he identified as the rampant sex, violence, and general antifamily tone of popular television, movies, and music. Clinton responded with his own critique of violence on television and the worldview it sells to children. Former Secretary of Education William Bennett made a media splash with his attack on media giant Time Warner for its distribution of "gangsta" rap. Finally, various members of Congress identified the newly emerging cyberspace as a site where images of sex and obscenity were rampant and in need of legislative action.

Radio, television, movies, music, and computer networks all came under attack during this brief period by politicians from different political perspectives, all of whom had little doubt that the media are ideological, selling certain messages and worldviews. Given that these critiques of the media were generally well received, there is good reason to believe that large numbers of the public also perceive the media as purveyors of ideology—even if they don't use the term. Media sell both products and ideas, both personalities and worldviews; the notion that mass media products and cultural values are fundamentally intertwined has gained broad public acceptance.

"Dominant Ideology" Versus Cultural Contradictions

Even though mass media texts can be understood in ideological terms, as forms of communication that privilege certain sets of ideas and neglect or undermine others, unambiguous descriptions of media ideology remain problematic. Research on the ideology of media has included a debate between those who argue that media promote the worldview of the powerful—the "dominant ideology"—and those who argue that mass media texts include more contradictory messages, both expressing the "dominant ideology" and at least partially challenging worldviews.

We prefer to think of media texts as sites where cultural contests over meaning are waged rather than as providers of some univocal articulation of ideology. In other words, different ideological perspectives, representing different interests with unequal power, engage in a kind of struggle within media texts. Some ideas will have the advantage—because, for example, they are perceived as popular or build upon familiar media images—and others will be barely visible, lurking around the margins of media for discovery by those who look carefully. For those engaged in the promotion of particular ideas, including such diverse groups as politicians, corporate actors, citizen activists, and religious groups, media are among the primary contemporary battlegrounds.

Media, in fact, are at the center of what James Davison Hunter (1991) has called the "culture wars" in contemporary American society, in which fundamental issues of morality are being fought. Hunter stresses the ways in which media—advertising, news, letters to the editor, and opinion commentary—provide the principal forms of public discourse by which cultural warfare is waged. The morality of abortion, homosexuality, or capital punishment is debated, often in very polarized terms, in the mass media, as cultural conservatives and cultural progressives alike use various media technologies to promote their positions.

But the media are not simply conduits for carrying competing messages; they are more than just the battlefield on which cultural warfare takes place. Much of the substance of the contemporary culture wars is about the acceptability of the images that the mass media disseminate. These struggles over morality and values often focus on the implications of our popular media images and the apparent lessons they teach about society. Among the more prominent examples are the struggles over the meaning of religion in films such as *Priest* and *The Last Temptation of*

Christ; the controversy surrounding the pregnancy of the television character Murphy Brown, who became a single mother; the broadcast by PBS of the documentary "Tongues Untied," which explored the experience of black gay men; and the battles over the use of "obscene" language in rap and heavy-metal music. These media battles often become quite fierce, with some voices calling for outright censorship, others defending free speech, and still others worrying about the consequences of cultural struggles that seem to represent a war of absolutes, with no possibility of compromise.

One of the principal reasons why media images often become so controversial is that they are believed to promote ideas that are objectionable. In short, few critics are concerned about media texts that promote perspectives they support. Ideological analysis, then, often goes hand in hand with political advocacy, as critics use their detection of distorted messages to make their own ideological points. As a result, exploring the ideologies of mass media can be very tricky.

The most sophisticated ideological analysis examines the stories the media tell as well as the potential contradictions within media texts, that is, the places where alternative perspectives might reside or where ideological conflict is built into the text. Ideological analysis, therefore, is not simply reduced to political criticism, whereby the critic loudly denounces the "bad" ideas in the media. Nor, in our view, is analysis particularly useful if it focuses on the ideology of one specific media text without making links to broader sets of media images. It may be interesting to ruminate over the underlying ideology of a popular movie like *Forrest Gump.* (Is it a nostalgic valorization of white men in the days before multiculturalism, or a populist story of the feats of an underdog?) However, this inquiry will move from party conversation to serious analysis only if we think more carefully about the *patterns* of images in media texts, rather than analyzing one film in isolation. At its best, ideological analysis provides a window onto the broader ideological debates going on in society. It allows us to see what kinds of ideas circulate through media texts, how they are constructed, how they change over time, and when they are being challenged.

Ideology as Normalization

What are the stakes in these battles over the ideology of media? From one standpoint, media texts can be seen as key sites where basic social norms are articulated. The media give us pictures of social interaction and social institutions that, by their sheer repetition on a daily basis, can play important roles in shaping broad social definitions. In essence, the accumulation of media images suggests what is "normal" and what is "deviant." This articulation is accomplished, in large part, by the fact that popular media, particularly television and mass advertising, have a tendency to display a remarkably narrow range of behaviors and lifestyles, marginalizing or neglecting people who are "different" from the mass-mediated norm. When such difference is highlighted by, for example, television talk shows that routinely include people who are otherwise invisible in the mass media—cross-dressers, squatters, or strippers—the media can become part of a spectacle of the bizarre.

Despite the likelihood of their having very different political stances, those who are concerned about media depictions of premarital sex have the same underlying concern as those who criticize the dominating images of the upper-middle-class family. In both cases, the fear is that media images *normalize* specific social relations, making certain ways of behaving seem unexceptional. If media texts can normalize behaviors, they can also set limits on the range of acceptable ideas. The ideological work lies in the *patterns* within media texts. Ideas and attitudes that are routinely included in media become part of the legitimate public debate about issues. Ideas that are excluded from the popular media or appear in the media only to be ridiculed have little legitimacy. They are outside the range of acceptable ideas. The ideological influence of media can be seen in the absences and exclusions just as much as in the content of the messages.

Media professionals generally have little patience with the argument that the media are purveyors of ideology. Instead of seeing media as places where behaviors are normalized and boundaries are created, those in the industry tend to argue that the images they produce and distribute simply reflect the norms and ideas of the public. This is not ideology, but simply a mirror that reflects the basic consensus about how things are. Since, as we saw in Chapter 2, mass media are commercially organized to attract audiences for profit, there is good reason to believe that popularity will be more important to media producers than a commitment to any specific ideology. However, our investigation of the ideology of media does not mean that producers are consciously trying to sell certain ways of thinking and being. Ideology is not only produced by committed ideologues. As we will see, we can find ideology in our everyday lives, in our definition of common sense, and in the construction of a consensus.

Theoretical Roots of Ideological Analysis

The analysis of ideology can be traced back to the works of Marx and, especially, to twentieth-century European Marxism. The analysis has evolved over time, maintaining some elements of its Marxist origin while developing more complexity and nuance.

Early Marxist Origins

For early Marxists, the discussion of ideology was connected to the concept of "false consciousness." Ideology was seen as a powerful mechanism of social control whereby members of the ruling class imposed their worldview, which represented their interests, on members of subordinate classes. In such a system, the subordinate classes who accepted the basic ideology of the ruling class were said to have false consciousness because their worldview served the interests of others. For Marx and early Marxists, social revolution depended on the working class breaking free of the ideas of the ruling class—moving beyond their false consciousness—and developing a "revolutionary" consciousness that represented their material interests as workers. This new way of thinking would then stand in opposition to the ruling ideology, which promoted the economic interests of the capitalist class.

In this context, ideology was understood to involve having ideas that were "false" because they did not match one's objective class interests. One of the ways capitalists ruled industrial society was by imposing upon the working class a worldview that served the interests of capitalists yet pretended to describe the experiences of all humankind. Ideology, then, was about mystification, the masking of interests, and the conflation of the particular and the universal. Moreover, ideology could be understood in straightforward economic-class terms. Capitalists had a class interest in the accumulation of capital through the exploitation of labor. Their ideology, which celebrated individualism and the free market, was a result of their economic interests. Workers had a class interest in fundamentally changing the conditions of their work and restructuring the social relations of production; this could be accomplished by a social revolution. Any system of ideas that did not recognize these economic realities, according to an early school of Marxism, was the result of the ideological power of capitalists. Ideological analysis, from this perspective, meant identifying the ways working people's ideas failed to reflect their class interests; in essence, it was about pointing out how consciousness was "false" and in need of correction.

The critique of ideology has evolved a great deal from its connections to the concept of false consciousness, but it still maintains some of the basic outlines of the early Marxist model. Ideological analysis is still concerned about questions of power and the ways in which systems of meaning—ideologies—are part of the process of wielding power. And ideological analysis continues to focus on the question of domination and the ways certain groups fight to have their specific interests accepted as the general interests of a society. But the contemporary study of ideology is more theoretically sophisticated, paying attention to the ongoing nature of ideological struggles and to how people negotiate with, and even oppose, the ideologies of the powerful. Ideas are not simply "false," and the connection between ideas and economic interest is not necessarily straightforward. In fact, much of the contemporary study of ideology has moved away from a focus on economic-class relations toward a more dynamic conceptualization of the terrain of culture.

Hegemony

The key theoretical concept that animates much of the contemporary study of the ideology of media is *hegemony*. Drawn from the work of Antonio Gramsci (1971), an Italian Marxist who wrote in the 1920s and 1930s, the notion of hegemony connects questions of culture, power, and ideology. In short, Gramsci argued that ruling groups can maintain their power through either force or consent, or a combination of the two. Ruling by way of force requires the use of institutions such as the military and the police in an effort to physically coerce—or threaten coercion—so that people will remain obedient. There is no shortage of historical examples of societies in which the use of force and the threat of even more severe forms of coercion have been the principal strategy of ruling. The military dictatorship is the most obvious example.

Gramsci noted, however, that power can be wielded at the level of culture or ideology, not just through the use of force. In liberal democratic societies like the United States, force is not the primary means by which the powerful rule. Certainly there are important examples of the use of force—turn-of-the-century efforts to crush the labor movement, the incarceration of members of the Communist Party in the 1950s, the violence directed at the Black Panther Party in the 1960s. But these examples stand out because the use of physical force is not the routine strategy for maintaining social order. Instead, Gramsci's work suggests that power is wielded in a different arena—that of culture, in the realm of everyday life—where people essentially agree to current social arrangements.

Consent, then, is the key to understanding Gramsci's use of hegemony, which is exercised through a kind of "cultural leadership." Consent is something that is won; ruling groups in a society actively seek to have their worldview accepted by all members of society as the universal way of thinking. Institutions such as schools, religion, and the media help the powerful exercise this cultural leadership, since they are the sites where we produce and reproduce ways of thinking about society.

Hegemony, though, is not simply about ideological domination, whereby the ideas of one group are imposed on another. Instead, the process is far subtler. Hegemony operates at the level of *common sense* in the assumptions we make about social life and on the terrain of things that we accept as "natural" or "the way things are." After all, what is common sense except for those things we think are so obvious that we need not critically evaluate them? Common sense is the way we describe things that "everybody knows," or at least should know, because such knowledge represents deeply held cultural beliefs. In fact, when we employ the rhetoric of common sense, it is usually to dismiss alternative approaches that go against our basic assumptions about how things work. Gramsci reminds us that one of the most effective ways of ruling is through the shaping of commonsense assumptions. What we take for granted exists in a realm that is uncontested, where there is neither a need nor room for questioning assumptions (Gamson et al., 1992).

Hegemony theorists remind us that commonsense assumptions, the taken-for-granted, are social constructions. They imply a particular understanding of the social world, and such visions have consequences. It is common sense, for example, that "you can't fight city hall" or that women are better nurturers than men or that "moderate" positions are more reasonable than "extreme" positions. When people adopt common-sense assumptions—as they do with a wide range of ideas—they are also accepting a certain set of beliefs, or ideology, about social relations.

A similar dynamic applies to what we think of as "natural." Nature is something that we define in opposition to culture, since nature is per-ceived to be beyond human control. We generally think that the "natural" is not a social construction; nature is more enduring and stable than the creations of human societies. Thus, if social structures and social relation-ships are defined as natural, they take on a kind of permanency and legiti-macy that elevates them to the realm of the uncontested. Think about the social relationships we call "natural" (or "unnatural"). Is it natural that some people are rich and some are poor, that people will not care about politics, or that people of different racial and ethnic backgrounds will prefer to live with their own groups? If these conditions are simply nat-ural, then there is little reason to be concerned about economic inequality, political apathy, or residential segregation, because they are not social problems but the natural order of things.

Let's look at some more controversial claims about the natural. One of the principal underpinnings of racist ideology is the belief that one race is naturally superior to others. Sexism rests on the assumption that men and women, by nature, are suited to different and unequal tasks. And contemporary discussions of sexuality are filled with claims about the "natural" status of heterosexual relationships and the "unnatural" status of gay and lesbian relationships. These examples illustrate how claims about nature work in the service of ideology. If such claims are widely accepted—if they are seen as the outcome of nature instead of culture—

then there may be legitimate reason for racial inequality, sexual discrimination, and the demonization of gays and lesbians, since these relationships are the result of the natural order of things. What we think of as natural and normal, then, is a central part of the terrain of hegemony.

Hegemony, however, is not something that is permanent; it is neither "done" nor unalterable. Gramsci understood hegemony as a process that was always in the making. In order to effectively wield power through consent, ideological work through cultural leadership was an ongoing necessity. The terrain of common sense and the natural must be continually reinforced because people's actual experiences will lead them to question dominant ideological assumptions. People are active agents, and modern society is full of contradictions; therefore, hegemony can never be complete or final. Some people will not accept the basic hegemonic worldview, some people may resist it, and changing historical conditions will make certain aspects of hegemonic ideology untenable. Ultimately, Gramsci saw hegemony as a daily struggle about our underlying conceptions of the world, a struggle always subject to revision and opposition. Rulers, who try to maintain their power by defining the assumptions upon which the society rests, work to bring stability and legitimacy and to incorporate potentially opposing forces into the basic ideological framework. In a striking example, images of rebellion from the 1960s have become incorporated into our democratic story and now are used to sell cars and clothing.

Sociologist Stuart Hall, the leading voice of British cultural studies, has provided a sophisticated analysis of how mass media institutions fit into this conception of hegemony. He argues that mass media are one of the principal sites where the cultural leadership, the work of hegemony, is exercised. Media are involved in what Hall calls "the politics of signification," in which the media produce images of the world that give events particular meanings. Media images do not simply reflect the world, they *re-present* it; instead of reproducing the "reality" of the world "out there," the media engage in practices that define reality. As Hall (1982, p. 64) puts it, "representation is a very different notion from that of reflection. It implies the active work of selecting and presenting, of structuring and shaping; not merely the transmitting of an already-existing meaning, but the more active labour of *making things mean*."

Media representations are intertwined with questions of power and ideology because the process of giving meaning to events suggests that, potentially, there are multiple definitions of reality. Media have, as Hall says, "the power to signify events in a particular way." The question, then, is "What are the patterns by which events are represented?" This is fundamentally a question about ideology, because it suggests that media are places where certain ideas are circulated as the truth, effectively marginalizing or dismissing competing truth claims. Many scholars argue that media generally adopt the dominant assumptions and draw upon the commonsensical views of the world that everyone knows. As a result, media representations, while not fully closed, have the tendency to reproduce the basic stories and values that are the underpinnings of this hegemony.

Media are, without doubt, not simple agents of the powerful, and, as we will explore further in Chapter 8, the ideas of the powerful are not simply imposed upon readers or viewers. Media are cultural sites where the ideas of the powerful are circulated and where they can be contested. As we move from a theoretical discussion of media, ideology, and hegemony to specific cases that illustrate the ideology of mass media products, we will see the complex ways in which media products are a part of larger ideological debates.

News Media and the Limits of Debate

For decades, Americans have debated the politics of the news media, with criticisms of the news coming with equal vigor from both sides of the political spectrum. The underlying assumption in this debate is that news media are, in fact, ideological; the selection of issues, stories, and sources is inescapably value-laden. While media outlets fend off attacks from the political right that they are too liberal and attacks from the left that they are too conservative, journalists find themselves precisely where they want to be: in the middle. This middle ground serves as a haven for reporters, a place that is perceived as being without ideology. After all, if ideological criticism comes from both sides, then the news must not be ideological at all. Attacks from both sides make the center a defensible place.

Since we generally associate ideology with ideas that are perceived to be extreme, those in the middle are viewed not as ideological but as pragmatic. And since ideology is something to be avoided, the journalistic middle ground becomes safe. There is good reason for journalists to want to occupy this territory. It insulates them from criticism and gives the news legitimacy with a wide range of readers and viewers who see themselves as occupying some version of a middle ground.

However, the notion that the news reflects the "consensus" is itself ideological, because news does the active work of defining that consensus. Once that consensus is defined, the claim that reporting is a mere reflection of an already existing consensus is blind to the ways such definitions work to solidify it. We might say the same thing about the journalistic center. The news does not so much occupy the middle ground as define what the middle ground is. In the process, news reporting effectively defends the legitimacy of this worldview, which is oriented to the reproduction of current social arrangements. In short, the middle ground is ideological precisely because it is a cultural site where commonsense assumptions are produced, reproduced, and circulated.

Elites and Insiders

A large body of scholarly literature has explored the ways in which news media produce ideological visions of the nation and the world. One of the principal findings of this research is that news focuses on powerful people and institutions and generally reflects established interests. Whether this makes news "liberal" or "conservative" is another matter; some claim "the establishment" is liberal, while others argue that it is conservative. In either case, our reading of the research literature suggests that news reaffirms the basic social order and the values and assumptions it is based on.

In his widely cited work *Deciding What's News*, sociologist Herbert Gans (1979) found that two of the most prominent enduring values in the news are "social order" and "national leadership." This focus on order and leadership gives the news a view of society that is both moderate and supportive of the established hierarchy. As Gans (p. 61) notes, "with some oversimplification, it would be fair to say that the news supports the social order of public, business and professional, upper-middle-class, middle-aged, and white male sectors of society. . . . In short, when all other things are equal, the news pays most attention to and upholds the actions of elite individuals and elite institutions."

With its focus on elites, news presents images of the world that are significantly lacking in diversity. This has substantial consequences for the way the news depicts the political world. Politics, according to most major news media, is not about broad questions of power—who wields it, in what arenas, under what circumstances, with what consequences—nor is it a forum for wide-ranging debate and controversy about current events. Instead, politics is framed as an insiders' debate, with only a privileged few invited to the table.

The "insider" nature of political news means that a small group of analysts are regular commentators and news sources, regardless of the wisdom of their previous commentary or of their prior actions when they occupied positions of power. To be—or to have been—an insider, with access to powerful circles, makes one a de facto "expert" as far as the news is concerned. As a result, individuals are qualified to comment on and analyze current events to the extent to which they are or have been insiders. The "debates" we see in the news, therefore, are often between insiders who share a common commitment to traditional politics, to the exclusion of those outside the constructed consensus.

The range of insiders invited to discuss issues is often so narrow that a host of unaddressed assumptions are implicit in their approach. For example, debating whether the United States should have used ground troops or relied solely on air power to drive Iraqi troops from Kuwait in 1991 ignores a variety of assumptions about the desirability of the use of military force in the first place. Debating President Clinton's 1993 "managed care" approach to heath care reform versus Republican attempts to limit reform neglects other possible alternatives, such as a single-payer system. The result is that contrasting perspectives in the news frequently represent the differences—generally quite narrow—between establishment insiders. This approach to the news does little to inform the public of positions outside this limited range of opinion. More important, it implicitly denies that other positions should be taken seriously. Ultimately, one principal way the news is ideological is in drawing boundaries between what is acceptable—the conventional ideas of insiders—and what is not.

Economic News as Ideological Construct

News coverage of economic issues is remarkable in the way it reproduces a profoundly ideological view of the world. Most news coverage of the economy is by and about the business community (Croteau and Hoynes, 1994). While individuals can play a range of roles in economic life—worker, consumer, citizen, or investor—economic news focuses overwhelmingly on the activities and interests of investors. One of the most striking examples of this phenomenon is the fact that virtually every newspaper has a Business section, while almost none have a Consumer or Labor section. As a result, economic news is largely business news, and business news is directed at corporate actors and investors.

In this kind of news, the ups and downs of the stock market are often the centerpiece, serving as an indicator of the economic health of the country. By equating economic health with the fortunes of investors, news tips its ideological hand. Such definitions fail to recognize that different groups of people can have different economic interests. Although a rise in the stock market is depicted as positive economic news for the country as a whole, there are clearly losers even when the market soars. For example, a rise in corporate profitability may be the result of an increase in productivity, which in turn may be accompanied by extensive layoffs. For example, AT&T's stock rose upon the announcement of the elimination of 40,000 jobs in early 1996. This is not an unequivocally positive development, especially for those workers who lose jobs or take pay cuts.

Let's hypothetically turn the tables on economic news. What if coverage of the economy focused predominantly on the experiences and interests of workers, evaluating economic health from the standpoint of working conditions and highlighting the economic analysis of labor union officials? It would likely be labeled "anti-business" or "pro-labor" and be targeted by critics for its "biased" reporting. It would, in short, be identified as providing a fundamentally ideological view of the economy. It is striking, however, that the news media's emphasis on the corporate and investor perspective is generally accepted as the appropriate way to cover the economy. Indeed, the dominance of the business worldview in economic news coverage is so complete that it seems natural. We take it for granted, assuming that the economy equals corporate America and that economic health is equivalent to investor satisfaction. No conscious effort at manipulation is being made here, but it is a clear example of the ways media products draw upon and reproduce a hegemonic ideology.

Movies, the Military, and Masculinity

One of the difficulties of ideological analysis of media products is that there is no singular "mass media." The term *mass media*, we should reiterate, is plural, signifying the multiple organizations and technologies that make up our media environment. As a result, we have to be careful when we make generalizations about the ideological content of media, in large part because we are usually talking about a specific medium and perhaps even specific media texts. Another challenge for ideological analysis is that media texts are produced in specific historical contexts, responding to and helping frame the cultural currents of the day. Mass-mediated images are not static; they change in form and content in ways that are observable. Ideological analysis, therefore, needs to pay attention to the shifts in media images—sometimes subtle and sometimes quite dramatic—in order to allow for the dynamic nature of mass media.

If the study of media and ideology needs to be both historically specific and wary of overgeneralizing from single texts, what analytic strategies have proved useful? One of the most common approaches is to focus on specific types or "genres" of media, such as the television sit-com, the Hollywood horror film, or the romance novel. Because texts within the same genre adopt the same basic conventions, analysts can examine the underlying themes and ideas embedded within these conventional formats without worrying that any contradictions they might uncover are the result of the distinct modes of storytelling of different genres. The result is that most scholarly studies of media ideology are both quite specific about their subject matter and narrow in their claims, focusing on issues such as the messages about gender in the soap opera (Modleski, 1984) or the ideology of the American Dream in talk radio (Levin, 1987).

In addition, scholarly studies of media texts generally either focus on a specific historical period—for example, foreign policy news in the Reagan era (Herman and Chomsky, 1988)—or provide comparisons of one genre of media across several time periods—for example, best-selling books from the 1940s through the 1970s (Long, 1985). These analyses provide, on one hand, an understanding of how a specific medium displays a particular worldview or ideological conflict and, on the other hand, an understanding of how such stories about society change over time, in different historical contexts.

Two film genres, action-adventure and military/war films of the 1980s and early 1990s, are worth exploring for their underlying ideological orientation because of their popularity. With action-adventure movies such as *Raiders of the Lost Ark* and *Romancing the Stone* and military movies such as *Rambo* and *Top Gun* attracting large audiences—and inspiring sequels and seemingly endless imitators—scholars have used an ideological framework to understand the underlying messages in these films. What are these movies about, and why are they so attractive to American audiences? In other words, what are the ideologies of these films, and how do these ways of seeing the world fit within broader ideological currents? These questions help both to interpret the films and to locate their meanings in a social context.

Action-Adventure Films

Action-adventure films were among the most popular movies of the 1980s. The three Indiana Jones films, starring Harrison Ford, are the archetype of this genre, in which the male hero performs remarkable feats that require bravery and skill throughout a fast-paced 90-minute struggle with an evil villain. The hero ultimately emerges triumphant after several close calls, defeating the villain, saving the day, and usually winning the affection of the female lead. One version of this genre places the hero in faraway, exotic lands, making the villains and the action more unpredictable. But the basic story line can be found in films set in the United States, such as *Die Hard* and *Speed*. On one level, these kinds of movies can be thrilling, suspenseful (even though we know, deep down, that the hero will triumph), and even romantic as we watch the hero overcome new challenges and seemingly impossible odds on the road to an exciting and satisfying finish. However, if we dig below the surface of the action, we can explore the kinds of stories these movies tell and how the stories resonate with our contemporary social dilemmas.

Gina Marchetti (1989) has argued that the key to the ideology of this genre is the typical construction of the main characters, the hero and the villain, which leads to specific stories about the nature of good and evil, strength and weakness, and courage and cowardice. One underlying theme of the action-adventure genre is the drawing of rigid lines between "us" and "them," with the villain representing the dangers of difference. There are, of course, many different versions of the central determinant of the in-group and the out-group. Nationality and ethnicity are frequent boundary markers, with white Americans (Michael Douglas, Bruce Willis) defeating dangerous foreigners. In other versions, civilized people triumph over the "primitive" (*Indiana Jones and the Temple of Doom*), or representatives of law and order defeat the deranged (*Speed*).

Ultimately, the hero effectively eliminates the danger represented by "the other"—the difference embodied by the villain—usually by killing the villain in a sensational climactic scene. Metaphorically speaking, social order is restored by the reassertion of the boundaries between what is acceptable and what is not, with the unacceptable doomed to a well-deserved death. The films go beyond xenophobic demonization of difference, however, by demonstrating the terms on which people who are different can become part of mainstream society. The hero's local accomplices—such as Indiana Jones's child sidekick Short Round in *Temple of Doom*—demonstrate that it is possible to be incorporated into mainstream society. This is the flip side of the violent death of the villain: The difference represented by the friend or "buddy" can be tamed and made acceptable (Marchetti, 1989). Difference, then, must be either destroyed or domesticated by integrating the other into the hierarchical social relations of contemporary society, where the newly tamed other will likely reside near the bottom of the hierarchy. Ultimately, the action-adventure genre, with its focus on the personal triumph of the hero, is a tale about the power of the rugged male individual, a mythic figure in the ideology of the American Dream.

Vietnam Films

One particular 1980s version of the action-adventure genre was the "return to Vietnam" film, symbolized most clearly by the hit movie *Rambo*. In these films—which also include the *Missing in Action* trilogy and *Uncommon Valor*—the hero, a Vietnam veteran, returns to Vietnam a decade after the war to rescue American prisoners-of-war that the U.S. government has long since abandoned. In the process, the Vietnamese are demonized as brutal enemies who deserve the deaths that the heroes—most notably Sylvester Stallone and Chuck Norris—inflict upon the captors as they liberate the prisoners.

The ideological work of these films is not very subtle, and given that they were popular during Ronald Reagan's presidency their ideological resonance should not be surprising. In essence, these films provide a mass-mediated refighting of the war, in which Americans are both the good guys and the victors. The films serve as a kind of redemption for a country unable to accept defeat in Vietnam and still struggling with the shame of loss. If the United States did not win the Vietnam War on the battlefield, the movies allow its citizens to return in the world of film fantasy to alter the end of the story. In these stories, there is no longer shame or defeat but instead pride, triumph, and a reaffirmation of national strength. This outlook was, to be sure, part of the appeal of Ronald Reagan, whose campaign for President in 1980 called for a return to a sense of national pride, strength, and purpose that would move the nation beyond "the Vietnam syndrome."

The back-to-Vietnam films are, perhaps most fundamentally, part of the ideological project to overcome the Vietnam syndrome by providing a substitute victory. Susan Jeffords (1989) has argued that these films are about more than our national pride and the reinterpretation of defeat in Vietnam. She makes a persuasive case that the return-to-Vietnam films are part of a larger process of "remasculinization" of American society, another key component of the ideology of the Reagan years, in which a masculinity defined by its toughness is reasserted in the face of the twin threats of the defeat in Vietnam and the growth of feminism.

These Vietnam films are, to Jeffords, fundamentally about the definition of American "manhood" at a time when the traditional tough image had been challenged by the social movements of the 1960s and the defeat in Southeast Asia. The Sylvester Stallone and Chuck Norris characters—Rambo and Braddock—return to Vietnam in order to recapture their strength and power, all the while resisting and chastising the government for being too weak (read: "feminine") to undertake such a courageous mission. The "return" is as much about returning to a mythical past in which a strong America ruled the world and strong American men ruled their households as it is about rescuing POWs. Rambo and Braddock symbolize the desires of, and provide a mass-mediated and ideologically specific solution for, American men struggling with the changing social landscape of the 1980s.

Such popular media images are not simply innocent fantasies for our viewing entertainment. If we read these films in ideological terms, both the film texts themselves and their popularity tell us something about American culture and society in the 1980s. The masculine/military films of the time both reflected the fears and desires of American men and helped reproduce a new brand of toughness that became prevalent in the 1990s. The films were part of a political culture that created the conditions for the popular 1989 invasion of Panama and the even more popular 1991 war in the Persian Gulf, where TV news images did not differ much from those in the 1986 hit film *Top Gun*. Americans did overcome the "Vietnam syndrome" in the late 1980s, as symbolized by the willingness of the population to support military action in Panama and Iraq. Part of the ideological work necessary for that transformation was performed by popular Hollywood films.

Television, Popularity, and Ideology

While certain genres of popular films have been the subject of ideological analysis, it would be fair to say that the whole range of network television programming has been studied for its ideological content. In fact, ideological analysis of media is sometimes reduced to the study of television, just as claims about "the media" are often claims about televised images.

This state of affairs is not the result of some simple misunderstanding of terminology. Instead, such equations of media and television are implicit arguments that television is the dominant form of media in the late twentieth century. (A single top-rated program is viewed by 15–20 million households, while a major newspaper chain like Gannett reaches a combined total of 6 million readers through its 80-plus newspapers.) Television occupies so much of our leisure time and seems to so routinely dominate the cultural landscape of the United States that claims about its preeminence among media technologies rarely seem overstated. From presidential politics to the O. J. Simpson trial, from war in the former Yugoslavia to the Los Angeles earthquake, ideas and images circulate most widely (and rather quickly) through television.

Television is more than just the most popular medium in terms of audience size. It also regularly comments on popular media. In fact, an astounding number of TV shows have been, at least in part, about the media. "Frasier" was about a psychiatrist turned talk-radio host; "WKRP in Cincinnati" and "NewsRadio" focused on rock and news radio stations, respectively; "Lou Grant" was about the workings of a big-city newspaper; "The Naked Truth" was about a tabloid newspaper photographer; "Lois and Clark" featured the exploits of mild-mannered newspaper reporters; "Caroline in the City" starred a newspaper cartoonist; "Dave's World" was based on a (real!) newspaper columnist; and one costar of "Mad About You" was a documentary filmmaker. A host of programs since the 1960s have been about television itself. The "Dick Van Dyke Show" was about a team of sit-com writers; the father in "Family Ties" was the manager of a public television station; the "Mary Tyler Moore Show" was about a TV news station; the "Larry Sanders Show" spoofed late-night talk shows; "Home Improvement" was about a cable TV program; and "Murphy Brown" centered on the staff of a news-magazine show. In addition, talk shows and entertainment-oriented programs focus on the lives of media celebrities and the ins and outs of the television, film, and music worlds. With popular media as the subject and setting for so much programming, television is a virtual running commentary on the media world. Television is often so self-referential—or at least media-centered—that the programs assume that viewers are deeply engaged with the culture of media, and the humor often requires a knowledge of the specific media reference.

As we will see in Part Four, the centrality of television in the media landscape has given audiences ample resources for interpreting televised messages. In short, our exposure to television and its self-referential "winking" about popular culture have made most of us rather skilled viewers who catch the references and know what they are all about.

Television and Reality

If television is as central to our mass-mediated culture as a broad range of scholars maintain, then the underlying ideas that television programs disseminate are of substantial social significance. What stories does television tell us about contemporary society? How does television define key social categories, depict major institutions, or portray different types of people? What is "normal" in the world of television, and what is "deviant"?

One reason why television is often considered to be so ideologically charged is that it relies, almost exclusively, on conventional "realist" forms of image construction that mask the workings of the camera. As a result, the family sit-com invites us to drop in at the home of our electronic neighbors, and the courtroom drama allows us to sit in on a trial. Most of us do not consciously mistake such families and courtrooms for "real life"; we would not confuse these televised images with our real neighbors, for example. Still, part of the allure of television is that it *seems* real; we routinely suspend disbelief while we are watching. The pleasures of television are a result of our ability to temporarily ignore our knowledge that there are no FBI agents named Mulder and Scully, no such thing as Klingons, and no newsmagazine show called "FYI."

The ideological work of television, then, lies in the ways it defines and orders its pictures of "reality"—in its claims to reflect the humor and hardships of family life, the dangers of police work, the fun and confusion of "twenty-something" single life, or the drama of the courtroom. This reality is created and packaged by writers and producers with the goal of attracting a mass audience. The images are not simple reflections of an unproblematic reality but representations of a world that is not as orderly as a 30- or 60-minute program.

In striving for popularity, the television producers have often adopted the strategy of "least objectionable programming," whereby programs are intended to avoid controversy and remain politically bland. This approach is, itself, ideological; blandness favors certain images and stories and pushes others to the margins or off the air entirely. This is one reason why television programs, despite the widespread belief that Hollywood producers are committed liberals, have included so few gay and lesbian characters on prime time.

It is difficult, however, to make broad generalizations about the ideology of television programming beyond the observation that network executives want popularity without controversy. This formula for programs reaffirms the dominant norms of contemporary society. For a more nuanced understanding of how television programs are ideological and how they respond to the often volatile social and political world, we need to look more carefully at a particular genre of programming. Ella Taylor's (1989) study of the changing image of the family on prime-time television from the 1950s through the 1980s provides a clear example of the ideological twists and turns of network television.

Television and the Changing American Family

Beginning in the 1950s and 1960s, domestic life as represented by programs such as "Leave It to Beaver," "Ozzie and Harriet," and "Father Knows Best," along with zanier fare like "Bewitched" and "I Dream of Jeannie," was predominantly white, middle class, happy, and secure. Network television presented the suburban family as the core of the modern, post-scarcity society, a kind of suburban utopia where social problems were easily solved (or nonexistent), consensus ruled, and signs of racial, ethnic, or class differences or conflict were difficult to find. Taylor suggests that if, indeed, such families existed, they were precisely the people whom network advertisers sought. Still, this image of the postwar family—and the not-so-subtle suggestion that this was what a "normal" family looked like—was a particular story masked as a universal one. Certainly, these families were not typical American families, no matter how often they were served up as such.

The television family did not remain static, however; changing social conditions and new marketing strategies in the television industry helped create competing domestic images. The biggest change came in the 1970s, with what Taylor calls the "turn to relevance," when the television family became a site where contemporary social and political issues were explored. The program that epitomized the new breed was Norman Lear's "All in the Family," which was expected to flop yet became one of the most popular and profitable shows of the decade. The program revolved around the ongoing tension among a cast of diverse characters in their Queens, New York, home. On one side were Archie Bunker, a stereotypical white, working-class bigot, and his strong but decidedly unliberated wife, Edith. On the other side were Archie's feminist daughter, Gloria, and her husband, Michael, a sociology graduate student with leftist political views. From week to week, Archie and Michael argued over race relations, the proper role of women in society, American foreign policy, and even what kind of food to eat. Throughout the political debates, the main characters traded insults and vented their anger at each other while Archie waxed nostalgic over the good old days of the 1950s and Gloria and Michael looked nervously at their futures. Programs such as "The Jeffersons" and "Maude," both "All in the Family" spin-offs, as well as "Sanford and Son" and "Good Times"—among the most popular programs of the mid-1970s—may have been less acerbic than "All in the Family," but they were all a far cry from the previous generation of conflict-free, white, middle-class family images.

By the middle of the 1970s, the image of the family was neither all white nor all middle class, and domestic life was no longer a utopia; instead, the family was depicted as a source of conflict and struggle as well as comfort and love. In short, social problems made their way into the television family. Taylor argues that the key to this change was the networks' desire, particularly at CBS, to target young, urban, highly educated viewers—an audience that was highly coveted by advertisers. The new image of the family, self-consciously "relevant" instead of bland and nostalgic, was perceived to be attractive to the youthful consumers who had lived through the social turbulence of the 1960s. But television's ideological change was slow and in many respects subtle. Nostalgic programs that presented the ideal middle-class family were also popular in the 1970s—"Happy Days" is a classic example.

At the same time that the television family was losing its blissful image in the 1970s, a new version of family appeared in the world of work. In programs such as "M*A*S*H," "Mary Tyler Moore Show," "Taxi," and "Barney Miller," the setting was not the home; instead the programs revolved around the relationships between co-workers that Taylor calls a "work-family." In these programs, the workplace became a place where people found support, community, and loyalty and served as an often warm and fuzzy kind of family for people who were much more connected to their work than to their home lives. Taylor argues that the image of the work-family was popular precisely because of broad cultural anxiety about the changing boundaries between private life and public life in the 1970s, particularly for young professionals seeking prestige and success. Work-families, in essence, provided a picture of a safe haven from domestic conflicts in both the world of television and the experiences of viewers.

Given the growing rationalization of the American workplace in the 1970s, when more men and women came to work in large, bureaucratic organizations, finding images of the family in the workplace is surprising. Taylor (1989, p. 153) argues that the popularity of the work-family programs tells us a great deal about the social role of television. "If we understand the television narrative as a *commentary* on, and *resolution* of, our troubles rather than a reflection of the real conditions of our lives, it becomes possible to read the television work-family as a critique of the alienating modern corporate world and an affirmation of the possibility of community and cooperation amid the loose and fragmentary ties of association."

Of course, the neat and orderly resolution of social dilemmas is precisely the area in which television is ideological. In this case, network television presented images of domestic conflict but resolved them in the workplace through a professional, career-oriented ideology that reassured us that, despite change, everything would be okay. In the end, even as it incorporated conflict and relevance into its field of vision, television still gave viewers satisfying families and happy endings that affirmed the basic outlines of the American Dream.

In more recent years, conflicting visions of family life—from the nostalgic "Wonder Years" and the idyllic "Cosby Show" to the cynical "Married With Children" and the sober "Grace Under Fire"—have vied for viewer attention. In addition, a new 1990s kind of "family" image, the close-knit friendship circles depicted in hits such as "Seinfeld" and "Friends," has become a regular staple in prime time. These new family images show that television programs and the ideology they circulate are far from static. In the midst of cultural conflict over the meaning of family in the 1990s, network television images are, themselves, part of the ongoing ideological contest to shape the definition of a proper family. Even here, of course, there are significant limits to television's portrayals. For example, we rarely see interracial or gay and lesbian families in popular television. But conflict and diversity, even in limited form, are part of the post-Cosby television family of the 1990s.

Rap Music as Ideological Critique?

We have seen that mass media can be analyzed in ideological terms, but media products are not ideologically uniform. They are both contradictory and subject to change. In short, there is no single ideology embedded within mass media texts. Even so, most mass media can be seen as sites where facets of the dominant version of the American story—an ideology that essentially sustains the current social order of our capitalist/democratic society—are displayed, reworked, and sometimes contested. At the same time, conventional norms and mainstream values are generally reaffirmed, even if in slightly modified form, by those mass media texts—news, popular films, and network television—that seek a large audience. Thus, hegemony is constructed, perhaps challenged, and reasserted on a daily basis through the products of our mass media. But is it possible for widely circulating mass media texts to be oppositional or counterhegemonic? Can mass media provide challenges to the dominant ways of understanding the social world?

Tricia Rose (1994), in her study of the meanings of rap music in contemporary America, argues that rap should be understood as a mass-mediated critique of the underlying ideology of mainstream American society. Rap presents an alternative interpretation—a different story—of the ways power and authority are structured in contemporary society. For example, on an album called "It Takes a Nation of Millions to Hold Us Back," Public Enemy has a song titled "Black Steel in the Hour of Chaos." In one verse, the singer describes receiving a draft registration notice from the government. He responds, "They wanted me for their army or whatever/Picture me given' a damn—I said never/Here is a land that never gave a damn/About a brother like me and myself/Because they never did."

Much of rap music is a critique of institutions such as the criminal justice system, the police, and the educational system, all of which are reinterpreted as sites that both exhibit and reproduce racial inequality. These alternative interpretations are not always explicit; often they are subtle, requiring a form of insider knowledge in order to fully understand what they are about. Rose (p. 100) suggests that rap "uses cloaked speech and disguised cultural codes to comment on and challenge aspects of current power inequalities. . . . Often rendering a nagging critique of various manifestations of power via jokes, stories, gestures, and song, rap's social commentary enacts ideological insubordination." While public attention focuses on the anger of "gangsta" rap, Rose points out that a much larger body of rap music acts in subtle and indirect ways to refuse dominant ideological assumptions about black youth, urban life, and racial inequality by articulating opposing interpretations of current social relations.

Rap's ideological displacement of the conventional story with new stories is rooted in the inequalities of the social world. Rose argues that rap's

stories—its ways of understanding society in alternative, even oppositional ways—come from the life experiences of black urban youth. In
essence, rap presents an ideological critique from below; it is a musical
form that criticizes social institutions from the perspective of those who
have comparatively little power in contemporary society.

At the same time, rap is full of ideological contradictions. While some
politically radical male rappers critique the institutions of society as being
racist, the lyrics and imagery of their music are often sexist and homo-
phobic. They often depict women in degrading ways, including references
to violence against women. So even as they are challenging the dominant
ideology about race, some black male rappers generally accept and reinforce traditional ideological assumptions about gender roles and sexuality.
The discourses within rap music, then, are not unambiguously oppositional in ideological terms.

Rose notes, however, that the alternative interpretations of social reality in rap lyrics, while partial and contradictory, only partly explain why
rap can be understood as a form of ideological critique. Rap music, even
that not expressly political in its lyrical content, is part of a broader struggle over the meaning of, and access to, public space. In short, the dominant discourse about rap—one frequently encountered in news media
coverage of the rap scene—is connected to a broader discourse about the
"spatial control of black people." In the case of rap, the focus is on ways
in which the culture of rap, particularly the gathering of large groups of
black youth at concerts, is a threat to social order. Rose contends that the
very existence of public rap events, at which black youth make claims to
their right to occupy public space, is part of an ideological struggle in
which the rap community refuses to accept the dominant interpretation of
its "threat" to society. It is in such large gatherings, already politicized by
the kind of resistance implied by the use of public space, that new forms
of expression and new ideas have the potential to emerge. This fight for
public space is at the center of what Rose calls rap's "hidden politics."

Rap, of course, is much more than a form of political expression, however contradictory, that circulates within the black community. It is also a
highly profitable commercial industry. In fact, rap's commercial success is
due, in large part, to the fact that the music is popular among white suburban youth. Whites actually buy more rap and hip-hop music than
Blacks. This complicates the ideology of rap, making it difficult to simply
accept the argument that rap can be "counterhegemonic," a form of resistance to dominant ideological constructions. Such media messages are
unlikely to be attractive to upper-middle-class white suburbanites or corporate record companies. Central to Rose's argument is that the ideology

of rap is often masked and is most accessible to those who know the black urban culture that forms its roots. Therefore, black youth may interpret the meaning of rap in ways very different from white youth, even though both may enjoy the music. As we will explore in Part Four, there is good reason to believe that the meanings of rap will be multiple and contested. Even so, we are still stuck with the dilemma posed by commercialization.

Is it possible for corporate-produced, commercial mass media products to be fundamentally oppositional in ideological terms? Even rap music—with its critique of the police, schools, and mainstream media—is part of the corporate sector and, as such, is subject to the rules that govern the culture industry. In particular, this means that rap is a commercial product that is packaged and marketed to be sold to demographically specific sets of buyers. To the extent that the music does not sell, it will not be available in the mass market for very long; the musical packages and marketing strategies that do work will lure record companies into a strategy of imitation until profits dry up. In short, rap is as much a commercial commodity as it is an intervention in ideological contests.

As it did with the commercialized images of rebellion from the 1960s —Janis Joplin's tongue-in-cheek prayer for a Mercedes is now used in ads for Mercedes-Benz cars—the culture industry is capable of incorporating potentially oppositional forms of expression into the mainstream by turning them into commercial products subject to the rules of the market. By becoming a prominent commercial product that is now routinely used in national advertising campaigns, rap may have lost a good deal of its critical impact. Rap music is now about selling records and products as much as it is a forum for potentially oppositional expression. Still, incorporation into the marketplace is not likely to entirely empty a cultural form, like rap, of its potential to provide ideological critique, particularly if that critique is disguised in the ways Rose suggests.

Ultimately, the example of rap music demonstrates the workings of hegemony. Mass media texts are contradictory; they can be oppositional, presenting ideological alternatives, even as they reproduce specific dominant ideological assumptions. But maintaining even this limited form of critique is difficult. Commercialization is part of the process through which the ideological struggle is waged; even critical media products have a tendency to be (at least partially) incorporated into mass, commercial products that accept the boundaries of mainstream definitions of social reality. This is, of course, an ongoing process, and incorporation is never total. But the media industry has proved to be remarkably resilient and innovative—it seems that virtually any form of expression can be tamed enough to be sold to a mass market.

Advertising and Consumer Culture

Each day, we are bombarded with advertisements in our homes, cars, and workplaces and on the street. As businesses seek new places to advertise their goods and services, ads can be found just about everywhere. Buses and subways have long been prime advertising spaces, catching the eyes of riders and passersby alike. At least one airline now sells ad space on the outside of its planes. Don't be surprised if you see an image of Bart Simpson on the side of a plane the next time you go to an airport! Television and radio have long been chock-full of ads. When you log onto the Internet, you will find that colorful advertisements are also part of the cyberspace experience. Ads surround sporting events, both on television and in sports arenas. They arrive in the mail and via fax. We wear advertising logos on our clothes and hum advertising jingles in the shower. In short, ads are so deeply embedded in our environment that we are likely to see, hear, and even smell them (in the form of magazine perfume ads) without thinking twice (see Exhibit 6.1).

What kinds of stories do advertisements tell about ourselves and our society? Certainly, on one level, ads are specific to their product or service. They tell us that if we drink a particular brand of beer we will meet attractive women or that if we wear the right makeup we will meet handsome men, if we purchase a certain automobile we will gain prestige, if we use specific cleansers we will save time, and if we wear certain clothes we will find adventure. Ads may also tell us that a particular item will save us money, that a specific service will make us healthier, or that a new product will make a great gift for a loved one. There is a wide range of specific messages in these ads, suggesting connections between products and lifestyles and between services and states of mind and presenting a host of information about prices, availability, and the like. We are not simply passive participants in all of this. We recognize advertising conventions and don't expect the connections depicted in ads—cosmetics and love, suits and success, for example—to be taken literally.

Despite the diversity of advertising messages and their frequent use of irony and humor, there is an underlying commonality to almost all advertisements: They are fundamentally about *selling*. They address their audiences as *consumers* and celebrate and take for granted the consumer-capitalist organization of society. This perspective is, of course, decidedly ideological. Ads tell us that happiness and satisfaction can be purchased, that each of us is first and foremost an individual consumption unit, and that market relations of buying and selling are the appropriate—perhaps the only—form of social relations outside the intimacy of the family. Sometimes even the intimacy of the family is seemingly up for sale. One recent commercial implied that a father could spend more quality time

EXHIBIT 6.1 *Advertising in Public Space*

Advertisements occupy increasingly large amounts of public space. This photo shows a particularly striking example of ads towering over and moving within an urban setting. Ads also populate our daily landscape in less dramatic ways. In addition to the regular mass media, T-shirts, bumper stickers, grocery bags, junk mail, and many other sites all carry ads. Where have you seen advertisements today? *(Photo by Serge Levy)*

with his son if he bought a direct-TV satellite dish! Advertising presumes and promotes a culture of consumption, normalizing middle- or even upper-middle-class lifestyles and making buying power a measure of both virtue and freedom.

In the process, advertising elevates certain values—specifically, those associated with acquiring wealth and consuming goods—to an almost religious status. Moreover, advertising promotes a worldview that stresses the individual and the realm of private life, ignoring collective values and the terrain of the public world (Schudson, 1984). The values that advertising celebrates do not come out of thin air, but this does not make them any less ideological. Whether or not ads are successful at selling particular products—some ad campaigns succeed and others fail—the underlying message in advertising, which permeates our media culture, is the importance of the values of consumerism.

Selling Consumerism in the Early Twentieth Century

Stuart Ewen (1976) has explored the historical roots of what we now call consumer culture, tracing the role of early-twentieth-century advertising in its creation. Turn-of-the-century capitalists, captains of industry, saw mass advertising as a means of shaping the consciousness of the American population in a way that would give legitimacy and stability to the rapidly industrializing society. The key to this new consciousness was the creation of a new way of life based on the pleasures of consumption. Mass advertising emerged in the 1920s when leaders of the business community began to see the need for a coordinated ideological effort to complement their control of the workplace. Advertising would become the centerpiece of a program to sell not only products, but also a new, American way of life in which consumption erased differences, integrated immigrants into the mainstream of American life, and made buying the equivalent of voting as a form of commitment to the democratic process.

From the start, then, advertising was more about creating consumers than selling individual products. If a mass-production economy was to be profitable and if those who worked for long hours under difficult conditions in the factory were to be pacified, new needs and habits had to be stimulated. This was the job of advertising. Its early practitioners built on people's insecurities about their lives and their appearances to shape desires for new consumer products. Solutions to personal problems were to be found in the world of consumption, an early version of the currently prevalent attitude that views a day of shopping as a way to cheer up oneself. Ads suggested that new products such as mouthwash, hand lotion, and deodorant would protect people from embarrassment and give them a ticket to the modern world. Old habits and folkways—the traditions that recent immigrants brought to the United States—were to be discarded in favor of the new "American way," participation in a consumer society. Ads sold consumerism as a gateway to social integration in twentieth-century America and as an ideology that would smooth over social conflicts —especially class conflict—and serve as a form of social cement.

One way advertising tried to sell a cross-class ideology of consumerism was through its focus on the realm of consumption and its neglect of production. The industrial workplace might be unsatisfying, even degrading, but advertising offered a world that was far removed from the drudgery of work, emphasizing the wonders of the consumer lifestyle. It was, after all, that lifestyle and associated worldview that ads were selling, regardless of whether people had the means to really live it. As Ewen (1976, p. 108) puts it, while the ideology of consumerism "served to stimulate consumption among those who had the wherewithal and desire to consume, it also tried to provide a conception of the good life for those who did not. . . . In the broader context of a burgeoning commercial culture, the foremost political imperative was *what to dream.*" Such dreams could be realized only by consuming goods, and even this was only a temporary realization, requiring continuous consumption in search of the lifestyle promoted by advertising. Our culture of consumption, then, is intimately connected to advertising, which helped create it and continues, in new forms, to sustain consumerism as a central part of contemporary American ideology.

Women's Magazines as Advertisements

The "women's magazine" is one medium that is particularly advertising-oriented and consistently promotes the ideology of consumerism. Its emphasis on ads—which often seem to make up the bulk of the content —has led one critic to label this genre the "women's advertising magazine" (McCracken, 1993). Publications such as *Vogue, Glamour, Redbook, Cosmopolitan,* and *Modern Bride* include page after page of glossy ads featuring products targeted specifically at women.

More generally, the magazines promote the consumer lifestyle by showing how beauty, sexuality, career success, culinary skill, and social status can be *bought* in the consumer marketplace. Social problems, from the standpoint of consumer ideology, are redefined as personal problems that can be solved by purchasing the appropriate product. Women's magazines, in addressing a specific social group, identify women as a consumption category with special product needs. The magazines link an identity as a woman with a set of specific consumer behaviors, making the latter the prerequisite for the former. To be a "woman," then, is to know what to buy; the ad content in women's magazines both displays the specific products and celebrates the pleasures and needs of consumption.

But there is more to women's magazines than just the ads, even though a common reading strategy is to casually leaf through the pages, glancing at the ads and headlines. Ellen McCracken (1993) argues that the editorial content—the nonadvertising articles—is itself a form of "covert advertising" that promotes the same kind of consumer-oriented ideology. The most visible ad is the cover of the magazine. The standard image of the ideal woman on the cover suggests that purchase of the magazine will provide clues to how and what to buy in order to become the ideal woman. Additionally, covers are often reproduced inside the magazine along with information about the products displayed, suggesting that the image depicted is one that can be purchased.

Even the "editorial advice" provided by women's magazines is a form of covert advertisement, selling the consumer ideology. Beauty advice, for example, routinely suggests the consumption of various forms of makeup as a way to achieve beauty. Such advice often identifies brand names that are most effective—brands frequently promoted in ads in the same magazine. The regular "makeover" feature, in which an "average" woman is turned into a glamorous model look-alike, is, in essence, an endorsement of the beauty products advertised elsewhere in the magazine. Advice, then, really concerns appropriate consumption habits. Just as early ads identified newfound needs, the women's magazine suggests what women need. In the end, women's magazines use both direct and covert advertising to sell magazines and promote an ideology that celebrates the consumption of gender-specific products as a means to identity formation and personal satisfaction—the dream of the "good life."

Advertising and the Globalization of Culture

The dreams that advertisements sell within the United States are also exported all around the globe. American-made ads for American brands —from Coca Cola to Levis—circulate through the growing global media culture. More generally, American media products, from television programming to Hollywood films, are consumed by a vast international audience. Both the ads and the programming serve as a kind of international promotional vehicle for the American way of life by focusing on the material abundance and consumer opportunities available in the United States.

While different products use different sales pitches and the entertainment media explore a range of themes set in various locations, most American media—especially those that are exported—share an underlying frame of reference that defines America by its combination of consumer capitalism and political freedom. Because media are owned and operated by profit-making companies, it should not be surprising that the cornucopia of images converges in the promotion of the benefits of a consumer society. Given the rapidly growing global economy, American-based companies see the international market as one of the keys to twenty-first-century success.

If advertisements and exported entertainment promote the American way of life, what exactly are they selling? After all, it is difficult to reduce the United States, a diverse and fragmented culture, to simple, unambiguous themes. The images on global display, like much domestic advertising, are about dreams. America is portrayed as a kind of dreamland where individuals can fulfill (or buy?) their desires. The images of the dreamland do not require a rigid uniformity, because central to the ideology on display are the notions of individuality and freedom, which merge into the concept of *consumer choice*. Dreams are fulfilled by individual consumers who make choices about what to buy: Coke, Pepsi, or 7 Up; Calvin Klein, The Gap, or Ralph Lauren; Nike or Reebok; Macintosh or IBM; Avis or Hertz. The route to happiness in this electronic dreamworld is consuming the "right" product. Think about how happy the diners are in McDonald's commercials or how peaceful the world is in the Ralph Lauren magazine ads.

The world portrayed in television programs like "Friends" or "Beverly Hills 90210" and on MTV similarly displays images of attractive people living comfortable lives surrounded by contemporary consumer goods. Both advertisements and entertainment media promote a commitment to the latest styles—for example, in clothes, cars, leisure activities, and food —that requires not only consumption but continuous consumption in order to keep up with stylistic changes. The focus on style is directed particularly at youth, who are increasingly the most coveted market and who are particularly avid media users. The international advertising, television, and music scenes have helped generate an emerging cross-national, global youth culture in which teens in different countries adopt similar styles in clothes and appearance; consume the same soda, cigarettes, and fast food; and listen to and play the same kind of music. The international teen market may cross national boundaries, but, with the help of American media products, youth style is based to a great degree on American images and consumer goods.

American media products may be the most prominent in global circulation, but they are not the only media images out there. Various European and Japanese companies also produce media and advertising for an international market, often in concert with U.S.-based companies. Herbert Schiller (1992), one of the early critics of the export of American mass media, argues that globally circulating media images all promote a similar ideology, regardless of their national origin. While the use of mass media as a tool for marketing lifestyles may have had its origins in the United States, it has become a global phenomenon. Although global media images may display national cultural differences as part of the sales pitch, they highlight difference as part of the promotion of the value of consuming and acquiring things. Ironically, cultural differences in global media images—like multicultural images in American media—attract audiences for the promotion of a consumerist ideology that most fundamentally aims to bring different cultures together into an increasingly homogeneous, international consumer culture. If "we are the world," as the 1980s hit song for famine relief asserted, it is because we all buy, or dream about buying, the same things.

Culture has become increasingly global, with media images circulating across national boundaries. At the same time, U.S. media images display more difference than they did a generation ago. But what messages do U.S. media images present about the status of Americans and the status of foreigners in this global culture? This question fundamentally addresses ideology.

In his study of advertising images of foreigners, William O'Barr (1994) argues that the ideological analysis of ads requires us to look at what he calls the "secondary discourses" within the advertisements. As opposed to the primary discourse, which concerns the specific qualities of the advertised product, secondary discourses are those ideas about social relationships that are embedded within the ads. The ideology of advertising images, from this perspective, is to be found in the ways the images convey messages about social life at the same time that they try to promote a specific product. Context, setting, characteristics of the principal actors, and the interaction between actors within the ad are central to these secondary discourses.

In contemporary print ads, according to O'Barr, there are three main categories of ad that feature images of foreigners: travel ads, product endorsements, and international business ads. The foreigners within travel ads are depicted as the "other"—different from the "us" that the ad is targeting—and the ads suggest that these others are available for the entertainment of American tourists. Implicit both within the images of local people dancing, painting, and smiling with American tourists and within the ad copy that invites tourists as "honored guests" or offers to "open both our homes and hearts" to visitors is a message that foreign lands are in the business of serving American visitors. Such images, by offering satisfaction from local people who aim to please, suggest that the needs and desires of Americans are the key to the potential relationship. The pattern in travel ads is unambiguous; the American tourist dominates the relationship with foreign cultures, particularly when the ads promote travel to Third World countries.

Product advertisements that draw upon images of foreigners make connections between the advertised commodity and associations we have with foreign lands. O'Barr suggests that images that, for example, link lingerie to Africa through the use of a black model in apparently "primitive" clothing or that connect perfume to China or India by associating the product with Chinese art and characters or the Taj Mahal tell us stories about these foreign societies. The irony is that the products—in this case the lingerie or perfume—have nothing to do with societies in Africa, China, or India; the images of "others" are used to promote products made and used in the West.

Why, then, do ads draw upon such images? O'Barr argues that the images of foreign lands are intended to suggest that the products are exotic or romantic. In so doing, they suggest that Africans, Chinese, or Indians are different from Americans, often depicting them as more primitive, and particularly, more sexual. These associations are intended to make the products attractive while simultaneously reaffirming that foreigners are fundamentally different.

Images of foreigners in ads for travel and products highlight difference, depicting an "other" who is subordinate to, but a source of pleasure for, American tourists and consumers. The ideology underlying these images about the place of the United States in the contemporary global order differs little from the messages in earlier ad images of foreigners. But the globalization of the economy has produced a new ad image of the foreigner: the potential business partner.

When the issue is international business, ad images no longer suggest difference, which might be an obstacle to conducting business. Instead, images of foreigners in international business ads emphasize that Americans and foreigners share a perspective and have a common set of goals. Foreign businesspeople are depicted not as "others"—as an exotic or threatening "them"—but as people just like us. These ads are directed at a much more limited audience—international businesspeople—than are the travel or product ads. Business ads, however, do suggest that there is an alternative to the depiction of foreigners as others, even if it is now limited to the global corporate community.

The most widely circulating images of "otherness" in advertising convey messages about foreigners from a distinctly American point of view and suggest that there are fundamental differences between "us" and "them," that we have power in our relationships with "them," and that "they" are available to stimulate, entertain, and serve "us." Media in a global culture may provide more images of foreign people and lands—and international business ads suggest that new kinds of images are emerging—but the underlying message in advertisements about *who we are* and *who they are* draws upon age-old assumptions about the relationship between powerful Americans and subordinate foreigners.

Conclusion

This chapter has looked at the content of mass media by adopting an ideological approach. We have reviewed the underlying theoretical frameworks of ideological analysis and examined several specific cases to detect ideology at work in mass media. As our examples suggest, there is no singular ideology that is promoted by popular media. Researchers who study the ideology of media are interested in the underlying stories about society that the media tell, the range of values that the media legitimize, and the kinds of behaviors that are deemed normal. Most popular media promote, often in subtle and even contradictory ways, perspectives that support our basic social arrangements and endorse the legitimacy of social institutions, marginalizing attitudes and behaviors that are considered to be out of the "mainstream."

Media images can and sometimes do challenge this mainstream, status quo–oriented ideology by providing a critique of contemporary social organization and norms, but commercialization makes it difficult for media to maintain a critical voice. The search for popularity, wider distribution, and profitability tends to dull the critical edges of media imagery, pushing media back toward more mainstream (and marketable) ideologies. There are, to be sure, media that consistently promote alternative ideological perspectives. Local weekly newspapers, journals of opinion, public access television, and independent films are often quite self-conscious about providing perspectives that differ from the dominant popular media. These alternatives, however, remain on the margins of the media scene, reaching small audiences and lacking the capital to mount a serious challenge to the dominant media.

We have explored the ideology of the media texts themselves, examining the underlying perspectives within the images that confront us every day, but we have not yet taken up the potential *impact* of media messages. To fully understand the ideology of media, we must look at the meanings actual audiences attach to the media they read, watch, and listen to. We also need to explore the ways in which media are a part of the political world and our everyday social interaction. Having examined media production and media content, we turn in Part Four to the ways the media influence contemporary social and political life.

Audiences
Meaning and Influence

Part Four focuses on the relationship between audiences and the mass media. Building upon our previous discussion of media production and media content, we round out our sociological analysis of media by examining both how the media influence the social world and how human activity shapes the interpretation and use of media.

Chapter 7 explores the indirect influence of mass media on our political life, focusing on how news media coverage has helped transform elections and on how various political actors use the media as a strategic resource. Chapter 8 turns directly to mass media audiences—people like us—who ultimately view, read, and listen to mass media. The chapter explores the ways audiences actively construct meaning from media messages rather than passively receiving prefabricated messages. Chapter 9 shifts the focus to the role of media technologies and examines the different kinds of interaction that are facilitated by the different forms of media. The chapter explores how media technologies shape social communication as well as how people influence the development of media technologies. ■

CHAPTER 7

Media Influence
and the Political World

In the past half-century, the mass media have helped to fundamentally alter the nature of American politics. Among the most important political events in each of the last five decades were the McCarthy hearings in the 1950s, the Vietnam War in the 1960s, Watergate in the 1970s, the election of Ronald Reagan in the 1980s, and the Persian Gulf War in the 1990s. Each of these developments was profoundly influenced by mass media exposure. Through nationally televised congressional hearings and press conferences, Senator Joe McCarthy used the media's soapbox to peddle his extreme and often unsubstantiated brand of anticommunism. The conflict in Vietnam was America's first "television war"; the media brought the brutal realities of modern warfare—and the widespread opposition to it—into American living rooms. The print media, especially the *Washington Post*, played the central role in exposing the Watergate scandal. The Reagan era set the standard for mediated politics as a former Hollywood actor and his staff skillfully manipulated news coverage. Finally, the Gulf War featured a massive government effort to manage the media by strictly controlling the flow of information and images available to them.

As we saw earlier, media are affected by the constraints of legal and informal political pressures, as well as by the economic forces that shape the media industry. However, the media's impact on the political world is real and undeniable. The media are formidable actors who, within the structural constraints already examined, influence the political world in a variety of ways. This influence reaches not only presidents and political elites, but also ordinary citizens.

The media industry, most directly, is a powerful lobbyist for its interests. Media corporations have organized themselves into specialized lobbying groups that cater to different segments of the media industry. The Motion Picture Producers and Distributors Association of America, the Magazine Publishers Association, the National Association of Broadcasters, and the American Newspaper Publishing Association are but a few examples of these groups. When legislation that might affect a particular segment of the industry is being discussed in Congress, the media's political lobbyists spring into action—and sometimes even draft sections of proposed legislation.

The media industry has long lobbied for the elimination of regulations that constrain its activities. In the 1993–94 election period, the political action committees of the telecommunications industry contributed nearly $7 million to politicians from both parties (McChesney, 1995). It was no accident, then, that media "deregulation" became a key legislative priority of the newly elected Republican majority in Congress, culminating in the 1996 Telecommunications Act. Such is the power of the industry's direct lobbying.

This chapter, however, focuses on the media's more *indirect* influence on political life. The bulk of the chapter is devoted to the role of print and broadcast news media in the electoral process. We look at both how media involvement has changed the behavior of politicians and how media coverage has affected voters. In turn, we consider how political actors have adapted by incorporating the media into their repertoire of political strategies. Like other social relationships, that between the media and the political world involves both structural constraint and human agency.

However, politics is more than just voting, and the political impact of the media emanates from more than just the news media. Therefore, we also consider the media's impact on social-movement efforts and look briefly at the political implications of film, entertainment television, music, and new media technologies. Again, we highlight the structure–agency dynamic. This time we explore how media can be active agents in affecting the political structure while at the same time serving as an institutional structure used by political actors to achieve success.

Media and Political Elites

Too often, commentators discuss media influence solely in terms of the potential impact on regular citizens. For example, the question of whether the news media affect voting behavior is a perennial favorite among researchers. However, the most profound and direct influence of the media on the political world probably takes place at the level of political elites. The media's influence on a hundred politicians has much more significant and pronounced implications than their influence on a hundred regular voters. It is insiders—politicians, lobbyists, campaign managers, financial contributors, and so forth—who pay closest attention to, and are most likely to be influenced by, the media. Nowhere is this more evident than in the changes in political campaigns in response to media coverage.

Politicians have long understood the potential power of the mass media. The print media, for a time, were directly associated with political parties. When broadcast media emerged, politicians quickly saw their possibilities for influence. Herbert Hoover launched a successful presidential bid over the radio. Franklin Roosevelt used radio "fireside chats" to communicate with the public during the Depression. Dwight Eisenhower used television campaign commercials in 1952, and the Kennedy campaign in 1960 solidified the influence of television on American politics that has continued to this day. Today, we can hardly overestimate the media's influence on election campaigns and the running of government.

The Media in Political Campaigns

Media considerations are perhaps the single most important factor around which candidates organize electoral campaigns. This is especially true for presidential and congressional elections, but many of the following observations apply to state and local elections as well.

At its simplest level, we see the importance of media in the fact that a telegenic style and appearance greatly enhance a candidate's chance of success. That is, looking and acting comfortable on television can aid a candidate's cause. All major campaigns have media "handlers," consultants who coach candidates on improving their appearance in the media. An early indication of the importance of appearance was the infamous presidential debate between Kennedy and Nixon in 1960. The debate was televised, but Nixon declined to wear the heavy makeup that aides recommended. On camera, he appeared haggard and in need of a shave, while Kennedy's youthful and vibrant appearance was supported by the layer of television makeup he wore. The significance of this difference in appearance became apparent after the debate. Polls showed that a slim majority of those who heard the debate on the radio thought Nixon had won, while an equally slim majority of those who watched the debate on television gave the edge to Kennedy. After this dramatic event, the fear of not performing well in televised debates so intimidated presidential hopefuls that it was 16 years before another debate was televised.

The lesson was clear: Appearance matters. Telegenic individuals who have experience in dealing with the media are at a decided advantage in the political realm. Media coverage of elections, especially on television, tends to highlight images. News accounts of elections emphasize personal stories, personalities, and preplanned campaign events and are less likely to explain the background and implications of substantive issues and policy debates (Graber, 1980). The result of expanded media coverage has, in many ways, been a loss of substance in favor of appearance.

Celebrity politicians from former actor (and later president) Ronald Reagan to former basketball player (and later senator) Bill Bradley to former pop music star (and later member of Congress) Sonny Bono have all used their media skills and celebrity in pursuing political careers. Ronald Reagan's reputation as the "great communicator" was surely in part the result of the training he received as actor, radio personality, and ad salesman. His oratorical skills were largely limited to scripted events. He was notorious for misstating facts and for rambling, sometimes incoherently, when faced with spontaneous speaking situations. On occasion, he even confused his movie roles with real-life experiences. The ability of his staff to maintain the president's polished public image was central to his success.

After the first two years of poor showings in the polls, the Reagan presidency was marked by high public popularity—even though polls showed most Americans disagreeing with many of Reagan's key policy positions. Some took this result to be the ultimate triumph of image over substance. As Reagan's own chief of staff, Donald Regan (1988, p. 248), admitted, "Every moment of every public appearance was scheduled, every word was scripted, every place where Reagan was expected to stand was chalked with toe marks. The President was always being prepared for a performance, and this had the inevitable effect of preserving him from confrontation and the genuine interplay of opinion, question, and argument that form the basis of decision."

The 1996 presidential election once again highlighted the importance of being telegenic in contemporary politics. Youthful and publicly affable Bill Clinton had a distinct advantage over the older and more sullen Bob Dole, who often appeared uncomfortable in the media spotlight.

The significance of television images goes well beyond the specific appearance of the candidate to include the more general visual context in which a candidate appears. In this regard, too, observers generally point to Ronald Reagan's campaign and presidency as the epitome of the masterful use of visuals to enhance a candidate's image. Both during the campaign and after the election victory, the Reagan team showed remarkable skill at manipulating media coverage by providing television with an irresistible visual to support the "line of the day"—the message the White House wanted the media to emphasize in that day's reporting. In this way, they could direct media coverage—at least in visual terms—by making it efficient for the news media to use the visual settings they had orchestrated. The administration even coordinated the 1986 bombing of Libya to coincide with the start of the evening news (Kellner, 1990). Michael Deaver, the Reagan White House media specialist, later pointed out that he and his staff found television reporters quite "manageable" because he gave "the nightly news good theater, a good visual every evening and pretty much did their job for them" ("Nightline," September 27, 1989).

The use of media by presidential candidates is not a partisan matter. Democratic president Bill Clinton lifted a page or two from the Reagan playbook during his tenure in the Oval Office. When Clinton had a credibility problem with the military, he dressed in a leather flight jacket and visited U.S. troops on an aircraft carrier—creating strong visual images for the evening news. To promote Clinton's image as a world leader, his staff took advantage of a New York visit by Russian president Boris Yeltsin to stage a photo opportunity. The evening news and the next day's newspapers featured the image of the two men sitting outdoors deep in conversation, with an idyllic fall foliage backdrop. The careful construction of such photo opportunities has become a routine part of presidential politics. Most of the pictures we see of the president are likely to have been scripted ahead of time by collaborative "advance teams" of reporters and political aides who scout out the best angles for photo opportunities at upcoming events. Using stand-ins for the president and his entourage, these advance teams often stage practice photos that they later distribute to the media. These photos, along with notes about the camera lenses likely to produce the best results, are then used by photojournalists in planning their coverage of the "real" event.

Postmodernist theorists, especially Baudrillard (e.g., 1983), have argued that the rising importance of images signals a new kind of "reality." In postmodern society, they argue, the image has come to replace the "real." As a result, the public is often unable to distinguish between image and reality. While most postmodernists ignore the central economic issues that affect the rise and prominence of media, they alert us to the troublesome growth in the manipulation of media images. The practical application of postmodernist theory to the political world suggests that substantive policy debates will continue to take a backseat to polished, telegenic candidates and scripted photo opportunities. For example, as the visuals of television news coverage have increased in importance, the use of excerpts from candidates' speeches has declined. The average "sound bite" on network television has shrunk over the years to just a few seconds. Also, the 1996 national political conventions marked an unprecedented level of media manipulation as tightly scripted control of the proceedings resulted in virtual "infomercials" for each party.

Candidates have complete control over media images when they produce their campaign commercials. Television advertising has become a central part of most electoral campaigns. In 1992, billionaire Ross Perot spent millions of dollars on his first presidential bid. In 1996, multimillionaire and political newcomer Steve Forbes made a serious bid for the Republican presidential nomination based largely on his ability to personally pay for millions of dollars worth of television advertising. While it's easy to dismiss the impact of such clearly self-interested efforts, some evidence suggests that voters receive more information about candidates from campaign commercials than from news coverage (McClure and Patterson, 1976).

Increasingly, campaign ads have relied upon negative "attack" formats to achieve maximum effect. The infamous "Willie Horton" ad used to support the Bush campaign in 1988 is one example of a powerful—and, many argued, racist—political ad. Willie Horton was a black prisoner who had attacked a white woman while on a prison furlough. The ad featured the mug shot of Horton and the image of prisoners leaving through a revolving door. It attacked Democratic candidate Michael Dukakis for being soft on crime by supporting the furlough program. After the 1988 campaign, pollster Lou Harris (in Kellner, 1990, p. 133) suggested that "the simple story of this election is that the Bush commercials worked and the Dukakis commercials have not."

More generally, staffs now organize campaigns with two primary tasks in mind: fund-raising and media exposure. Campaign organizers develop a candidate's schedule according to media needs. They are highly conscious of media markets they are trying to reach and media deadlines they are trying to accommodate. Often the only handshaking and baby-kissing that take place in today's campaigns are those staged for maximum media coverage. Campaign staffs time speeches, rallies, and personal meetings with voters on the street to coordinate with media deadlines. Press releases and photo opportunities, of course, are also part of the routine.

Polls and Pundits

The American news media are notorious for their "horse race" coverage of elections. Too often, critics contend, the media are less interested in where candidates stand on the issues than in their electability as measured by polls. Such coverage highlights tactics rather than substance.

Highly publicized poll results have potential implications for knowledge about, interest in, and support for candidates, but definitive empirical evidence of these effects does not yet exist. The impact of media polls can be especially important to campaign consultants, staff, journalists, and especially financial contributors. Candidates who can demonstrate their electability by doing well in early polls are much more likely to attract the campaign contributions—before any votes are cast—that are essential to run an effective campaign. Thus, poll results may represent a self-fulfilling prophecy.

The effect on regular voters, though, is less clear. The danger is that, especially for those with little involvement with or knowledge about candidates, poll results can signal how people *ought* to vote instead of reflecting existing voter preference. This would make it extremely difficult for third-party candidates and other "dark horses" to be successful. Some studies provide evidence that voter judgment of what others believe does affect candidate preference and that polls showing a clear front-runner depress voter turnout (Traugott, 1992). Both of these findings suggest that publicized polls may have a potentially significant impact on voters.

The media's emphasis on winners and losers continues even after the campaigns are over. Journalists and pundits on public affairs programs often interpret political news through a lens that highlights the ups and downs of political careers rather than the substantive content of policy proposals (Fallows, 1996). The sports metaphor of "winning" and "losing" dominates political life. When journalists ask "Who won the week?" they inevitably give *their* interpretation of events. According to critic Jay Rosen (1993, p. 9), "The question . . . permits the media to play time-keeper, umpire, and finally, judge. The question would not occur to an ordinary citizen, but it remains a favorite of pundits and reporters because it appears to place the press on the outside of a process—the shaping of perceptions—that is profoundly affected by what the press itself does." The negative impact of such media coverage permeates political life. "By now even the denizens of the White House think they've achieved something by 'winning the week.' They fret and fuss when the week, according to the pundits, has been lost." These comments by Rosen highlight the dual impact of media coverage—it potentially affects voters and political elites alike.

The Decline of Political Parties and Institutions

As the media have become more important in political campaigns, political party organizations have become less important. In American politics, political parties used to maintain a grassroots organization that contacted voters, educated them about candidates, and encouraged them to vote. This system resulted in an intricate infrastructure of party workers, often organized down to the urban "block captain." For the most part, such organizational structures have ceased to exist. Also in decline are a range of other "mediating institutions" (Greider, 1992)—especially labor unions —that used to serve as structures to organize and mobilize groups of ordinary citizens. These institutions served as links between the public and the political process.

Now, mass media serve as the vehicles for conveying political messages and mobilizing voters. Candidates spend the vast bulk of campaign finances on producing and airing campaign commercials. Rather than being active participants in dialogues about issues and candidates, citizens increasingly are becoming an audience for televised debates and political commercials that sell the latest candidate. Public service campaigns to encourage voting (as seen on MTV, for example) do nothing to create any lasting political structure. Instead, such endeavors promote voting as an individual act devoid of any long-term political commitment. Ads sell candidates/products to voters/consumers in a way that blurs the line between politics and commerce.

The decline of party structures has been accompanied by a decline in party allegiance. In the 1940s, when researchers conducted early studies of voters, the most important determinant of a person's vote was party affiliation, followed by group allegiance, perception of the candidate's personality, and consideration of issues. After a half-century of media coverage, the order of importance has changed. Now, in presidential campaigns, the candidate's personality is of greatest importance to voters, followed by the issues, party membership, and group membership (Graber, 1980). The media, which communicate a great deal about personality and issues, have taken on an increasingly significant political role, while the influence of other institutions has declined.

Media and Individual Citizens

We usually cannot, or do not, experience firsthand the goings on of public life. Consequently, as citizens, we are partially reliant on the news media for an informative and accurate account of what is happening in the world around us. That is why the media are such an important element of the democratic process. Citizens in a democracy need adequate information to make informed decisions and to take appropriate political action.

Media Effects: From Influence to Interaction

Given the media's central role in the political process, it's no wonder that researchers have repeatedly asked questions about how the media affect that process. The answers that have emerged over the decades range from simple models emphasizing direct media influence to more sophisticated analyses highlighting the interaction of media and audience.

The Hypodermic Model

The earliest speculation about media effects suggested a direct and powerful influence on the public. Some commentators wrote of a "hypodermic" (or "silver bullet") model, with the media injecting a message directly into the "bloodstream" of the public. The anecdotal evidence for this belief dates at least as far back as the Spanish-American War in 1898 when, as one historical account (Palmer and Colton, 1978, p. 612) puts it, "The newspapers, especially the new 'yellow' press, roused the American public to a fury of moral indignation and imperial self-assertion."

The introduction of broadcast technology only raised further concern about the media's influence. Everything from government propaganda efforts during the two world wars to the famous panic caused by Orson Welles's 1939 radio broadcast of *War of the Worlds* suggested that the media could directly manipulate a passive and gullible public. In the 1990s, when some popular critics warned against violent rap lyrics *causing* anti-social behavior or against portrayals of lesbians and gays *promoting* homosexuality, they hearkened back to this vision of all-powerful media.

Mass Society Theory

A broader current of sociological theory that also suggested the potential for dramatic media influence was the mass society theory of the post–World War II years (e.g., Kornhauser, 1959; Reisman, 1953). Although it existed in various forms, at the core of the theory was the argument that then-contemporary society was characterized by growing homogenization of the population and a decline in interpersonal and group relations. At its base, the theory suggested the decline of more traditional personal bonds. The traditional extended family was giving way to smaller (and, later, fragmented) nuclear families whose members, because of work and school, spent less time with one another. Strong religious ties gave way to more perfunctory religious, or even secular, identities. A "melting pot" culture discouraged ethnic-group identity. Cohesive neighborhoods and community participation declined with the rise of dispersed and isolated suburbs. Work in large, corporate-owned organizations became more and more alienating.

While mass society theorists saw trends toward isolation and depersonalization in postwar America, they also noticed the rise in mass media, especially television. They argued that these mass media played a crucial role in uniting (and homogenizing) a disparate and atomized population. Stripped of significant personal ties, the mass population was especially susceptible to the influence of media messages. The language of mass society was perhaps best suited to totalitarian regimes. Indeed, it was concern over the use of propaganda in Nazi Germany and the Soviet Union that motivated much of the early research. However, the notion of an alienated public tuned in to mass media to gain some semblance of collective identity may not seem farfetched in today's media-saturated society. Although mass society theory per se has not continued as a vibrant thread of thought, many of the concerns raised by the original theory have lived on in other research traditions.

The Minimal Effects Model

Belief in an all-powerful media did not hold up under the scrutiny of early empirical research. In a classic study of voters, *The People's Choice,* Lazarsfeld, Berelson, and Gaudet (1948) argued that the media's impact on individuals was weak and short-lived. This "minimal effects" model suggested that media messages acted to reinforce existing belief rather than to change opinion. The authors suggested that social characteristics such as class and religion were more important than the media in explaining voter behavior. In part, this is because people who pay close attention to the news media tend to already have strong political beliefs, and thus media messages are less likely to affect them. People who are more likely to be undecided and uninterested are less likely to pay attention to media coverage.

Whatever effect the media did have, they argued, was often achieved through a "two-step flow of influence." The media transmitted information to opinion leaders who tended to pay close attention to the news media. These leaders, in turn, could influence those with whom they had personal contact. Some theorists also argued that interpersonal contact was more influential than the media in effecting a change in belief, because it involved the desire for social acceptance that is part of all direct human interaction.

The problem with the earlier hypodermic model was that it left out the active agency of the reader of media messages. Taken literally, this early model ignored the preexisting ideas and orientation of the reader. The minimal effects model gave more weight to the ability of the reader to select, screen, and judge media information. The reader, after all, is not a passive sponge soaking up media messages but an active, thinking individual capable of ignoring or resisting media messages.

Agenda Setting

The minimal effects approach to the media reigned until the late 1960s, when researchers increasingly accepted the "agenda-setting" role of the media. In a classic phrasing of the argument, Bernard Cohen (1963, p. 13) claimed that the news "may not be successful in telling people what to think, but it is stunningly successful in telling its readers what to think about." This ability to direct people's attention toward certain issues became known as agenda setting. It highlighted the important role that journalists play in selecting and shaping the news. Researchers empirically examined Cohen's claim by studying undecided voters in the 1968 presidential election (McCombs and Shaw, 1972; 1977). They found a remarkable similarity between the media's issue focus and the issue agenda of undecided voters. While this finding showed a correlation between the media's agenda and the agenda of voters, the study's design did not allow for determining a causal relationship.

Funkhouser (1973) tackled the issue by looking at three sources of data: (1) public opinion polls regarding the most important issues facing the nation, (2) media coverage in the nation's top three weekly news-magazines, and (3) statistical indicators measuring the "reality" of key issue areas. Confirming earlier findings, Funkhouser found substantial correlation between public opinion and media coverage. More important, he found that neither public opinion nor media coverage correlated well with statistical indicators of the "real" world. For example, media cover-age and public concern regarding the Vietnam War peaked *before* the greatest number of U.S. troops were sent there. Media coverage and pub-lic concern about unrest on college campuses and in urban areas also peaked *before* the period in which the greatest number of campus demon-strations and urban riots took place. This suggested that the media's cov-erage of issues affected public opinion more than the issues' objective prominence in the "real" world. It also showed that media coverage did not necessarily reflect real-world trends.

Simple experimental work examining this agenda-setting function of the media later confirmed a causal relationship between media coverage and the issue agenda of the audience. Iyengar and Kinder (1987) showed test participants different videotapes of edited television news broadcasts. The different versions of the broadcasts were the same, with one excep-tion. The researchers added stories to the tapes so that some participants saw pieces either on the environment, on national defense, or on inflation. Tests before and after viewing showed that those issues the researchers had highlighted in each of the doctored broadcasts were more likely to be chosen by participants as important. Researchers found some agenda-setting effects after the viewing of only a single broadcast. However, most effects took place only after participants had watched several of the altered newscasts.

While the agenda-setting function of the media is now firmly estab-lished, it is neither simple nor complete. Brosius and Kepplinger (1990) coupled a year-long content analysis of German television news programs with weekly public opinion polls on the most important issues of the day. They found strong agenda-setting effects on some issues. However, on other issues, either public concern largely *preceded* media coverage, or the two simply didn't correlate well. This kind of finding suggests the neces-sity for caution in assessing the media's role in setting the public agenda. Perhaps agenda setting is most pronounced when individuals have no direct contact with an issue and thus are dependent on the media for information. Perception of issues that directly impact an individual's life may be more resistant to media influence.

The agenda-setting approach has traditionally looked at who sets the public agenda. Evidence points convincingly to the news media. However, this begs the question of who sets the news media's agenda. The answer here is not so simple. As we have shown at various points in this book, a number of important influences affect the functioning of the media, including the demands imposed by corporate owners to ensure economic profitability, the role of sources and public relations agencies in initiating stories, and the "gatekeeping" and professional norms of journalism. This last factor is highlighted in a comparative study of U.S. and British media coverage of national elections (Semetko et al., 1991). In Britain, the study found a close correlation between the media's agenda and the issues being promoted by the political parties. In the United States, the correlation between media and party agendas was much weaker. The researchers found that U.S. journalists use more professional discretion in framing a campaign, often by discussing its strategic and tactical features. We can interpret this reportorial stance of the U.S. media either as independence or as renegade negativism. Whether such a stance serves the public well is a question for debate.

The Gap Between Theory and Popular Perception

For some time, many researchers accepted the idea that media could influence the public's agenda while having little impact on what people believed—in essence, a move from "minimal effects" to "limited effects." This idea contrasted sharply with the public's general perception that media play a *very* influential role in society. There are three major reasons for this gap in perceptions (Graber, 1980).

First, most research has looked only at a narrow range of media effects issues. For example, researchers looked at the most convenient unit of analysis: voters. If voters did not change their minds as a result of media exposure, the argument went, then there was no media influence. Since researchers conducted these influential early studies at a time when party loyalty was strong, they found little change in voter preference based on media influence. However, this research did not gauge the range of possible media effects in other, less predetermined situations.

Second, research sometimes mistakenly equated the absence of factual learning from the media with the absence of media influence, in essence ignoring more complex or unintended effects. For example, a study of a media campaign to promote awareness of environmental pollution found that people learned very few of the facts highlighted in the campaign. However, there was an unintended effect. After the campaign, people were more likely to blame big business for most pollution (Graber, 1980). By overemphasizing the transmission of factual information, researchers may be missing some of the evidence of media influence.

Finally, researchers have had great difficulty clearly measuring media effects, because media stimuli routinely interact with other social stimuli. Disentangling these multiple influences is extremely difficult, and, as a result, clear evidence of direct media influence is difficult to obtain. Still, more recent trends in media research seem to point toward a dual concern with the power of audiences to interpret media and with the subtler influences of media.

Media–Reader Interaction

As we will highlight in Chapter 8, recent trends in media research have paid more attention to how the audience actively uses information. This focus shines the light of inquiry on the dynamic interaction between media and reader.

Various studies, using a range of methods, have also shown that media information is but one element that citizens use in developing political beliefs. Over the course of a year, Doris Graber (1988) monitored the media while at the same time conducting intensive interviews with 21 participants. Her interviews revealed that while people used media information to make sense of public issues, what they knew about these issues was not limited to the information the media supplied. Silvo Lenart (1994) used experimental data to argue that media information and interpersonal communication "are complementary halves of the total information whole." William Gamson (1992) showed how regular working people in his focus-group study constructed meaning by combining media-based information with popular wisdom and experiential knowledge. His study treated the media as a tool or resource which people can use, to varying degrees, to help them make sense of current events. While accepting the potential influence of the media, this approach balances media power with the creative agency of readers.

Political Socialization Theory

We must understand media effects in subtler terms than simply their ability to change the mind of a potential voter. The long-term, cumulative effect of exposure to mass media needs to be considered as well.

Media influence may be especially strong in the early political socialization of adolescents, who are old enough to seriously consider political issues but have not yet fully developed a political orientation. For example, high school students say they rely on the mass media more than on families, friends, or teachers in developing attitudes about current events such as economic or race issues (Graber, 1980). This runs counter to the "two-step" model of influence, which sees personal interaction as more influential than media exposure. We can speculate that the influence of the media may have increased since the 1950s and 1960s as children and adolescents have spent more and more time with the mass media. Exposure to the mass media is now a central means by which young people learn and internalize the values, beliefs, and norms of our political system, a socialization that lays the foundation for much of later political life. As we will see below, the lessons of such socialization sometimes emanate from entertainment television as well as news and public affairs media. Research suggests that children's early support for the political system usually gives way to growing disillusionment in the teen years, but this skepticism often dissipates as teens become young adults (Graber, 1980).

Cultivation Theory

Another brand of theory that addresses the cumulative impact of media on the public is cultivation theory. This theory is based on a project by George Gerbner and his associates (1994; Signorielli and Morgan, 1990) that for over 20 years examined the impact of growing up and living with television. They argue that, through its regular and almost ritualistic use by viewers, television plays a homogenizing role for otherwise heterogeneous populations. Influence occurs because of continued and lengthy exposure to television in general, not just exposure to individual programs or genres.

They suggest that immersion in television culture produces a "mainstreaming" effect, whereby differences based on cultural, social, and political characteristics are muted in heavy viewers of television. The result is that heavy television viewers internalize many of the distorted views of the social and political world presented by television (such as those discussed in Chapter 5). For example, compared to the real world, television programs drastically underrepresent older people, and heavy viewers tend to similarly underestimate the number of older people in society. Television portrays crime and violence much more frequently than it occurs in real life, and these television portrayals seem to influence heavy viewers in this area as well. Heavy viewers are more likely than moderate or light viewers to believe that most people cannot be trusted and that most people are selfishly looking out for themselves (Gerbner et al., 1994).

The impact of television cultivation on political belief seems to be in a conservative direction (Gerbner et al., 1982; 1984). A journalistic pose of an "objective" balancing of views seems to encourage heavy viewers to avoid calling themselves either "conservatives" or "liberals." However, self-described "moderates" who are heavy television viewers actually hold beliefs that are closer to those of conservatives than to those of liberals on a whole range of social issues, such as race, abortion, and homosexuality. On economic issues, heavy viewers are more likely than moderate or light viewers to adopt the conservative call for lower taxes, but they are also more likely to support a populist call for more social services.

Lessons from the Research

Research on the media's impact on citizens highlights the tension between media influence and reader agency. Media messages are negotiated by readers, but these messages can have an impact. Media influence what people think about and, to a lesser extent, how they understand the world.

For example, one of the most talked about issues in the 1990s was the growth of cynicism and alienation in the American electorate. For some time, observers have argued that media coverage of the political world has contributed to this rise in cynicism, undermining the democratic process (Entman, 1989; Goldfarb, 1991; Robinson, 1976; Rosen, 1993). Among the arguments is the claim that the press promotes cynicism and undermines its credibility when it focuses superficially on the ups and downs of individual politicians. Too often, critics argue, the media suggest that "yet another president is a bumbling clown, that government is a hopeless mess, that politics repays no serious effort to attend to it. Mindlessly, the press contributes to these perceptions and then stands back to survey the damage as if it were some naturally occurring disaster" (Rosen, p. 9).

However, the influence of the media is neither blatant nor unqualified. Perhaps the most significant effects of media exposure come about after long-term, heavy use. As we will see in Chapter 8, readers approach media products with a preexisting set of beliefs and experiences through which they filter media messages. Readers also occupy specific social positions that affect how they interpret the media. In order to understand the impact of media, therefore, we must remember that media consumption is often an active processing of information, not just a passive reception of media words and images.

Media and Social Movements

We have highlighted media effects on political elites and individual citizens. We now turn our attention to the media's coverage of social movements—groups of citizens who have banded together to promote a social or political cause. Social movements are an especially important part of the political landscape because they can mediate between individual citizens and political elites.

We can think of the relationship between media and social movements as a transaction between two complex systems, each trying to accomplish a particular goal. Movements ask the media to communicate their message to the public, while the media look to movements as one potential source of "news." However, the media hold the upper hand in their relationship with social movements. Movements usually need the mass media to widely publicize their activities. Such coverage helps social movements mobilize support, achieve validation as a significant political player, and expand the scope of conflict to attract potential allies or mediators. The media, on the other hand, have many alternatives to social movements as news sources (Gamson and Wolfsfeld, 1993).

The task that faces social movements, therefore, is twofold. First, they must convince media gatekeepers that they are worthy of coverage; that is, that they represent an interesting story angle or are a significant "player" in the issue at hand. This task involves the direct issue of media access. Small grassroots organizations that do not achieve what the media consider to be "player" status often have to resort to dramatic actions, such as demonstrations and protests, to attract the media's attention.

Second, social movements must work to influence the nature of the media coverage they receive. This task involves the struggle over "framing" messages (Gamson and Modigliani, 1989; Gitlin, 1980; Snow et al., 1986; Tuchman, 1978). A frame generally refers to the context into which the media place facts. Frames organize information and help make it intelligible. For example, imagine the case of an environmental group suing a corporation to prevent the construction of a new facility that it believes will harm the local environment. The news reports about this issue might frame it as a story of David versus Goliath—the little local environmental group versus the big multinational corporation. However, the news reports could also frame the story as a handful of unreasonable extremists trying to stop rational progress. The first frame might help the movement mobilize support. The second frame would probably hurt their efforts. Movements, then, try to influence the coverage they receive in the media.

Gaining access to media coverage by staging dramatic actions can be counterproductive for a movement if the media use a discrediting frame in their coverage. Discrediting techniques used by the media include downplaying content in favor of emphasizing the spectacle of an event, painting demonstrators as deviant and unrepresentative of the population, granting comparable coverage and thus "false balance" to a tiny number of counterdemonstrators, and undercounting the attendance at demonstrations (Parenti, 1986).

As with electoral politics, the media's desire for succinct sound bites and interesting visuals has a significant impact on social-movement efforts. Mass media will usually ignore movements that are unable to accommodate journalists' needs. Although pandering to media desires for dramatic visuals risks undermining the effective communication of a movement's message, proactive planning is a necessity if movements are to do all they can to develop favorable media coverage (Ryan, 1991). Grassroots citizens' organizations with few resources for public relations and media strategizing are at a distinct disadvantage when they face off against well-funded government agencies, corporations, and other organizations, especially when these movements are challenging mainstream norms.

"New Media" and the News

Television and newspapers continue to dominate the world of news. However, the nature of these media is being changed and supplemented by the introduction of so-called "new" media. The problem with specifying "new" media is, of course, that such lists quickly become dated. These lists also miss the point of new media, since one of the most important aspects of these media is their "convergence" into a single form of multimedia communication. While complete convergence is unlikely to occur for some time, some of the more recent technologies—computers and cable television with interactive capabilities, for example—have already changed the political landscape.

Since the early 1980s, political actors, especially political elites, have been using new technologies in their attempt to communicate with the public. In a combination of campaign advertising and direct-mail solicitation, presidential candidates have distributed videocassettes to voters. Candidates have used satellites to set up interviews on local television stations, thereby avoiding the more aggressive (and, usually, better informed) national news media. Electronic mail and fax machines are already staples of election campaigns. The computer Internet is the site of many "home pages" for political candidates and public officials. These few examples demonstrate how agency by political actors has influenced the application of media.

Social movements, too, have tried to use some of these new technologies. The declining cost of computers and laser printers has allowed desktop publishers to more easily produce alternative media products such as newsletters and magazines. The computer Internet is also home to many discussion groups and home pages that focus on political issues.

The future of these new technologies is being intensely debated. Some see great hope for new technologies, while others warn about potential dangers (Abramson, Arterton, and Orren, 1988). For example, videotext involves delivering text and graphic material through telephone or cable wires to a home computer–like terminal. Users of such a system could develop "personalized" newspapers that present information only on stories in which a reader had already expressed an interest. Responding to your pattern of interests, your electronic "paper" might deliver baseball scores, but not golf or tennis results; it might feature stories on the environment, but not on crime. Would such capabilities encourage learning about social and political issues by tailoring information to individual needs and interests? Or would such a system further fragment society by eliminating the possibility for common ground among citizens?

Other technologies, too, could have an impact on our political process. Interactive television could be used for "electronic town meetings," incorporating instant plebiscites on issues of the day. Could this be a technological fix for our ailing democracy, or would those with the power to set the agenda for these programs manipulate such an arrangement? Would instant polling or voting be a positive development, or would such a technique simply record emotional responses devoid of serious deliberation? Would people become more engaged in contemporary affairs, or would electronic town meetings just contribute to the further decline of face-to-face debate and deliberation? Such questions haunt the arrival of new technologies on the political landscape.

However, though studded with potential pitfalls, recent media technologies offer the potential for expanding useful political communication. For example, because it is transmitted through wire rather than the airwaves, cable television presents the intriguing possibility of specifying viewership. A station could broadcast a local school board meeting, for example, to all wired homes in that particular school district—but not to viewers in other districts. Because the meeting is unlikely to interest viewers outside the district, regular broadcast television stations would probably not carry it at all. Cable channels set aside for public affairs programs, though, could easily transmit such meetings, making them accessible to a larger number of people. Of course, not all homes have cable, and those that do not are disproportionately lower-income. Also, watching a meeting at home is not the same as being present and able to make one's views known. Still, such a simple step could be part of a larger move toward using media to enhance democratic participation.

Politics and Entertainment Media

Our discussion about the media's impact on political life has emphasized the most obvious and immediately relevant form of media: the news. Such "serious" media were long the focus of academic research. Until the 1980s, the academic community did not take "pop" culture or entertainment media very seriously. That situation, however, has changed. Recent work on nonnews media has begun to suggest that they have a profound importance in shaping (and often distorting) our understanding of the world. This section briefly considers a few examples of the political significance of nonnews media.

Television and Film

While it features some "newsmagazine" shows, we usually associate prime-time television with a variety of entertainment programs ranging from made-for-television movies to dramas and situation comedies. Such programs attract much larger audiences than news broadcasts. Most people usually think of such shows as "only entertainment," but they feature characters and storylines that directly or indirectly have political significance. All TV, in fact, is political. Not all writers and producers of television fare have an explicit political agenda—though many do—but we can interpret all media content from a political viewpoint. Most obviously open to political interpretation is programming that directly tackles social issues. Increasingly, TV movies, dramas, and sit-coms have addressed a wide range of social issues such as sexual abuse, racism, and homelessness (Lichter, Lichter, and Rothman, 1994).

However, political implications lie behind every type of cultural product, including entertainment television that is not explicitly political. Television programs were just as political when they *avoided* issues such as sexism and corporate corruption. Even situation comedies featuring characters who have nothing to do overtly with political issues make a normative political statement by their avoidance of politics. Refusing to take a stand is, in fact, taking one. Indeed, "nonpolitical" programs may be making the strongest political statements of all. In not questioning the status quo, such programs reinforce it by contributing to its "taken-for-granted" nature. Sometimes, by disparaging all politics or efforts at change, these shows may foster a cynicism and a fatalism that are dismissive of real efforts to promote change. Therefore, we can find much of the political implication of prime-time television in unstated assumptions.

A word of caution is in order when we are discussing the political role of entertainment television. There is no conspiracy at work to indoctrinate prime-time viewers. Instead, as we have seen, programming decisions are usually made on the basis of trying to satisfy the tastes of the viewing public—whatever the popular sentiment happens to be at the time (Gitlin, 1985). Commercial television, remember, is a for-profit enterprise in the business of delivering audiences to advertisers. It is not in the business of political proselytizing. Ratings and profits are the bottom line.

When researchers study viewers and not just the content of prime-time programming, they find the political impact of television to be complicated. The content of media does matter; however, audiences play an important role in interpreting what they see. For example, in the 1970s sitcom "All in the Family," heated arguments between the two main characters covered such political ground as the Vietnam War, race relations, and the status of women. How did such a program affect viewers? According to one study (Vidmar and Rokeach, 1974), the effects depended on the preconceptions of the viewer. On race, for example, the views of both liberals *and* the prejudiced were reinforced by watching the program.

"All in the Family" may have been unusual in the degree to which it routinely articulated clashing views. Most shows do not regularly feature views that are such polar opposites. However, even when they suggest a more singular worldview, entertainment programs are open to interpretation. Such was the case with the late-1980s hit "The Cosby Show." The program was a traditional professional-class family situation comedy, with one major exception: All the leading characters were black. Many critics hailed the program as a positive portrayal of African Americans rarely found on television. However, Jhally and Lewis (1992) found in their interviews with viewers that many of them were interpreting the show in a quite different light. White viewers interpreted the location of black characters within the elite world of the professional class (the mother was a lawyer, and the father was a doctor) as a sign that racial barriers no longer existed. The authors argue that, ironically, the program contributed to a new "enlightened racism" among these viewers. Black viewers, on the other hand, tended to welcome the positive portrayal of a sensitive, intelligent, and, most of all, successful black family. Jhally and Lewis, though, suggest that this reaction reinforces the stereotype that a positive image must equal a prosperous image.

Anecdotal evidence suggests that widely divergent interpretations of media content are common. For example, the comedy show M*A*S*H was a hit on CBS for 11 years. As it chronicled the trials and tribulations of a surgical unit during the Korean War, it presented antiauthoritarian and antiwar humor. The show's original writer, Larry Gelbart, wanted the program's message to be that war was futile. However, he left the show after four years because he feared that the original intent of the series had been defeated. Ironically, he felt that the show's long-term success routinized the characters' fatalistic acceptance of war. He may have been right.

One of the series' main actors, Mike Farrell, learned from his fan mail that audiences could interpret the same material in a multitude of ways. As he recounted, he received some letters that said, "'Boy, you guys make war look like fun,' and/or, 'After watching your show I've decided I'm going to sign up.'" Farrell commented, "I read those and I kind of shake my head, and I've written back and said, 'I don't quite understand how you can watch our show and come to that conclusion.'" But Farrell reported that he "also got a wonderful letter from a kid who said that he had intended to be a professional soldier, and after watching our show over the years he had seen that that's not what he wants to do, and as a matter of fact he's decided to become a priest" (in Gitlin, 1985, p. 217). One lesson is that, perhaps more so than with news coverage, viewers can interpret the ambiguous political messages of entertainment television in many different ways. We explore this topic in more depth in the next chapter.

As with television programs, the political content of popular films takes a back seat to their ability to turn a profit. Big-budget Hollywood films, especially, must appeal to a broad and diverse audience in order to be profitable. The political content of such films is often left ambiguous so as not to offend potential moviegoers (Prince, 1992). As a result, the biggest box-office hits—blockbusters like *ET, Star Wars, Raiders of the Lost Ark,* and *Batman*—are usually upbeat, feel-good, action-adventure films with cartoonlike characters and little serious content, political or otherwise.

While the political messages in the entertainment media may be ambiguous, some argue that they generally have conservative implications. In his review of political films of the 1980s—including films with Cold War, Vietnam, Latin American, and science fiction themes—Stephen Prince (1992) argues that such films are more likely to reinforce dominant political views than to promote alternatives for change. Even popular science fiction films of the era, such as *Blade Runner, Aliens, Robocop,* and *Total Recall,* which projected social problems into the future, generally did not offer political alternatives. By failing to explore possible alternatives, such films "can be viewed as reinforcing existing trends toward political passivity and feelings of social helplessness in the face of economic crisis" (p. 193).

Music

The world of music and music videos has its own set of political implications. Like television and film, music is generally a commercial product sold for profit. As such, producers must be cautious about promoting messages that alienate too many in the audience. Mainstream radio hits, therefore, are full of platitudes about love and—well—little else. It might be argued that, as a diversion from the problems of the day, such music helps maintain the status quo, though it does not contain an overt political message. Some forms of music, however, attract an audience precisely because they promote politically charged, controversial, or alternative views. Such music is especially significant because it tends to be much more meaningful to people who listen to it.

We can use the example of music to highlight a point about the construction of meaning in media (which we explore more fully in the next chapter). An ongoing interactive process is involved in the production and consumption of media products (Gottdiener, 1985). The producers of music (the corporate owners, not necessarily the bands) are usually interested in the creation of profit. In more theoretical terms, what is important to producers is the *exchange value* of the product (what it can be sold for). People who buy music have a totally different motivation. They want to play the CDs and enjoy the music. What is important to consumers is the *use value* of the product (the function it serves).

The process does not stop there. Those buying the music infuse the product with symbolic meaning (or *sign value*). Saying that you regularly listen to country music performer Garth Brooks or the band Hole or composer Philip Glass suggests something significant that goes beyond a difference in musical tastes. Music fans often infuse the music they like with meaning. Musical taste—especially a taste for music that is outside of the mainstream—can also signal a political orientation or a set of values. That is why alternative music is often associated with a broader subculture marked, for example, by fashion and style. Heavy metal's leather and chains, punk rock's dyed hair and body piercing, rap's hip-hop clothes, and grunge's flannel shirts all are relevant in this respect.

Producers—in the form of the corporations that sell music—do not attach the same kind of meaning to the products as consumers do. Many baby boomers have had the unpleasant shock of hearing a rock song that had special meaning for them transformed into supermarket Muzak. A media product with meaning to a consumer has been repackaged and stripped of meaning by producers.

Often, the meaning that is attached to music has political significance. But even in this case the music industry has learned how to adeptly manipulate articulations of dissent into viable, profitable commercial products. In some cases, these products may maintain the veneer of a rebellious alternative lifestyle, but in fact they have become well-controlled sources of corporate profit. For example, music that at one time may have represented anger toward and rejection of authority figures and the status quo—we are thinking here, especially, of rock, punk, and rap music—has been absorbed by corporate America and transformed into a commodity stripped of its political significance.

In the 1980s, punk rock, which thumbed its nose at the commercial slickness of mainstream music, was smoothed around the edges and repackaged as "New Wave" music. As we've seen, not long after rap's appearance as a powerful music of resistance, it was incorporated into corporate advertising strategies. The "Pillsbury Doughboy" even began rapping in order to sell cookie dough! The "grunge" movement of the early 1990s was grounded in local music scenes; featured low-cost, used-clothing fashions; and was seen by many of its fans as a rejection of corporate-dominated rock and fashion. However, grunge quickly became a major profitmaker for multinational corporations. By the mid-1990s, the grunge sensibility had been repackaged under labels such as "alternative" and "buzz" and represented a mainstream trend in the rock music industry. In just a few short years, the music industry transformed a voice of rebellion into a highly marketable commodity, usually divested of political significance. By the time you read this, there is likely to be a newly emerging music trend that, once again, attempts to resist the corporate pressures of commercialization. The active resistance of audiences to being co-opted by the mainstream may well be one of the prime forces behind creativity in the music industry.

Drawing upon an even earlier period of time, the media industry has enlisted the rock and roll of the 1960s and 1970s to enhance sales. Corporate advertising has appropriated music that once represented a countercultural critique of the status quo. Bob Dylan's political anthem, "The Times They Are A-Changing," now sells financial services. While keeping the catchy tune, a seafood chain has turned the Allman Brothers' countercultural refrain, "love is in the air," into "lobster everywhere." Lou Reed's "Walk on the Wild Side" sells motor scooters. The Beatles' "Revolution" sells sneakers. Steppenwolf's "Born to Be Wild" sells cars. "Paranoid," from the early heavy-metal bad boys Black Sabbath, sells beer. (You can't help but wonder which meaningful songs of today will be the commercials of tomorrow.)

While profit-seeking corporations largely co-opt mainstream commercial music for their own purposes, there is a long, rich history of music associated with different political causes. The labor and civil rights movements, for example, each developed a distinct repertoire of political music that was a cornerstone of each movement. Conservative religious movements also draw on a wide range of "Christian" music aimed at promoting a biblically inspired political message. Some forms of rap and hip-hop music continue to be a forum for the expression of political views. The 1980s saw a series of music-based charity and political projects, including Live Aid for famine relief in Ethiopia, Farm Aid for U.S. farmers facing foreclosure, Sun City opposing apartheid and promoting human rights in South Africa, and several Amnesty International tours for human rights worldwide. To varying degrees, each of these efforts has made a political statement out of music. But when huge corporations control the major distribution and marketing of music, it is often difficult to tell whether music is closer to being a political soapbox for challenging views or a musical bar of soap to be packaged and sold for profit like any other commodity.

It is important to remember that audiences appropriate music for their own purposes, regardless of how it is marketed. The sale of some music can profit a corporation while simultaneously serving a different function for the consumers of that music. In many cases, the social and political commentary in the music of Metallica or Ice Cube or Tracy Chapman has significant meaning for those who listen—regardless of the corporate label for which the music is recorded. This demonstrates another aspect of the complex tensions involved in the social process of media creation and consumption.

The genres of music continue to multiply. The music scene has permutated into hip-hop, house, rap, baggy, techno, industrial, gothic, death metal, thrash, speed metal, and numerous other genres that come and go with passing fads. World music, too, has taken on a multitude of forms. Coupled with old standbys like folk and country (which themselves harbor a variety of strains), the fragmentation of popular music has been the story of recent decades. It is important to note that we cannot speak of a single version of any of these musical genres. Each consists of many different, sometimes contradictory, tendencies. For example, as we have seen, some forms of rap are well known for their angry and progressive political sentiments regarding racism, economic inequality, and police brutality. Other rap artists have incorporated messages of misogyny and anti-Semitism and seem to glorify violence. Still other rap music is concerned with personal themes of love and relationships, not with political issues. Thus, there is no single political message promoted by rap—or any other genre of music.

Whatever the genre, the political impact of music is mixed. Musicians and fans endlessly struggle to claim their music as something different and, in some cases, as a political statement of alternative views. The music industry, however, is less interested in *why* music sells than in *how well* it sells. The result is oppositional cultures that are endlessly being absorbed into the commercial marketplace, which transforms what were once vibrant political statements into product jingles, movie soundtracks, and elevator Muzak. At the same time, enclaves of local and noncommercial ventures—college radio stations, small alternative clubs, and independent record labels—continuously nurture newly emerging alternatives.

Global Media, Global Politics

The global dimension of the media's political impact has become all the more significant in recent years as the media industry itself has taken on global proportions. We can divide the growing body of transnational research into studies of the Western (especially U.S.) media's impact on other societies and, more recently, studies of indigenous media. Critics have often examined Western media in the context of "cultural imperialism," an approach with which we begin this discussion.

The Cultural Imperialism Thesis

For a number of years, the discussion of global media was influenced by the argument that media products of the West, especially of the United States, so dominated the rest of the world that they amounted to a form of cultural imperialism. In recent years, for example, American products have made up 40 percent of the European film market and nearly a quarter of the TV market. U.S. media corporations also control 60 percent of the film distribution networks in Europe (Hirsch and Petersen, 1992). Over half of all movies shown on European television are made in the United States (De Bens, Kelly, and Bakke, 1992). The basic argument of the cultural imperialism thesis was that Western media products introduced into other countries, especially "developing" countries, contributed to a decline in local traditional values and promoted, instead, values associated with capitalism. In addition, ownership and control over media was maintained in U.S. hands, and other nations became more dependent on the United States for cultural production. Early articulations of this position emphasized the role of television (Schiller, 1971) and were an important antidote to ethnocentric and sometimes racist thinking about the superiority of American culture.

However, the argument that U.S.-owned media hardware and programs were part of a plan to culturally subjugate the world seems overdrawn in the 1990s. Evidence suggests that the imperialism thesis is problematic on at least two counts (Tunstall, 1977). First, researchers questioned the early claims of powerful effects, pointing out that the media capacities of other nations quickly allowed them to produce their own programming, reducing their reliance on U.S. shows. More recently, as we examine in Chapter 8, research has shown that media audiences in different countries make local interpretations of U.S. media products. The program might be the same, but the local meaning of the program in two countries could be quite different. Over time, researchers made cultural imperialism theory more subtle by recognizing such variation in impact. Theorists recognized that the type of society into which media products were introduced, the forms and volume of media products, and many other variables affected the strength and particular characteristics of the media's impact.

Second, interest shifted away from a focus on television toward a broader, more generalized understanding of the influence of different media—including everything from radio to music to comic books. For some capital-intensive media products, especially film, American dominance truly did reach global dimensions. However, in less expensive and more easily produced formats, such as television, local indigenous programming grew, and regional export centers developed.

At century's end, the situation has become quite complex. U.S. media still have a significant impact on foreign nations, and some TV programs have become popular worldwide. At this writing, for example, "Baywatch" is a global hit. American film is also very popular, with action-adventure films making the biggest splash. Is there a trend here? Sex and violence seem to cross cultures easily, whereas comedy and some forms of drama have a more difficult time. As American producers and film studios become increasingly reliant on overseas distribution to make a profit on expensive "blockbusters," the ease with which a film crosses cultural barriers becomes a relevant factor. Thus, violence-packed action-adventure films are still a hit with Hollywood producers even though they are often less successful in the U.S. market than more family-oriented fare.

Meanwhile, in the area of pop music, American artists are sometimes heavily influenced by other cultures. Western musicians such as Paul Simon, David Byrne (formerly of the Talking Heads), and Sting (formerly of The Police) are among the best-known mainstream artists who have incorporated African and South American sounds and musicians into their work. Observers have sometimes criticized the process of Western musicians drawing on indigenous cultures as being exploitative, because it represents a raiding of local culture for the profit of Western artists and record conglomerates. Critics have also accused musicians of creating a "watered-down" or homogenized musical sound. However, others argue that the increased exposure of indigenous music has led to a greater appreciation of it by a wide variety of audiences. In fact, "world music" has grown in popularity to become a recognizable music category that represents both music produced in particular parts of the world and an amalgam of varied instruments and rhythms resulting in a generic "global" sound ungrounded in any single tradition.

The meeting of Western and international music can be complicated. Various elements of South African "township jive," mbaqanga, kwela, and Zulu choral music dominated the sound on Paul Simon's hit album *Graceland.* Simon's interest in South African popular music was sparked in part by the fact that the sound reminded him of 1950s American rock and roll. In fact, American rock music and other African-American musical styles of the 1950s and 1960s were distributed in South Africa (Garofalo, 1992). Thus, local cultures had absorbed the infusion of 1950s American rock and roll and had produced new sounds that, in turn, were the inspiration for popular American music in the 1980s and 1990s. A simple model of cultural imperialism cannot account for the complicated interconnections that have become world music.

The Politics of Media in Other Nations

The 1990s have been a time of enormous global change. The growth in communication technologies has been a major element of this change. O'Neil (1993) contends that factors such as the increased "range of public knowledge across the barriers of space, illiteracy, and national sovereignty" have helped promote mass-based "people power" politics. Such politics is not inevitably democratic, but it does tend to restrict the license of rulers while opening the way for potentially democratic action. O'Neil also notes that global media have changed the nature of leadership by making strong visual and emotional appeal more important than knowledge or experience.

Communications media have clearly become central to political action. However, we need to take care in assessing their impact. Consider one famous image from the 1989 student uprising in China's Tiananmen Square. In grainy footage, a single unknown youth stood defiantly in front of an oncoming tank. The tank stopped, turned, and tried to go around the youth. He moved over, again blocking the tank. The standoff continued in this manner until bystanders dragged the youth to safety. The image has become an inspirational one in the West. (One of our colleagues has a poster-size print of the incident on the wall of his office.) However, the film was also shown—repeatedly—on state-sponsored Chinese television. Why? Because the government wanted to show how cautious it had been in putting down the rebellion. In the eyes of the Chinese government, the film showed foolish defiance by a youth and restrained response by government officials (see Exhibit 7.1).

EXHIBIT 7.1 *Culture, Meaning, and Images*

The same media content may be understood quite differently in different cultural contexts. The well-known photo above was taken during the 1989 Tiananmen Square political demonstrations in Beijing, China. It shows a lone demonstrator briefly preventing a tank from proceeding on its way. As the tank tried to go around the demonstrator, he moved and again blocked the tank's progress. Friends pulled the demonstrator away shortly after this photo was taken. *(Photo © Magnum Photos, Inc./Stuart Franklin)*

In the West, the incident came to symbolize heroic individual defiance in the face of overwhelming power. In China, though, the video of the incident was shown repeatedly on state-controlled television to illustrate the great restraint used by the military in dealing with demonstrators. The meaning of the same image was quite different for people of different cultural sensibilities.

Clearly, however, modern communication technologies have become a central part of political activity. When leaders of a 1991 coup against Soviet president Gorbachev knocked out the transmission capabilities of some media outlets in Moscow, some Russians were able to receive news of developing events by way of satellite dish, courtesy of CNN. When government officials essentially blacked out coverage of the events in Tiananmen Square, Chinese students studying abroad faxed newspaper stories to the student leaders in China. In January 1995, the Iranian parliament approved a ban on satellite TV dishes in an attempt to control reception of popular Western TV programs that Islamic clerics claimed were promoting moral decay. In 1994 and 1995, the conflict in Chechnya brought Russian citizens their first "TV war" as evening news coverage showed graphic images of fighting and death. One U.S. account noted that "the images of Russia's first major televised conflict appear to be stirring bitter opposition to what was already an extremely unpopular war" (Los Angeles Times/Washington Post News Service, 1995). Thus, the media that helped make Russian president Boris Yeltsin a popular hero during the 1991 coup attempt contributed to his dramatic decline in popularity just four years later. The Russians were experiencing the impact of media in a manner reminiscent of the American experience in Vietnam almost thirty years earlier.

Conclusion

The media's influence on the political process has utterly transformed the way politics is conducted in many countries. It reaches beyond the content of political coverage in the news and entertainment media, extending into the social process of political deliberation and transforming the physical, social act of conducting politics. The media have facilitated the development of a mass audience for political spectacles. This audience usually has no serious affiliation with political parties, labor unions, or other political organizations. It learns about candidates through the media lens.

The structure of the mass media enables politicians to reach a broad audience. However, to do so, politicians must play by the ground rules set by the media. Parties and platforms matter less in a glossy, mediated politics, while personality and image matter more. Politicians, acutely aware of this fact, tailor their activities accordingly. They often steer away from substantive policy to a politics of sound bites and photo opportunities.

Mass media and emerging media technologies have the potential to facilitate information sharing and political discussion. However, as the experience of recent history indicates, the detrimental impact of these media may well counteract the benefits. In addition, the potential role of the media in promoting a more vibrant political process remains unrealized.

As should now be clear, discussion of the role of mass media in political life must be tempered by the realization that audiences are not passive receptors of media messages. As we explore in Chapter 8, audiences are active participants in the construction of meaning.

Active Audiences and the Construction of Meaning

Until recently, scholars and critics did not take media audiences very seriously. Concern about the potentially manipulative nature of media images led researchers to focus on the media messages themselves, which were subjected to rigorous scrutiny. Some research and debate focused on the ways media messages "cause" specific behaviors. Does television viewing lead teenagers to have sex at an early age? Does heavy-metal music cause listeners to commit suicide? Do violent movies make people use violence in their lives? Audiences, from this perspective, were the recipients of a form of external stimulus—a movie, song, or television program—that elicited an observable response.

Certainly, researchers who focused on media effects were asking a significant question. Perhaps you can recall seeing a particularly violent movie or TV show that was so graphic it made you wonder how it might affect other viewers. What the effects research highlighted, and what virtually all observers now accept, is that *media messages matter*. They are not somehow separate from our "real" lives, picked up for fun and discarded when we turn to the important things. On the contrary, media messages are central to our everyday lives. This is, indeed, one of the basic premises of this book.

But there is a crucial difference between this position and one that focuses on the direct "effects" of media on audiences. In large measure, the discussion of media effects ignores living, breathing people. People exist only as receptacles for media messages, passive groups whose behaviors and attitudes are the result of a powerful external force: the media. The implicit assumption is that in order to understand the media's effect on people all we need to know is what the messages say. Certainly, this image is a bit overdrawn. Few researchers would explicitly take this position. But it does point out the underlying problem of the "effects" framework. By focusing on the effects of media, this perspective largely strips members of the audience of any human agency.

In many respects, *audience* is an unfortunate term. It evokes the image of a mass of passive receivers ingesting their daily dose of media products. This is, not surprisingly, the media-industry image of audiences, who need do nothing except purchase a CD, go to a movie, or turn on the right channel. What audiences actually think or do is irrelevant, as long as they show up.

For our purposes, however, this view of audiences is insufficient. We prefer to think of audiences as active readers rather than passive recipients. We see the meaning of media texts as something that these active audiences construct rather than something that is prefabricated by media producers. There are two good reasons for conceptualizing the audience in this way. First, it fits with our own experiences as media consumers and as members of various audiences. Second, a large body of recent research demonstrates that media audiences are active interpreters of meaning. Real people with lives, histories, and social networks are the audiences for mass media products. The notion of the active audience brings these real people into our model of media and the social world. This chapter explores the ways audiences actively interpret mass media.

The Active Audience

A long line of media research has argued that mass media serve simply to transmit the ideas of the dominant groups in society to the mass of the population. In this view, people are indoctrinated by media in ways that are often so thorough they do not even realize they are being dominated. The idea that the audience is active arose in opposition to the notion of all-encompassing ideological domination. It is driven by a kind of populism that views people, not only media institutions, as wielders of power in their relationships with media messages. Proponents of the active audience theory argue that media cannot tell people what to think or how to behave in any direct way (even if state-run media may be trying to do just this), because people are not nearly as stupid, gullible, or easy to dominate as the media indoctrination perspective would have us believe.

The phrase "active audience" appeals to our belief in the intelligence and autonomy of people. The term is both a critique of cynicism about the power of media and an expression of faith in the power of people. For those of us who do not want to simply dismiss people—especially those who partake in devalued forms of media such as soap operas, entertainment-oriented magazines, and action films—the concept of the active audience is a significant step forward.

While the idea of an active audience fits with our sensibilities by granting people some power and agency in their use of media, we still have not explained what kind of activity the audience engages in. We need to move beyond the general label to define what we mean by an "active audience." There are three basic ways in which media audiences have been seen as active: through individual interpretation of media products, through collective interpretation of media, and through collective political action. We examine each of these areas of audience activity below.

Interpretation

The first kind of audience activity is *interpretive*. The meanings of media messages are not fixed; they are constructed by audience members. This construction comes from a kind of engagement with media texts, generally through routine acts of interpretation. There is nothing necessarily heroic here, nor does interpretive activity require some special set of skills. It is part of the process whereby media messages come to *mean* something to us; it is how we derive pleasure, comfort, excitement, or a wide range of intellectual or emotional stimulation. We engage in interpretive activity, to various degrees, each time we turn on the television, read the paper, or go to the movies.

This interpretive activity is crucial, because it is in the process of audience reception that media texts take on meaning. Producers construct complex media texts, often with a very clear idea of what they intend to say, but this intended message is not simply dumped into the minds of passive audiences. Instead, audiences interpret the message, assigning meanings to its various components. Sometimes there will be a very close correspondence between the intended meaning and the ways a particular audience interprets the message. This correlation may be the result of fine craftsmanship on the part of the producer, the use by producer and audience of a shared interpretive framework, or just plain luck. But there is no guarantee that producers will get their message across in the ways they want. Audiences may not know the implicit references, they may draw upon a different interpretive framework, or they may focus on different components of the message than the producer had planned. Audiences, then, may not construct the meaning intended by the producer, nor will all audience members construct the same meaning from the same media text.

The Social Context of Interpretation

The second kind of audience activity grounds us firmly in daily life. Audiences are active in the sense that they interpret media messages *socially*. That is, audiences do not simply watch, read, or listen to a media text, develop independent interpretations of what it means, and stick to them. On the contrary, media are part of our social lives, and we engage with media in social settings. Sometimes we partake of media in groups; we go to the movies with a date, watch television with our family, or go to a concert with friends. Other times our media use is initially an individual activity but later becomes part of our broader social relationships. We talk with friends, roommates, or co-workers about the book we have just finished, the album we have recently bought, or the news article we have just read. Perhaps we pass along the book, album, or paper to a friend in order to pursue the discussion further. If you stop to think about it, you might be surprised at how much of your everyday conversation is related to mass media.

Many people even engage with media that focus on other media: Book and film reviews in newspapers and magazines, radio commentaries about new music, television programs that evaluate news media, and computer networks that provide commentary on virtually every form of mass media are all widely available. The cynic might say that this abundance of media commentary is all about marketing; in a clever move, the media industry has created a whole sector of media that are principally geared to selling other media. This is certainly part of the story, but it misses the ways audiences use these media-about-media in the social act of interpreting and evaluating media texts. In both kinds of activity—the ways audiences construct meaning and the ways audiences engage with others as they interpret media texts—we can see that audiences are far from passive.

Collective Action

There is an additional sense in which audiences can be active. As we saw in Chapter 7, audiences sometimes organize collectively to make formal demands on media producers. Whether they are outraged by the images they see in a popular film, distressed by the exclusion of their point of view from the news, or concerned about the advertising directed at their children, audiences can engage in collective action to change media texts.

Meanings: Agency and Structure

The notion of active audiences does more than throw into question the traditions that identify meaning as something imposed on audiences by media texts. It undermines the very idea that media texts have a singular meaning. If audiences are active interpreters of media and if different audiences have different backgrounds, social networks, and defining experiences, then it is likely that there will be multiple interpretations of the same media text. This certainly complicates any analysis of media texts and their impact, because it destabilizes the meaning of media. No longer is it enough to ask media creators what they had in mind in making a movie or writing a book. Nor is it enough to use the skills of the literary critic to uncover the hidden meaning of texts. Understanding media requires that we explore the interpretive strategies of real people as they encounter various forms of mass media.

Agency and Polysemy

In the field of cultural studies, scholars use the term *polysemy* to describe the notion of multiple meanings in media texts. Media are said to be polysemic—to have multiple meanings. But where do these meanings come from? Is polysemy the result of audience activity, or is it the result of the properties of the media themselves? In other words, are multiple meanings simply the result of different audience members constructing different interpretations, or do they exist because the texts themselves are "open"— that is, structured in such a way as to allow for multiple readings?

One of the leading scholars in cultural studies, John Fiske (1986), has argued that media texts contain an "excess" of meaning within them. Many of the components of a television program, for example, will fit together into one relatively consistent interpretation that is likely to be the dominant interpretation. But lots of bits and pieces around the edges of the program do not quite fit, and the dominant interpretation cannot completely contain them. Humor and irony are particularly tricky, because they are full of the kind of ambiguity that can be interpreted in different ways. Media, from this perspective, contain the raw materials for multiple interpretations; the texts are structured in ways that facilitate, even if they do not encourage, people's "reading against the grain."

Movies, music videos, magazines, and even short advertisements are packed with potentially meaningful images and words. It is no wonder, then, that each and every piece of a media message does not fit perfectly into a coherent whole. We are not talking about a simple jigsaw puzzle; a better metaphor would be a jigsaw puzzle with far too many pieces. You need only some of the pieces to create a picture; but choosing different pieces will result in different pictures. The same can be said of media texts.

Let's look at an example: What makes a movie an "antiwar" film? The most straightforward response is that a movie is antiwar if its message is critical of or in opposition to warfare. But who is to determine that the message is critical of warfare? The filmmaker? The leading film critics? The trained media scholar? All of these people may have quite sophisticated analyses of why a specific film should or should not be considered antiwar. In fact, we might even be comfortable relying upon such prominent analysts to decide whether or not we should label the film "antiwar." But even a film that seems to have all the qualities of an antiwar film and leads us to question the morality of organized warfare (for example, Vietnam films such as *Platoon, Full Metal Jacket,* or *Casualties of War*) will likely contain elements that can be used as the basis for a much different interpretation. Perhaps the film depicts soldiers brutally and indiscriminately killing a group of defenseless noncombatants. Is there more than one way to interpret this scene? Although many, perhaps even most, people would likely find this scene horrific, it is likely to provide the seeds of an alternate interpretation, suggesting, for example, the necessity of war, the commitment of soldiers, or the evil of our enemies. Perhaps the victims did not speak the same language as the soldiers, or the soldiers expressed fear or confusion, or the battle is proclaimed a victory later in the film. Any of these circumstances can be the key to different readings of even an apparently straightforward text.

Is one interpretation of the film "correct" and another just plain wrong? Can we say that the film is *really* an antiwar film and those who see otherwise just don't get it? Of course we can, and, in fact, we regularly do when we talk—perhaps argue—with friends and family about a movie we have just seen. Even if we are sure our interpretation is correct, this conviction is ultimately of little consequence if the film means something else to others. It is likely, then, that media texts do have some degree of "openness" in their very structure, making widely divergent readings possible—even though difficult.

Given the substantial competition for the attention of audiences, this openness is a highly desirable feature for mass market media. The most successful texts will have components that appeal to different audiences. Jhally and Lewis (1992) explore this issue in their study of audiences of "The Cosby Show," which was the most popular show in the United States for several years. As we have seen, white audiences either interpreted the Huxtable family to be, for all intents and purposes, "white" because they were upper middle class or saw the Huxtable family's success as an indication of the end of racism in the United States, providing evidence that black families can be just like white families. Black audiences expressed pride in the portrayal of a successful black family on national television, and many were pleased to see such a positive representation of Blacks. For black audiences, this positive image did not mean that the Huxtables were "white," nor did it signify the end of racial discrimination. In short, the black and white audiences drew very different lessons about race relations from "The Cosby Show." From the standpoint of the producers of the program, however, this ambiguity is its very beauty. It may be that popularity in a diverse society requires ambiguity; in this case, both Blacks and Whites could enjoy the program even though they interpreted it in very different ways.

You can see how the meaning of media has been opened up by the notion of the active audience and the polysemic text. Does that mean that audiences are interpretive "free agents," that they can derive any meaning they want, or that the meaning of texts is limited only by the number of audience members? There is a tendency in some branches of cultural studies to really push the boundaries, arguing that ways of making meaning are so diverse that we can neither fully understand them nor control them and that, in fact, audience members have the ultimate power in their interactions with media because they can make the media texts mean whatever they like. In this view, social structure is almost completely wiped away, and audiences are no longer constrained at all. The texts themselves matter very little. They are not simply open, they are wide open—to be interpreted in a limitless number of ways.

This view substitutes one oversimplified perspective (meaning is given) with an alternative (meaning is entirely open) that suffers from the same basic flaw. In essence, this latter view is all agency and no structure. In disputing the notion that media texts have any meaning prior to their interpretation, this view makes the texts themselves irrelevant. And in arguing that interpretations are virtually limitless, this position neglects the social context in which we experience and interpret media, the often familiar conventions that media representations use, and the underlying patterns these interpretations have.

Structure and Interpretive Constraint

We are not simply "free" of constraints when we experience media; we do not live in some electronic netherworld. We experience media as part of daily life, not separate from it, and our lives unfold in specific social locations. Our age, occupation, marital and parental status, race, gender, neighborhood, educational background, and the like help structure our daily lives and our media experiences. Media texts are not a random hodgepodge; those that seek a mass audience are built around familiar images and traditional themes that regular mass media users are likely to have experience interpreting. Media messages matter, but so does our location in various social groups. Social location matters because it shapes whom we talk to about different media, what we perceive to be our own best interests and most important concerns, and what kind of interpretive framework we bring to the mass media.

The task, then, is to be mindful of the ways in which meaning is constructed by socially located audiences under specific historical circumstances. This means that we have to understand both the role of agency —audiences constructing meaning—and the role of structure—the patterns of interpretation and the social locations that shape them. Who we are does not determine how we will interpret media texts, but neither is our social identity irrelevant. At the same time, media texts do not have a singular meaning to be detected by audiences, but neither do they have limitless meanings.

Some meanings will be easier to construct because they draw upon widely shared cultural values and sets of assumptions about the way the world works. Other meanings will be less commonly derived because they require substantial rethinking or depend upon the use of alternative informational resources. As a result, meaning may be actively constructed by audiences, but in most cases one interpretation is likely to be most common and fit with the underlying values of the culture. We can think of this as the "preferred" reading, in that the text itself is most amenable to this interpretation. Of course, the possibility still exists for alternative readings, and one's "interpretive community," or web of social networks, is one of the keys to whether people interpret media in line with the "preferred" reading or with some divergent reading.

Decoding Media and Social Position

Our discussions with friends and family about the meaning of media messages provide strong evidence that audiences indeed interpret media in diverse ways. At the same time, as we explored in Chapter 6, media products are often ideological in the sense that they consistently promote certain messages over others. These ideological representations are most powerful when they pervade the realm of "common sense" such that competing meanings are no longer even entertained. This is an apparent contradiction. How can we negotiate the terrain between the active audience and the ideological nature of many media texts? By pointing to the role of social structure, several studies have helped reconcile the forces of ideological constraint and audience agency in the interpretation of media.

Class and "Nationwide"

As we have seen, the notion of the active audience raised serious questions for the study of media. It was no longer enough, for example, to study the content of media messages, because such messages are at least partially open to different interpretations. But where do these different interpretations come from? One answer is in the relationship of meaning to social position. David Morley (1980) tackled this question in his study of the British television "magazine" program "Nationwide." In short, Morley analyzed the text of the "Nationwide" broadcast to determine the "preferred" meaning of the messages, and he interviewed groups of people from different social backgrounds who had viewed the program to see if and how social position and meaning-making are related.

If we are to understand the relationship between media and society, Morley's question is a profound one. A focus on the individual act of interpretation may be preferable to the notion of a passive audience, but it tells us little about what media messages will mean to different audiences.

It is tempting to believe that people are free to construct their own interpretations, because this radically individualist position assigns great power to each of us. However, research on audiences suggests that social position affects interpretation. It acts as a central mediator of the interpretive process—not as a determinant of meaning, but as a key provider of the resources we use to decode media messages.

Morley explores this terrain, paying particular attention to the role of social class. In his study of "Nationwide," he makes use of Stuart Hall's "encoding–decoding" model, a method that highlights both messages and their interpretation by audiences. One of the key contributions of this model is the way it conceptualizes media—borrowing from linguistics—as messages that are constructed according to certain "codes." Understanding or "decoding" these messages requires knowledge of the conventions of the medium and the workings of the culture. Since we are all connected in various ways to our media-saturated culture, much of this competence is so taken for granted that we do not even think about it.

Even though our competence may seem "natural" when we watch television, read the newspaper, or pick up a fashion magazine, our ability to interpret these media depends upon our familiarity with the basic codes of each medium. (We saw this in our discussion of photography in Chapter 4.) We know about beginnings and endings of programs and articles, about the relationship between pictures and words, about the presence (or absence) of the author, about the difference between advertisements and the articles or programs, and so on. Imagine what television viewing would be like if we did not understand the ad–program relationship. It would seem like a random jumble of images. Or what if we had no idea about the codes of supermarket tabloids? We might be shocked by the newest "revelations" instead of being entertained by them (see Exhibit 8.1). Think about what MTV would look like to someone who has never seen a music video. Without some implicit knowledge about the codes of music video, it is likely that the newcomer would be baffled by the presentation and perhaps even puzzled as to why anyone would find it fun to watch.

Media messages also draw upon broader sets of cultural codes about how the world works. These codes build on assumptions that do not have to be articulated. In other words, the meaning of media texts depends, to a great degree, on the taken-for-granted. News stories about the president's day do not have to explain why he is important; magazine images assume certain definitions of beauty or success; and films and television programs draw upon layers of assumptions about relationships between men and women, parents and children, the rich and the poor. Decoding, then, is the process whereby audiences use their implicit knowledge of

EXHIBIT 8.1 *Decoding Media*

Supermarket tabloids, like those pictured here, have many loyal readers. These readers for the most part are aware of the distinctive "codes" of tabloids. Even though tabloids and mainstream newspapers or newsmagazines are both print media, most people do not read them the same way. Most readers know that tabloids are full of images and stories that are entertaining, bizarre, and fantastic rather than necessarily "true" stories that depict "reality." Active audiences interpret the tabloids; they understand tabloid conventions and take them into account in making sense of and enjoying supermarket tabloids. *(Photo by Serge Levy)*

both medium-specific and broader cultural codes to interpret the meaning of a media text.

The "encoding–decoding" model focuses on the relationship between the media message, as it is constructed or "encoded" by a media producer, and the ways that message is interpreted or "decoded" by audiences. Encoding and decoding are connected because they are processes that focus on the same media text, but a particular decoding does not necessarily follow from a specific encoded meaning. According to this model, producers create media texts in ways that encode a preferred or "dominant" meaning—the interpretation that will most likely follow from a decoding based on the codes of the medium and the dominant assumptions that underpin our social life. Morley suggests a very simple approach: People can read the preferred meaning, they can develop a "negotiated" reading, or they can draw upon extratextual resources to construct an "oppositional" reading. The question for Morley, then, focuses on which groups decode messages in line with the preferred meaning and which groups produce negotiated or oppositional meanings.

The "Nationwide" study indicated that there was a tendency for people from different socioeconomic classes to interpret the meaning of the television program in different ways. There was no direct correlation between class and interpretation, and Morley was reluctant to draw definitive conclusions from this study. Still, the general pattern is worthy of our attention. In decoding "Nationwide" coverage of economic issues, workers and managers constructed very different interpretations. The bank managers whom Morley interviewed read the preferred meaning. They saw so little controversy in the presentation of the economy that they focused their attention on the program's style rather than its content. Morley argues that the "Nationwide" framework was a perfect fit with the commonsense views of the bank managers. The group of trade unionists he interviewed saw the economic coverage as entirely favoring management. At the same time, younger management trainees also saw the coverage as ideological, but they saw it as favoring the unions. Morley reports that these distinctions between the interpretations of the bank managers, management trainees, and trade unionists are rather sharp. He concludes that "these examples of the totally contradictory readings of the same programme item, made by managers and trade unionists, do provide us with the clearest examples of the way in which the 'meaning' of a programme or 'message' depends upon the interpretive code which the audience brings to the decoding situation" (Morley, 1992, p. 112).

Students from different social classes also derived different meanings from the items in "Nationwide." Groups of middle-class students criticized the program for failing to include enough detail in its coverage of issues. They viewed it as lacking the seriousness that would make an informational program worthwhile. It was, in their view, a trivial program. The mainly black working-class students used an entirely different evaluative scheme. They suggested that the program was too detailed and, ultimately, boring. For these students, the program was also viewed as largely worthless, not for its trivial nature but because it lacked the entertainment value that makes television worthwhile. In short, the groups of students from different classes approached "Nationwide" with distinct interpretive frameworks—one group focused on information, the other on entertainment—and thus viewed the program in dramatically different ways.

In evaluating the meaning of this study, Morley makes an important qualification about his results to which we should pay careful attention. Social class, Morley argues, *does not determine* how people interpret media messages. Meaning is class-stratified but not in ways that are constant or entirely predictable. If we reduce meaning-making to some simple formula focused on social class, we deny audiences the agency that the active audience theory has so usefully brought to our attention.

How, then, does class influence interpretation? Social class—and we would add age, race, ethnicity, and gender—plays a key role in providing us with cultural "tools" for decoding. Some class-based tools are useful for navigating the world of politics (Croteau, 1995). Others are helpful for decoding media. Among the media-related cultural tools are what we might call *discursive* resources, for example, the language, concepts, and assumptions associated with a particular subculture or a political perspective. Different groups of people will have access to different discursive resources for decoding media messages. The distinction between "negotiated" and "oppositional" readings is significant in this context, because oppositional readings require that audiences have access to discursive resources that allow them to make meanings opposing the preferred one. For example, trade union activists bring a discourse of union politics—involving "the introduction of a new model, outside the terms of reference provided by the programme" (Morley, 1992, p. 117)—to bear on their interpretation of messages about the economy. This allows them, in Morley's study, to produce readings critical of the economic organization of society. We can easily imagine oppositional readings among other groups with sufficient discursive resources. Perhaps a feminist perspective—again, a set of discursive resources—provides some women with the tools to make oppositional readings of the images in popular women's magazines.

It should not be surprising that people occupying different social positions possess different kinds of discursive resources. Our social position provides the frame through which we view the world, making some things visible and others more difficult to see. If, indeed, social position shapes the tools we have available for interpreting media images, then the meanings we assign to different media products will ultimately be related to social position. Audiences are still active in this view; they still have to do the decoding work, and access to particular tools does not guarantee a particular interpretation. But the same cultural tools are not available to everyone. Our social position provides us with differential access to an array of cultural tools, which we use to construct meaning in more or less patterned ways. The result is a model of humans as active agents constrained by specific structural conditions.

Gender, Class, and Television

Morley's study of "Nationwide" was, of course, only a start; the study raised some enduring questions and provided tentative answers. Most important, it provided an example of audience research that was both cognizant of the interpretive activity of audiences and grounded in the social world. Other researchers followed this fruitful path, examining the ways different audiences interpreted similar media texts. Andrea Press's (1991) study *Women Watching Television* is one of the well-known studies that have focused on the relationship between social structure and audience interpretation. Press interviewed middle-class and working-class women, focusing on their backgrounds, their attitudes toward gender issues, and their television viewing histories and preferences.

Press suggests that middle-class women watch television differently from working-class women in that they use a different set of criteria for evaluating programs and identifying with television characters. The first difference is in assessing the degree of "realism" of television programs. Women from different classes view this issue in widely disparate terms. Working-class women place a high value on images they believe to be realistic, while middle-class women do not expect television to be realistic. Working-class women are likely to view televised depictions of middle-class life as realistic, especially in comparison to what they see as the "unreal" (and uncommon) depictions of working-class life. Middle-class women are much less likely to think about whether the programs are realistic, since, for the most part, they assume (and accept) that they are not.

The results of these differences, Press argues, are substantial. In short, the combination of a focus on realism and a sense that common television images of the middle-class household are realistic portrayals leads working-class women to an interpretation that devalues their own class position. In other words, as Press (1991, p. 138) puts it, "working-class women are particularly vulnerable to television's presentation of the material accoutrements of middle-class life as the definition of what is normal in society."

While middle-class women may be cynical about the realistic nature of television depictions, they are much more receptive to depictions of women on television than their working-class counterparts. Working-class women were consistently critical of the image of both the independent working woman and the stereotypically sexy woman—two stock images for television characters—in large part because they perceive them to be unrealistic. Working-class women belittled, and even dismissed, popular images of women because these images bear little resemblance to their sense of what it means to be a woman in American society. Middle-class women, however, were much more likely to focus on the positive nature of these images, either defending such televised characters or indicating a sense of identification with them. The result is that middle-class women's interpretations of televised images of women are part of their own definitions of womanhood, whereas working-class women show a tendency to resist these interpretations.

The point is that class plays a central role in how audiences make sense of television images. We can use Press's work to make a broader speculative connection between social class, production, content, and audience interpretation—all elements of our media/society model. Because of their lived experience, working-class women know that most television programs present a distorted, unrealistic picture of working-class life in general and working-class women in particular. However, without extensive lived experience of middle-class life, working-class women are more likely to accept the media's portrayal of the middle class as plausibly realistic. Middle-class women, on the other hand, are more likely to have a background similar to that of middle-class media producers, including having a shared and taken-for-granted understanding of class. Middle-class women, therefore, largely ignore questions of class and find the media's depiction of women's roles as "normal" since the images more closely reflect their own middle-class perspective. Thus, we have more evidence that social position and meaning-making are connected, albeit in complex and indirect ways.

Race, Gender, and *The Color Purple*

Morley's and Press's studies are representative of a much larger body of work on television audiences, their interpretive strategies, their cultural tools, and their relationship to the media industry. Scholars have used a similar approach to study the meaning of a broad array of media texts beyond television. For example, Jacqueline Bobo (1988) examined the ways black women decoded the popular film *The Color Purple*. Based on Alice Walker's award-winning book of the same title, Steven Spielberg's film version did well at the box office but was subjected to substantial criticism. The premiere of the film was picketed by activists in Los Angeles, and prominent black male critics called the film racist. Others noted that the film reproduced stereotypical images of Blacks and was part of a long tradition of unflattering depictions of Blacks in Hollywood films.

Despite this criticism, Bobo found that black women had a very favorable response to the film, the result, in large part, of a sense of identification by black women with the main characters in the film, most notably Whoopi Goldberg's character, Celie. This identification stems from the overwhelming absence of black women on the big screen. *The Color Purple* provided black women with strong lead characters, something the women in Bobo's study found empowering. Also, the film was released at a time when a community of black women writers and artists was growing and finding an enthusiastic audience, especially among other black women. Ultimately, the combination of Hollywood's historic treatment of black women and the growth of a black feminist literary culture helps explain the positive response of black women to the film—in contrast to other interpretations, particularly those of black men. The sense of identification led the women to become engaged with the film, and the cultural tools provided by the black feminist literary scene gave them resources for an alternative interpretation of the film.

International Readings of American Television

If you have traveled outside the United States, you probably know that American television programs are very popular in other countries. Dozens of countries broadcast either reruns of classic programs or current network ratings leaders. Since, as we have seen, meanings are multiple and are constructed by socially located audiences, what do these popular television programs actually mean to viewers outside the United States? How do people in Italy, for example, interpret programs like "LA Law" or "NYPD Blue"? What do these programs mean to audiences who have little or no experience with Los Angeles, New York, or the cultural context within which these programs are viewed by people in the United States? What about situation comedies? Are "Seinfeld" and "The Simpsons" seen as humorous by people in Singapore, Argentina, or Russia? If so, how do audiences interpret the programs in ways that make them laugh? What does it mean that, as of 1995, "Baywatch" was the most popular program in the history of international television, watched by viewers in 144 countries and translated into 15 different languages? And what lessons about life in the United States do international audiences draw from these popular television programs?

These are classic sociological questions about the relationship between culture and meaning—what do popular media images mean in different cultural contexts?—but we are only beginning to study this relationship. It is too simple to assert that American television images indoctrinate international viewers to support American consumer capitalism or to argue that international audiences adapt these foreign images to their own social situations. It is more difficult, and ultimately more rewarding, to explore the complex ways in which active audiences make use of images that often are heavily laden with ideological messages.

The most sophisticated effort to study this terrain is Liebes and Katz's (1993) study of the 1980s television program "Dallas," which was popular with audiences in dozens of countries. This evening drama—some refer to it as a nighttime soap opera—chronicled the lives of a wealthy Texas oil family named Ewing and its lead character/villain J. R. Ewing. The program followed family members through ups and downs, with a regular focus on secret love affairs, back-room business deals, and an almost constant tension between loyalty and betrayal. What was the underlying message in the program? Was it ultimately about the corrupting influence of wealth or the power of money? Was it about the control of women by the men in their lives or the prevalence of self-interest in all social relationships? These are difficult questions, but they become even more complicated when we recall that the program was watched vigilantly by people all over the world.

Liebes and Katz compare the "decodings" of six different ethnic groups from three different countries: Americans from Los Angeles, Japanese, and four different communities in Israel—recent Russian immigrants, Moroccan Jews, Arab citizens of Israel, and kibbutz members. The study is based on several "focus group" discussions within each ethnic group; groups of friends watched the program together at one viewer's home and participated in a guided discussion about the program upon its completion. Liebes and Katz found substantial differences among the ethnic communities, both in how they watched the program and how they interpreted it.

In each focus group, viewers were asked to "retell" the story of the just-completed program as if they were explaining it to a friend who had missed the episode. The different ethnic communities used very different storytelling approaches. Both Arabs and Moroccan Jews were most likely to retell the episode on a scene-by-scene basis, often in great detail. The Americans and kibbutzniks were more likely to focus on the characters instead of the plot line. And the Russians explained the message of the program instead of either the action or the characters. Of course, not all members of each ethnic group fit neatly into a box, all using the same interpretive strategy, but the interpretive patterns were very clear.

Where do these different approaches come from? This is a much more difficult question to answer. Liebes and Katz suggest that the distinct strategies can be explained by the cultural position of the different groups. Arabs and Moroccan Jews are the most "traditional" groups in the study, and their linear storytelling draws connections between their own culture and the perceived reality of the lives of the extended family living in Dallas. Russians, on the other hand, draw upon their skill at reading between the lines for the underlying message, a skill that was well developed in the former Soviet Union. And the American and kibbutznik groups build upon their cultures' interest in psychology and "group dynamics" to explore the attitudes and actions of the characters. In each case, the "retelling" approach does not come out of thin air—it is anchored in underlying cultural dynamics that provide the different audiences with culturally specific resources.

Viewers from all ethnic groups talked about the connections between the program and real life much more frequently than they subjected the program to critical analysis. Even here, however, significant differences were evident. The Russian, American, and kibbutz groups were three times as likely to use "critical," or analytical, statements as the Arab or Moroccan Jewish group. Discussions focused on a consistent set of themes —human motivations, family relations, moral dilemmas, and business relations—in all the groups. Although the groups discussed similar themes, however, they talked about them in very different terms. For example, the Americans and kibbutzniks employed a "playful" approach in these discussions, "relating the story to imagined situations" or "trying on the characters," much more frequently than the other groups, who almost always discussed the story in a straightforward way, relating the story more directly to life.

Additionally, the Arab groups were much more engaged with the program than the other groups. In fact, the Arab groups were the only ones to make regular use of a normative interpretive framework, making moral judgments about the activities depicted in the program. Liebes and Katz suggest that the more frequent use of an analytical framework by the "Western" audience members is likely a result of their greater experience with television as a medium and their greater familiarity with the society portrayed in "Dallas." In short, the American, Russian, and kibbutz groups have different resources for analyzing the images in "Dallas" than do their Arab and Moroccan counterparts.

The distinctive "retellings" of the program indicate that, while the different ethnic groups may have watched the same program, they did not see the same thing. For example, the Americans were playful and detached in their reading of the program, while the Arabs were emotionally engaged, asserting their opposition to the program's values. As a result, the Arabs were most likely to read the meaning of the program as "Americans are immoral," while the Americans were most likely to assert that the programs meant little beyond entertainment. Ultimately, the broad depiction of family relations—their triumphs and tragedies—makes the program widely popular, even if people use different cultural resources to interpret what these images mean about people, society, or the United States.

Although it was an international hit, "Dallas" was not popular everywhere. In Japan, where "Dallas" was a bust, viewers made more "critical" statements about the program than any other ethnic group and made very few comments that connected "Dallas" to their own lives. This might help explain why "Dallas" never caught on in Japan; viewers were never able to really engage with the program. Instead, "Dallas" was perceived as full of inconsistencies that the Japanese could not accept—inconsistencies with the genre of the evening drama, with the viewers' perception of American society, with their sense of their own society, and even with their view of the characters' motivations.

Ultimately, we might sum up this study by noting that the Japanese viewers focused on very different aspects of the program than did other groups, interpreting "Dallas" in ways that led viewers to prefer other programs. They did not exhibit the playfulness of the Americans, the detective work of the Russians, or the moral disapproval of the Arab viewers. The program, in short, had very little meaning to the Japanese beyond its utter inconsistency. While its openness to diverse interpretations might help explain why the program was popular in so many different countries, with the text itself allowing very different viewers to engage with it, the possibilities were not limitless. In a Japanese cultural context, "Dallas" evidently had very little to offer viewers.

The Social Context of Media Use

When and where do people watch television, listen to the radio, or read the newspaper? It is not surprising that many people "watch" television or "listen" to the radio without really paying attention to the program or song. We can all probably recall instances when, after an hour or more, we realized that we had no idea what we had been watching or listening to. What is the "meaning" of this kind of media experience? If we are interested in the media experience of audiences, we need to think about both the active interpretation of media messages and the act of media use itself.

Romance Novels and the Act of Reading

One of the most influential studies of media "audiences" is Janice Radway's (1984) now classic book, *Reading the Romance*. One of the principal reasons why Radway's work has been so influential is that it challenges many of our basic assumptions about "lowbrow" mass media such as romance novels. Radway's work helps clarify the basic tension between structure and agency that we have emphasized in this book, and it serves as an exemplar of what it means to study the active yet socially located media audience.

Romance novels may seem an odd topic for a serious study of mass media. They are widely denigrated by academics, who are not likely to read them. They are culturally devalued, like the soap opera, in part because they are seen as the exclusive domain of women. Moreover, the romance genre is widely associated with traditional, sexist visions of society: the damsel in distress, the woman who is incomplete without her heroic man, even the woman who finds love with the man who has sexually assaulted her. All this makes it easy to dismiss the romance novel as frivolous trash with straightforward, sexist messages that serve only to oppress women.

However, do we know what romance novels mean to those who regularly read them? Is the common assessment of this medium as traditional, sexist, and even dangerous a reasonable description of the meaning of the romance novel? Radway turns to a group of white, middle-class romance-novel readers to find out. Instead of assuming that her skillful interpretation of the texts uncovers their "true" meaning, she compares her formal analysis of the texts with the interpretations of women readers of the romance novels. Her findings suggest that the question of meaning is rather complex: Readers are certainly active, but they are also responding to their fundamental social situation.

One of Radway's principal findings is that women answer her questions about "why" they read romance novels by focusing on the *act of reading* instead of on the content of the stories. These readers, who do not work outside of the home but are busy with the demands of the full-time roles of wives and mothers, suggest that the activity itself is meaningful as an escape from the demands of their daily lives. In essence, reading romance novels gives women time to themselves, peace and quiet, and a break from the emotional work of nurturing others. It provides what Radway calls a "free space," away from the social world that the women occupy.

But why romance novels? Couldn't this "free space" be created by reading books about computers or women's history? Radway argues that the romance novel allows the women to "escape" from the constraints of their social existence by taking time each day to do their own thing and enter the fairy-tale world of the romance heroine, who has all of her emotional needs satisfied. It is both a literal escape, through the act of reading, and a figurative escape, through the fantasy of the romantic plots. The romance novel, then, represents a kind of freedom for these women, a place where they can assert their independence and vicariously experience the kind of nurturance they seek in their own lives.

We can see the meaning of the romance novel for these women only if we understand their social roles as wives and mothers. The lives of romance readers are tightly circumscribed by traditional cultural norms that specify what it means to be a good wife and mother. While the women largely accept these norms, their own emotional needs are not satisfied by their daily existence, precisely because of cultural restrictions on the activity of women. Reading romance novels, then, is a way for women to refuse, if only temporarily, to accept these norms. The romance novel "compensates" women by helping them meet their own need for nurturance and by allowing them to focus on themselves instead of others. According to the readers, romance reading also makes the women more assertive in their domestic relationships, in part because they have to defend their reading time. Some even mention that they are inspired to become romance writers themselves.

Ultimately, Radway finds that reading romance novels is both a small protest against the social conditions of women and participation in a "ritual of hope" that men can meet the needs of women and traditional relationships can provide the blissful existence of the romantic heroine. Romance novels, then, are not simply sexist trash that reaffirms cultural restrictions on female behavior. Indeed, Radway finds that her readers attach a much different meaning to these texts, one that is a kind of critique of their own social conditions. The act of reading is based on dissatisfaction. It implicitly suggests that heterosexual marriage cannot meet all of the women's needs even as the romance stories provide a vision of how women can be fulfilled. At the same time, this protest is both subtle and partial; it does not become outright rebellion against the wife/mother role. In fact, the protest is bound by a basic acceptance of gender roles within the traditional family. Romance reading does not challenge these roles but instead provides vicarious pleasures that help satisfy needs not met by these highly circumscribed roles.

Romance novels, then, do not mean only one thing. The women Radway interviewed—white, middle-class, midwestern women—interpret romance novels in ways that help explain their own social world and compensate for its shortcomings. This is likely to be a very different reading from the interpretation of trained academic literary critics or even of potential male readers, who inhabit different social worlds. Of course, the content of the novels themselves is significant. Radway's readers actively seek out books that allow them to escape and to hold onto the hope that men can satisfy women's needs, that the heroine and hero will live happily ever after, and that the woman's commitment to the relationship will prevail over the traditionally male commitment to public achievement. As a result, the women make rigid distinctions between romance novels they like and those they dislike. They are not so free to interpret the texts that any romance novel will meet their needs. Because the texts provide the raw materials for the women's interpretations, making some more likely and others next to impossible, part of the art of romance novel reading is to be able to find, or at least quickly determine, those novels worth reading.

Radway's study of romance readers is a good example of how audiences make meaning out of media texts under conditions not of their own choosing. Audiences may be active, but they exist within particular social worlds and are interpreting media texts with specific properties. The nurturance and hope that the women get from the romance novel may surprise some of us, but we should be able to see that Radway's readers draw upon their own experiences, their assumptions about the social world, and the messages in the books to reach their understanding of what these novels mean. At the same time, Radway's study should make us sensitive to the conditions under which people consume mass media. The very act of reading the romance novel is central to the meaning of the text.

Watching Television with the Family

In a work subsequent to the "Nationwide" project, David Morley adopted Radway's focus on the act of media use. Morley's (1986) *Family Television* explores the domestic context of viewing television and shows how television use is embedded within the social relations of the household. If we are to understand what television messages mean, we have to focus on the social experience of watching television. Most of us watch television in a domestic setting, with members of our families or with household partners. These domestic relations help shape what we watch, how we watch, and what meanings we assign to the programs. The social practice of watching television—often in a collective setting—is, like the act of reading a romance novel, central to what its text means to audiences.

According to Morley, gender is one of the keys to understanding how people experience television. If we focus our attention on the use of television in a family context, this statement should not surprise us. After all, roles in the family are structured, to a great degree, by gender, and Morley's study focuses on relatively traditional British families, in which gender roles are likely to be clearly defined. Since men have a tendency to control the program selection process, television is a potential site for domestic power struggles.

One result of gender roles within the family is that adult men and women watch television very differently. Men indicate that either they are very attentive when they watch or they don't watch at all. Women, on the other hand, see television viewing as a social act that is accompanied by conversation and other household activities. For women, just sitting down to watch television without doing anything else seems like a waste of time. In addition, men and women generally view the same programs because they watch television together in the evening, but they do not view them with the same attentiveness. In short, our interpretations of television programs are connected to our engagement with the program. We may tune in to get information, to relax, to find excitement, to tune out the noises of the highway next to our house, or to gather the family for a rare moment of togetherness. These different approaches to television will help shape the meaning we attach to different programs.

Television is a great conversation generator. Because it is so widely viewed, television is the subject of much small talk. When we talk about television or other forms of media with our friends and family, we engage in a kind of collective interpretive activity. We recount what happened, why it happened, what it means, and what is likely to happen next. All of this is part of a process by which we construct meanings for television programs—or movies, songs, magazines, and so on. After watching a particularly interesting or funny television program, attending a provocative movie, or reading a shocking magazine article, we tend to seek out others to talk with, hoping that they have seen or read the same item. Perhaps this is why people go to the movies or a concert with others; even though the viewing or listening in these settings allows for little conversation, you can talk with your friends about the event on the way home.

According to Morley, talking about television, while common among women, is rarely admitted by men. Men either do not talk with friends about television or are unwilling to admit that they engage in a behavior they define as feminine. Morley (1986, p. 158) suggests that this has real consequences: "Given that meanings are made not simply in the moment of individual viewing, but also in subsequent social processes of discussion and 'digestion' of material viewed, the men's much greater reluctance to talk about (part of) their viewing will mean that their consumption of television material is of a quite different kind from that of their wives."

Interaction with media and discussions about media products are important parts of the process of meaning-making. Here again, we can see how meanings are generated in social settings by active audiences. Radway and others have adopted the term "interpretive community" to suggest both the social structural forces at work—our membership in communities—and the forces of human agency—the act of interpretation. When we think about audiences, then, we need to remember that the meanings people make of apparently omnipresent media products are connected to experiences and social structures outside the world of media. Media are, in essence, part of our lives and must be understood in the context of the relationships that constitute our lives.

Active Audiences and Interpretive "Resistance"

The meaning of media messages, as we have seen, cannot be reduced to the "encoded" or "preferred" or even most common reading of a particular media text. Audiences, drawing on specific sets of cultural resources and located in specific social settings, actively interpret media products. The distribution of social and cultural power remains significant, for it structures the discursive resources at our command, the context in which we use media, and the production of media texts. But this power is not absolute or uncontested. The power to define social reality, of which the media are a part, is not something that is simply imposed on unwitting audiences. If media messages circulate versions of a "dominant" ideology, these messages are only the raw materials of meaning; they require construction and are subject to revision.

It is clear that the relationship between media messages, audiences, and meaning is a complex one. We cannot treat the media as some simple vehicle for brainwashing people. This realization has led many scholars to investigate the possibility that some audiences interpret media texts in an "oppositional" way or engage in a kind of interpretive "resistance." Some critics argue that a political struggle is occurring at the level of individual interpretation, thereby rescuing "the people" from a perception that they consent to current social and political arrangements. In other words, audiences "resist" the imposition of preferred meanings, actively reinterpreting media messages in contrary, even subversive, ways.

These claims of interpretive resistance employ an image of audiences as "semiological guerillas," fighting a daily war against the symbolic power of the media industry (Carragee, 1990). Rather than small arms and sneak attacks, the weapons these guerillas use are their own interpretive skills, which they deploy against the purveyors of ideological conformity. The war is waged each day in small, virtually invisible ways in the very act of reading the newspaper or going to the movies. However, with its focus on the almost unlimited agency of audiences, the resistance thesis has a tendency to be far too casual in its dismissal of social structure.

Instead of simply assuming that media audiences consistently behave as symbolic resistance fighters, we need to examine more specifically the ways particular audiences produce from media texts meanings that can be characterized as oppositional. Theorists have argued that individuals resist the definitional power of authorities by reinterpreting media messages, but research has demonstrated neither the process by which such interpretations become oppositional nor the conditions under which such resistance occurs. Instead, the argument for the possibilities of resistance is largely the result of faith in the power of citizens to think and behave as active subjects rather than passive objects of history. Such faith and optimism, while admirable political qualities, do not adequately explain the relationship between active audiences and a powerful culture industry, nor do they provide the basis for understanding the possibilities for and conditions conducive to actual resistance.

If audiences do engage in interpretive resistance by constructing oppositional meanings from media products, we should be able to look at specific examples of these practices. Indeed, several important cases touch on these issues; as we have seen, Morley's study of "Nationwide" and Radway's study of romance readers certainly suggest that audiences have the capacity to produce meanings that are at least partially oppositional.

Interpretive Resistance and Feminist Politics

Resistance can be said to occur when people read media messages in ways that oppose their preferred or commonsensical meaning, articulating a kind of refusal to accept dominant meanings. That is, audiences resist the imposition of meaning and construct new readings that stand in political opposition to the preferred meanings. Linda Steiner's (1988) study of the "No Comment" feature of the original *Ms.* magazine provides a good example of oppositional decoding among a community of readers. *Ms.* was a glossy feminist monthly founded in 1972 and subsequently reincarnated as an advertising-free, less slick bimonthly in 1990. It published "No Comment" each month as a compilation of reader-submitted items —mostly advertisements—that were offered as evidence of sexism in American society. The submissions came from a wide range of sources, including large and small newspapers, magazines, catalogs, and billboards, and often several people submitted the same item.

"No Comment" was a space where readers of *Ms.* could identify images from mainstream media and "expose" their underlying sexism.

One common set of images depicted women as the property of men; an insurance ad, for example, suggested that wives were "possessions," and a news article identified a female politician simply by citing her husband's name. Other themes included images that dismissed feminism, advertising that blatantly exploited women's bodies, images that implied that women enjoy sexual violence, and items that trivialized women's accomplishments. One of the more popular items—submitted to *Ms.* by more than 40 people—was a 1977 quote from a prominent U.S. Army general that appeared in *Parade* magazine; it criticized women for entering West Point because this deprived men of their positions.

Ms. readers likely either gasped in outrage or had a good laugh, or perhaps both, when they read the items in "No Comment." But what does this have to do with resistance? Steiner argues that the point of "No Comment" was precisely for the community of feminists around *Ms.* to collectively resist media messages that reinforced a sexist image of the world. The items were put on display in "No Comment" and decoded in ways that opposed their dominant meaning precisely so that the traditional definitions of what it means to be a woman could be resisted by *Ms.* readers.

No doubt, in this case, those who submitted the items were interpreting the messages in ways contrary to their intended meaning. And since *Ms.* is a feminist publication, it is likely that readers of "No Comment" drew upon a set of cultural tools that would lead to a widely shared oppositional reading of the images as "sexist." Readers may give themselves a pat on the back for their critical interpretive skills and wink knowingly at others who read such texts oppositionally. But does exposing images as sexist provide a means for readers to actually "resist" the culture and society they define as sexist?

There is good reason to see this action as more than just "oppositional decoding" of media images and to define the public presentation of these interpretations in "No Comment" as a kind of resistance. While such resistance may not change social structures, it helps create a feminist group identity. Collective refusal to accept traditional interpretations of femininity gives strength to such an oppositional identity, with real potential consequences. In this case, when mass media images of women were read in oppositional ways by the feminist community, the decodings help solidify a feminist identity opposing the traditional norms and roles that are the underpinnings of the media images being exposed.

These decodings were not, however, solitary acts of interpretation; they were both public and collective. When readers submitted items to the "No Comment" section as a way of sharing their oppositional decodings with like-minded feminists, they helped build a shared meaning system that could serve as a basis for social solidarity within the feminist community. In so doing, they drew upon and helped reproduce a feminist discourse that served as a key resource for such oppositional readings. If there is resistance here, it is not just at the level of individual interpretation. We need to locate the oppositional decodings in the context of a feminist community that provided the cultural resources for such interpretations and served as a site where meaning-making became a more explicitly political act.

Resistance and Identity

Other feminist scholars have explored the ways women respond to and resist media images. In her discussion of the relationship between media images of dancing and the activity itself, Angela McRobbie (1984) argues that teenage girls construct interpretations of dance films such as *Flashdance* in ways that oppose the dominant meaning of the film. Rather than reading the film as a story about a woman who marries her boss's son, using her sexuality to please men in the process of becoming a successful dancer, the girls in McRobbie's study decoded the film in ways that highlighted their own autonomy and sexuality. Dancing, in this interpretation, is not about pleasing or displaying one's body for men; it is about enjoying one's own body and is an expression of sexuality. This reading opposes the dominant interpretation of female sexuality by asserting a sexual identity that does not require the approval of men. The girls drew upon their own experiences of dancing in clubs to reinterpret *Flashdance* in ways that supported their own identities as strong, independent, and sexual females.

Teenage fans of performers such as Madonna and Cindy Lauper, according to Lisa Lewis (1990), engaged in a similar kind of interpretive resistance. Performances that built upon apparently traditional images of female sexuality and male pleasure—and styles of dress that drew on the same images—were interpreted by teenage fans as expressions of their own desires. For female teenage fans, the sexuality of these videos—which differed dramatically from the traditional MTV video—was a sign of female power, because women were the subjects, not the objects. Female fans who imitated the style of these female performers, rather than adorning themselves for men, were asserting their demands for fame, power, and control without giving up their identity as girls. This was the core of their interpretation of the music video texts—texts routinely dismissed in the broader culture as negative portrayals of women.

What connection do these examples have to resistance? Both suggest that there is a relationship between oppositional forms of decoding and social action. These oppositional decodings are part of the construction of a subcultural identity that embodies a resistance to traditional norms and roles. The female fans, in the case of MTV, were principal players in the struggle over music video images—their demands on the music industry helped open the door for female musicians. Also, in both cases, the oppositional decoding is not free-floating; it is part of the collective activities of audiences in specific social settings.

Ultimately, the key question about the possibility of resistance concerns the social consequences. How are these interpretations linked to social action? We have seen three examples that provide a clear analysis of the relationships between oppositional decoding, human activity, cultural tools, and social setting. Such examples suggest that oppositional decoding and resistance are useful concepts, but they need to be used with care (Condit, 1989). Instead of admiring the almost unlimited capability of people to resist domination, we need to take the notion of resistance seriously by looking at the conditions under which concrete audiences engage in such resistance and what consequences follow.

The Pleasures of Media

Perhaps the principal reason we spend so much time with the mass media is that it is fun. We listen to our favorite album, go to the movies, pick up a popular magazine, or spend the evening in front of the television because these activities are enjoyable or relaxing. The media world is, in large part, a world of entertainment, offering us a wide range of choices for how to entertain ourselves. We spend a large portion of our lives having fun and seeking pleasure from the media. But making a rigid distinction between entertainment ("it's only entertainment") and the serious stuff that "really matters" would be a mistake. We need to take fun seriously and explore what it is that makes media a source of pleasure.

Media scholars historically have tended to be suspicious of the pleasures of media. On one hand, media research through the 1970s paid almost exclusive attention to "serious" forms of media, particularly news. On the other hand, pleasure itself was seen as the problem: Media entertained people as a means of distracting them from the more important arenas in life. After all, how could people challenge the social order if they were busy each evening watching "Dynasty" or "The Cosby Show"?

Instead of dismissing fun or assuming that it makes people content with the status quo, more recent work has examined the specific sources of media pleasure and the conditions under which people derive fun from media. Feminists, in particular, have focused their attention on the realm of pleasure, arguing that the pleasures associated with mass media can be liberating for women (Walters, 1995).

We began to see this in Radway's romance novel study, in which the pleasures of the act of reading are taken seriously. The enjoyment that the romances provide and the reasons for seeking such pleasure are connected to the social position of the women readers. Romance novels are enjoyable because reading provides a free space and vicarious fulfillment of the women's romantic fantasies. Indeed, Radway suggests that such mass-mediated pleasures may obviate any need to change the social world. Even so, the women use romance reading as a means of asserting their right to pleasure in a social situation where pleasure is routinely neglected.

Pleasure and Fantasy

Ien Ang's (1985) study of Dutch viewers of "Dallas" provides a more in-depth study of the pleasures of media. The key questions here concern why people enjoy media experiences such as viewing "Dallas." In the case of "Dallas," we are presented with a potentially troubling contradiction. Women are the primary viewers, yet the female characters on the program are depicted as powerless. As Ang suggests, women viewers can both perceive the women characters as powerless and find great pleasure in watching the program. What is it, then, that makes these television images fun for women?

It certainly is tempting to think that "Dallas" is, by definition, an anti-feminist program and that feminists will find little pleasure in such a program. Ang argues, however, that feminists can enjoy "Dallas." The key to explaining the pleasures of a media product like "Dallas," even for those who might seem like unlikely enthusiasts, is the status of the program as fantasy. Fantasy allows us to imagine that we are different, that social problems can be solved, or that we can live in a utopia. It is worth quoting Ang (1985) at length on this point:

> Here it is not primarily a matter of the content of the fantasy, but mainly of the fact of fantasizing itself; producing and consuming fantasies allows for a play with reality, which can be felt as "liberating" because it is fictional, not real. In the play of fantasy we can adopt positions and "try out" those positions, without having to worry about their "reality value.". . . It may well be, then, that these identifications can be pleasurable, not because they imagine the Utopia to be present, but precisely because they create the possibility of being pessimistic, sentimental or despairing with impunity —feelings which we can scarcely allow ourselves in the

battlefield of actual social, political and personal struggles, but which can offer a certain comfort if we are confronted by the contradictions we are living in. (p. 134)

The meanings of such media pleasures, then, cannot be perceived simply by analyzing the media texts; media audiences can incorporate media texts into complex fantasies that can make daily life much more enjoyable.

Celebrity Games

The world of entertainment celebrity is also connected to questions of pleasure. Who are these famous people, where do they come from, and why are they worthy of our attention? If we look around at contemporary American society, there can be little doubt that these are important questions. How can we explain the national and even international fascination with the O. J. Simpson trial, which became the most prominent news story of 1994 and 1995? Why do so many of us pay attention to the details of the lives of actors, musicians, and other media personalities, keeping up with their relationships, weight changes, and hairstyles?

Serious scholars might be inclined to dismiss the celebrity world as meaningless trivia or, worse yet, to sound an alarm about the dangerous distraction that captivates the American public. This doesn't tell us much about either celebrity or its meaning to audiences. Let's face it—celebrity watching is not confined to a small number of obsessed fanatics. Many people pay some attention to the celebrity scene, whether by reading a newspaper interview with a favorite movie star, reading profiles of musicians in the music press, or watching "Entertainment Tonight" on occasion. In fact, for the vast majority of Americans who engage, in various ways, with the mass media, the world of entertainment celebrity is likely to be a regular feature.

Joshua Gamson (1994) suggests that celebrity watching is a complex act and that audiences use a range of interpretive strategies in these mass-mediated interactions with the celebrity world. Some audiences essentially believe what they see, take the celebrities at face value, and focus on their great gifts or talents. Others see celebrity as an artificial creation and enjoy the challenge of seeing behind the images, unmasking these celebrity "fictions." Other audiences are what Gamson calls the "game players," who neither embrace the reality of celebrity nor see it as simple artifice, but who adopt a playful attitude toward the celebrity world.

This playfulness revolves around two kinds of activities: gossip and detective work. For some, the fun of celebrity comes from the game of gossip. In this game, it does not matter whether celebrities are authentic people or manufactured creations, or whether they deserve their fame or not. The fun lies in the playing of the game, and the game is sharing information about celebrity lives. This game of gossip is fun because the truth of each comment is irrelevant; friends can laugh about the bizarre or enjoy evaluating celebrity relationships with the knowledge that there are no consequences.

Other game players focus their energy on detecting the truth about celebrities. This game is animated by the ever-present question of what is real in this world of images, even though the game players are not certain whether they can ever detect the reality. As a result, the fun lies in the collective detective work, not in any final determination of truth or reality. The game itself is the source of pleasure, as players scrutinize celebrity appearances and entertainment magazines, sharing their knowledge with one another as they peel away the never-ending layers of the proverbial onion. Each performance or news item adds to the story, and the detective game continues. The pleasure comes with the speculation, the moments of "aha," and the search for additional information—which the celebrity system produces almost endlessly.

Ultimately, the world of celebrity is a place where the real and the unreal intermingle and where the boundaries between the two are blurred. Game-playing audiences know that the game is located in a "semifictional" world, which makes it both fun and free. Moreover, the pleasure of these games comes from the very triviality of the celebrities themselves. According to Gamson (1994):

> It is the fact that the game-playing celebrity watchers don't really care about the celebrities—contrary to the stereotypical image of the fan who cares so much and so deeply—that makes the games possible and enjoyable. . . . [Celebrities] literally have no power of any kind over audiences. If they did, the "freedom" of the games would be dampened. What matters to celebrity-watching play is that celebrities do not matter. (p. 184)

We see that mass-mediated pleasure can come from a recognition by audiences of media's trivial nature, which makes them perfect sites for fun and games.

Pleasure and Resistance

We have seen that audiences derive pleasure from their use of various forms of mass media. But is there a relationship between the interpretive activity of audiences and their enjoyment? The research in this area has produced a healthy debate but certainly no consensus on the matter. Here we return to the notion of the active audience, which is a requirement for the mediated pleasures we have been discussing. The pleasure of media use comes precisely from interpretive engagement with media texts; media are fun because we actively participate in the making of meaning, not because we simply turn off our brains.

Even if we accept the argument that it is interpretive activity itself that is a source of pleasure, we still need to ask whether all interpretations are equally enjoyable. Does it matter whether we accept the "preferred" meaning or "resist" it? Do both kinds of interpretive strategies result in our having fun? In his study of television, John Fiske (1987) argues that the act of interpretive resistance itself produces pleasure. In this view, the fun of media use and the "popularity" of popular culture are the result of assertions of independence by audiences; the media allow audiences a kind of freedom to understand the world on their own terms. Resistance is fun, we might say, because it empowers those who do not wield power in their daily lives.

While this "pleasure of resistance" view is a provocative hypothesis, we in fact know very little about how widespread such pleasurable resistance actually is. The studies we have identified in this chapter certainly suggest that pleasure and resistance are not necessarily connected. Media use can be fun in situations where audiences are not resisting dominant meanings. Some critics argue that it requires more work to produce oppositional interpretations (Condit, 1989). Such interpretations may be a source of great pleasure because of the hard work involved, but this interpretive work may be an obstacle that will prevent many audience members from making oppositional meanings. Interpretive resistance may be fun, but it may also be comparatively rare.

We do know that media can be fun, that audiences are active, and that meanings can be variable. If the social position of audiences and a corresponding set of cultural tools help explain the patterns of interpretation, they may also help clarify the nature of mass-mediated pleasure. Media can be fun because reading or watching offers a space away from the demands of daily life. Feminist media theorists have argued that this is a particularly significant issue for women, whose social roles give them little space. Pleasure can also come from entrance into a world of fantasy; here, again, social position will shape the kinds of fantasy worlds that are attractive and the ways audiences engage with fantasy images. Pleasure can also come from asserting autonomy in the face of conformity and from seeing through media in ways that are empowering. More generally, media can be fun because they are a forum for play in a society that values work far above leisure.

Conclusion

This chapter has examined the ways in which audiences are active inter-preters of media messages. The central contribution of much of the recent audience research lies in its interest in individual and collective forms of human agency. The active audience tradition has brought real people back into focus in media research by exploring the interaction between people and media texts and locating meaning in those interactions.

Although audiences are active, their activity is still subject to a variety of structural constraints. The media messages themselves matter—even if they can have multiple meanings—because they make some interpreta-tions more likely than others. The cultural tools that audiences bring to the interpretation of media are not uniform; different people from differ-ent social locations will not have the same resources at their command. By ordering the distribution of cultural tools, social structure serves as a constraint on the process of meaning-making.

Audiences, then, are active, but they are not fully autonomous; a soci-ology of the media needs to be sensitive to both the interpretive agency and the constraints of social structure. In the 1990s, audience research has been particularly useful when it has clarified the intersection of agency and structure in the analysis of what media messages *mean*. Research that compares the interpretive work of audiences from different social locations has been particularly useful in this regard. But what about the different kinds of *media*? Do the specific properties of a medium affect this interpretive work? We turn, in Chapter 9, to a consid-eration of media technology.

Media Technology and Social Change

In previous chapters, we have explored the industries and organizations that *produce* our mass media, the *content* of the media images that circulate widely, and the *meaning* of these media images for both audiences and the broader political system. We have also addressed a range of media forms, from newspapers and magazines to film and broadcasting to the rapidly expanding world of computer networks. However, we have not paid in-depth attention to the specific communication *medium* upon which the various media industries rely. Since we cannot have newspapers without printing presses, or television programming without equipment to transmit and receive visual images, we need to examine media technologies themselves. What kinds of information do the different forms of media communicate? How do different media forms shape the ways we think or influence the character of our social relationships? These questions focus specifically on media's technological apparatus—the medium itself.

The importance of media technology is rarely underestimated. In fact, a body of work has focused almost exclusively on technology as a driving force of social change. While changing technology certainly has consequences for society, a more sociological perspective examines the broader context in which technology exists. Thus, in this chapter, while we consider the different properties of the various media and their social implications, we go further and examine how the direction and application of media technology are socially constructed. This discussion takes into account the dynamic tension between media technologies and the various social forces that have shaped their evolution and use.

The Nature and Consequence of Media Technology

For most of us who are not engineers, the technologies that form the basis of our mass media seem remarkable. Even early-nineteenth-century printing presses are splendid machines. Electronic communication is even more technologically impressive and more difficult to understand. We might have a good sense of how printing is done, but how does radio or television really work? Many of us will not be able to answer this question, at least not in technical terms. However, we can still enjoy television and radio. In fact, the sets are so user-friendly that the only thing we have to do is plug them in and turn them on.

Computers and computer networks also are advanced technologies that most of us know very little about beyond what is required to use them. Though they are much more complicated than television sets, we can use our home, school, and office computers without knowing how their chips and operating systems work, how they process and store data digitally, or how they link up with networks and other media. Computers are getting easier to use, and, with generations of children being introduced to them in grammar school, more and more people are becoming computer literate.

One important characteristic of media technology, then, is that it is usable by almost anyone with access to it; it does not require elaborate technical knowledge on the part of users. The significance of media technology, as a result, is far-reaching.

Differing Technological Capabilities

Each medium has its own technological capabilities that affect the delivery of text, sound, and visual images. (See Exhibit 9.1.) For example, imagine a music concert performed by one of your favorite artists. A radio station could offer a free live or recorded broadcast of the concert. You would hear the sound but not be able to see the performers. A magazine could not bring you the sound, but for a price it could provide still pictures—after the fact—to show you what the event looked like; it could also have a printed story providing background information about the event. Broadcast television could bring free live video (moving pictures) and sound, but it would not be very useful for delivering text. (A cable TV program would cost money to receive and might even be offered only as a "pay-per-view" event.) A recording of the concert on compact disk or cassette would provide sound and would likely be packaged along with printed text, but it would not include video, and it, too, would cost money to purchase. An "enhanced" CD—which is basically a CD-ROM that is playable on a computer as well as on an audio CD player—would have all the sound of a regular CD plus printable text (such as song lyrics and artist profiles) and video images that could also be printed on a computer printer. However, this multimedia presentation is not the free live concert broadcast on radio and would be available only well after the original concert date.

We can see that the various media technologies provide different ways of "communicating" the concert experience, both in the kinds of information they present and in the ways we experience it. As we noted in

EXHIBIT 9.1 *Select Characteristics of Different Media*

	"Live"?	Text?	Sound?	Picture?	Video?	Interactive?[1]
Print	No	Yes	No	Yes	No	No
Radio	Yes	No	Yes	No	No	No
Film	No	No[2]	Yes	Yes	Yes	No
Broadcast TV	Yes	No[2]	Yes	Yes	Yes	No
Cable TV	Yes	No[2]	Yes	Yes	Yes	Yes
Music recording (CDs, cassettes, etc.)	No	No	Yes	No	No	No
CD-ROM (for computer)	No	Yes	Yes	Yes	Yes	No
Computer networks	Yes	Yes	Yes	Yes	Yes	Yes

The technological limitations of each medium set the parameters for their use. With the rise of digitization, though, the boundaries between different media are falling as they "converge" toward a single, digital form of multimedia.

[1] By interactive, we mean a medium that provides for two-way communication, not simply one that offers a range of choices. Computer menus, CD-ROM software, and programmable CD players offer the user options, but they are not truly interactive.
[2] While film and television can show text on the screen, they are not primarily textual mediums, and the text cannot be transferred to paper. Cable or digital television linked to a computer, though, does offer textual capabilities.

Chapter 3, though, digital capabilities are making it possible for different media to converge, as seen with "multimedia" computer CD-ROMs. (CD-ROM stands for "compact disk—read-only memory," which indicates that the material on the disk cannot be altered by the user, only "read.") The computer Internet even offers the possibility of receiving a live concert, with audio and video, along with accompanying text documents that could be printed. Experiments along this line have already been done, although current technology limits the quality and practicality of these efforts.

As our example shows, technology clearly matters. But, given our sociological approach, we should ask, *Why* does it matter? That is, what is it about mass media technology that has social significance? We can answer this question by reminding ourselves of the nature of mass media.

Mediating Communication

Media technologies are a structural constraint. Like all structures, they have been developed by humans and, subsequently, both enable and limit human action. How they do this is at the center of a sociological understanding of media technology.

Let's begin our discussion by returning to the roots of the term *media*. As we noted in Chapter 1, it is derived from the Latin word for "middle." This signifies that the media are in the middle of a communication process, specifically, in between the sender and the receiver of a message. The early use of the term *media* was as part of the phrase "mass media of communication." By now we have dropped the explicit reference to communication in everyday language and talk simply of "the media." Still, we need to bear in mind that our mass media communicate from one place to another. Thus, media technologies have social significance because they affect human communication.

We can see how technology affects communication by reminding ourselves of some of the defining characteristics of mass media. The word *mass* suggests that the communication is sent from one place and received in many places by a large audience. A newspaper, for example, is produced by a relatively small group of individuals who work for a particular news organization, and it is sold to a large group of readers. There is one sender, the news organization, and there are many receivers, all of the readers. Films, television, and music are also centrally produced, and they are distributed in theaters, through broadcasting, by cable lines, and through the sale of compact disks to large and often diverse audiences. Traditional forms of mass media, then, have a *one-to-many* orientation.

Another property of mass communication is that the senders are known but the receivers are not. Readers know the author of the book they are reading, but authors clearly cannot know who is buying or reading their book, except in the form of sales statistics. When we watch a television program or go to the movies, the names of the producer, director, and actors are prominently displayed—even though only real fans know much about them. Of course, with moviegoers and television viewers all over the country (or the world), audiences are anonymous. So another characteristic of most mass media is that they involve a *known sender* and generally *anonymous receivers*.

Additionally, most mass communication is not amenable to direct feedback from receivers of the messages. (Computer networks and some cable TV are partial exceptions.) When we read a book or a magazine, listen to the new CD we just bought, or turn on the television, there is no way to directly respond to the messages we are receiving. We can, if we want, take the time to write or call the distributor, producer, or author to let them know how much we liked or disliked their movie or book. (Or we can simply stop watching, listening, or reading.) But letters or phone calls are separate—and not "mass"—forms of communication. The traditional forms of mass communication are not interactive. Thus, mass communication is usually a *one-way* communication from a known sender to a mass of anonymous receivers.

The social significance of mass communication is that it differs substantially from unmediated face-to-face interaction. Here we get to the crux of the issue. When we take a sociological look at media technology, we are asking how these technologies shape the ways we interact and communicate with one another. One important influence of technology on communication is the compression of time and space.

Rethinking Time and Space

If we stop to think about it, a live television image of an event that is hundreds or thousands of miles away is an astonishing manipulation of time and space. We can "be there" without being there. For example, if someone who lives a block away from a stadium is not tuned in electronically, out-of-towners will know the outcome of the ballgame before the local neighborhood resident does. Physical distance becomes irrelevant.

The 1989 Loma Prieta earthquake near San Francisco demonstrated how television alters our relationship to time and space. Because major league baseball's World Series was under way in the Bay Area when the tremor occurred, the national media—blimp and all—were on hand. For those in the area whose electricity and phone service were knocked out by the earthquake, information about the size and scope of the earthquake was hard to come by. For those with family members living across town, it took considerable time, perhaps even hours, to get information about these family members' whereabouts. However, the live television shots gave the national audience virtually instant pictures of the damage, along with quick updates on the status of various neighborhoods. In short, residents of Boston or Dallas who had their television turned on received more and faster information about the earthquake than local San Francisco residents. Many San Franciscans who still had phone service made long-distance calls to relatives across the country to find out what had happened in the Bay Area and to learn how the situation was unfolding. This example suggests that our sense of "distance" in a television age is far different from that in previous eras. As we will see in the next chapter, this compression of space and time has become a key dimension of "globalization."

Computers also challenge our traditional notions of time and space, particularly as the virtual world of cyberspace evolves. The concept of "virtual community" (Rheingold, 1993) suggests that communities no longer need to be geographically based. People all over the globe can, according to many proponents of electronic interaction, become "virtual" neighbors through the space-bridging technology of the Internet. Friends, support groups, and professional colleagues can now communicate in the virtual world of computer networks, often without any face-to-face interaction at all. And high-tech jobs no longer need to be located in an office in a particular geographic location. A growing number of professionals are finding ways to "telecommute" to work—using phone, fax, and computer networks—so that they can work from home or avoid rush-hour traffic. Here, again, we can see how communication technology allows us to rethink the meaning of distance.

Given the technological sophistication of our media, its importance in communications, and its widespread utilization by broad segments of the population, we should not be surprised that discussions of media technology often emphasize the awesome power of the newest machine to affect society. While it may seem easy to recognize a medium's potential social impact, it is also easy to overstate the determining role of media technologies. In fact, the tendency to focus on the raw power of technology leads us down the well-blazed but analytically impoverished path to technological determinism, which claims that media technologies have a determining role in processes of social change. This position fails to recognize that technology is only one element of the media process in the social world. Still, the arguments of technological determinists must be considered.

Technological Determinism

We can think of technological determinism as an approach that identifies technology, or technological advances, as the central *causal* element in processes of social change. Sociologist Claude Fischer (1992) characterizes the most prominent forms of technological determinism as "billiard ball" approaches, in which technology is seen as an external force introduced into a social situation, producing a series of ricochet effects. From this perspective, technology causes things to happen, albeit often through a series of intermediary steps. For example, the invention of the automobile might be said to cause a reduction in food prices, because the automobile "reduced the demand for horses, which reduced the demand for feed grain, which increased the land available for planting edible grains," making food less expensive (Fischer, 1992, p. 8).

The problem, however, is that there is no human agency in this picture. In the technological determinist's lens, people exist only as rational employers of technology or pieces on the proverbial chess board who will be moved by the requirements of the technologies. In other words, this view is all structural constraint and no human action. It argues that technological properties demand certain results and that actual people do not use technologies so much as people are used by them. In this view, society is transformed according to a technical, rather than a human, agenda.

In his impressive social history of the telephone, Fischer (1992) argues that we should not even ask what "impact" a technology has had on a particular society, for this question implies from the outset that the technologies do something to us. Instead, Fischer suggests that we focus our attention on the people who use the technologies, sometimes in surprising ways. Actual users of technology, then, become the focus of the analysis, but they are not free-floating; technology users operate within specific social contexts, and they are working with technologies that can be used in limited ways.

The point is that the analysis of media technology cannot ignore the various, perhaps even contradictory, ways people make use of new technologies. Nothing inherent in the technologies forces us to adopt them in a particular way. In fact, people may find unexpected uses for certain technologies. Many early radio enthusiasts, for example, thought that its principal use would be point-to-point communication—a kind of wireless telephone—rather than broadcasting. And, before the development of broadcasting, early developers envisioned telephone technology as a way to bring news and entertainment into the home, not as a device for personal communication. New technologies enter social settings that are home to often deeply ingrained habits and cultural practices that shape the use of media. Therefore, to understand the relationship between media and society, we cannot ask only what a new *technology* does to people. We must also ask what *people* do with the new technology.

Technology and the Media Environment

Joshua Meyrowitz (1994) uses the term "medium theory" to refer to the body of literature that focuses on the technological aspects of media beyond their content. Medium theorists identify media as more than conduits for the transmission of messages. In essence, the basic rationale for looking beyond the content of media is that the very nature of the medium can be the key to its social impact. From this perspective, media technologies can be powerful social forces; their power lies in the ways they help organize and allow us to construct the cultural environment.

McLuhan's Message

Perhaps the most widely read medium theorist was the Canadian literary scholar Marshall McLuhan. McLuhan is best known for his claim, in sound-bite form, "the medium is the message." Briefly, McLuhan argued that if the influence of media interests us, then we should focus our attention on the ways each new medium disrupts tradition and reshapes social life. The real message, for McLuhan, was not the formal content of media but the ways the media themselves extend our senses and alter our social world. McLuhan (1964, p. 32) was quite insistent about this position, arguing that "the 'content' of a medium is like the juicy piece of meat carried by the burglar to distract the watchdog of the mind."

If content is, according to McLuhan, a peripheral issue, then what is it about the medium that is of such concern? In an early work, *The Gutenberg Galaxy* (1962), McLuhan focused on the shift from oral to print societies, exploring the social implications of the fifteenth-century invention of the printing press by Johannes Gutenberg. He argued that new media technologies rework the balance of our senses, isolating and highlighting certain senses at the expense of others. Print, from this perspective, intensified the visual—we use our eyes to read—and separated it from other senses, in particular, sound. McLuhan even argued that print media helped create a sensory environment that produced Western capitalist societies—an environment that was bureaucratic and organized around mass production, an ideology of individualism, and a commitment to the nation-state as the fundamental social unit.

In another work, McLuhan (1964) turned to the shift from print to electronic media, arguing that television could help reconnect the senses that had been fragmented by print. Electronic media could, in this view, bring us back to a kind of preprint state of harmony. It is this perspective that leads to utopian predictions of the development of a new "global village" based on the wonders of communication technology—a claim we explore in the final chapter. In the end, McLuhan advanced an unconventional but not very sophisticated version of technological determinism in which each medium was seen to shape our senses in such a way that certain social outcomes would be almost inevitable. And since the dominant media of an era are so all-encompassing, it would be virtually impossible for citizens to see the ways technology was influencing them. Despite McLuhan's now famous claim, we would argue that the message cannot be reduced to the medium. Such a proposition oversimplifies the complexities of the media process.

Images and Public Life

Others have followed McLuhan's approach, focusing on the consequences of the change from one medium to another. For example, some critics argue that the rise of television is the central cause of the decline in the seriousness of our public life (Postman, 1985). According to this view, the substance of democracy—participation by an informed citizenry—has been undermined by the rise of television because the medium has transformed the ways we talk and think about public issues. The underlying premise is that what we say is, in large part, the result of the form—or technology—we use to say it. The properties of television encourage, perhaps even dictate, particular ways of talking and thinking.

This kind of critique of the television age is often a nostalgic lament for the bygone days when print was the dominant form of media in American society. Following McLuhan, Neil Postman (1985) argues that print-based societies—and he identifies eighteenth- and nineteenth-century America as the most thoroughly print-based culture in history—encourage rationality, seriousness, and coherence in both our ways of thinking and the content of public discourse. Reading creates a mind in which analytic thought, based on logic and clarity, is premium. Societies that rely upon the printed word as the central means of both private and public communication, therefore, will develop a rational, serious population. Others have made similar arguments about the connection between print and rationality, suggesting that, for example, the development of the printing press played a key role in the rise of scientific thinking (Eisenstein, 1979).

Postman (1985) is concerned with the ways television challenges the rationality and coherence of print-based modes of thinking by holding up entertaining and trivial images, but the most interesting part of his book is the discussion of the role of the telegraph and the photograph in cultural change. By altering our sense of physical place—specifically, by making it possible to communicate with people who were physically distant—the telegraph, according to Postman, challenged the world defined by print in three fundamental ways. First, because they could get information from faraway places, newspapers were full of stories that were largely irrelevant to their readers. News no longer had to have any relationship to its audience, nor did information have to be functional in any way—it just had to be "new." Daily news consisted of new things, and novelty became more important than relevance. Second, since the telegraph made it easy to transmit so much information, little of which was relevant to the lives of readers, news no longer had any connection to action. People could not do anything about the things they read about in the paper. Information may have been abundant, but events were happening so far away and were so disconnected from people's lives that the news encouraged feelings of powerlessness. Third, in privileging speed and abundance of information, the telegraph sacrificed context. No longer did news have to be linked to any broader, historical framework. There was no need to connect one story to the next, or one day's headlines to the next day's.

The point was to keep the information flowing—to report the new things that happened—rather than to contextualize messages or events by linking them to prior messages or events. Quantity became more important than either quality or depth.

The photograph extended what Postman sees as a revolution in the ways we understand the world. Photos do not encourage logical argument or contextual knowledge. Instead, as Postman (1985, p. 73) puts it, "the point of photography is to isolate images from context, so as to make them visible in a different way." As the saying goes, a picture is worth a thousand words. But Postman argues that, when we trade words for pictures, we lose something in the deal. The very meaning of information, of truth, is altered by a focus on the visual image of the photograph. Truth is no longer something we understand from logical thought, the kind of thinking that reading produces. Instead, truth is in the seeing, not in the thinking; or, as the saying goes, seeing is believing.

A generation before Postman, historian Daniel Boorstin (1961) argued that the pervasiveness of visual images was changing the very meaning of "reality." Images have become so embedded in our consciousness, in this view, that it is becoming harder to discern the difference between image and reality. It is not that we are losing our ability to think; it is that image-oriented pseudoevents blur the distinction. Pseudoevents are events planned for the express purpose of producing dramatic images that can be disseminated or reported. In effect, they are events that have no independent existence; they take place only to be publicized. Pseudoevents include press conferences, televised debates between political candidates, and "photo opportunities"—all events staged in order to produce dramatic images. Pseudoevents, however, are neither true nor false; they actually happen, but only to produce dramatic images. Appearance, not substance, is what matters. Indeed, pseudoevents may be more interesting than spontaneous happenings, a state of affairs that suggests that our definition of reality may be changing.

Postmodernists suggest that contemporary society is increasingly characterized by this kind of "hyperreality," in which the boundary that used to separate reality from its representation has "imploded," leaving images with no real-world referents (Baudrillard, 1988). One does not have to be a postmodernist, however, to see the significance of image making. In 1961, in the early years of the television age, Boorstin was exploring the relationship between the medium of communication and our ways of knowing. In a similar vein, Postman identifies our image-dominated world as a "peek-a-boo" world; things come and go, with little coherence, but our lives are always chock-full of entertainment. In a world where the dominant medium is television, fast-paced entertainment may have become the model for all of society. As other realms of experience increasingly compete with, and even imitate, television, pretelevision ways of knowing the world may be becoming more and more marginal.

There can be little doubt that critics like Postman and Boorstin are correct about the significance of images in American society and the centrality of television in our lives. This represents, to be sure, a dramatic change from life in the first half of the twentieth century. The analysis of how the telegraph reorients our relationship to physical space—and therefore makes new kinds of information available—is a helpful example of how new forms of media provide resources for changing social patterns, particularly with respect to who and what we know.

Still, the causal claims—that inherent properties of media technology are the key determining force—are much more difficult to accept. The problem is that this viewpoint ignores people, except perhaps as victims of an all-powerful medium. Even though it is rarely explicit, most critics of television write about *commercial television,* not simply television technology (Hoynes, 1994). The claims that television, as a technology, must be about entertainment, attractive images, and rapid movement from one idea to the next are not some technological law of nature. They are the result of a broadcast industry—driven by people—in which the need to sell products and make profits has dominated.

Certainly, there is nothing "natural" about our television industry or the kinds of programs that dominate the airwaves. The commercial organization of broadcasting did not just happen naturally; it was developed—in the face of rarely mentioned opposition—by people who would profit from the commercial organization of the industry (McChesney, 1994). Medium theorists often fail to explore the ways human actors or public policy have shaped the uses of technology. In addition, this perspective has little room for any kind of critical, intellectual activity on the part of television audiences. As we saw in Chapter 8, there is good reason to believe that the decoding of television messages, including a kind of reading between the lines, requires active engagement and interpretive work.

Electronic Media and Social Identity

Other researchers have employed subtler versions of medium theory, exploring questions of determination and causality more carefully. Meyrowitz (1985), for example, has argued that the primary social impact of television is the way the medium radically breaks the connection between *physical place* and *social place,* making physical location much less significant for our social relationships. With television, we can be "there" without actually being there. We can watch sporting events, courtroom verdicts, and political speeches, and even go shopping without leaving our homes. And vast numbers of people living in different parts of the country can all be doing the same thing at the same time in very different places. Before the development of electronic media, our social roles and identities were closely tied to the physical places where we performed these roles. With the advent of electronic media, especially television, old roles and identities became blurred or reconfigured in response to new kinds of social situations. This view, with its focus on place, stresses the ways the media are part of and help shape our environment—the "situational geography" of social life.

One of Meyrowitz's principal examples is what he calls the "blurring of childhood and adulthood," which is a result of the new patterns of information flow initiated by television. Television brings adults and children together in social situations that were once distinct and allows children to see parts of the social world that were previously hidden or difficult to access. In particular, according to Meyrowitz, television permits children to be "present"—socially, if not physically—at "adult interactions." The result is that an important barrier between adults and children, which in the past was reinforced by different levels of reading skill, no longer holds.

The new domestic information environment brought on by television does more than remove barriers and reshape previous patterns of communication, however. Television gives children a much clearer view of the world of adult secrets; they see more closely the "backstage" behaviors of adults. (This may have a good deal to do with the popular belief that children today grow up too fast.) As a result, the adult world is much less mysterious to television-age children, in large part because they know that there is an adult backstage that is at least partially hidden. Schools do not have the same kind of power today as in the past, because television provides an alternative source of information. As a socializing agent, then, television does not simply supplement parents and schools; it competes with them by providing children with ideas and images that often contradict the stories and myths handed down in the family and at school. Also, the ability to understand television is not connected to age; children can read and understand television as well as adults—a dramatic change from print-oriented cultures, in which information was connected to largely age-specific reading skills.

Our information environment and our sense of place have changed quite dramatically in the twentieth century, and the growth of electronic media has clearly played a role in this change. Still, we need to be careful. It is too easy to simply identify television as the cause of these changes—whether we celebrate or deplore them. Technology does not drive culture in so straightforward a manner. As we will see later in this chapter, when we look at the incorporation of television into the home in the 1950s, the cultural practices of the people who adopt a particular technology shape the development and uses of that technology.

Medium Theory in a Computer Age

By the late 1990s, new technological developments extended the forms of electronic communication and began to erase the distinctions between different forms of media. Digital communication now links text, image, and sound; personal computers, for example, are fast becoming new versions of home entertainment centers. The trend is likely to continue. Sven Birkerts (1994) picks up the questions asked by prior medium theorists and applies them to the posttelevision, digital age. The title of his book, *The Gutenberg Elegies*, suggests that he is working in the tradition of McLuhan. If McLuhan's *Gutenberg Galaxy* was about identifying the characteristics of print culture, Birkerts is writing about an era—one in which the printed word was the dominant medium—that he considers to be dead. His elegies are both a celebration of a bygone era and a warning about the future digital age.

Drawing upon the notion of social life as a web of interaction, Birkerts argues that new media technologies "reweave" social and cultural life. New modes of communication require new ways of receiving and reacting to the content of those communications. Electronic media gave us a new sense of time and space by allowing for a much faster flow of information and by breaking the spatial connection between the physical and the social. Digital media have taken us much farther down that road. The virtual world of computer networks is a new social space, cyberspace, that allows for new forms of interaction with little connection to the physical world. People can take on new identities in cyberspace, transcending the limits and the responsibilities of their physical environment —at least temporarily.

The new media take us so far from the natural world that our sense of time changes as we become increasingly committed to the instantaneous nature of computer-mediated communication. Indeed, it was not long ago—the late 1970s—that overnight mail seemed an absurd luxury. As late as 1985, the fax machine seemed to be an unnecessary gadget. Now we view both overnight mail and fax as increasingly essential; computer networks and the ability to send files instantaneously around the globe are making overnight mail the slow boat these days. Regular e-mail users even refer to the U.S. postal service as "snail mail," since (comparatively) it is so slow.

In this high-tech age, where data seem virtually limitless, Birkerts argues that our ways of thinking are in the process of changing. No longer do we value deliberation; decisiveness rules the day. We do not need to know about the world; instead, we need to know how to access the data that will tell us about the world. The abundance of information and the complex ways of storing and manipulating it put a premium on a new set of skills—retrieving and referencing, rather than understanding.

The development of hypertext, in this view, is the strongest signal of a change in our culture. Using hypertext is different from the experience of reading. With hypertext, "readers" use a computer to choose from a range of "links" to follow in an electronic document. Each link leads to another text with even more links. Even though we are using our eyes and looking at words, Birkerts argues that the hypertext activity needs a new name, perhaps "texting" or "word piloting." Reading is an activity in which we engage with ideas, listen to an author, and consider an argument. In the social space created by reading, authors have a kind of cultural authority, at least while we are reading their book. Hypertext challenges the very idea of authorship; the author no longer matters in the same way when "readers" are "piloting" from one link to the next. The writer–reader relationship, in short, is no longer the same in the world of hypertext.

Birkerts has the same fear as many other medium theorists: that as we become more and more enmeshed in advanced computer technologies we will lose any sense of unmediated experience, making the social world of media the only world we know (or value). Newer, faster, space-altering media will squeeze out prior cultural forms, including reading and rigorous thinking. We will define freedom as freedom from the constraints of the physical world, which we will seek to accomplish by an even deeper commitment to mediated experience. This may sound like a cheap science fiction movie, but such changes are already in full swing.

The question, of course, is what role particular media technologies play in these developments. A McLuhanesque approach focuses on the impact of the new medium itself. But we also need to pay attention to the commercial forces that are driving the development of these technologies and shaping their distribution in particular ways. In fact, the growth of mega-media giants and the culture industry's focus on the short-term bottom line are central to explaining the "superficial" nature of media culture. Certainly, the technologies provide new opportunities for media corporations by giving them new profit-making resources and the enhanced ability to link different kinds of media. And some users of the newer media have focused on creating new spatial relations in the electronic world of cyberspace. But largely because of the economics involved, cyberspace at the end of the twentieth century is still a relatively exclusive community.

Medium theorists raise provocative questions and identify changes in broad social patterns that are clearly linked to changes in media technology. However, these approaches tend to overlook both the actual *users* of the technologies and the *economic, organizational, and political forces* that shape the development of the new media. The strength of medium theory is that it looks at the social environment the media help create and at how that environment shapes human action. At its best, it is not overly deterministic but focuses on the ways in which a medium facilitates some actions and discourages others.

The Social Construction of Media Technologies

Technologies do not simply appear on the scene, fully developed and ready to be implemented, nor do the technical properties of emerging technologies predetermine their use. People must use new technologies, and in capitalist societies this use usually must be profitable. Media technologies, therefore, are embedded in ongoing social processes, and, as a result, their development and application are neither fixed nor fully predictable (Douglas, 1987). Technological development is the result of several interacting variables: the capacities of new machines, the priorities of owners and investors, the cultural practices and traditions that the new technologies confront, the uses of potentially competing machines, and the specific ways people actually talk about and use the new technologies. To understand the social significance of media technology, then, we should pay attention to the social forces that shape their development and adoption.

In order to address these issues, scholars have closely examined the earlier introduction of new technologies, such as the development of radio and the rapid spread of television. These assessments confirm that our now taken-for-granted ways of using radio and television were in fact the result of complex social processes. As we have seen, the technical properties of each medium do matter. They place constraints on the ways people can use media by providing parameters within which human agents must operate. But humans do have agency, and they have a range of options with respect to how to use media technology.

The Early Years of Radio

In its earliest years, people knew "radio" by a different name and understood it as a very different form of communication. What we now take for granted—a model of broadcasting music, news, and entertainment programming —took two decades to evolve (Douglas, 1987; Schiffer, 1991; McChesney, 1994). For 10 years after its invention by Marconi in 1895, people called radio the "wireless." Early radio was essentially the same technology we know today; it used the electromagnetic spectrum to transmit audio signals from sender to receiver. But the *meaning* of the technology was different. Radio technology existed, but the social forces that later shaped the direction of radio technology had not yet coalesced. Corporate consolidation of the radio industry had not yet occurred; the government had not yet regulated the use of the electromagnetic spectrum; investors had not yet recognized the profitability of producing household radio receiving devices. The "wireless" had not yet become "radio."

When Marconi first demonstrated his "wireless" in 1899 at the America's Cup in New York City, he thought of the technology as a telegraph without wires. In the eyes of its inventor, then, the wireless was an improvement of an existing communication technology that sent messages from one point to another. The remarkable achievement had nothing to do with broadcasting music or entertainment; it was concerned with the ability to communicate point to point through the airwaves. Marconi's business acumen directed his attention to those institutions, particularly newspapers and steamships, that had come to rely upon the telegraph in their routine business practices. Perhaps his wireless could serve as a substitute, or an upgrade, providing a less cumbersome means for long-distance communication.

The primary users, in Marconi's vision, would be large commercial interests with a regular need for transmitting information to and receiving information from a distance. There was little sense that *individuals* would use wireless and, therefore, little reason to produce equipment for individual use. In addition, early developers conceived of wireless as a two-way communication device—wireless users would both send and receive messages. At the beginning of the twentieth century, the notion that receive-only devices—what we call radios—would be the core of the technology was still far off. A century after the invention of the wireless, this early vision of its utility may seem naive. However, the future of wireless—later called "radiotelegraphy," then "radiotelephony" when it began to transmit voice instead of Morse code, and finally just "radio"—was uncertain for more than 20 years (Douglas, 1987).

In the early years of the twentieth century, a struggle over the control of radio—and over the definition of its proper uses—brought corporate interests, the U.S. military, and amateur operators into conflict. Corporate interests, including the American Marconi Company, sought private control of the airwaves in order to use them for profit. The Navy sought government control of the airwaves in order to use them for official purposes, particularly during wartime. And amateur radio enthusiasts, mostly young men and boys in the years between 1906 and 1920, saw the airwaves as a form of public property to be used by citizens to communicate with one another. As amateurs learned how to use the new technology and how to construct their own transmitters and receivers, a radio subculture emerged in which sending and receiving long-distance communications became an increasingly popular hobby. As listeners tuned in at night, seeking transmissions from sites hundreds of miles away, it was amateurs who planted the seeds of the broadcast model and made the act of listening a leisure activity.

In the years prior to 1920, corporate and government radio operators still saw radio as a form of point-to-point communication, even as the airwaves became increasingly populated by amateurs. The sinking of the *Titanic* in 1912 highlighted the difficulty of communicating distress signals by wireless because of the jumble of overlapping transmissions. The Marconi Company complained about the use—and what it saw as abuse—of the airwaves by amateurs. The result was the Radio Act of 1912, which regulated the use of the airwaves by requiring all transmitting stations to be licensed by the federal government.

This outcome had been in the making for several years; because the airwaves have limited space, it was becoming increasingly clear that the government would have to organize and delimit their use. For Marconi, the Radio Act certified the central role of his company, since the government would curtail access for amateurs. According to Douglas (1987, p. 233), "the amateurs had to be purged from the most desirable portion of the broadcast spectrum. They had to be transformed from an active to a passive audience, allowed to listen but not to 'talk.'" Even before the notion of broadcasting had taken hold, therefore, the institutional structure of broadcasting was in place: centralized, licensed senders and large numbers of individual listeners.

Despite these restrictions, amateurs continued to operate radios in even larger numbers. Some made use of the short-wave frequencies that the government allocated, others were granted government licenses to use the airwaves, and still others continued to operate without licenses. In 1917, when the United States declared war on Germany, the government ordered all amateur radio operators to shut down and dismantle their equipment. Douglas (1987) reports that the police closed down more than 800 stations in New York alone. In need of skilled radio operators, the Navy recruited amateurs, many of whom served in World War I. They returned home after the war even more skilled in radio technology. By 1920, amateurs were experimenting with playing music and providing information over the air to other amateurs, who were encouraging their families and friends to listen along. Several amateur transmitters built up substantial audiences for their "programming," while the corporate radio industry continued to focus on point-to-point communication.

All of this changed when, in the hope of increasing sales of their radio equipment, a Pittsburgh department store ran a local newspaper advertisement for a musical program broadcast by amateur Frank Conrad. Shortly thereafter, Westinghouse, one of the major manufacturers of radio sets, began financing Conrad's station as a means of selling its radios. Radio manufacturers AT&T and General Electric, along with department stores, quickly jumped into the business of broadcasting by setting up stations to stimulate the sale of radio sets. The market for the broadcast model was much larger than for the point-to-point model. As news coverage of radio programming increased, owning a radio set and being able to listen to the programs became highly popular. In 1922, AT&T began selling access to the airwaves as Marconi had done for private communication, but with a much larger audience. The broadcast model, with programming financed by the sale of advertising, was finally in place.

The route to radio broadcasting of music, news, and serials, all surrounded by ads, was not the straightforward result of some technological imperative. It was full of twists and turns with apparently minor players performing major roles, a series of miscalculations by inventors and entrepreneurs, and historically specific actions on the part of government and the corporate community. For decades after the consolidation of the broadcasting model, amateurs stoked the flames of an alternative way of thinking about radio. "Ham" radio enthusiasts built their own sets that allowed them to transmit as well as receive programming and messages. This ham radio subculture was, in important respects, the cultural antecedent of the contemporary computer hacker scene. Others—so-called "pirate" radio operators—mounted even more direct challenges to the official broadcast model, using the airwaves without a license to transmit alternative music and sometimes politically radical ideas.

When we include factors beyond technology in our understanding of radio, we can see that what we often take for granted as the natural order of things is in fact the result of a complicated social process. Moreover, we can see that things could have turned out differently. Basic wireless technology might have been applied or further developed in a different direction. In short, alternative arrangements, with distinct social consequences, are always possible.

What if corporate capital had not been inclined to develop—or had been prevented from developing—a commercial radio industry? What if the government had maintained exclusive control of radio, as some urged in the post–World War I years? Or consider the flip side. What if government had stayed entirely out of radio, enacting no regulations at all to control the use of the airwaves? In each of these cases, the development and ultimate meaning of radio would likely have taken their own path, making some uses more likely than others. In other countries, radio has played a different role than in the United States. In some countries, radio has served as a more distinct form of top-down communication, providing official information (i.e., propaganda) from the government to its citizens. In others, listeners have much more widespread access to the airwaves, which are not used to sell products with the same zeal as in the United States.

Playing "what if" games certainly does not change the outcome, but it suggests the contingency in technological development. Events had to unfold in a particular way for radio to turn out as it did. We cannot understand the meaning of radio in American society simply by looking at its technological component, because this ignores the social processes that shaped its use. The goal, then, is to understand how media technologies develop, how people use them, and what this means for broader patterns of social communication. We must remember that media technologies are processes that both are influenced by and, in turn, shape social life.

Introducing Television into the Home

Twenty-five years after the consolidation of the radio industry, television was available as a mass consumer item. Manufacturers marketed it as a new form of home entertainment that would bring public amusement right into the home. Families would not even have to leave the house to have fun. Instead, television would bring the family together to enjoy leisure activities. If sales of television sets are any measure, this pitch worked quite well. Television became a household staple—a virtual necessity—faster than any previous home appliance. The percentage of American households with television sets skyrocketed from just 0.02 percent in 1946 to almost 90 percent in 1960. In relatively short order, television became a central part of American life.

The remarkably rapid adoption of television, however, did not simply change home life. Instead, television both accommodated to already existing family practices and tried to mold these practices to make television a central part of domestic life (Spigel, 1992). Producers directed most early television programming at women viewers, whom they considered to be the largest and most accessible audience. Daytime radio programming had already demonstrated the broad interest of women in home entertainment. The 1950s family ideology did not distinguish between women's labor time and their leisure time; there was always housework to be done, but it was not defined as "work." And while women were perceived as having a great deal of "free time" during the day, that is, time for leisure or relaxation, there was always plenty of work around the house that required women's attention. Radio, a purely aural medium, could provide entertainment while women worked, since listening did not distract women from other activities. Television, however, was a different story; it had to adapt to the 1950s family ideology. As a result, television was marketed to women as something they could enjoy at the same time as they were doing housework (Spigel, 1992).

One concrete example of this adaptation of television to the family ideology was the development in 1952 of a TV-Stove, a machine that allowed women to watch television while they cooked. The TV-Stove demonstrates that cultural practices can shape the development of a communications medium. Leaders of the television industry feared that the new medium might not fit into women's lives and therefore might be underused or ignored altogether. By designing the apparatus in line with cultural practices and traditions, the television industry hoped to attract loyal viewers.

The content of programming also reflected the practices of 1950s middle-class women. In the formative years of television, producers developed the "soap opera" and the "variety show" as programming that would not conflict with women's work roles in the home. Soap operas contained little action but a great deal of verbal explanation. Also, they often repeated the same themes. Viewers could miss episodes or listen from an adjacent room without losing track of plot developments. Variety shows, while more visually oriented, moved from one act to the next, making it easy for viewers to watch only parts of the program; there was no need to pay attention from beginning to end. This, too, was ideal for women working around the house.

In order for television to be successful, then, it had to make itself fit into the routines of its viewers. Television was not an external force that colonized the home and our ways of thinking, in part because there was widespread anxiety about the impact of television in the early years. To prevent resistance or outright rejection, television evolved as a medium that was compatible with the 1950s family ideology.

Thus, television was shaped by a set of cultural practices and traditions about family life—the practices of the white, middle-class families that producers saw as the core of the consumer market. But this is only one side of the story. The television industry also tried to reshape family routines to be compatible with television viewing. As Spigel (1992, p. 85) puts it, "Not merely content to fit its programming into the viewer's rhythms of reception, the network aggressively sought to change those rhythms by making the activity of television viewing into a new daily habit." Promoters billed NBC's "Today Show" as the TV equivalent of the morning newspaper; the networks routinized their schedules, previewed upcoming programs, and linked program times to the household activities of women and children.

Much of television, including the domestic sit-coms of the 1950s, focused on how to *consume* various products, including television itself. The medium of television certainly helped consolidate the United States as a consumption-oriented society. In fact, television became the centerpiece of American consumer culture. There is good reason to believe that television has influenced, and even disrupted, our traditions and practices as well as our buying habits. Still, television itself was shaped by both the emerging consumer culture and the commercial organization of broadcasting. Television was not a predetermined entity; cultural practices shaped its early development and uses, just as the medium in turn influenced these practices and encouraged new uses of the technology.

The Future of Interactive Media Technologies

A whole new generation of media, based on computer technologies, emerged in the 1980s. These disparate forms of media, often called the "new media," have capabilities that differ significantly from the previous generation of mass media. One principal difference is that the new media can be used for interactive communication. This breaks with the one-way nature of "mass" communication and has many of the characteristics of face-to-face communication (Rogers, 1986). In essence, new media technologies provide citizens with the technical apparatus to do more than just receive information. They can respond to messages they receive, select which images they want to receive, or even send out their own messages.

For example, citizens can use new media for "electronic town meetings" (Abramson et al., 1988), which allows them to speak to one another from different locations. Corporations use a similar technology on a smaller scale for "teleconferencing," which brings people together via television screen even when they may be thousands of miles apart. And the Internet, the World Wide Web, and commercial computer services such as Prodigy and America Online provide computer links between people for either electronic conversation or the transfer of data and images. In all these examples, the distinction between sender and receiver is blurred, because all who have access to the technology can be more than passive audiences.

The differences between "new" and "old" forms of media are substantial in themselves. As with the introduction of previous technologies, however, the new forms of communication have produced often wild speculation about their social impact. One critic, representing the extreme view, has argued that innovations in computer networking technology are producing "the most transformative technological event since the capture of fire" (*Harper's Magazine*, 1995), fundamentally changing the way we live. However, such predictions adequately conceptualize neither the social forces that influence the development of technology nor the cultural practices that shape how people use them. New media do, indeed, provide resources and opportunities for new forms of social interaction and new ways of relating to, or even manipulating, the limitations of time and space. But, again, this is only part of the story. If we are to understand the social significance of the new media, we must look at how their technological properties intersect other social forces.

Rather than focusing on only one causal element, the technology, W. Russell Neuman (1991) suggests that we need to understand the relationship between the "technological drivers," the social psychology of media use, and the economics of the media industries. He uses the metaphor of a tug-of-war: The new media have technical capabilities that pull in one direction, but social psychological and economic forces pull back hard in the other direction. The short-run outcome will likely be only small social changes, even if opportunities for more significant changes emerge in the long term. In other words, change will be evolutionary, not revolutionary.

The key to understanding the new media is that they all connect with one another. According to Neuman (1991, p. 12), "We are witnessing the evolution of a universal interconnected network of audio, video, and electronic text communications that will blur the distinction between interpersonal and mass communication and between public and private communication." Neuman argues that these integrated media networks have several key capabilities:

- The new media will become increasingly less expensive.
- They will once again alter the meaning of geographic distance.
- They provide the possibility of increasing the speed of communication.
- They allow for a huge increase in the volume of communication.
- They allow for more channels of information flow.
- They provide opportunities for interactive communication.
- They provide more control for individual users.
- They allow forms of communication that were previously separate to overlap and interconnect.

In short, new technologies allow for more, faster, diverse, two-way communications between users who have both more control and more choice. These properties of the new media provide resources for increased media diversity and give communications power to citizens instead of to central authorities. Were the story to end here, we might agree with those who celebrate the new media as guarantors of a renewed democracy that empower citizens and reinvigorate participation in public life.

However, we have looked only at one side of the tug-of-war. The new media may pull toward diversity and participation, but other social forces pull toward uniformity and spectatorship. Most of us have deeply ingrained media habits that are not likely to change dramatically simply because of new technological capabilities. We spend a great deal of time with media, sometimes using more than one medium at the same time. Also, most of us use media for entertainment purposes, not for strictly informational or political purposes. Developments in interactive media already accommodate these habits; many of the widely used services are versions of high-tech shopping and other consumer-oriented activities. The Internet, for example, is becoming increasingly commercialized as companies produce "home pages" advertising their products and make it easy for consumers to buy these products via cyberspace.

Long-standing media habits will shape how most of us use the new media. The new media will certainly not change our behavior and thinking overnight. Instead, our behaviors and attitudes will influence the development of the new media, especially with respect to the vast majority of the population, who will relate to new media in much the same way they do to existing media.

Some people will make use of the full range of capabilities offered by the new media. For these individuals, new media technology can offer a significantly different way of accessing, manipulating, and using information. But any communication advantage provided by the new media is likely to be distributed unevenly, replicating existing informational inequalities. Those who are already better educated, more familiar with emerging technologies, and better able to afford devices such as sophisticated home computers will be precisely the people who benefit most from the new media. New media may even inadvertently expand the gulf between the technological "haves" and "have nots."

Economic forces like those examined in Chapter 2 will also pull away from diversity and toward sameness. The new media are being developed as for-profit channels and products of communication. Owners and investors are likely to promote their wares to a mass audience, imitating already popular products and avoiding products that lack demonstrated appeal. The shift from broadcast to cable television is a good example of this dynamic. We now have 50 or more channels, but *more* programming has not meant *diverse* programming. Instead of a couple of hours a week of "Wide World of Sports," we now have the sports networks, ESPN and ESPN2, 24 hours a day. Instead of Saturday morning children's cartoons, we now have a cartoon network. The cable coming into our homes can do more than bring us programs; it can easily transmit out of the home, as well. However, experiments with interactive cable programming have shown little profit potential beyond home shopping. In short, market forces will greatly constrain the vast technological potential of the new media.

Neuman (1991, p. 165) sums up his analysis by arguing that "the anticipated impacts of the new media are neither inevitable nor self-evident." This is a good guideline for the analysis of the social implications of any new technology. If we weigh the technological properties of the new media along with media habits and market forces, the new media, despite vastly increased volume, seem unlikely to rapidly change the communication environment, which is characterized by least-common-denominator mass audience content. The situation is not static, however. Media habits may change, albeit slowly, and larger numbers of citizens may begin to take advantage of new media, providing new markets. In the short run, larger changes are likely to occur at the margins, as small numbers of citizens use interactive, digital media in new and intriguing ways.

The communications revolution, despite daily predictions of its imminent arrival, will probably be slow, partial, and full of contradictions. The real question is not what these technologies can do but how their capacities intersect with other social forces and cultural trends. Media technology ultimately may not be the driver of social change; it might be more helpful to look at our changing political culture for insight into technology's potential uses. In this regard, the growing focus on multiculturalism —as both beliefs and a set of practices—should direct our attention to the rapid increase in media produced by and directed to defined groups. Some have dubbed these "special interest" media; others refer to *narrow*casting in contrast to *broad*casting. Regardless of the label, we can already see that new media technologies are being used for targeted communication. Cable television channels, small book publishers, special interest magazines and newsweeklies, computer newsgroups, and even advertising and direct mail focus products on relatively small groups defined by characteristics such as race, gender, age, sexual orientation, and lifestyle. This marketing strategy is an example of how the technological properties of new media—especially their flexibility and relatively low cost—work in concert with both social developments, such as multiculturalism and a growing identity politics, and economic forces, such as the search for new consumer markets, to produce new patterns of social communication.

The implications of targeted, rather than mass, media are far from clear. Some see a fragmentation of American society, a breaking of the common cultural bonds—reinforced and reproduced by mass media—that formed the basis for a national identity in the United States. Others see the seeds of a new cultural democracy in which alternative meanings circulate and communication patterns are as much people-to-people as they are top-down, creating spaces for new forms of public communication and participation. In either case, media technologies do not stand on their own; we must locate the new media in specific social and historical contexts. This approach insists on avoiding the tendency to reduce the question of causality to straightforward technological forces; instead, it sees technologies as resources that people can use in varying ways or ignore. Different forms of media may allow, and even facilitate, certain uses that influence our social roles and identities; they do not determine them.

Conclusion

We have traveled a long way in this chapter, from the invention of the printing press to the new world of digital, electronic communication that is collapsing the distinctions between the different forms of media. We have seen the pitfalls of a technologically deterministic view that denies even the most rudimentary forms of human agency. At the same time, we have explored how media systems contribute to the social environment in which we live. Indeed, media are a central element of social structure. To understand the dynamic relationship between technology, culture, and social change, however, analysis of past technological developments and predictions of future change must weigh the forces of both social structure, which media technologies both help constitute and are shaped by, and human agency, the actual use of technologies and the broader cultural practices that shape their use.

As we think about the implications of new media technologies, we should remember that social change is not linear and that we are likely to find it in unexpected places. Take, for example, the efforts to sell weekly newsmagazines in multimedia form on CD-ROM. *Newsweek Interactive,* one of the pioneers in this field, has found that readers and advertisers alike have been reluctant to jump on board. After all, many of us enjoy the opportunity to hold a magazine or newspaper; the feel of the publication is part of the reading experience. While products such as *Newsweek Interactive* have not yet had much impact on our reading habits, however, other changes are appearing around the edges, especially within the institutions that produce multimedia products. The journalists and editors who actually produce *Newsweek Interactive* have "shed traditional identities of both reporter and editor. They've started creating entirely new roles, behaving more like film producers and directors" (Oppenheimer, 1993, p. 34). This is, of course, not a simple effect of multimedia technology. On the contrary, it demonstrates how media professionals make use of and adapt to technological resources and suggests that discussions of new technologies must look at the organizations that employ them as well as at the everyday lives of citizens.

PART FIVE

Globalization and the Future

CHAPTER 10

Media in a Changing Global Culture

In the mid-1960s, Canadian cultural scholar Marshall McLuhan (1964, p. 19) wrote that with the rise of electronic media "we have extended our central nervous system itself in a global embrace." McLuhan believed that the rise of electronic media marked a new phase in human history. For the first time, physical distance was no longer a barrier, and instantaneous mass communication across the globe was possible. The result was McLuhan's notion of the "global village," in which the people of the world would be brought closer together as they made their voices heard. Such an information environment, according to McLuhan, "compels commitment and participation. We have become irrevocably involved with, and responsible for, each other" (McLuhan and Fiore, 1967, p. 24).

In the years since McLuhan wrote, the mass media *have* moved steadily toward becoming truly global in nature. Cable News Network (CNN) provides news via satellite to over 100 nations in all corners of the globe (Mowlana, 1993). Major sporting events are broadcast to hundreds of millions of viewers worldwide. For example, over one *billion* people around the globe watched the 1990 World Cup match between Germany and Argentina (De Mooij and Keegan, 1991, p. 4). Satellite transmissions across continents and oceans are now routine. However, the consequences of increasingly global media have not been as straightforward as McLuhan's work suggests. In fact, the trends in media globalization are marked by distinct ambiguity and contradiction. Some developments seem likely to produce positive changes of the sort envisioned by McLuhan; others seem cause for alarm. Some trends seem certain, others more tenuous. What is clear, though, is that whatever future direction the mass media take, it will have a global facet. There is no turning back. Understanding some of the basic global dimensions of media, therefore, is central to consideration of the future of *all* mass media.

This chapter explores the nature and potential consequences of mass media globalization. We have already addressed some global dimensions of media in earlier chapters. It is impossible to separate globalization from the issues with which we have been concerned. However, this chapter allows us to do two things. First, we discuss media globalization as a distinct social force that both contributes to social change and is influenced by global changes. Second, we reintegrate concepts that in earlier sections of this book we separated for analytic purposes. In the real world, media ownership, production, content, ideology, politics, audiences, and technology are all inextricably intertwined. We had to separate these and other concepts in order to discuss them coherently. In this final chapter, though, we move freely from one topic to another in a more integrated manner that more closely resembles the real—and complex—world of mass media.

What Is Globalization?

We can think of globalization as having two central components. The first relates to the changing role of geography and physical distance. As we saw in Chapter 9, with electronic media, instantaneous communication and interaction can be carried out over far distances. Globalization carries this phenomenon to its global limits. The second dimension of globalization involves the content of this communication. With electronic media, the ideas, images, and sounds of different cultures are potentially available to vast networks of people outside the culture from which the message originated. In this sense, culture becomes more accessible to larger numbers of people. We examine each of these components of globalization, beginning with time and space.

Crossing Limits of Time and Space

When humans began orbiting the earth, photographs taken from space allowed people for the first time to see the planet in a single image—a tiny blue ball amid the vast darkness of space. Perhaps nothing better captures the symbolism of globalization than these now well-known pictures. In the click of a camera's shutter, the vast expanses of the earth, which had taken humankind centuries to explore and map, suddenly seemed small and fragile. A single photographic image captured the great distance between the plains of Africa and the plains of the American Midwest, suggesting that perhaps the distance was not so great after all.

The ability to capture an image of the entire globe was symbolic of the move toward globalization in many spheres. By now, *globalization* has become a common buzzword. The "global economy," "global politics," and the "global environment" are just a few contexts in which people use the term. Environmentalists in the 1970s encouraged us to "think globally, act locally." The idea was that we needed to be aware of the implications of our actions because of the interconnected nature of global societies and ecosystems. Radiation clouds spewing forth from the Soviet Union's Chernobyl nuclear power plant paid no attention to national borders as they drifted across parts of Europe. CFCs manufactured and used in industrialized countries adversely affected the ozone layer upon which people in *all* nations depend for protection from the harmful elements of the sun's rays. What environmentalists have known for a long time is that we are interdependent and interconnected. This interconnectedness—whether good or bad—has been highlighted by the process of globalization.

Globalization, of course, signifies more than environmental interconnectedness. It also includes political globalization, as embodied by the United Nations, and economic interdependence, as seen in the growth of multi- or transnational corporations. Improvements in transportation and communication have facilitated the coordinated production and distribution of products over vast distances. (The clothes and shoes you are wearing are likely to have been produced outside the United States—even if they bear the brand name of an "American" corporation.) International monetary policies and trade agreements also speak to the globalized nature of our contemporary economy.

Globalization in many spheres has driven home the fact that our interaction and interdependence extend beyond local, regional, and national boundaries to encompass the far reaches of the planet. We can no longer live in isolated enclaves, unaffected by the actions of those beyond our immediate community. Instead, globalization implies that populations are not limited by physical proximity. Space, in the form of physical distance, has come to have less practical significance. Physical transportation to all corners of the globe is now easier than ever, making international travel and the transportation of goods commonplace. More important for our purposes, electronic communications often make the need for physical travel obsolete.

Electronic communication has been a feature of globalization at the same time as it has facilitated other forms of globalization such as international finance and manufacturing, which would be impossible without international communication networks. Global communication has compressed both space and time. While sitting in an office in the United States, we can pick up a telephone or type an e-mail message and communicate over a vast distance. In fact, it is just as easy to communicate via e-mail with someone on the other side of the globe as it is to do so with someone across town or across campus. Technology has reduced the significance of the distance between the sender and receiver of a message. (Using electronic mail and the telephone, the authors collaborated to produce this book, even though one of us was in New York and the other was in Virginia. We wrote and revised chapters by sending them back and forth via the Internet. There was no need for us to be physically in the same place, nor was there a need to mail a printed "hard copy" of the chapters. Digital communication via the Internet largely eliminated the practical significance of the distance between us. It would have been just as easy to collaborate via e-mail if we had been in different corners of the globe instead of different parts of the United States.)

Telephones and e-mail also compress time. Communication happens almost instantaneously. Indeed, what now most concerns observers is not the production and distribution of information but rather the glut of information at our fingertips. The speed and ease with which we can access information means that our biggest task is often sifting through it all to find what is useful to us. Anyone who has "surfed" the Internet to try to find a useful bit of information can tell you that the vast quantities of information—much of it the equivalent of electronic junk mail—can be overwhelming.

Crossing Cultural Boundaries

Globalization is not just about the technological innovations used to communicate over long distances. In addition, and perhaps more important, it also refers to the exchange and intermingling of cultures from different parts of the globe. The globalization of mass media, especially, refers to the content—the cultural products—available globally.

Let's use music as an example. Music is one of the easiest media products to sell globally because its language is universal. Print media may be international to a degree, but the barriers of language and literacy limit their reach. Producers must translate print media in order to cross cultural boundaries, and a significant literate audience must be available to receive the product. Visual media, such as television and movies, are more accessible because an audience does not have to be literate to enjoy them. Usually, though, these media have dialogue that must have subtitles or be dubbed in the local language. Music, however, can sell across national and cultural borders even when the lyrics are in an incomprehensible foreign tongue. The music, not the lyrics, generates sales.

The globalization of music has resulted in at least three developments. First, music that would not normally have traveled beyond a particular culture is now more readily available to different cultures. Listeners can hear American music worldwide. Buyers can find recordings of Madonna in China's prolific bootleg music scene. Fans can hear American jazz and blues around the globe. Cajun and Zydeco music are popular well beyond the Louisiana region where they originate. As rap has become a global phenomenon, artists now accompany its distinctive rhythms with lyrics in many different languages. Music from other cultures is also more readily available within the United States and elsewhere. Most major record stores feature a wide variety of music from different cultures. European gypsy music, as popularized by the group the Gipsy Kings, has a significant audience in the United States. The reggae of Jamaica has been a major musical force for decades. With little effort, we can find traditional music of many sorts in major music stores. This diversity represents the broad distribution of many different kinds of music across cultures.

A second development has been the exchange of musical elements between different cultures. Contemporary Afro-pop sometimes combines the electric guitars of Western rock and roll with melodies and rhythms reminiscent of more traditional African music. Western rock drummers, on the other hand, have long used a tradition from Africa whereby the sounds of many different drums are combined. In some traditional African cultures where music performances were part of communal events, a large number of drummers would each play a single drum, allowing mobility for dance. In Western rock, with its typical small bands of only four or five musicians, a musician assembles a collection of drums in a drum kit accessible to a single drummer. In both these cases, artists have incorporated and adapted components of one culture within the context of another. Afro-pop and Western rock still have their distinct sounds, but they also share a good deal. We might say that the cultural distance between them has been compressed.

Globalization of music has also resulted in a third development, a hybrid form of music that incorporates many different cultures in its new, unique sound. By using a wide variety of instruments and incorporating melodic and rhythmic sensibilities from many cultures, musicians produce new music that is not clearly identifiable with any single culture—thus the name "world music." For example, in the 1980s, the Do'a World Music Ensemble, a United States–based band, incorporated the sounds of instruments from many different cultures. Even the name of the group reflects its emphasis on global culture; "Do'a" is an Arabic-Persian word signifying a call to prayer, meditation, chanting, and worship. The liner notes to one of their albums list the following instruments: acoustic and classical guitar, West African balafons, mandolin harp, nyunga nyunga mbira, mbira dzavadzimu, tabla, Bolivian charango, adodo drum, gankogui bell, high-string guitar, Brazilian berimbau, dumbe drum, concert and alto flutes, piano, Oberheim OB-Xa synthesizer, C-soprano saxophone, ocarina, Chinese reed flute, acoustic bass, French horn, and cello. The music produced with all these different instruments tends to have a vaguely "ethnic" sound that is clearly not mainstream American pop but also is not grounded in any particular culture. Critics disagree as to whether this synthesis represents a positive integration of different cultures or the "melting" of distinct cultures into a more homogeneous blend. Whatever the verdict, the globalization of music has resulted in the crossing of cultural boundaries in yet another way.

The Promise and Reality of Media Globalization

Some of the observations we have made regarding globalized two-way communication, such as electronic mail, are applicable to our topic of concern, the mass media. Most mass media, such as the music discussed above, generally involve only the one-way flow of information. The digitization of information is opening the doors to more interactive mass media, blurring this distinction. In the near future, we will probably be able to "talk back" to television, for example, by choosing our own programs and movies to watch from a massive bank of options and by electronically "voting" to express our opinion on subjects being discussed. At best, though, this is a very limited notion of "communication" that is inevitably constrained by the "mass" nature of many audiences.

What we remain primarily concerned with is the global role of traditional mass media—movies, television, books, recorded music, and so on. Global media have carried words, sights, and sounds across vast geographic and cultural distances. The promise of such globalized media is the "global village" of McLuhan's vision in which media offer an electronic soapbox for differing voices to speak from. This multiplicity of voices, in turn, extends the range of publicly available knowledge about many different areas and aspects of the world. Finally, the airing of voices and knowledge can promote greater understanding between different nations and cultures.

The promise of the global village, however, remains largely unfulfilled. Indeed, global media have led to a series of developments that may be more a cause for concern than a source of hope. The globalization of mass media has included the rise of centralized media conglomerates of unprecedented size and influence. Commercial interests, rather than educational concerns or altruistic motives, have almost always fueled the globalization of mass media. This has meant the emergence of a global marketplace in which advertisers hawk their wares to international audiences measured sometimes in hundreds of millions of people. Often, global media as a commercial venture have simply highlighted the global nature of inequality.

In short, the globalization of mass media has been neither democratic nor egalitarian. The dream of a global village in which equals share information and culture does not describe the reality of today's global media.

While mass media globalization continues to offer some promises that are worth holding onto, we must also be aware of the social impact of these enticing developments. We explore below three key areas of concern related to media globalization: ownership and control, content, and consumption.

The globalization of mass media has been largely a centralized affair, resulting in a concentrated global media industry. The ownership and control of these global media corporations remain firmly rooted in a few prosperous industrialized nations. Since wealthier nations dominate the ownership and control of the media industry, they also dominate the production of global media products. The content of media produced by more developed nations for distribution worldwide, along with the sheer volume of media products flowing from wealthy industrialized countries to poorer nations, has caused deep tensions between industrialized and developing countries. As mentioned in Chapter 7, the dominance of Western media products has led some to claim that media globalization equals "cultural imperialism." However, some significant countertrends should be noted when we assess the impact of global media. The stratified nature of globalization suggests that the term is in some ways a misnomer. Not only are ownership and production concentrated in wealthier nations, but consumption, too, is skewed heavily toward the wealthier segment of the world's population—those with the necessary material resources to fully participate in the global media culture.

The Global Media Industry

The first area we explore is that of ownership. As we saw in Part One, ownership and control of production must be understood in order to understand the overall nature of mass media.

Global Products, Centralized Ownership

We return to our example of music to examine the globalization of media. As we discuss the global media, we will draw from Barnet and Cavanagh's (1994) description of the key media players in the international economy.

Walk into a major music store, and the sights—and more importantly the *sounds*—can be overwhelming: thousands of different compact disk (CD) and tape offerings divided into a dozen or more major categories. In fact, the categories alone can be overwhelming: classical, funk, new age, world, rap, swing, country, house, gospel, jazz, reggae, folk, rhythm and blues, and rock in ever-changing subcategories (punk, classic, speed, thrash, gothic, alternative, death, buzz, metal, southern, grunge, and so on).

This cornucopia of diversity, however, obscures an underlying reality: just six megacorporations dominate the popular music industry worldwide. The "big six" are Warner (United States), Bertelsmann (Germany), Thorn-EMI (United Kingdom), Polygram (Netherlands), MCA (Canada), and Sony (Japan). These "big six" distribute *95 percent* of all music carried by record stores in the United States and *over half* of the music in Europe. This includes "independent" labels who must rely on these major music conglomerates for distribution. In fact, the "big six" increasingly require an ownership share in the "independent" labels whose titles they distribute. (See Exhibit 10.1.)

Music is big business. In 1990, the recording industry sold about $20 billion worth of music worldwide (Barnet and Cavanagh, 1994). Europe accounted for $8 billion, the United States $6.5 billion, Japan $3 billion, and developing countries over $2 billion. CDs have been an especially lucrative product. The huge volume of production has driven down the manufacturing costs for CDs, but the retail price of a CD has remained steady. Industry observers estimate that it costs about $4.20 to produce a CD, including royalties to the artists. Manufacturers sell this CD wholesale for as much as $10.70, and retail prices can range from $13 to as high as $18. The lucrative profits generated by the sales of actual music recordings are sometimes supplemented by ancillary revenue generated by the use of music in commercials, movies, and television.

The major music corporations that dominate this field are themselves often part of even larger global corporations. Warner Music is owned by Time Warner, one of the world's largest media conglomerates. Warner is the best-known and only U.S. company among music's "big six." Bertelsmann Music Group, owners of the popular BMG music club, is a German company that owns RCA and Arista records in addition to publishing houses, book clubs, printing operations, television and radio operations, magazines, and newspapers. Sony, a Japanese company, owns what used to be CBS records and is now Sony Music. Thorn-EMI is a British electronics company and defense contractor in addition to being a music company. Polygram is a British-based branch of the Dutch electronics company Philips, which sells about half of all the classical music sold worldwide. Seagram, a Canadian company, owns MCA which also produces motion pictures, television and home video products, and books, in addition to operating theme parks and retail stores. Seagram is also a global power in the beverage industry where it produces and distributes spirits and wine (including brands such as Chivas Regal and Crown Royal), fruit juices (including Tropicana products), and coolers and mixers that are sold in over 150 countries and territories.

EXHIBIT 10.1 *Select Labels at the "Big Six" Music Companies, 1996*

Warner Music Group (Time Warner)	Bertelsmann Music Group (Bertelsmann)	Sony Music Entertainment (Sony)	Thorn-EMI	Polygram (Philips)	MCA Entertainment (Seagram)
■ Asylum Records	■ Ariola Records	■ Columbia Records	■ Angel Records	■ A & M Records	■ Dreamworks
■ Atlantic Records	■ Arista Records	■ Epic Records	■ Blue Note Records	■ Atlas	■ Gasoline Alley Records
■ Curb Records	■ BMG Classics	■ Legacy	■ Capitol Nashville	■ Chronicles	■ Geffen Records
■ Discovery Records	■ Iguana Records	■ Relativity Records	■ Capitol Records	■ Def Jam Records	■ Giant Step Records
■ East/West Records	■ Indolent Records	■ Sony Classical	■ Christian Music Distribution	■ Deutsche Grammophon	■ GRP Records
■ Elektra Records	■ Laface Records	■ Sony Music	■ Chrysalis Records	■ Go! Discs Records	■ Impulse Records
■ Mammoth Records	■ Paradise Records		■ EMI Classics	■ Hollywood Records	■ Interscope Records
■ Matador Records	■ Private Music		■ EMI Latin	■ Island Records	■ Krasnow Entertainment
■ Maverick Records	■ RCA Records		■ EMI Records	■ London Records	■ MCA Records
■ Qwest Records	■ RCA Victor		■ Guardian Records	■ Margaritaville Records	■ Radio Active Records
■ Reprise Records	■ Reunion Records		■ I.R.S. Records	■ Mercury Records	■ Silas Records
■ Rhino Records	■ Windham Hill		■ SBK Records	■ Motown	■ Universal Records
■ Sire Records	■ Zoo Entertainment		■ Virgin Classics	■ Polydor	■ Uptown Records
■ Slash Records			■ Virgin Records	■ Polydor Nashville	■ Way Cool Records
■ Tag Recordings				■ PolyGram Classics & Jazz	■ 510 Records
■ Tommy Boy					
■ Warner Bros. Records					

This is just a sample of the (primarily U.S.) record labels at the corporate "big six." This chart does not reflect the actual corporate structure of these conglomerates; most companies have divisions that operate the different labels.

Source: Corporate communications offices and Internet web sites of the "big six" companies.

The "big six" in music illustrate one of the central ironies in the globalization of mass media: While the distribution of media products has spread out across the globe, the ownership and control of media production are largely centralized in a few megacorporations usually composed of dozens, if not hundreds, of different companies. Consumers, seeing a wide variety of company names on the products they buy, may not realize that these different brands are often divisions of the same multinational corporation with production and distribution facilities dispersed in many different countries. These transnational corporations can shift resources from country to country in the pursuit of higher profits, which usually makes meaningful regulation by individual countries extremely difficult, if not impossible.

The Case of Bertelsmann

A brief look at one of the "big six" music companies will illustrate the vast expanse of these corporations. Most people have never heard of Bertelsmann, yet it is one of the largest media conglomerates in the world. In 1996 it owned 375 different companies operating in 30 countries. (See Exhibit 10.2.) The vast holdings of this one company include the following:

- *Music:* Bertelsmann has music operations in 27 countries. As noted, the company owns RCA and Arista records, and its stable of artists has included diverse musicians such as the Grateful Dead, Arturo Toscanini, Dave Matthews Band, Carly Simon, Cowboy Junkies, Whitney Houston, and James Galaway. Bertelsmann also produced the soundtracks of many movies, including *Dirty Dancing* and *Reality Bites.* It operates the BMG (Bertelsmann Music Group) record club; you may have seen its offer "get ten CDs for the price of one" in newspapers and magazines. It also owns facilities for producing tapes, CDs, and music videos.

- *Publishing and Printing:* Bertelsmann operates book clubs around the globe, including the Literary Guild in the United States, and owns publishing houses in a half dozen countries, including Bantam Doubleday Dell in the United States. It publishes over a hundred different magazines and newspapers throughout the Western hemisphere. It owns paper and printing plants in seven countries, including a plant in Pennsylvania that prints 20 percent of all paperback books produced in the United States. Another of its companies prints 140 different magazines, including *Time, Sports Illustrated,* and *Fortune.* The company's full vertical integration allows it to create, manufacture, distribute, and sell printed products of all types, including books, magazines, newspapers, maps, calendars, diaries, and brochures.

EXHIBIT 10.2 *Global Media: The Case of Bertelsmann*

BERTELSMANN PRODUCT LINES

BOOKS (32% of total sales)	BMG ENTERTAINMENT (32% of total sales)	GRUNER+JAHR (PRESS) (20% of total sales)	INDUSTRY (16% of total sales)
▪ Book and record clubs (Germany) ▪ Book and record clubs (international) ▪ Encyclopedia publishing ▪ Hardcover and paperback books ▪ Professional and trade magazines Information services ▪ How-to books Cartography	▪ Record labels ▪ Music clubs ▪ Music publishing ▪ Licensing ▪ Storage media production ▪ Commercial TV ▪ Pay-TV ▪ Film and TV productions ▪ Multimedia products ▪ Radio	▪ Magazines (Germany) ▪ Magazines (international) ▪ Newspapers ▪ Printing plant ▪ Trade	▪ Offset printing ▪ Rotogravure printing ▪ Paper production ▪ Distribution and services ▪ Special publishing

The sheer size and number of companies owned by a single media conglomerate can be staggering. Bertelsmann employs 57,400 workers, owns well over 300 companies, and had revenues in the 1994–95 fiscal year of over $14 billion. About one-third (35 percent) of its revenues came from Germany, another third (33 percent) came from the rest of Europe, a quarter (24 percent) came from the United States, and the remaining revenues (8 percent) came from elsewhere. At the time of this writing, Bertelsmann is the third largest media corporation in the world. The table above shows the structure of the corporation's product lines.

Following are just a few of the companies owned by Bertelsmann, organized by industry. Companies without figures indicate 100% ownership.

BOOKS (32% of total sales)	LOCATION
Literature and Specialized Books	
C. Bertelsmann Verlag	Munich, Germany
Albrecht Knaus Verlag	Munich, Germany
Plus 3 other companies	
Reference Books/How-to Books/Cartography	
Bertelsmann Lexikon Verlag	Munich, Germany
Verlagshaus Stuttgart	Stuttgart, Germany
Officina Nova	Budapest, Hungary
GeoCenter International	Basingstoke, Great Britain
GeoCenter Prague	Czech Republic
GeoCenter Warsaw	Poland
Buch- und Schallplattenfreunde	Zug, Switzerland
Plus 18 other companies	

EXHIBIT 10.2 *(continued)*

Book Europe/Asia

Euroboek	Utrecht, Netherlands
Euroboek	Borgerhout, Belgium
BCA (50%)	London, Great Britain
Bookclub of Ireland (50%)	Dublin, Ireland
Doubleday Australia	Sydney, Australia
Doubleday New Zealand	Auckland, New Zealand
France Loisirs (50%)	Paris, France
France Loisirs (Suisse) (50%)	Crissier, Switzerland
Quebec Loisirs (50%)	Montreal, Canada
Euroclub Italia (51%)	Novarra, Italy
Circulo de Lectores	Barcelona, Spain
Lexicultural	Lisbon, Portugal
Plus 12 other companies	

North America

Bantam Doubleday Dell Publishing Group	New York, USA
Doubleday Book and Music Clubs	New York, USA
Doubleday Canada (30%)	Toronto, Canada
Doubleday Book and Music Clubs (30%)	Toronto, Canada
Transworld Publishers	London, Sydney, Auckland

Professional Information

AZ Direct Marketing Bertelsmann	Vienna, Austria
Edition Securite Routiere	Paris, France
Editorial Trafico Vial	Madrid, Spain
Bertelsmann Information Services	Munich, Germany
Medi-A-Derm Verlagsgesellschaft	Hamburg, Germany
Plus 27 other companies	

BMG ENTERTAINMENT (32% of total sales)	LOCATION

Music

Arista Records	New York, USA
BMG Ariola	in 35 countries
(including Greece, Thailand, Colombia, Belgium, Hungary, Argentina, Germany, Hong Kong, Finland, South Africa, Denmark, Malaysia, Philippines, Mexico, Brazil, Chile, Korea, Singapore, Sweden, Taiwan, Poland, and Switzerland)	
BMG Classics/RCA Victor	New York, USA
BMG Musique Quebec (66.6%)	Montreal, Canada
BMG Records	London, Great Britain
BMG U.S. Latin	Miami, USA
BMG Victor (90%)	Tokyo, Japan
Hansa Musik	Berlin, Germany
Private Music	New York, USA
RCA Records Label	New York, USA
Reunion Records (50%)	Nashville, USA
Windham Hill (50%)	Palo Alto, USA
Zoo Entertainment	Los Angeles, USA
Plus 7 other companies	

EXHIBIT 10.2 *(continued)*

Music Publishing
BMG Songs — Los Angeles, Nashville, New York, USA

BMG Music Publishing — In over 20 countries
Killer Tracks (50%) — Hollywood, USA
Reunion Music Group (50%) — Nashville, USA
Plus 5 other companies

Video and Other Activities
BMG Video — New York, USA
ION (Multimedia) (50%) — Los Angeles, USA
Ufa Video — Munich, Germany
Plus 4 other companies

Film
UFA Film — Hamburg, Germany

Television
RTL plus Deutschland — Hanover, Cologne, Munich
Plus 5 other companies

Radio
Antenne Bayern — Munich, Germany
Berliner Rundfunk — Berlin, Germany
Plus 6 other companies

Production
G+J Film Produktion — Berlin, Germany
Geo Film — Berlin, Germany
Westdeutsche Universum-Film — Cologne, Germany
Plus 16 other companies

Storage Media
Sonopress — Gutersloh, Germany
Sonopress — Sao Paulo, Brazil
Sonopress — Weaverville, USA
Plus 8 other companies

GRUNER+JAHR (PRESS) (20% of total sales)	**LOCATION**

Magazines
Druck- und Verlagshaus Gruner+Hahr (74.9%) — Hamburg, Germany
Borse Online Verlag (74.9%) — Munich, Germany
G+J (UK) (74.9%) — London, Great Britain
Plus 14 other companies

EXHIBIT 10.2 *(continued)*

Newspapers	
Berliner Verlag (74.9%)	Berlin, Germany
Morgenpost Verlag (90%)	Hamburg, Germany
Morgenpost Sachsen Verlagsgesellschaft (60%)	Hamburg, Germany
Printing and Technical Companies	
Brown Printing Company (74.9%)	Waseca, USA
G+J Images (74.9%)	New York, USA
Plus 4 other companies	
Services	
Berliner Pressevertrieb	Berlin, Germany
Plus 4 other companies	

INDUSTRY (16% of total sales)	**LOCATION**
Printing/Technical Companies	
Berryville Graphics	Berryville, USA
Delta Lithograph	Valencia, USA
Dynamic Graphic Finishing (90%)	Horsham, USA
Offset Paperback Manufacturers	Dallas, USA
Printer Colombiana (51%)	Bogota, Colombia
Printer Industria Grafica	Barcelona, Spain
Plus 10 other companies	
Paper Production and Services	
Cartiere del Garda	Riva, Italy
Bertelsmann Distribution	Gutersloh, Germany
Bertelsmann Electronic Printing Services	Gutersloh, Germany
Special Publishing	
Deutscher Supplement Verlag (75%)	Nuremberg, Germany
Editoriale Johnson (60%)	Seriate, Italy

Source: Bertelsmann documents for the 1994–95 fiscal year from the company's online Internet site (www.bertelsman.com).

- *Broadcast and Films:* Bertelsmann owns two major radio stations in Germany and a radio news agency based in Bonn. It has three film companies, which produce mostly made-for-TV movies that are syndicated and reach audiences of over 200 million people in Europe. It owns a pay-TV channel in Germany and major interests in other cable and broadcast operations, including RTLplus, Europe's most powerful private-broadcasting radio and TV network.

The example of Bertelsmann illustrates that, while the tentacles of global corporations extend to all sectors of the mass media and to all corners of the globe, the control of the megacorporations remains centralized in wealthy developed nations. Recall that the corporate home bases of the music "big six" are Canada, Germany, Great Britain, Holland, Japan, and the United States. Globalization of the mass media clearly does not extend to ownership, which has not yet gone beyond a few prosperous nations. The importance of centralized ownership and control is that decision making related to the purpose and content of the mass media, as well as the benefits that accrue from owning what are often highly profitable ventures, remains firmly in the hands of a few major corporations based in the wealthiest nations.

Global Media Content

In this section, we sample the global dimension of the debates over media, in particular the "cultural imperialism" thesis and the controversy over global information flow.

The Debate over "Cultural Imperialism"

In Chapter 7, we briefly introduced the "cultural imperialism" thesis, the argument that the media products emanating from the West, especially the United States, so powerfully shape the cultures of other nations that they amount to a cultural form of domination. Here the link between ownership and media content is made explicit. Values and images of Western society, according to this argument, are embedded in the media products sold by Western corporations. Norms of individualism and consumerism, for example, pervade media products exported by the West and often conflict with the traditional values in the nations where such products are sold. The flow of media products, the argument continues, results in the erosion of local cultures and values.

There is no denying the profound impact that U.S. culture has had in other countries. In 1991, the *Christian Science Monitor* asked its reporters around the world to comment on the role of American culture in each country to which they were assigned. The result was an eclectic assortment of observations concerning the varied role of American cultural influence abroad.

- The television program "America's Funniest Home Videos" has been copied as "Smile, Please" in Germany, as "Australia's Funniest Home Video Show," and as "Beadle's About" in England.

- In China, an intellectual who had been jailed for several months complained in writing to his captors that when arrested he had not been read his rights. He recalled, "I said they should have done it the way they do on the U.S. television show 'Hunter.'" The detective program is very popular in China.

- In Mexico, middle- and upper-class viewers regularly receive cable that includes all of the U.S. television networks and movie channels featuring dubbed Hollywood movies.

- In India, the death of U.S. comedian Lucille Ball deeply saddened many people. Her slapstick brand of humor on the "I Love Lucy" show translated well and was quite popular.

- CNN has been a popular television addition in a growing list of African nations, including Kenya, Ghana, and South Africa. However, its reach is limited to the more prosperous segments of society who can afford a television set and the nearly $20-per-month fee needed to receive CNN.

- In Russia and other parts of the former Soviet Union, *Rambo* and more recent U.S. action-adventure films have been extremely popular. In the early 1990s, after the Soviet breakup, theaters showed many old American films for the first time, including *Gone With the Wind* and *One Flew Over the Cuckoo's Nest*.

- American disco became a major fad in China in the mid-1980s. By the 1990s, the elderly were using it to accompany their early-morning exercises in public parks.

- In Germany, well over 90 percent of the films being shown in theaters had been made in Hollywood. A particular cult favorite was *The Blues Brothers*, which regularly had midnight showings in most cities.

To return to our example of music, we might add that the overwhelming majority of music in the global marketplace is sung in English. For example, in Brazil, where people speak Portuguese, nearly three-quarters of the songs played on the radio are in English. In Germany, English songs make up 80 percent of radio playlists. In Japan, about half the songs are in English (Barnet and Cavanagh, 1994).

Eastern Europe has afforded marketers enormous new opportunities to sell Western mass media products. For example, romance novels translated from their original English have become enormously popular in Poland and other parts of Eastern Europe. Western producers of the genre, such as Harlequin (or Arlekin, as it is known in Poland), have launched major campaigns to promote the romance novel. Despite the fact that the genre was unknown in Poland until recently, Arlekin sold 24 million romance novels there in 1993 (Spolar, 1995).

One reason why some U.S. media products have been so successful is that U.S. projects tend to have substantial budgets, resulting in very slick and attractive production values. The Hollywood blockbuster, for example, typically relies on dramatically photographed scenes, pyrotechnics, and gripping chase sequences to hold an audience's attention. All these things are very expensive to produce—more expensive than most non-U.S. production studios can afford. The irony is that in order to finance increasingly expensive blockbuster productions, Hollywood must rely on substantial revenues from foreign markets. In 1995, for example, the movie *Waterworld,* starring and directed by Kevin Costner, was estimated to cost an incredible $175 million to produce but was projected to generate only about $93 million in U.S. revenue. These numbers would spell financial disaster for the movie studio if it were not for the international revenue expected to be generated, about $150 million (Pond, 1995). Added to the money received from video rental, those numbers mean a tidy profit for the studio.

The issue of money has also affected the receipt of U.S. media products abroad in another way. Some nations simply do not have the resources to develop the infrastructure necessary to produce high-quality media products. Even for those nations that do have major production facilities available, it is almost always cheaper to buy U.S.-made media products than to produce their own. When a for-profit market model drives media-related decision-making, as it does in many nations, it generally makes good short-term business sense to import U.S.-made cultural products. The impact on local cultures, critics contend, can be devastating (Mattelart, 1979; Schiller, 1992).

The Fight to Preserve Local Cultures

In the early part of the century, many French-Canadians immigrated to the New England states from Quebec. Owners often recruited them to work in their paper and textile mills. The workers usually lived in nearby ethnic neighborhoods. They formed French-speaking Catholic parishes, which set up schools—taught in French—for their children. These immigrants, like all immigrants, tried to maintain their culture by preserving their language, religion, and traditions. The grandparents of one of us

(Croteau) made that trip from Quebec, and growing up I experienced the remnants of what was once a vibrant French-Canadian culture. My parents' first language was French, although they also spoke English. I remember vividly the *soirées* that family members occasionally hosted. These were house parties at which family and friends gathered to talk, play cards, dance, and play French-Canadian music.

When I was a child, the French-Canadian culture was still alive in my family. But even then I thought of this music and culture as old-fashioned. I spoke only English and listened to American rock and roll. Thus, I grew up not learning about French-Canadian music, not learning the French language, and not adopting the "old" customs of the past. In my family, I was in the first generation of fully assimilated Americans. I lost the French-Canadian culture of my heritage.

This individual tale of cultural loss was repeated for tens of thousands of Franco-Americans throughout New England. On a collective level, the story describes how cultures become homogenized and assimilated. They are bleached of their distinctive elements, leaving behind faded colors of only slightly different shades.

On October 30, 1995, the province of Quebec held a referendum on whether or not to secede from the rest of Canada. The referendum, which failed by just one percentage point, symbolized the continued importance of culture in contemporary life. The major difference between Quebec and the rest of Canada, which led to the vote on secession, is that Quebec is predominantly (82 percent) French-speaking. French-Canadians have feared for decades that their distinct culture would be assimilated into the culture of the English-speaking majority in Canada, just as the New England French-Canadian culture has largely been lost in the English-speaking United States.

The fact that Canada shares a border with the world's largest producer of English-language media products only exacerbates the concerns of French-Canadians—and of all Canadians. Canadian culture, even its English component, is overwhelmed by the U.S. products that flood the market. Ninety-five percent of films in Canadian theaters are from the United States. Almost all major U.S. channels are available on Canadian cable systems. U.S. firms control music distribution. Two-thirds of all books sold are from the United States, as are 80 percent of magazines (Escobar and Swardson, 1995).

Like the early French-Canadians in New England, Quebec and the rest of Canada have tried various defensive measures to protect their culture. Some of these tactics have included French language requirements, taxes on some imported cultural products, and even a law mandating that 30 percent of the music played on AM radio must be Canadian. However, the global nature of media products has made it virtually impossible to stem the tide of U.S. products.

The Canadian experience of trying to protect local culture has been echoed in many other countries. France, for example, has opposed international free trade treaties because of the perceived threat posed by the flow of products from the U.S. media industry. The European Union has stipulated that half of all broadcast programming must be produced within the union. Some governments give financial support to fledgling domestic artists and media companies in an effort to provide an alternative to imported foreign fare.

The fight to preserve local cultures comes in the wake of both anecdotal and more systematic evidence suggesting the widespread, varied, and pervasive influence of foreign media in many countries. The fear is that the globalization of media is resulting in the homogenization of culture. Like sand castles on a beach, local cultures are being eroded and flattened by the gradual impact of the endless tide of U.S. and other Western media products. A Sri Lankan musician notes:

> My fear is that in another 10 or 15 years' time what with all the cassettes that find their way into the remotest village, and with none of their own music available, people will get conditioned to this cheap kind of music. . . . However small a nation we are, we still have our own way of singing, accompanying, intonating, making movements and so on. We can make a small but distinctive contribution to world culture. But we could lose it . . . .
> (in Barnet and Cavanagh, 1994, p. 150)

The idea of cultures losing their "distinctive" element is perhaps what critics fear most. If music, literature, film, and television become globally mass produced and homogenized—like so many standardized McDonald's restaurants strewn across the international cultural landscape—then the world as a whole loses.

The Imperialism Thesis: Some Complications

The signals pointing to cultural imperialism are more mixed than might be apparent at first glance. Some signs suggest that local cultures are more resistant than we might expect and that the wave of U.S. media products flooding foreign markets may be reaching its peak as local media industries begin competing for national markets. To complicate matters even further, Western corporations are developing new strategies to cope with this changing global reality, sidestepping some of the earlier charges of cultural imperialism.

While U.S. culture has had a massive impact abroad, as we noted in

Chapter 7, the traditional cultural imperialism thesis has two key limitations. First, it generally does not take into account the multiple interpretive strategies used by audiences in different cultures, as our example of the television program "Dallas" in Chapter 8 suggested. The meaning a particular product holds for local audiences may vary widely because of local cultural values. Thus, we cannot assume that foreign audiences interpret U.S. media products in any single way. The circulation of U.S.-produced global media products does not seem to be creating any singular Americanized consciousness, as some had feared. Nor is it creating any singular "global consciousness," as some had hoped. Barnet and Cavanagh's (1994) comments on this latter point are worth quoting at length:

> Although hundreds of millions of children and teenagers around the world are listening to the same music and watching the same films and videos, globally distributed entertainment products are not creating a discernible global consciousness—other than a widely shared passion for more global goods and vicarious experience. Because of the great range of personal experience consumers bring to global cultural products, the emotional impact on fans can differ widely in unpredictable ways. . . . Hearing the same music, playing the same globally distributed games, or watching the same global broadcast do not appear to change people's sense of who they are or where they belong. Serbs and Croats, Sinhalese and Tamils, listen to the same Michael Jackson songs as they take up arms against each other. The exotic imagery of music video offers the illusion of being connected to cultural currents sweeping across the world, but this has little to do with the consciousness philosophers from Kant to Marshall McLuhan have dreamed of, an identification with the whole human species and the planet itself. (p. 138)

At best, we need to reexamine the belief that exposure to media products fundamentally changes people.

The second limitation of the cultural imperialism thesis, as we pointed out in Chapter 7, is that in its simple version the thesis often does not distinguish between different types of media. U.S. products clearly dominate some media, while other media continue to be local in nature. As we explore below, recognizing difference, subtlety, and shades of influence is a vital part of discussing something as complex as the world's cultures.

Additional indications suggest that the cultural imperialism thesis presents only a partial picture. Consider the following examples:

- In Brazil, the American prime-time soap opera "Dallas" never caught on. Brazilians preferred their own unique "telenovelas" (soap operas).

These series generally run for about six months and are a romantic mix of humor and drama. They usually feature the downfall of a rich character who becomes poor and the success of a poor character who becomes rich. The programs have set fashion trends, made hits out of theme songs, and promoted products written into the script. Brazil now exports these programs to China, Cuba, and many other countries. This trend toward locally produced programs also holds in other countries, such as Taiwan and Mexico (*Christian Science Monitor,* 1991; Landler, 1994).

- In Britain, the 1980s infatuation with American programming such as "Dallas," "Dynasty," and "L.A. Law" was replaced in the early 1990s with interest in more homegrown fare. Most popular was the BBC's evening soap opera "Eastenders." The program focuses on a group of families living in London's East End. It regularly addresses social issues such as race relations, crime, and unemployment—topics studiously avoided in most American television programs (*Christian Science Monitor,* 1991).

- India has the most productive movie industry in the world, producing more than 900 films in 1985, even though the foreign distribution of these films is generally limited to markets in Africa and Asia. Also enormously popular are television serials based on Indian classics, which air on Sunday mornings (*Christian Science Monitor,* 1991; Sreberny-Mohammadi, 1991).

- Despite the influence of American artists, local music stars are still a significant part of most markets. For example, three-quarters of the Japanese records sold in Japan feature Japanese artists (Barnet and Cavanagh, 1994).

- We must also note the influence of other cultures on U.S. media. As with the globalization of music discussed at the beginning of this chapter, simultaneous trends seem to be occurring. The sounds of a multiplicity of cultures are being made more accessible to American listeners in a variety of ways. Recordings of music from different cultures are now more readily available than ever, although they generally still appeal to a relatively small audience. Perhaps more significant, the music of other cultures is being recombined in new ways to produce hybrid forms of music, some of which are still rooted in a distinctive culture. Others, however, are no longer grounded in a single culture but instead are better characterized as "world music."

These examples illustrate something that is now common knowledge among media corporations: There are limits to the appeal of Western, and especially U.S., culture in other nations. One industry account of television programming suggests that we are at a new phase of media development. "First, technology, privatization, and economic growth vastly expand the distribution channels for media. Then, because local economies are not yet big enough to finance homegrown programming, America rushes in to fill the void. But as these markets mature . . . local producers are able to make better and more ambitious shows" (Landler, 1994, p. 187). These locally produced programs, finely attuned to the local culture, tend to be very popular. Thus, local producers have in some cases successfully competed with the global media conglomerates by providing localized alternatives that differentiate themselves from the homogenized international media fare.

In response to the changing circumstances, many multinational corporations are becoming more sophisticated in addressing local markets in foreign countries. Most media conglomerates have adopted some variation of a two-pronged approach to selling cultural products. The first prong of the strategy is the promotion and distribution of Western artists as global superstars. For example, the pop stardom of Michael Jackson and Madonna in the 1980s and early 1990s marked the sale of a commodity that was popular in many different countries.

The second prong of the corporate strategy is to devote resources to working within the parameters of local culture. MTV, which in 1993 reached 210 million households in 71 countries, has taken this approach. MTV Europe and MTV Latino, for example, are exports of the American music video format altered to fit the regional cultures they serve. Another version of this second-prong strategy is to nurture indigenous talent, which companies can then package and sell to local or regional markets, if not a global market. The company we profiled earlier, Bertelsmann, uses this approach in developing new musical artists.

This second approach, of course, is itself a double-edged sword. Even as major media conglomerates acknowledge the importance of local cultural tastes, they may be contributing to the decimation of local media companies by moving into local media markets. Sometimes, this means being in outright competition with local companies, creating a David and Goliath scenario. In some cases, this movement has taken the form of joint ventures in the co-production of cultural products such as television programs.

The irony is that the corporate drive for profit—the very force that has fueled fears of cultural imperialism—has also forced companies to pay attention to local cultures and customs. Altruistic concern about preserving local cultures has not been the motivation. Instead, companies have realized that locally customized media products often sell better than standardized global products. Thus, an article in a leading business magazine notes that U.S. media companies, when they expand into Latin America and Asia, can no longer "view these regions monolithically—a tabula rasa on which to project Western movies, news, and television shows." As a sign of things to come, the piece features a company that is "tailoring its programs for its ethnically and linguistically diverse audience" (Landler, 1994, p. 186).

Even textbooks on advertising in a global market now routinely discuss the difference between techniques of global standardization and techniques of "local adaptation." The latter approach explicitly takes into account differences in infrastructure, economics, and technology, as well as cultural differences that influence the behavior of consumers. One advertising textbook advises, "The international advertising executive will have to cooperate with people of different cultures. He or she will have to build strategies for communicating with consumers who have different values, attitudes, and buying behavior. Knowledge of the basic aspects of culture is essential in order to understand why people in different countries behave differently" (De Mooij and Keegan, 1991, p. 73). For many global corporations, the trend is toward trying to adapt to and exploit these different cultures. However, in many cases, the accommodation to local cultural tastes is superficial, merely disguising the export of U.S. or other Western products.

One consequence of "local adaptation" has been that in some parts of the world the resistance to foreign culture has waned. In Latin America, for example, the old cries of "cultural imperialism" are now heard only from a few. In Chile, a folklorist who directs an academic cultural center says, "This country is occupied, and there is no consciousness of that" (Escobar and Swardson, 1995). The most recent wave of television and other cultural products into the region has not met with the kind of opposition that marked earlier influxes of foreign culture. As one article states, "More and more, the Americas are accepting a universal, homogenized popular culture in which touches of Latin rhythm or Spanglish accent a dominant North American diet of songs, words and images" (Escobar and Swardson, 1995). In the past, this trend would have been widely considered to be cultural imperialism. However, in an era when more governments are adopting market capitalism and when global corporations are careful to at least superficially tailor their products to local cultural tastes, it is now widely considered to be inevitable.

The trends in global media, therefore, are mixed. The ability to innovate and adapt quickly to changing social and cultural tastes favors decentralized, locally produced products. The ability to pour massive resources into the production, promotion, and distribution of cultural products favors the global media corporations. It remains to be seen whether, in the long term, vibrant, locally produced media will successfully compete with global products from the major corporate conglomerates. It also remains to be seen whether some form of partnership between global and local producers will become the wave of the future.

The Politics of Information Flow

The formal political concern with media globalization dates back at least as far as 1925. In that year, the League of Nations adopted a resolution to create a committee charged with "determining methods of contributing towards the organization of peace, especially: (a) by ensuring the more rapid and less costly transmission of Press news with a view to reducing risks of international misunderstanding; (b) And by discussing all technical problems the settlement of which would be conducive to the tranquillisation of public opinion" (in Gerbner, Mowlana, and Nordenstreng, 1993, p. 183). The dissemination of information worldwide through the media, therefore, was endorsed as a tool for the promotion of peace and understanding. These and subsequent discussions of global information flow were not limited to mass media, but that is our concern here.

The uses of propaganda during World War II once again prompted concern over the distribution of information in the mass media. The United States used the forum of the United Nations to promote a policy that allowed for the international collection, sale, and distribution of information worldwide. The Final Act of the 1948 UN Conference on Freedom of Information argued that "freedom of information is a fundamental right of the people, and it is the touchstone of all the freedoms to which the United Nations is dedicated without which world peace cannot well be preserved." The act further stipulated that, in order to be valid, freedom of information depended on "the availability to the people of a diversity of sources of news and opinion," and it condemned the use of "propaganda either designed or likely to provoke or encourage any threat" to peace (in Gerbner, Mowlana, and Nordenstreng, 1993, pp. 179, 181).

While the idea that information should flow freely across national boundaries sounds benign to Western ears, many developing countries came to understand it as privileging the "first world's" market-driven perspective of information flow. At the time, "first-world" and developing nations had very different levels of infrastructure development and capital resources. As a result, the operating reality of "free" international information flow was that major advertiser-funded news organizations from developed nations dominated the collection and dissemination of information. It was as if everyone had been invited to contribute to a multicultural mural, but only some people were equipped with paint and brushes. Those with advantages in resources were able to express their vision, while those lacking resources were effectively silenced.

Western wire services such as the Associated Press (AP) and United Press International (UPI) in the United States and Reuters in the United Kingdom dominated the news accounts that traveled around the globe. They collected information and wrote news stories from what has been described as "a limited perspective reflecting the economic and cultural interests of the industrialized nations" (MacBride and Roach, 1993, p. 6). This criticism extended to entertainment media as well as to the use of emerging technologies, such as satellites, to directly transmit news and entertainment.

Developing nations, which did not have the private investment needed to support major commercial media, looked to their governments to nurture media that served public, rather than private, needs. These public needs covered a vast and varied territory. In some cases, fulfilling public needs involved the dissemination of basic information on everything from public health to agricultural practices to child education. In other cases, the concern was with more generalized access to information as a central element of a democratic society.

To many Westerners, the involvement of government in the organization and production of media immediately raises the specter of censorship and state domination—which in some cases did occur. However, in many developing nations, government involvement with local media represented the only way to ensure the existence of an alternative to Western media conglomerates. In addition, many developing nations did not want to be simply flooded by the "free flow" of information from the West. Instead, they wanted a free and *more balanced* flow of information. The intervention of government was needed to regulate the vast quantity of information flowing from more developed nations, an action that Westerners found antithetical to the idea of a "free" information flow.

The call by poorer nations for a "new world information and communication order" (NWICO) was taken up by UNESCO (United Nations Educational, Scientific, and Cultural Organization). While reaffirming the right of journalists to "have freedom to report and the fullest possible access to information," a 1978 UNESCO declaration on the mass media also suggested, among other things, that mass media contribute to peace and understanding "by giving expression to oppressed people who struggle against colonialism, neo-colonialism, foreign occupation and all forms of racial discrimination and oppression and who are unable to make their voices heard within their own territories." It went on to declare that "it is necessary that States facilitate the procurement by the mass media in the developing countries of adequate conditions and resources enabling them to gain strength and expand, and that they support cooperation by the latter both among themselves and with the mass media in developed countries" (in Gerbner, Mowlana, and Nordenstreng, 1993, pp. 176, 178). The declaration was suggesting a need to hear those voices that had not been included in the established media—a position that threatened the status quo.

Developing nations often saw their efforts as an attempt to balance the scales of information production and distribution that had always been tipped sharply in favor of wealthier Western nations. Many in the West saw such efforts as a form of censorship that threatened their freedom to interpret the world and to communicate their interpretation globally. Western nations, threatened by the proposals, responded with a powerful campaign aimed at discrediting the idea of a new information and communication order—and UNESCO. (The United States announced its resignation from UNESCO at the end of 1983.) Critics of the ideas being aired in UNESCO argued that these ideas were controversial, political, and opposed to freedom. The campaign was successful, stalling any progress for NWICO and paralyzing the work of UNESCO. In the late 1980s and early 1990s, the United Nations and UNESCO backed away from the promotion of NWICO, although most analysts suggest that the debate is far from over.

One reason for the ongoing debate is that Western domination of the international flow of information has continued despite advances in communications in many developing countries. Many developing nations have had enormous difficulty creating and supporting effective communication infrastructures that reach their populations, especially in rural areas. In the absence of such structures, Western media often continue to dominate. Writing about the case of Africa, Francis Kasoma (1993) observes:

> The deluge of Western flow of information through the media to Africa has not abated. African television and cinemas are almost totally dependent on American, British, and French soap operas and films. The news on radio and television as well as in some newspapers is full of stories from the West sent by Reuters, Agence France Presse, United Press International, and Associated Press. On the other hand, Western, as well as Eastern, media are almost devoid of any information from Africa except for the occasional bad news which is meant to show how inefficient, unfortunate, and in dire need of help Africans are. . . . All the continent has strived for is to get a hearing in Western, and even Eastern, media, so that the people of these regions can learn about their people and

their problems. This knowledge is key to the attainment of peace in Africa. (p. 78)

The ability to "get a hearing" in the international media is precisely what McLuhan believed would be inevitable in the global village. The fact that this clearly is not the case raises significant doubts about the appropriateness of the "global village" metaphor.

Global Media Consumption: Limits of the "Global Village"

In the mid-1980s, a group of mostly American pop musicians got together to record a song to raise money for famine relief in Ethiopia. The song, titled "We Are the World," was meant to suggest the interdependence and mutual responsibility of the world's populations. However, the title also is open to a more cynical interpretation. American pop artists were affirming the global nature of their efforts—sung in English—with very little participation from the rest of the world. "We Are the World" was, to say the least, an overstatement.

We can make a similar point about media "globalization." For example, if the world's major media conglomerates are all from North America, Europe, and Japan—wealthy, industrial nations—can such a media system truly be called "global"? If the dominant ownership and control of the "global media" remain firmly in the hands of media conglomerates based in a few wealthy nations, wouldn't it be more accurate to describe the process as the international *export* of "first-world" media? When was the last time you saw a television program produced in Asia, watched a movie made in Africa, or read a book written by a South American author? Asking someone from Asia, Africa, or South America about the last time they saw, read, or heard a U.S. media product would elicit a quite different response.

Without belaboring the point, the term "global media" is misleading insofar as it obscures the fact that ownership and control of the "global" media industry are not really spread out globally but instead are centralized and concentrated in a few wealthier nations. We must remember that global communications are highly stratified. Those with substantial resources—the corporations of the wealthy nations of the world—are able to benefit most from the globalized media culture. McLuhan's "global village" suggested an even playing field occupied by equally influential actors. That image certainly does not describe the state of affairs that exists today in media production.

One could argue, however, that ownership and production are not necessarily the focus of the term "global media." Even though major corporations in a few wealthier nations still disproportionately control media production, these media products are being distributed and consumed worldwide. That universal consumption, one could argue, is the essence of "global media." We would agree that the application of the label "global" to the consumption of media products is more justified than its application to the production of media. However, here, too, we must be careful not to overgeneralize.

Media are not equally accessible around the globe. The consumption of media requires money, whether for the purchase of equipment such as radios and television sets to receive media (hardware) or for the purchase of actual media products such as books and music recordings (software). Globally, patterns of media consumption follow the same pattern as economic inequality. The richer nations that disproportionately own and produce mass media also disproportionately consume mass media. The egalitarian image of a "global village" once again obscures reality.

With all the talk of global media and instantaneous communication, it is easy to forget that illiteracy, disease, and hunger mark daily life for significant segments of the earth's population. J. V. Vilanilam reminds us, "If there were 100 residents in this global village, only one would get the opportunity for education beyond [high] school level, 70 would be unable to read and write. Over 50 would be suffering from malnutrition, and over 80 would live in sub-standard housing. Six of the 100 would hold off the entire income of the village"(in Mowlana, 1993, p. 60). Despite rhetoric to the contrary, consumption of media is still limited by the staggering degree of economic inequality that exists globally. (See Exhibit 10.3.)

When we think of "global media," televisions and computers immediately come to mind. But in some parts of the world, more basic technologies reign. In 1995, for example, a company in South Africa began marketing newly patented wind-up radios to meet demand in areas where electricity was unavailable and batteries were too costly (McNeil, 1996). The fact that such a market existed speaks to the enormous disparity between wealthy and poor nations. When it comes to music, for example, the United States, Europe, and Japan collectively spend about nine times as much as the rest of the world, even though these countries make up less than one-seventh of the world's population. Exhibit 10.4 shows the massively skewed distribution of television sets, radios, and newspapers around the world. In 1991, there was one television set for every 1.2 Americans but only one set for every 32 Chinese or every 56 Pakistanis.

Such vast disparities indicate that we cannot analyze the consumption of mass media in any uniform global manner. Only the middle- and

EXHIBIT 10.3 *The Globalization of Mass Media*

The spread of global media adapts to differing circumstances in different countries. In India, there are only 35 television sets for every 1,000 people. Since most people cannot afford to own television sets, "video vans," like the one shown here, bring entertainment and commercial advertising to rural populations. This illustrates both the massive global inequality in media access and the seemingly relentless expansion of mass media into previously isolated areas of the globe. *(Photo © Magnum Photos, Inc./Raghu Rai)*

EXHIBIT 10.4 *Newspapers, Radios, and Televisions per 1,000 People in Select Countries*

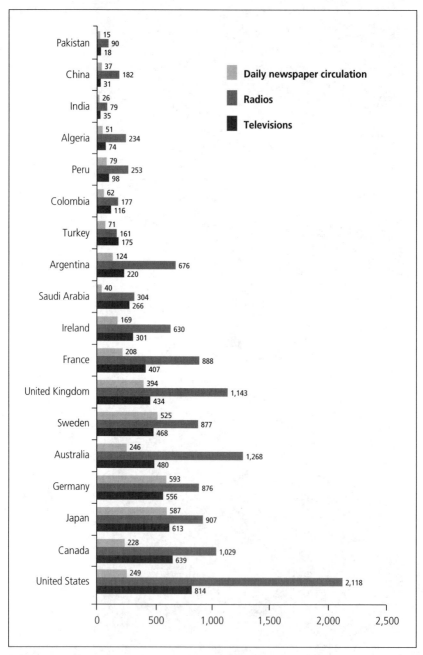

Source: *Statistical Abstract of the United States,* 1995.

upper-class segments of many countries are able to afford regular access to global media products. Writing about South America, one commentator noted, "In a continent where so many are still poor, the mass culture tends to accentuate differences. . . . [I]t makes a student in Buenos Aires much closer to a counterpart in New York than to someone in a poor province 300 miles away" (Escobar and Swardson, 1995). The people in many poorer nations who are tuned in to the global media are the relative elites of those nations. In this way, too, the use of global media reflects broader patterns of national and international inequality.

Even with all the above qualifications, however, we cannot forget that the mass media *are* having a global impact. While in many countries regular media consumption is limited to the relatively privileged, these are the very people who are most able to influence the future direction of their societies. Through their consumption by the middle and upper classes, the words, images, and sounds of mass media are likely to have an impact that in the future will reverberate ever more widely, in ways we cannot predict.

Afterword: The Ubiquity of Change and the Future of Mass Media

Change is one of the great constants of human history. The discipline of sociology emerged, in large measure, in response to the political, economic, and intellectual changes that marked nineteenth-century Europe. Social thinkers of the day were trying to make sense of the revolutionary change that was taking place around them as modern industrial societies replaced traditional agrarian societies.

With industrialization, urban centers replaced rural farming communities. Population densities grew, as did the social problems now associated with urban life. The emergence of factory wage laborers, who replaced farmers and artisans, brought fundamental changes in family life and child-rearing practices. No longer did children learn basic work skills alongside their parents in the home or the field. Parents now left the home to work in shops and factories. The bustling diversity of city life replaced the relative homogeneity and isolation of rural life. Different ethnic, religious, and racial groups intermingled as never before. The haphazard rise of industrial centers brought incredible wealth to a few people in the emerging capitalist class and laid the foundations for a mass-production economy. The price paid for this dramatic transformation included poverty, urban slums, exploitative child labor practices, dangerous and underpaid work, and a host of other social problems.

At the end of the twentieth century, the economic and social changes that provided the impetus for early sociological thinkers have largely run their course. In American society, industrialism has, in many ways, given way to a new and perhaps equally fundamental change. Just as the rise of industrial society rested on technological innovations that made factory production viable, new technological developments are part of contemporary processes of profound social, economic, and political change. The rise in electronic communications and computerization has enabled the emergence of a U.S. economy rooted less in manufacturing and more in services and information. We are living, as some label it, in a "postindustrial" or "information-based" society.

Computers are perhaps the single most widely recognized symbol of the new technological society. The incredible capacity that computers offer for the storage, manipulation, and retrieval of information is closely connected to changes in the workplace, government, schools, and even the home. The digitization of information is increasingly blurring the distinctions between computers and mass media. We are moving toward a future of more media, more information, more images, more sounds, more words, and more data.

The changes that will come are likely to be as profound as those that marked the dawning of industrialization. But, as with all technological change, the direction taken by future media changes will depend on the decisions made by members of society. There is nothing inevitable about the march of technology or of the mass media.

Our argument for a sociological analysis of mass media began in Chapter 1 with a sketch of a model for approaching the study of media and the social world. We have tried to show that understanding the media involves understanding a series of social relationships. By now it should be clear that looking only at media content—the most common way to talk about "the media"—provides us with an incomplete picture of the media and their significance for society. Instead, we must be alert to the relationships that exist within our model, relationships that involve the media industry, media messages or products, technology, active audiences, and the social world beyond the media. Even in the years to come, understanding the media will mean understanding these social relations in all their complexity.

REFERENCES

Abramson, Jeffrey B., F. Christopher Arterton, and Gary R. Orren. 1988. *The Electronic Commonwealth: The Impact of New Media Technologies on Democratic Politics.* New York: Basic Books.

Ang, Ien. 1985. *Watching Dallas.* London: Methuen.

Auletta, Ken. 1991. *Three Blind Mice: How the TV Networks Lost Their Way.* New York: Random House.

Bagdikian, Ben. 1992. *The Media Monopoly,* 4th ed. Boston: Beacon Press.

Baker, C. Edwin. 1994. *Advertising and a Democratic Press.* Princeton, NJ: Princeton University Press.

Baldasty, Gerald J. 1992. *The Commercialization of News in the Nineteenth Century.* Madison: University of Wisconsin Press.

Ballard, Ian Matheson, Jr. 1995. "See No Evil, Hear No Evil: Television Violence and the First Amendment." *Virginia Law Review, 81*(1), 175–222.

Barnet, Richard J., and John Cavanagh. 1994. *Global Dreams: Imperial Corporations and the New World Order.* New York: Simon & Schuster.

Baudrillard, Jean. 1983. *Simulations.* New York: Semiotext(e).

Baudrillard, Jean. 1988. *Selected Writings.* Mark Poster, ed. Stanford, CA: Stanford University Press.

Becker, Howard S. 1982. *Art Worlds.* Berkeley: University of California Press.

Bennett, W. Lance. 1988. *News: The Politics of Illusion,* 2nd ed. New York: Longman.

Bennett, W. Lance, and David Paletz, eds. 1994. *Taken by Storm: The Media, Public Opinion, and U.S. Foreign Policy in the Gulf War.* Chicago: University of Chicago Press.

Bielby, William T., and Denise D. Bielby. 1994. "'All Hits Are Flukes': Institutionalized Decision Making and the Rhetoric of Network Prime-Time Program Development." *American Journal of Sociology, 99*(5), 1287–1313.

Birkerts, Sven. 1994. *The Gutenberg Elegies.* Boston: Faber and Faber.

Bobo, Jacqueline. 1988. "*The Color Purple:* Black Women as Cultural Readers." In E. Deidre Pribram, ed., *Female Spectators,* pp. 90–109. London: Verso.

Boorstin, Daniel. 1961. *The Image.* New York: Atheneum.

Branch, Taylor. 1988. *Parting the Waters: America in the King Years 1954–1963.* New York: Simon & Schuster.

Brenner, Daniel, and William L. Rivers. 1982. *Free but Regulated: Conflicting Traditions in Media Law.* Ames: Iowa State University Press.

Bridge, Junior. 1995. "Females Finding Glass Ceiling Under Repair." *The Quill, 83*(6), 16.

Brosius, Hans-Bernd, and Hans Mathias Kepplinger. 1990. *Communication Research, 17*(2), 183–211.

Brown, J. D., and D. Campbell. 1986. "Race and Gender in Music Videos: The Same Beat but a Different Drummer." *Journal of Communication,* 36(1), 94–106.

Butsch, Richard. 1992. "Class and Gender in Four Decades of Television Situation Comedy: Plus ça change. . . ." *Critical Studies in Mass Communication,* 9, 387–399.

Carlson, James M. 1985. *Prime Time Law Enforcement: Crime Show Viewing and Attitudes towards the Criminal Justice System.* New York: Praeger Publishers.

Carlson, James M. 1995. "Political Socialization Through Media." In Jan P. Vermeer, ed., *In "Media" Res: Readings in Mass Media and American Politics.* New York: McGraw-Hill.

Carragee, Kevin M. 1990. "Interpretive Media Study and Interpretive Social Science." *Critical Studies in Mass Communication,* 7(2), 81–96.

Cassata, Mary B., and Molefi K. Asante. 1979. *Mass Communication: Principles and Practices.* New York: MacMillan.

Cheney, Richard. 1992. "Media Conduct in the Persian Gulf War: Report to Congress." Washington, DC: Department of Defense, Public Affairs Office.

Chiuy, Yvonne. 1995. "FTC Settles Car Ad Boycott Case." *The Washington Post,* August 2, p. F3.

Christian Science Monitor. 1991. "Cultural Dispatches from Around the Globe." The [Nashua, NH] *Telegraph,* July 8, p. 7.

Clark, Charles S. 1991a. "Advertising Under Attack." *CQ Researcher,* 1(18), 659–679.

Clark, Charles S. 1991b. "The Obscenity Debate." *CQ Researcher,* 1(31), 971–991.

Clark, Charles S. 1993. "TV Violence." *CQ Researcher,* 3(12), 267–284.

Cohen, Bernard. 1963. *The Press and Foreign Policy.* Princeton, NJ: Princeton University Press.

Cole, Williams. 1995. "Readers for Sale!: What Newspapers Tell Advertisers About Their Audience." *Extra!,* 8(3), 6–7.

Collins, Ronald K. L. 1992. *Dictating Content: How Advertising Pressure Can Corrupt a Free Press.* Washington, DC: Center for the Study of Commercialism.

Condit, Celeste M. 1989. "The Rhetorical Limits of Polysemy." *Critical Studies in Mass Communication,* 6(2), 103–122.

Cooley, Charles Horton. 1902/1964. *Human Nature and the Social Order.* New York: Scribner's.

Coontz, Stephanie. 1992. *The Way We Never Were: American Families and the Nostalgia Trap.* New York: Basic Books.

Coser, Lewis A., Charles Kadushin, and Walter W. Powell. 1982. *Books: The Culture and Commerce of Publishing.* New York: Basic Books.

Crane, Diana. 1992. *The Production of Culture.* Newbury Park, CA: Sage.

Crawford, Alan Pell. 1993. "Finis to Fin-Syn." *Mediaweek,* April 12, p. 15.

Cripps, Thomas. 1993. "Film." In Jannette L. Dates and William Barlow, eds., *Split Image: African Americans in the Mass Media,* 2nd ed., pp. 131–185. Washington, DC: Howard University Press.

Cronauer, Adrian. 1994. "The Fairness Doctrine: A Solution in Search of a Problem." *Federal Communications Law Journal,* 47(1), 51–77.

Croteau, David. 1995. *Politics and the Class Divide: Working People and the Middle Class Left.* Philadelphia: Temple University Press.

Croteau, David, and William Hoynes. 1994. *By Invitation Only: How the Media Limit Political Debate*. Monroe, ME: Common Courage Press.

Croteau, David, William Hoynes, and Kevin M. Carragee. 1996. "The Political Diversity of Public Television: Polysemy, the Public Sphere, and the Conservative Critique of PBS." *Journalism and Mass Communication Monographs, 157*, 1–55.

Curran, James. 1977. "Capitalism and Control of the Press, 1800–1975." In James Curran, Michael Gurevitch, and Janet Woollacott, eds., *Mass Communication and Society*. London: Edward Arnold.

Dates, Jannette L. 1993. "Commercial Television." In Jannette L. Dates and William Barlow, eds., *Split Image: African Americans in the Mass Media*, 2nd ed., pp. 267–327. Washington, DC: Howard University Press.

Dates, Jannette L., and William Barlow, eds. 1993. *Split Image: African Americans in the Mass Media*, 2nd ed. Washington, DC: Howard University Press.

De Bens, Els, Mary Kelly, and Marit Bakke. 1992. "Television Content: Dallasification of Culture?" In Kareen Siune and Wolfgang Truetzschler, eds., *Dynamics of Media Politics: Broadcast and Electronic Media in Western Europe*. London: Sage.

DeFleur, Melvin L., and Sandra Ball-Rokeach. 1989. *Theories of Mass Communication*, 5th ed. New York: Longman.

De Mooij, Marieke K., and Warren Keegan. 1991. *Advertising Worldwide*. New York: Prentice-Hall.

Denton, Robert, ed. 1993. *The Media and the Persian Gulf War*. Westport, CT: Praeger.

Douglas, Susan J. 1987. *Inventing American Broadcasting, 1899–1922*. Baltimore: Johns Hopkins University Press.

Duckworth, M., L. Lodder, M. Moore, S. Overton, and J. Rubin. 1990. "The Bottom Line from the Top Down." *Columbia Journalism Review,* July/August, pp. 30–32.

Editor & Publisher. 1995. "Minorities in the Newsroom." April 29, p. 39.

Eisenstein, Elizabeth. 1968. "Some Conjectures About the Impact of Printing on Western Society and Thought." *Journal of Modern History, 40*(1), 1–56.

Eisenstein, Elizabeth. 1979. *The Printing Press as an Agent of Change*. Cambridge: Cambridge University Press.

Entman, Robert. 1989. *Democracy Without Citizens*. New York: Oxford University Press.

Entman, Robert. 1992. "Blacks in the News: Television, Modern Racism, and Cultural Change. *Journalism Quarterly, 69*(2), 341–361.

Epstein, Edward J. 1973. *News From Nowhere*. New York: Vintage.

Escobar, Gabriel, and Anne Swardson. 1995. "From Language to Literature, a New Guiding Lite." *Washington Post*, September 5, pp. 1, A18.

Ewen, Stuart. 1976. *Captains of Consciousness*. New York: McGraw Hill.

Fallows, James. 1996. "Why Americans Hate the Media." *Atlantic Monthly*, February, pp. 45–64.

Faludi, Susan. 1991. *Backlash: The Undeclared War Against American Women*. New York: Crown.

Federal Communications Commission. 1995. "Comments Sought on November 1995 Expiration of Fin-Syn Rules." News Report No. DC 95-54, April 5. www.fcc.gov.

Fejes, Fred. 1992. "Masculinity as Fact: A Review of Empirical Mass Communication Research on Masculinity." In Steve Craig, ed., *Men, Masculinity, and the Media*, pp. 9–22. Thousand Oaks, CA: Sage.

Fejes, Fred, and Kevin Petrich. 1993. "Invisibility, Homophobia and Heterosexism: Lesbians, Gays and the Media." *Critical Studies in Mass Communication, 20*(6), 396–422.

Fischer, Claude. 1992. *America's Calling*. Berkeley: University of California Press.

Fishman, Mark. 1980. *Manufacturing the News*. Austin: University of Texas Press.

Fiske, John. 1986. "Television: Polysemy and Popularity." *Critical Studies in Mass Communication, 3*(4), 391–408.

Fiske, John. 1987. *Television Culture*. London/New York: Routledge.

Flint, Joe. 1993. "Networks Win, Hollywood Winces as Fin-syn Barriers Fall." *Broadcasting & Cable*, November 22, pp. 6, 16.

Folbre, Nancy. 1995. *The New Field Guide to the U.S. Economy*. New York: The New Press.

Foote, Cornelius F., Jr. 1994. "Minority, Total Newsroom Employment Shows Slow Growth, 1994 Survey Says." *ASNE Bulletin*, April/May, pp. 20–25.

Frank, Reuven. 1993. "Fairness in the Eye of the Beholder." *The New Leader*, November 15–29, pp. 20–21.

Freeman, Michael. 1994a. "A Last Gasp for Fin-Syn?" *Mediaweek*, November 28, p. 5.

Freeman, Michael. 1994b. "Producers Fight for Fin-Syn." *Mediaweek*, December 5, pp. 10, 12.

Frith, Simon. 1981. *Sound Effects*. New York: Pantheon.

Funkhouser, G. Ray. 1973. "The Issues of the Sixties: An Exploratory Study in the Dynamics of Public Opinion." *Public Opinion Quarterly, 66*, 942–948, 959.

Gamson, Joshua. 1994. *Claims to Fame*. Berkeley: University of California Press.

Gamson, William. 1992. *Talking Politics*. Cambridge: Cambridge University Press.

Gamson, William, David Croteau, William Hoynes, and Theodore Sasson. 1992. "Media Images and the Social Construction of Reality." *Annual Review of Sociology, 18*, 373–393.

Gamson, William, and Andre Modigliani. 1989. "Media Discourse and Public Opinion on Nuclear Power." *American Journal of Sociology, 95*, 1–37.

Gamson, William, and Gadi Wolfsfeld. 1993. "Movements and Media as Interacting Systems." *The Annals of the American Academy of Political and Social Science, 528* (July), 114–125.

Gans, Herbert J. 1979. *Deciding What's News*. New York: Vintage.

Garofalo, Reebee, ed. 1992. *Rockin' the Boat: Mass Music and Mass Movements*. Boston: South End Press.

Gerbner, George, Larry Gross, Michael Morgan, and Nancy Signorielli. 1982. "Charting the Mainstream: Television's Contributions to Political Orientations." *Journal of Communication, 32*(2), 100–127.

Gerbner, George, Larry Gross, Michael Morgan, and Nancy Signorielli. 1984. "Political Correlates of Television Viewing." *Public Opinion Quarterly, 48*(1), 283–300.

Gerbner, George, Larry Gross, Michael Morgan, and Nancy Signorielli. 1994. "Growing Up with Television: The Cultivation Perspective." In Jennings Bryant and Dolf Zillmann, eds., *Media Effects: Advances in Theory and Research*. Hillsdale, NJ: Lawrence Erlbaum Associates.

Gerbner, George, Hamid Mowlana, and Kaarle Nordenstreng, eds. 1993. *The Global Media Debate: Its Rise, Fall, and Renewal*. Norwood, NJ: Ablex Publishing Corporation.

Gitlin, Todd. 1980. *The Whole World Is Watching: Mass Media in the Making and Unmaking of the New Left*. Berkeley: University of California.

Gitlin, Todd. 1985. *Inside Prime Time*. New York: Pantheon.

Goldfarb, Jeffrey. 1991. *The Cynical Society*. Chicago: University of Chicago Press.

Goldin, M. 1989. "Father Time: Who's on the Op-Ed Page?" *Mother Jones*, January, p. 51.

Goodwin, Andrew. 1992. *Dancing in the Distraction Factory*. Minneapolis: University of Minnesota Press.

Gottdiener, M. 1985. "Hegemony and Mass Culture: A Semiotic Approach." *American Journal of Sociology*, 90(5), 979–1001.

Graber, Doris A. 1980. *Mass Media and American Politics*. Washington, DC: Congressional Quarterly Press.

Graber, Doris A. 1988. *Processing the News: How People Tame the Information Tide*. New York: Longman.

Gramsci, Antonio. 1971. *Selections from the Prison Notebooks*. New York: International Publishers.

Gray, Herman. 1989. "Television, Black Americans, and the American Dream." *Critical Studies in Mass Communication*, 16(6), 376–386.

Gray, Herman. 1995. *Watching Race: Television and the Struggle for Blackness*. Minneapolis: University of Minnesota Press.

Greenberg, Bradley S., and Jeffrey E. Brand. 1994. "Minorities and the Mass Media: 1970s to 1990s." In Jennings Bryant and Dolf Zillman, eds., *Media Effects: Advances in Theory and Research*, pp. 273–314. Hillsdale, NJ: Lawrence Erlbaum Associates.

Greider, William. 1992. *Who Will Tell the People: The Betrayal of American Democracy*. New York: Simon & Schuster.

Hall, Stuart. 1982. "The Rediscovery of 'Ideology': Return of the Repressed in Media Studies." In M. Gurevitch et al., eds., *Culture, Society, and the Media*. London: Routledge.

Harper's Magazine. 1995. "What Are We Doing On-Line?" August, pp. 35–46.

Harrington, Richard. 1995. "Reviving the Label Movement." *Washington Post*, June 14, p. C7.

Herman, Edward, and Noam Chomsky. 1988. *Manufacturing Consent*. New York: Pantheon.

Hickey, Neil. 1995. "Revolution in Cyberia." *Columbia Journalism Review*, July/August, pp. 40–47.

Hills, Jill. 1991. *The Democracy Gap: The Politics of Information and Communication Technologies in the United States and Europe*. New York: Greenwood Press.

Hirsch, Mario, and Vibeke G. Petersen. 1992. "Regulation of Media at the European Level." In Kareen Siune and Wolfgang Truetzschler, eds., *Dynamics of Media Politics: Broadcast and Electronic Media in Western Europe*. London: Sage.

Hoynes, William. 1994. *Public Television for Sale: Media, the Market, and the Public Sphere*. Boulder, CO: Westview Press.

Hunter, James Davison. 1991. *Culture Wars*. New York: Basic Books.

Husseini, Sam. 1994. "NBC Brings Good Things to GE." *Extra!*, November/December, p. 13.

Iyengar, S., and D. R. Kinder. 1987. *News That Matters: Agenda-Setting and Priming in a Television Age.* Chicago: University of Chicago Press.

Jackson, L. A., and K. S. Ervin. 1991. "The Frequency and Portrayal of Black Families in Fashion Advertisement." *Journal of Black Psychology,* 18(1), 67–70.

Jeffords, Susan. 1989. *The Remasculinization of America.* Bloomington: Indiana University Press.

Jeffords, Susan, and Lauren Rabinovitz, eds. 1994. *Seeing Through the Media: The Persian Gulf War.* New Brunswick, NJ: Rutgers University Press.

Jessell, Harry A. 1993. "Networks Victorious in Fin-syn Fight." *Broadcasting & Cable,* April 5, pp. 7, 10.

Jhally, Sut, and Justin Lewis. 1992. *Enlightened Racism.* Boulder, CO: Westview Press.

Jost, Kenneth. 1994a. "The Future of Television." *CQ Researcher,* 4(48), 1131–1148.

Jost, Kenneth. 1994b. "Talk Show Democracy." *CQ Researcher,* 4(16), 363–375.

Kahn, Frank J., ed. 1978. *Documents of American Broadcasting,* 3rd ed. Englewood Cliffs, NJ: Prentice-Hall.

Kasoma, Francis. 1993. "Ironies and Contrasts." In George Gerbner, Hamid Mowlana, and Kaarle Nordenstreng, eds., *The Global Media Debate: Its Rise, Fall, and Renewal,* pp. 77–81. Norwood, NJ: Ablex Publishing Corp.

Kellner, Douglas. 1990. *Television and the Crisis of Democracy.* Boulder, CO: Westview Press.

Kellner, Douglas. 1995. "Cultural Studies, Multiculturalism, and Media Culture." In Gail Dines and Jean M. Humez, eds., *Gender, Race and Class in Media.* Thousand Oaks, CA: Sage.

Kornhauser, William. 1959. *The Politics of Mass Society.* New York: Free Press.

Krugman, Dean M., and Leonard N. Reid. 1980. "The 'Public Interest' as Defined by FCC Policy Makers." *Journal of Broadcasting,* 24(3), 311–323.

Kubey, Robert, and Mihaly Csikszentmihalyi. 1990. *Television and the Quality of Life: How Viewing Shapes Everyday Experience.* Hillsdale, NJ: Erlbaum.

Lafky, Sue A. 1993. "The Progress of Women and People of Color in the U.S. Journalistic Workforce: A Long, Slow Journey." In Pamela J. Creedon, ed., *Women in Mass Communication,* 2nd ed., pp. 87–103. Thousand Oaks, CA: Sage.

Landler, Mark. 1994. "Think Globally, Program Locally." *Business Week,* November 18, pp. 186–189.

Lazar, Bonnie A. 1994. "Under the Influence: An Analysis of Children's Television Regulation." *Social Work,* 39(1), 67–74.

Lazarsfeld, Paul, Bernard Berelson, and Hazel Gaudet. 1948. *The People's Choice: How the Voter Makes Up His Mind in a Presidential Campaign.* New York: Columbia University Press.

Lee, Martin, and Norman Solomon. 1990. *Unreliable Sources.* New York: Lyle Stuart.

Lenart, Silvo. 1994. *Shaping Political Attitudes: The Impact of Interpersonal Communication and Mass Media.* Thousand Oaks, CA: Sage.

Levin, Murray. 1987. *Talk Radio and the American Dream.* Lexington, MA: Lexington Books.

Lewis, Lisa. 1990. *Gender Politics and MTV.* Philadelphia: Temple University Press.

Lichter, S. Robert, Linda S. Lichter, and Stanley Rothman. 1994. *Prime Time.* Washington, DC: Regnery.

Liebes, Tamar, and Elihu Katz. 1993. *The Export of Meaning.* Cambridge: Polity Press.

Long, Elizabeth. 1985. *The American Dream and the Popular Novel.* Boston: Routledge & Kegan Paul.

Longley, Lawrence, Herbert Terry, and Erwin Krasnow. 1983. "Citizen Groups in Broadcast Regulatiory [sic] Policy-Making." *Policy Studies Journal,* 12(2), 258–270.

Lopes, Paul D. 1992. "Innovation and Diversity in the Popular Music Industry, 1969 to 1990." *American Sociological Review,* 57, 56–71.

Los Angeles Times/Washington Post News Service. 1995. "Deaths Are Live for Russians." *Richmond Times-Dispatch,* January 2, p. A4.

MacBride, Sean, and Colleen Roach. 1993. "The New International Information Order." In George Gerbner, Hamid Mowlana, and Kaarle Nordenstreng, eds., *The Global Media Debate: Its Rise, Fall, and Renewal,* pp. 3–11. Norwood, NJ: Ablex Publishing Corporation.

Marchetti, Gina. 1989. "Action-Adventure as Ideology." In I. Angus and S. Jhally, eds., *Cultural Politics in Contemporary America.* New York: Routledge.

Mattelart, Armand. 1979. *Multinational Corporations and the Control of Culture.* Atlantic Highlands, NJ: Humanities Press.

McAdam, Doug. 1982. *Political Process and the Development of Black Insurgency, 1930–1970.* Chicago: University of Chicago Press.

McChesney, Robert. 1994. *Telecommunications, Mass Media, and Democracy.* New York: Oxford University Press.

McChesney, Robert. 1995. "Telecon." *In These Times,* 19(17), 14–17.

McClure, Robert, and Thomas Patterson. 1976. *The Unseeing Eye.* New York: G. P. Putnam's Sons.

McCombs, Maxwell, and Donald L. Shaw. 1972. "The Agenda-Setting Function of the Mass Media." *Public Opinion Quarterly,* 36, 176–187.

McCombs, Maxwell, and Donald L. Shaw. 1977. *The Emergence of American Political Issues: The Agenda-Setting Function of the Press.* St. Paul, MN: West Publishing.

McCracken, Ellen. 1993. *Decoding Women's Magazines.* New York: St. Martin's Press.

McLaughlin, Margaret L., Kerry K. Osborne, and Christine B. Smith. 1995. "Standards of Conduct on Usenet." In Steven G. Jones, ed., *Cybersociety,* pp. 90–111. Thousand Oaks, CA: Sage.

McLuhan, Marshall. 1962. *The Gutenberg Galaxy.* Toronto: University of Toronto Press.

McLuhan, Marshall. 1964. *Understanding Media: The Extensions of Man.* New York: New American Library.

McLuhan, Marshall, and Quentin Fiore. 1967. *The Medium Is the Message: An Inventory of Effects.* New York: Bantam Books.

McNeil, Donald G., Jr. 1996. "Now Rural Africa Can Tune In." *Richmond Times-Dispatch,* February 19, p. A4.

McQuail, Denis. 1987. *Mass Communication Theory.* Newbury Park, CA: Sage.

McQuail, Denis, Rosario de Mateo, and Helena Tapper. 1992. "A Framework for Analysis of Media Change in Europe in the 1990s." In Kareen Siune and Wolfgang Truetzschler, eds., *Dynamics of Media Politics: Broadcast and Electronic Media in Western Europe.* London: Sage.

McRobbie, Angela. 1984. *Dance and Social Fantasy.* In A. McRobbie and M. Nava, eds., *Gender and Generation,* pp. 130–161. London: MacMillan.

Messner, Michael, Margaret Carlisle Duncan, and Kerry Jensen. 1993. "Separating the Men from the Girls: The Gendered Language of Televised Sports." *Gender & Society,* 7(1), 121–137.

Meyrowitz, Joshua. 1985. *No Sense of Place.* New York: Oxford University Press.

Meyrowitz, Joshua. 1994. "Medium Theory." In D. Crowley and D. Mitchell, eds., *Communication Theory Today,* pp. 50–77. Stanford: Stanford University Press.

Miller, Mark Crispin, ed. 1990. *Seeing Through Movies.* New York: Pantheon.

Mills, C. Wright. 1959. *The Sociological Imagination.* New York: Oxford University Press.

Modleski, Tania. 1984. *Loving With a Vengeance.* New York: Methuen.

Morley, David. 1980. *The Nationwide Audience.* London: British Film Institute.

Morley, David. 1986. *Family Television.* London: Comedia.

Morley, David. 1992. *Television, Audiences, and Cultural Studies.* London: Routledge.

Morris, Aldon. 1984. *The Origins of the Civil Rights Movement.* New York: Free Press.

Mowlana, Hamid. 1993. "Toward a NWICO for the Twenty-First Century?" *Journal of International Affairs,* 47(1), 59–72.

Mowlana, Hamid, George Gerbner, and Herbert Schiller, eds. 1992. *Triumph of the Image: The Media's War in the Persian Gulf.* Boulder, CO: Westview Press.

Neuman, W. Russell. 1991. *The Future of the Mass Audience.* New York: Cambridge University Press.

Noam, Eli M., ed. 1985. *Video Media Competition: Regulation, Economics, and Technology.* New York: Columbia University Press.

O'Barr, William. 1994. *Culture and the Ad.* Boulder, CO: Westview Press.

O'Neil, Michael. 1993. *The Roar of the Crowd: How Television and People Power Are Changing the World.* New York: Time Books.

Oppenheimer, Todd. 1993. "Newsweek's Voyage Through Cyberspace." *Columbia Journalism Review,* 32(6), 34–37.

Paik, Haejung, and George Comstock. 1994. "The Effects of Television Violence on Antisocial Behavior: A Meta-Analysis." *Communication Research,* 21(4), 516–546.

Palmer, R. R., and Joel Colton. 1978. *A History of the Modern World.* New York: Alfred A. Knopf.

Parenti, Michael. 1986. *Inventing Reality: The Politics of the Mass Media.* New York: St. Martin's Press.

Peterson, Richard A., ed. 1976. *The Production of Culture.* Beverly Hills, CA: Sage.

Peterson, Richard A., and David G. Berger. 1975. "Cycles in Symbol Production: The Case of Popular Music." *American Sociological Review,* 40, 158–173.

Pond, Steve. 1995. "Friendly Shores Abroad for 'Waterworld.'" *Washington Post,* October 3, p. B7.

Pool, Ithiel de Sola. 1983. *Technologies of Freedom.* Cambridge: Harvard University Press.

Postman, Neil. 1985. *Amusing Ourselves to Death*. New York: Penguin.

Powell, Walter W. 1985. *Getting Into Print*. Chicago: University of Chicago Press.

Press, Andrea. 1991. *Women Watching Television*. Philadelphia: University of Pennsylvania Press.

Prince, Stephen. 1992. *Visions of Empire: Political Imagery in Contemporary American Film*. New York: Praeger.

Prindle, David F. 1993. *Risky Business*. Boulder, CO: Westview Press.

Puette, William J. 1992. *Through Jaundiced Eyes: How the Media View Organized Labor*. Ithaca, NY: ILR Press.

Radway, Janice. 1984. *Reading the Romance*. Chapel Hill: University of North Carolina Press.

Regan, Donald. 1988. *For the Record*. New York: Harcourt Brace Jovanovich.

Reisman, David. 1953. *The Lonely Crowd*. Garden City, NY: Doubleday.

Rheingold, Howard. 1993. *The Virtual Community*. Reading, MA: Addison-Wesley.

Rhodes, Jane. 1993. "The Visibility of Race and Media History." *Critical Studies in Mass Communication, 20*(2), 184–190.

Robinson, Michael J. 1976. "Public Affairs Television and the Growth of Political Malaise: The Case of the 'Selling of the Pentagon.'" *American Political Science Review, 70,* 409–432.

Robinson, Michael J., and Andrew Kohut. 1988. "Believability and the Press." *Public Opinion Quarterly, 52,* 174–189.

Rogers, Everett. 1986. *Communication Technology*. New York: Free Press.

Rose, Tricia. 1994. *Black Noise*. Hanover, NH: Wesleyan University Press.

Rosen, Jay. 1993. "Who Won the Week?: The Political Press and the Evacuation of Meaning." *Tikkun, 8*(4), 7–10, 94.

Rosenblum, Barbara. 1978. *Photographers at Work*. New York: Holmes and Meier.

Ryan, Charlotte. 1991. *Prime-Time Activism*. Boston: South End Press.

Sandler, Adam. 1994. "Hollywood: 'R' Kind of Town." *Variety* (September 12), 356(7), 1, 7.

Schiffer, Michael. 1991. *The Portable Radio in American Life*. Tucson: University of Arizona Press.

Schiller, Herbert. 1971. *Mass Communications and American Empire*. Boston: Beacon Press.

Schiller, Herbert. 1989. *Culture, Inc.* New York: Oxford University Press.

Schiller, Herbert. 1992. *Mass Communication and American Empire*, 2nd ed. Boulder, CO: Westview Press.

Schlegel, Julia W. 1993. "The Television Violence Act of 1990: A New Program for Government Censorship?" *Federal Communications Law Journal, 46*(1), 187–217.

Schudson, Michael. 1978. *Discovering the News*. New York: Basic Books.

Schudson, Michael. 1984. *Advertising, the Uneasy Persuasion*. New York: Basic Books.

Seggar, J. F., J. Hafen, and H. Hannonen-Gladden. 1981. "Television's Portrayals of Minorities and Women in Drama and Comedy Drama, 1971–80." *Journal of Broadcasting, 25*(3), 277–288.

Semetko, Holli A., Jay G. Blumler, Michael Gurevitch, and David H. Weaver. 1991. *The Formation of Campaign Agendas*. Hillsdale, NJ: Lawrence Erlbaum Associates.

Shales, Tom. 1995. "The Fat Cat Broadcast Bonanza." *Washington Post,* June 13, pp. C1, C9.

Shapiro, Andrew L. 1995. "Street Corners in Cyberspace." *The Nation,* July 3, pp. 10–14.

Signorielli, Nancy, and Michael Morgan. 1990. *Cultivation Analysis: New Directions in Media Effects Research.* Newbury Park, CA: Sage.

Simmons, Steven J. 1978. *The Fairness Doctrine and the Media.* Berkeley: University of California Press.

Snow, David A., E. Burke Rochford, Jr., Steven K. Worden, and Robert D. Benford. 1986. "Frame Alignment Processes, Micromobilization, and Movement Participation." *American Sociological Review, 51,* 464–481.

Spigel, Lynn. 1992. *Make Room for TV.* Chicago: University of Chicago Press.

Spolar, Christine. 1995. "Romance by the Book in Poland." *Washington Post,* August 28, p. A19.

Squires, James. 1993. *Read All About It! The Corporate Takeover of America's Newspapers.* New York: Times Books.

Sreberny-Mohammadi, Annabelle. 1991. "The Global and the Local in International Communications." In James Curran and Michael Gurevitch, eds., *Mass Media and Society,* pp. 118–138. London: Edward Arnold.

Steeves, H. Leslie. 1993. "Gender and Mass Communication in a Global Context." In Pamela J. Creedon, ed., *Women in Mass Communication,* 2nd ed., pp. 32–60. Thousand Oaks, CA: Sage.

Steiner, Linda. 1988. Oppositional Decoding as an Act of Resistance. *Critical Studies in Mass Communication, 5*(1), 1–15.

Stone, Vernon. 1996. "Minorities and Women in Television News." University of Missouri. http://www.missouri.edu/~jourvs/gtvminw.html

Taylor, Ella. 1989. *Prime Time Families.* Berkeley: University of California Press.

Taylor, Phillip M. 1992. *War and the Media: Propaganda and Persuasion in the Gulf War.* New York: St. Martin's Press.

Tichi, Cecelia. 1991. *Electronic Hearth: Creating an American Television Culture.* New York: Oxford University Press.

Traugott, Michael W. 1992. "The Impact of Media Polls on the Public." In Thomas E. Mann and Gary Orren, eds., *Media Polls in American Politics.* Washington, DC: The Brookings Institution.

Tuchman, Gaye. 1978. *Making News: A Study in the Construction of Reality.* New York: Free Press.

Tunstall, Jeremy. 1977. *The Media Are American.* New York: Columbia University Press.

Tunstall, Jeremy. 1986. *Communications Deregulation: The Unleashing of America's Communications Industry.* Oxford: Basil Blackwell.

Underwood, Doug. 1993. *When MBAs Rule the Newsroom.* New York: Columbia University Press.

U.S. Census Bureau. 1992. *Statistical Abstract of the United States.* Washington, DC: USGPO.

Vidmar, Neil, and Milton Rokeach. 1974. "Archie Bunker's Bigotry: A Study in Selective Perception and Exposure." *Journal of Communication, 24,* 36–47.

Walters, Suzanna D. 1995. *Material Girls.* Berkeley: University of California Press.

Wenner, Jann, and William Greider. 1993. "The Rolling Stone Interview: President Clinton." *Rolling Stone,* December 9, pp. 40–45, 80–81.

Wiley, Richard E. 1994. " 'Fairness' in Our Future?" *Quill,* March, pp. 36–37.

Wilson, Clint C., and Felix Gutierrez. 1995. *Race, Multiculturalism, and the Media: From Mass to Class Communication,* 2nd ed. Thousand Oaks, CA: Sage.

INDEX

A

Abramson, Jeffrey B., 216, 281
Academics, 94
Acquisitions editors, 118–119
Active audience theory, 7–8, 230–232.
    See also Audience interpretation
Advertising, 53–62
    and audience as product, 53
    and children's television, 89–90
    and citizen activism, 95
    and class, 59–60, 152–153, 158,
        189–190
    and contemporary news media, 58–60
    content regulation, 90–91
    and cyberspace, 13, 283
    and gender, 149
    and globalization, 191–194
    growth of, 53–54, 189–190
    and ideology, 182, 186, 187–194
    and media political influence, 57, 218
    and "new media," 60–62
    nineteenth century, 54–58
    pervasiveness of, 187, 188
    photography, 111, 112–113, 114, 115
    and race, 140
    radio, 278
Africa, 304, 314–315
African Americans, 135, 140, 144, 145,
    146. *See also* Race
Agenda-setting theory of media influence,
    208–210
AIDS, 160
"All in the Family," 155, 181–182, 218
Alternative media, 55–57, 133, 146, 147
Amateur radio operators, 276–277, 278
American Marconi Company, 276, 277
American Medical Association, 89
American Newspaper Publishing
    Association, 199
American Psychological Association, 88
Ang, Ien, 256
AP. *See* Associated Press
Arterton, F. Christopher, 216
Asante, Molefi K., 8

Asian Americans, 139, 142. *See also* Race
Associated Press (AP), 106, 313
AT&T, 278
Audience
    fragmentation of, 61
    influence on content, 137, 167
    as product, 53.
        See also Audience interpretation
Audience interpretation, 229–260
    active audience theory, 7–8, 230–232
    and class, 239–242
    and cultural imperialism theory, 308
    encoding-decoding model, 237, 238,
        239
    and globalization, 243–246
    and identity, 253–255
    and ideology, 186
    and media political influence, 208,
        211, 218–219, 222, 225, 226, 227
    and pleasure, 255–259
    and race, 218, 234, 242–243
    and resistance, 251–255, 258–259
    and social construction of reality, 7–8,
        231
    and social context, 246–251
    and sociological perspective, 23–24,
        25–26
    and structure/agency dynamic,
        232–236
Auletta, Ken, 41
Autonomy, 23

B

Bagdikian, Ben, 34, 40, 42, 45, 46
Baker, C. Edwin, 59
Bakke, Marit, 223
Baldasty, Gerald J., 57–58
Ballard, Ian Matheson, Jr., 88
Ball-Rokeach, Sandra, 8
Barlow, William, 145
Barnet, Richard J., 295, 296, 304, 307,
    308, 309
Batman, 38, 219
Baudrillard, Jean, 203, 270

333